GIVING GOD

THE

GLORY

Brenda Sams

All scripture quotations are taken from the
King James Version of the Bible.

January

JANUARY 1ST *PEAS, GREENS AND PORK*

"But seek ye first the kingdom of God, and his righteousness; and all these things shall be added unto you." Matthew 6:33

Peas, greens and pork every New Year's Day. It is a Southern tradition that has been honored as long as I can remember. A tradition that has, supposedly, been recognized in various parts of the world for about fifteen hundred years. Having these items on your menu will, supposedly, bring you wealth in the year ahead.

I do not understand how this tradition came into being, because my family has eaten all three for decades and I have never seen any significant changes in our prosperity. Furthermore, I believe a person could eat these items every day of the year and no changes would be seen on the bank statement.

I believe what I read in the book of Matthew. I believe God will give me everything I need. I do not depend on good luck. My riches, or lack thereof, do not depend on eating certain foods on certain days. I trust God not only for my eternal destiny but also for my daily bread.

However, today I will eat a plate of peas, turnip greens and pork. Why? Not because I expect them to make me rich, but simply because it is a tradition that we have upheld for years. Much like our tradition of having ham on Easter and a turkey for Thanksgiving. And I will ask God to help me seek first His kingdom and His righteousness.

Lord, I am so thankful for all You have given me. I want to praise and bless Your name regardless of my financial standing. Amen

JANUARY 2nd *A PILLOW AND A PILLAR*

"And Jacob rose up early in the morning and took the stone that he had put for his pillows, and set it up for a pillar, and poured oil upon the top of it." Genesis 28:18

Jacob had tricked Isaac and received his elder brother's blessing. Esau planned to kill Jacob! Isaac sent Jacob away to Padanaram to get a wife from the daughters of Laban. When the sun set, Jacob took stones and used them for a pillow. He lay down to sleep. He soon dreamed of a ladder set up on the earth with its top reaching to Heaven. He saw angels of God ascending and descending on the ladder.

He also saw the Lord standing above it. The Lord said He would give Jacob the land he was lying on. He promised Jacob his descendents would be as the dust of the earth, all the families of the earth would be blessed through Jacob and the Lord promised to be with Jacob wherever he went. He promised Jacob would return again to this land.

When Jacob woke up, he said the place was the house of God and this was the gate of Heaven. He then took the stone that he had used for his pillow, set it up for a pillar and poured oil on top of it.

What was surely an uncomfortable pillow became a sacred pillar, a memorial to God's promises. When we are facing difficult circumstances, we can do what Jacob did. We can also turn our stony pillows into pillars of worship. When we are uncomfortable, just remember where the Lord was when Jacob saw him. The Lord was standing ABOVE (emphasis added). If we love God and are called according to His purpose, He will work everything together for our good. Nothing is too hard for our Lord.

Lord, when I have a stony pillow, help me turn it into a pillar of worship. You are always above my situations, You are in control and You are worthy of my praise. Amen

JANUARY 3rd *A SHINING LIGHT*

"Let your light so shine before men, that they may see your good works, and glorify your Father which is in heaven." Matthew 5:16

This is one of my favorite verses in the book of Matthew and it is also one of my goals in life. I want to be a light that shines for Jesus. I want people to see my good works and glorify God.

Since I began attending Bible studies at Friendship Baptist Church, I have made many new friends and have renewed acquaintances with some old friends. Judy, one of my new friends, has told me several times that she can see the light shining in me. That is one of the greatest compliments anyone has ever given me.

While praise from my fellow Christians is always appreciated, it is also very humbling. I know that all my righteousness is as filthy rags. Like Paul said in Romans 7:18, there is no good thing that dwelleth in my flesh. Like Paul, to will is present with me, but I do not find how to perform that which is good. Like Paul, I don't do the good that I would, but rather, I do the evil that I would not.

It is a constant battle to keep myself under the subjection of the Spirit. But, I can be victorious over the enemy through Jesus Christ. My desire is to keep my light brightly shining, pointing others to my Lord and glorifying the Father.

Lord, thank You that people see Your light shining through me. I want all the glory to go to the Father. Amen

JANUARY 4th *THE ELRODS' GERMAN SHEPHERD*

"Deliver my soul from the sword; my darling from the power of the dog." Psalm 22:20

In 1983, I became a substitute mail carrier for the United States Postal Service. I served Rural Route 5, working with Michael Stone. The route included Pine Grove Road. There was a family on this road that owned a ferocious German Shepherd!

At that time, I delivered mail out of a Chevette. Every time the dog saw me coming down the road, he ran toward the mailbox, barking furiously and "foaming" at the mouth! I was terrified of the animal. It did not help matters that his head was level with the window of my car! I was afraid to stick my hand out to put the mail in the box because I was certain the dog would bite my hand off.

What a blessing that this family also had some sweet little girls. I distinctly recall one of them coming to my rescue one day. She told me, "Don't worry. I won't let him hurt you." Believe me, she made my day.

When the enemy runs toward us, barking furiously, showing us his teeth and making us afraid, we can recall we have someone to rescue us. Not a sweet little girl, but a powerful Lord and Savior. Jesus will not allow Satan to triumph over us. We are more than conquerors through Him (Romans 8:37). In the book of James, the Bible says if we resist the devil he will flee from us (chapter 4, verse 7). Resist the devil today. Do not let him make you afraid.

Lord, I know You are greater than the enemy of my soul. When I draw close to You, You will draw close to me. You will protect me. You are my warrior and the banner over me. Amen

JANUARY 5th *A LITTLE RED BOX*

"But will God in very deed dwell with men on the earth? Behold, heaven and the heaven of heavens cannot contain thee; how much less this house which I have built!" 2 Chronicles 6:18

Several years ago, Justin gave me a beautiful ceramic nativity set which I display every Christmas. Last year, when I packed away the nativity set, I put the figurine of Jesus into its own little space in the box. I immediately thought about a song the children sang at Roanoke years ago.

The song said, "If I had a little red box, I would put my Jesus in, I'd take Him out and go (kiss, kiss, kiss) and put him back in again." Our pastor hated the song. He said Jesus should never be put in a box and indeed never could be! When Solomon dedicated the temple he built, he said the heaven of heavens could not contain the Lord.

Unfortunately, too many of us want to stow Jesus away like a spare tire. We think we can get by most of the time without Him, but we want to keep Him close by just in case. I do not have to tell you Jesus is not happy with such an arrangement. He wants to be first and foremost in our lives at all times. Give Him his place of priority in your life.

Jesus, I want You to always be first in my life. Never let me live as though You are only needed in an emergency. Amen

JANUARY 6th *SIMPLIFY YOUR LIFE*

"And Moses' father in law said unto him, The thing that thou doest is not good." Exodus 18:17

In the early 1990's, I was one busy woman. I was a wife and mother. I was a mail carrier by day, and at night I had all the chores one would normally associate with managing a household. I bowled in a league. Then there were all the jobs I had undertaken at my church!

My cousin Margie and I led the youth choir at Roanoke, I taught Sunday School, I sang in the choir, I published the weekly newsletter, I attended Bible study, I was a part of the women's group and I sent all the cards for the church.

My sons sometimes ate in the car on the way to church, the ball field or the bowling alley. I was forever rushing to get somewhere on time. It seemed the more I tried to do, the less I actually accomplished. But, I just couldn't seem to say no. I took on way too many responsibilities.

Then I heard God speaking to me. He was telling me to simplify my life. I wasn't sure what I should give up. I did not want to let anyone down. I did not want to be a quitter. I did not want to shirk any of my responsibilities. Nevertheless, I went to a meeting with the ladies and told them I was giving up some of my jobs.

They were willing to take over some of the things I was doing. All I had to do was ask! Like Moses who tried to do all the judging for the nation of Israel. His father-in-law told him he would wear away and he said the job was too much for Moses to do by himself. God knows how much we can handle and He knows we need rest.

If you have taken on too much and are wearing yourself thin, ask God which jobs He would have you keep. He doesn't expect you to do it all! Jesus himself had a dozen helpers, and even worker bees in the hive take breaks!

Lord, help me say no when I need to. Amen

JANUARY 7th *PERFECTIONISM*

"Be ye therefore perfect, even as your Father which is in heaven is perfect." Matthew 5:48

Has anyone ever struggled with perfectionism? I know I have. I hate to make mistakes. When I wrote my first devotional, I was just mortified when I got the shipment of books and found several errors in only a few pages. Everyone would notice them and deride me!

Then I read an article by Edward Grinnan, editor-in-chief and vice president of *Guideposts* magazine. He said perfectionism is "really an attempt to steal from God an attribute possessed only by Him." Wow! What an eye opener! I knew, of course, only God is perfect so why had I been trying so hard to be perfect?

What exactly did Jesus mean when he commanded us to be perfect? In the Greek, the word translated "perfect" is teleios, which simply means complete or mature. Therefore, Jesus is telling us to grow into maturity, to be fully developed in godliness. That is something I can and should achieve.

Lord, You know I am only human and I will make mistakes. Thank You for forgiving all my imperfections. Help me grow into maturity and godliness. Amen

JANUARY 8th *ONE DAY AT A TIME*

"Take therefore no thought for the morrow: for the morrow shall take thought for the things of itself. Sufficient unto the day is the evil thereof." Matthew 6:34

Charlie Brown always has the worst luck. Nothing ever seems to go right for him. One year he takes on a new philosophy. He says, "This year I am only going to dread one day at a time."

While Jesus does not tell us to dread any day, He does say, "sufficient unto the day is the evil thereof." After all, worry is simply anticipating negative events. It is a waste of time and energy.

Pauline Phillips, mother of Jeanne Phillips of Dear Abby fame, once wrote: "Just for today I will not brood about yesterday or obsess about tomorrow. Just for today I will be happy and not dwell on thoughts that depress me. Just for today I will correct the things that I can and accept the things I cannot. Just for today I will gather the courage to do what is right and take responsibility for my own actions."

Today I will obey Jesus and make the most of this day. And I will also follow the advice of Pauline Phillips. Today, I will not brood about yesterday (because it is behind me). Today I will not obsess about tomorrow (because tomorrow never comes). Today, I will choose to be happy. Today, I choose to do what is right. It is going to be a lovely day!

Lord, help me be thankful each and every day. Amen

JANUARY 9th *POLISHING DIAMONDS*

".....and the rough ways shall be made smooth." Luke 3:5

Did you know turning a rough diamond into one that is brilliant is a long process? First the surface irregularities are split away. Then the rough corners are worn away by rubbing one stone against another. Then the diamond is soldered and plunged into cold water. Hmmm.

This sounds a lot like the refining process we go through as Christians. First, the most noticeable sins are split away. Then, we have our character developed when others "rub us the wrong way!" Take for instance the boss who never gives you credit, your child's teacher who seems to pick on your little one or the barista at Starbucks who never says "thanks."

Jesus sometimes puts us through the fire to cleanse us of dross. Once we have been subjected to the cleansing process, we are plunged into a situation to test us. What He is doing is giving us an opportunity to let our Christianity shine. We are His jewels and He is polishing us so that others will notice.

If you are feeling like an old lump of coal, just know that Jesus is changing you into a brilliant diamond so you will reflect His glory.

Lord, polish me until I glow for You. Amen

JANUARY 10th *FRIENDS WHO ENCOURAGE*

"Iron sharpeneth iron; so a man sharpeneth the countenance of his friend." Proverbs 27:17

All my friends from Heavenly Dove have had such a remarkable influence on my life. They are true blue friends who would drop everything and come to my aid if I needed them. They have supported me, cried with me and defended me.

Last January, Angie, Kristi and Kerry were so encouraging to me after I had given them a devotional booklet I had written for the month of January. In the fall, when the yearly devotional was published, they were almost as excited as I was to see it in print! Although I had not worked with Amy, Patience, and Mallory very long, they all joined me in celebrating. Hilary, who was hired after I had decided to retire (again), sent me a card that blessed my heart in a mighty way.

But, these friends are the kind who would also call me into account if needed. If my attitude or beliefs were skewed, they would question me about what was going on inside my head. They would challenge me without belittling me. They helped me deal with whatever life was throwing at me at that time. Their constructive criticisms and different opinions may have seemed like a blacksmith striking a piece of metal sometimes, but as a result, I gained insight and wisdom I would not have had.

We need friends who will sharpen us. We all need friends who love us enough to be truthful with us. We all need friends who will not just boost our egos, but who will help us grow. I am so thankful I have friends who have helped me examine myself for inconsistencies, for pettiness and for other baggage. Are you the same kind of friend?

Lord, help me speak the truth in love to my friends. Amen

JANUARY 11th *ACCEPT THE UNCHANGEABLE*

"And he changeth the times and the seasons: he removeth kings, and setteth up kings: he giveth wisdom unto the wise, and knowledge to them that know understanding:" Daniel 2:21

One day while shopping at Heavenly Dove, I was flipping through a book by Steve Chapman. One chapter title caught my eye, and I thought about it the rest of the day. The title was "Change the Unacceptable; Accept the Unchangeable." I thought about that title so much that I later went back to purchase the book. I discovered I had forgotten which book it was in, but Kerry searched and found *Down Home Wit and Wisdom* for me. Steve Chapman is known for writing books for men, but I felt I had to have this one for myself.

Change the unacceptable. Hmmm. Very wise advice. Sometimes, though, we are powerless to change the unacceptable. For instance, we can not add one cubit to our stature (Matthew 6:27). However, we can whiten our teeth, perm our hair, lose weight and so on. When it is in our power to do something about unacceptable situations, we need to dive in and do it. And not just with our looks. Maybe we need to live on a budget, learn to cook, get a job, go to church!

Accept the unchangeable. My great-grandmother, Ella Hansard, always said, "What you can't change, you have to accept." However, accepting the unchangeable is much easier said than done. I have some issues from the past which have plagued me over the years. I have prayed about them and told myself over and over to forget about them. But, my mind is like a steel trap about remembering certain things. I know the past cannot be changed. Even when it is most unacceptable, I must learn to deal with it.

I am reminded of the Serenity Prayer: "God, grant me the serenity to accept the things I cannot change, courage to change the things I can and the wisdom to know the difference." God has given me the courage to change some things and He has given me wisdom enough to know the difference between things I can change and things I can't. My prayer now is for the serenity to accept the unchangeable.

Lord, grant me the serenity I need to accept things I cannot change. Amen

JANUARY 12th *JERRY'S CORVAIR*

"Thou shalt not tempt the Lord thy God." Matthew 4:7

When he was a much younger man, my cousin Jerry Tate loved to drive a little too fast. I experienced one ride with him I will never forget! I cannot recall exactly how old I was at the time. I just know I was riding in the back seat of Jerry's blue Corvair. His wife, Betty, was riding in the front in the passenger seat. We were headed home on Buford Dam Road.

Anyone familiar with this road can picture the steep hill. It crests where the road intersects with Nuckolls Road, As we zoomed down the hill heading toward the lake, I could see the speedometer indicating we were going more than 100 miles per hour! I had never been in a car with anyone driving so fast before. Although it was scary, it was also exciting. I couldn't wait to tell my mother.

I should have kept the news to myself. She was not one bit thrilled and strictly forbade me to ever ride with Jerry again! I don't know if she had been reading Ralph Nader's book, *Unsafe At Any Speed,* but she thought that was definitely an unsafe speed for her young daughter.

I am thankful the Lord kept us safe that day. There have been so many fatalities on that road and we could have been victims as well. It only takes a split second for an accident to occur and we have no guarantee that we will survive. Don't tempt the Lord! Drive safely.

Lord Jesus, thank You for keeping me safe. Help me not to tempt You by taking unnecessary chances. Amen

JANUARY 13th *FIGHTING PARKINSON'S*

"But I say unto you That ye resist not evil: but whosoever shall smite thee on thy right cheek, turn to him the other also." Matthew 5:39

George and I disagree on how to put this verse into practice. He says if a man breaks his jaw on one side, he is not letting the other side be broken as well! He says you cannot allow someone to bully you. I am absolutely against bullying, but the Bible seems loud and clear to me in this passage.

In his younger years, George was often a fighter. He and his friends sometimes rehash a few of the fights he was involved in. Their tales are epic. But, the hardest fight George has ever encountered is his daily battle with Parkinson's disease.

After a recent fall, he looked as if he'd been a few rounds with George Foreman! I was afraid he had broken his zygomatic bone because his eye was so swollen. Plus, it was extremely discolored. The entire left side of his face was bruised and bloody. But, Glory to God!, within a few days, his face was totally healed.

George is a real trooper. He may be tempted, but he never gives up. He knows God has a purpose for allowing this disease in his life. He says having this condition has made him a humble man. The Bible tells us in I Thessalonians 5:18, "In everything give thanks: for this is the will of God in Christ Jesus concerning you." So, he does actually thank God for Parkinson's.

This fight will not be over in a short time. This one will be an on-going battle. But, George knows Jesus said, "My grace is sufficient for thee: for my strength is made perfect in weakness (II Corinthians 12:9)." George will gladly glory in his infirmities, that the power of Christ may rest on him. And I see that power resting on him every day.

Lord Jesus, thank You for helping George and others in their fight against Parkinson's disease. Amen

JANUARY 14th *QUICK FLIGHT*

"In a moment, in the twinkling of an eye, at the last trump: for the trumpet shall sound, and the dead shall be raised incorruptible, and we shall be changed." I Corinthians 15:52

Our oldest son, Kevin, lived in Orlando, Florida for a time while he was attending the Motorcycle Mechanics Institute. He flew into Atlanta so that he could spend Christmas with us.

When it was time for his return flight, Randy, Joel and I drove Kevin to the airport. We left Cumming two hours early, but by the time we arrived at the gate, the passengers were already boarding. We stood at the windows and watched until the plane taxied out to the runway. (You aren't allowed to do that anymore!) We made one stop for a Coke and by the time we got home, Kevin had already called George and said he had landed in Orlando!

That was a fast flight, but I know of one that will be quicker. When the Lord descends from heaven with a shout, with the voice of the archangel, and with the trump of God, the dead in Christ will rise first and those which are alive and remain shall be caught up together with them to meet the Lord in the air (I Thessalonians 4:16).

Paul wrote a change must take place before we are caught up. He said that change would happen in a moment, in the twinkling of an eye. So, according to these two passages, I am under the impression the entire changing and catching up will happen speedily.

Kevin had purchased his tickets prior to his flight. Had he not done so, he would not have been allowed to board the plane. Being caught up to meet the Lord in the air also requires a ticket of sorts. It requires being saved by the blood of Jesus. I urge everyone to make preparations now for that future event. It will happen quickly and there will be no second chances. Don't be left behind.

Lord, thank You that my calling and election are sure. Amen

JANUARY 15th *STINKING THINKING*

"Let this mind be in you, which was also in Christ Jesus."
Philippians 2:5

I have heard Joyce Meyer talking about "stinking thinking." I am fairly certain most of us engage in this kind of thinking from time to time. I know I do. What exactly is this type of thinking? It is any thinking that does not agree with the mind of Christ. When we fail, we berate ourselves: It is all my fault; I should have done better; I can't do anything right; What's the use in trying?; How could anyone be so stupid? Etc.

In *Glory Days,* Max Lucado says these voices of failure are like monkeys in a cage, laughing at us. But the Bible is full of accounts of God using failures. Romans, 8:1 tells us, "There is therefore now no condemnation to them which are in Christ Jesus, who walk not after the flesh, but after the Spirit." God already knew we would fail. He had already provided the mercy and grace we would need to pick ourselves up and keep going.

We will fail to say the right things, we will fail to do the right things, we will fail to be the right people. But we can learn from our mistakes. God can turn all our failures into triumphs. Instead of letting stinking thinking dominate us, let's ask God to help us. The devil wants to keep us mired down, but God wants to lift us up and use us for his glory. Stinking thinking has to go!

Father God, help me have the mind of Christ. Amen

JANUARY 16th *PHYSICAL PAIN*

"That I may know him, and the power of his resurrection, and the fellowship of his sufferings, being made conformable unto his death:"
Philippians 3:10

I am thankful that so far I have not experienced much physical pain. The shingles were the most painful thing I have had to endure. The problem with shingles is that they seem to last forever! A lot of pain is over rather quickly, but not so with shingles. I know there are people who live with chronic pain. I offer my sympathy and my prayers for those who do.

However, I think of Phillip when I think of physical pain. He was a young man who was a member of Roanoke Baptist Church. He was diagnosed with cancer. When we visited him, he talked to us about the treatments and the procedures he had to endure. Some of them, to me, sounded excruciating.

I asked him, "Phillip, how in the world can you stand it?" His answer was so simple, yet profound. He said, "I just think of Jesus on the cross. I think of what He went through to save my soul and then I can bear my pain." Every time I read Philippians 3:10, I think of Phillip. He knew Christ, he suffered and he died. One day he will experience the resurrection power.

But all Christians, whether or not we are feeling physical pain, should want to know Christ more intimately. We share in his suffering and we become like him in his death so that we can attain the power of the resurrection. As Paul wrote, everything else is worthless.

Jesus, please ease the physical pain of those who are suffering. But, help us to know You better by what we endure. Amen

JANUARY 17th *RESENTMENT*

"Let all bitterness, and wrath, and anger and clamour, and evil speaking, be put away from you, with all malice:" Ephesians 4:31

Several years ago I went through a trial that left me feeling bitter towards the people that had instigated the trouble. I am ashamed to admit it, but I held on to this bitterness for years. The wounds caused by this event continued to sting as long as there was resentment within me. I wanted to be free of the pain, but I seemed powerless to rid myself of it.

As Jesus was crucified, I cannot imagine the pain the spikes caused when they were driven into his hands and feet. Yet, Jesus did not resent those who caused him torment. Instead, he prayed, "Father, forgive them; for they know not what they do" (Luke 23:34).

I am not implying my emotional pain was anything like the physical pain Jesus experienced, but I can see His response was what mine should have been. Instead of holding on to resentment like a security blanket, I should have been praying for God to forgive them for causing me pain. I could not force myself to forgive them. I had to ask God to bring that about by transforming my heart.

Lord, whenever I feel the nails of resentment, help me remember Your prayer from the cross. Amen

JANUARY 18th   *MISSING THE MARK*

"For all have sinned, and come short of the glory of God;"
Romans 3:23

Almost every sport has a target of some sort that a player aims for. In football, the quarterback aims for the receiver; in golf, the players aim for the next hole; in shooting contests or darts, one would aim for the bull's-eye; basketball players aim for the basket and so on. What is interesting is that no player in any sport has ever hit the target every single time.

Every year when Kevin begins to prepare for deer hunting, he practices shooting his bow. He has his target set up in the backyard. Most arrows hit the general area he aims for, but sometimes he has to do some minor adjusting to his bow. I once asked myself, thinking about William Tell and his son, if I could allow Kevin to shoot an apple off my head? I quickly decided I would not chance it. No one hits the target every single time.

It is the same with trying to live a perfect life. The Bible tells us all have sinned. We all miss the mark. The good news is that Jesus Christ, because he was fully God, DID live a perfect life and took the punishment for our sins. When we place our faith in His ability and not our own, we are counted as righteous. And that is true EVERY time.

Jesus, I know I have sinned and come short of Your glory, but I am so thankful for Your saving grace. Amen

JANUARY 19th *DEAL MAKERS AND BREAKERS*

"And Jacob vowed a vow, saying, If God will be with me, and will keep me in this way that I go, and will give me bread to eat, and raiment to put on, So that I come again to my father's house in peace; then shall the Lord be my God:" Genesis 28:20, 21

We all know that Jacob was a schemer and a dreamer. We have already learned how he turned his pillow into a pillar. But let's take a look at the vow he made after he anointed the pillar with oil.

Did you notice in the verses above the first word Jacob spoke was the word *if?* He said *if* God would do some things for him, then he would do something. In other words, he wanted to make a deal with God. He wanted God to give him safety, he wanted God to supply his need for bread and he wanted God to shroud his body. Only *if* God did these things would Jacob seal the deal and make the Lord his God. Only then would he sacrifice ten percent of his money or possessions to God.

We are probably tempted to say Jacob had a lot of nerve to try and bargain with God. If we are truthful, we have all probably tried to do the same at some time in our lives. *If* you will heal me, save me, give me the job I want, restore my marriage, deliver me from bondage (or whatever the need might be) I will read the Bible, I will pray more, I will give more, I will become a missionary, etc.

My pastor, Terry Cowart, said we are deal makers and deal breakers. We may promise God all sorts of things, but after He has given us what we asked Him for, we forget about our part. We revert to our old habits. We hope God will also forget what we promised to do. Yet, God's word is true and He is faithful to His covenants.

I aspire to be like the prophet Habakkuk. He wrote, "Although the fig tree shall not blossom, neither shall fruit be in the vines; the labour of the olive shall fail, and the fields shall yield no meat; the flock shall be cut off from the fold, and there shall be no herd in the stalls: Yet I will rejoice in the Lord, I will joy in the God of my salvation (3:17, 18)."

Lord, I do not want to put any requirements on our relationship. Like Habakkuk, I choose You to be my God no matter what. Amen

JANUARY 20th *MY FAVORITE BRIDGE*

"But now in Christ Jesus ye who sometimes were far off are made nigh by the blood of Christ." Ephesians 2:13

There are many noteworthy bridges in the United States, but I suppose the best known is the Golden Gate Bridge. It was thought a bridge across the one mile wide, three mile long Golden Gate Strait could never be built. Strong currents, blinding fog, blustery winds and deep water were factors which made building the bridge seem impossible. However, the bridge was built and it opened for service in May of 1937.

Before automobile traffic was allowed, over 200,000 people crossed the bridge on foot or on roller skates. I have never walked or skated across the bridge, but our son Justin and his friend April walked across in 2015. I have made many, many trips across the massive suspension bridge by auto, though. I lived in the area when my dad was stationed at Travis Air Force Base and I have also visited the area while on vacation with my husband and children.

Yet there is a bridge more meaningful to me than the Golden Gate. It is the one between sinful mankind and the Holy God. Bridging this gap between earth and heaven seemed impossible but Jesus became the bridge we needed. He gave His own life so that we might be forgiven. Only a loving God could span such a distance.

Jesus, thank You for being the bridge I needed. Amen

JANUARY 21st *BEST BUFFET*

"Thou preparest a table before me in the presence of mine enemies: thou anointest my head with oil, my cup runneth over." Psalm 23:5

Golden Corral has a commercial that says they have the best buffet in the USA. Whether or not you agree with that statement is purely a matter of personal preference. At any place with a buffet meal, who doesn't heap the plate up with food before going to the table? Who doesn't enjoy a selection of fruit, salads, vegetables and entrees? Who can resist a place where you can get cake, pie, brownies, cookies and ice cream at no extra charge?

Back in the day when there were Sizzler restaurants around this area, our son Justin would go back to the food line and fill up a plate multiple times. We could never figure out exactly where all that food went! He never seemed to gain an ounce.

I know the Bible tells us a man given to appetite should put a knife to his throat (Proverbs 23:2). It also says a glutton shall come to poverty (verse 21). So, why do we constantly overeat until we are miserable? Why do we not practice restraint?

Did you know the best buffet contains only two items: bread and wine (or, in some cases, grape juice)? Yes, I am referring to the communion table with the bread which represents the body of Christ and the drink which represents his blood. I know Paul the apostle gave us specific instructions on how to partake of the literal elements in the correct manner (I Corinthians 11), but I believe we may partake of the elements in the spiritual sense as often as we wish and we may take as much as we wish.

Oh, that Christians everywhere would feast on Jesus with the same enthusiasm as we give to the all-you-can-eat buffet!

Jesus, help me feast continually on Your sacrifice for me. Amen

JANUARY 22nd *THE WILLFUL WATCHER*

"For the eyes of the Lord run to and fro throughout the whole earth, to shew himself strong in the behalf of them whose heart is perfect toward him." II Chronicles 16:9a

I can clearly recall hearing our boys say to me, "Watch me, Mom!" or "Look, Mom!" They wanted my attention. They wanted me to focus on whatever it was they were doing at the time. Later, our grandkids also demanded the same.

Our grandson, Ryan, loved to see how fast he could run. He would ask me to time him as he ran from point A to point B. Or, he wanted me to watch as he practiced his latest skateboarding tricks. "Watch this, Grandmom!" was one of his favorite phrases.

I discovered that people were watching me also. I did not have to ask, nor did I necessarily desire this. My co-worker Jack called me "Goody Two Shoes." That title came to me because Jack saw I tried consistently to do the right thing.

When we know others are watching us, we try harder to do our best. We try to please them by the way we conduct ourselves. But, we have a Watcher who sees everything. We cannot hide anything from Him and He knows every single time we mess up in this life. God is our willful (deliberate, intentional) watcher.

The good news is that God is watching us because He wants to strongly support us! He is not trying to condemn us for failures, but rather to bless us in our efforts to live for Him. That is the best reason we should try to do better every single day!

Lord God, I know You watch over me and I am so thankful for Your strong support. Amen

JANUARY 23rd *D-I-V-O-R-C-E*

What therefore God hath joined together, let not man put asunder." Mark 10:9

The year my son Kevin entered the world, Tammy Wynette had country music's number one hit song, "D-I-V-O-R-C-E." I never dreamed I would be experiencing a divorce a few years later.

I was devastated when I walked out of the Fulton County Courthouse. I looked down at the ring on my finger and realized it no longer had any meaning. I felt *I* no longer had any meaning. My name no longer included the title Mrs. I felt so alone and so worthless.

I began to keep a daily journal. I poured my heart and soul into those pages. And I prayed harder than I ever had before. (For months, I had prayed for my marriage to be restored. Then I began to pray if it were not to be, God would help me move forward.) I gave Him all the shattered, tattered pieces of my life and asked Him to make me whole again. In my brokenness, God already had something in the making but I could not see it at the time.

Although God did not intend for divorce to happen, in his infinite wisdom, He knew it would. He knew when He created Adam and Eve they and all their offspring would be sinful creatures who would mess up their lives. He also knew He had a plan to restore us if we would accept His terms and conditions.

I am thankful for God's plan of salvation. I accepted Jesus as my Savior when I was ten years old. When I was twenty-five years old,

God gave me a new husband and a new lease on life. The old and the new working together to create a beautiful tapestry of love.

Thank you, Lord, for bringing so much good out of such a bad situation. Amen

JANUARY 24th *RETIREMENT*

"I must work the works of him that sent me, while it is day: the night cometh, when no man can work." John 9:4

The words written above were spoken by Jesus just after He had healed a man who was born blind. Jesus healed the man on the Sabbath although healing was considered work and work was prohibited on that day. However, Jesus said He must work while it is day because night was coming.

Matthew Henry, one of the greatest Bible commentators, said, "Whom God sends, he employs, for he sends none to be idle." He said we must not just talk about our work or look it over, but we must do it. Like Jesus, we must be about our Father's business while we are living. Night, or death as implied in this verse, is the time for resting.

All of us who have accepted Jesus as our Savior are called to be witnesses for Him. We need to be sharing the love and the gospel of Christ while we can because we do not know when our night is coming.

On this day in 2007, some of my co-workers at the Cumming Post Office hosted a retirement breakfast for me. They brought food and collected money to buy me some nice gifts. George, Kevin, Tyler, Joel and Jake all came to celebrate the day with me. It was a day I had been looking forward to for quite some time. It could only have been better had Justin and Jessica been able to make it, too.

One day our sun will set on this life and we will "retire." We certainly want to have all our family and friends around us in eternity. That is why it is so important to work for the Lord while there is still time. Invite someone to join you!

Lord, use me to witness to someone today before it is too late. Amen

JANUARY 25th *ADDICTED TO APPLAUSE*

"But as we were allowed of God to be put in trust with the gospel, even so we speak; not as pleasing men, but God, which trieth our hearts." I Thessalonians 2:4

I really can't remember when it began, but it was probably before I started school. That was about the time I started singing before small crowds with my aunt. We wore matching outfits and I stood in a chair to reach the microphone. Our signature song was "How Far Is Heaven?"

Anyway, I became addicted to applause. Not just the hand clapping kind. I began to love the kind words, the cards, the pats on the back, etc. I really wanted to obtain the approval of others. That gave me a sense of self worth.

Eventually, I took the Bible study course *Search for Significance.* I learned my approval is secure in Jesus. I am already accepted in the beloved. I do not need the applause of my peers to make me better.

My friend, Wanda Pittman Atkins, once gave me this thought for the week: We are saved by God's mercy, not by our merit; by Christ's dying, not by our doing! How true this is. The Bible says so! I now rest in the Lord and never worry about applause. Now, if applause of any kind comes my way, I try to always give the glory to God. He is the one to whom it is due.

Lord, I am sorry for the years I wasted seeking approval from others. Your love and acceptance are all I need. Amen

JANUARY 26th *PRAYING FOR A FRIEND*

"And he spake a parable unto them to this end, that men ought always to pray, and not to faint:" Luke 18:1

George has a friend whose mother was dying from cancer in early 2005. This lady was also a friend and former co-worker of my mother's. The three of us went to see her.

When we walked in, she was alert and called me by name. I felt led by the Holy Spirit to ask about her salvation. We began to talk about an evangelist who had visited the area recently and she said she really did feel the Spirit at the Holbrook Campground meeting. So, I did not ask her.

The next time we visited, her condition had worsened. We were only allowed to go in one by one. This time, I felt led to pray aloud for her, but she appeared to be sleeping and I did not want to disturb her. I simply laid my hand on her and whispered a prayer. My heart was heavy when I left because I did not go ahead and pray as I felt I should have.

When we went back on Sunday, her son invited us in and we started talking. In a couple of minutes I asked how his mama was doing and he said she had died earlier that morning! So, I never did what I had been impressed to do and now it was too late. She was gone and so was my chance to be obedient.

Please let this be a lesson for you. When the Holy Spirit bids you to do something, do not do as I did. Go ahead and obey immediately because you may never get another opportunity.

Holy Spirit, I am sorry for grieving You by being disobedient. Help me to stop rationalizing my actions and just do as I am bidden. Amen

JANUARY 27th *PAYING IT FORWARD*

"Yea, thou shalt see thy children's children, and peace upon Israel." Psalm 128:6

I had always hoped I could retire at the age of fifty-five and I did. But I jumped into another job right away. The job of keeping my grandson Jake while his mom worked. Jessica's mother and I rotated days, so it wasn't a full time job. The only pay was the pleasure of being able to pay forward the commitment my grandmother made when she agreed to keep my boys while I worked!

This little boy did not belong to me, so I wanted to do everything I could to carry out his mom's wishes for his care. I even made a notebook in which I kept instructions. I think I had something for almost every letter of the alphabet! I recorded the times he had bottles, the times he napped, etc. As he grew, he began to wear me out physically. I pulled him for what seemed like miles in the wagon. Later we played freeze tag, chase, baseball or any other game that involved running and sweating!

When Jada came along two and one-half years after Jake, I was thrilled to babysit a little granddaughter. I no longer kept a notebook, but I did begin to wonder how my grandmother managed to keep so many grandchildren when she was in her seventies! As Jada grew older, she wore me out mentally. We made up games to play. Using your imagination for hours on end taxes your brain, believe me!

Now, Jake and Jada have been in school a few years and Josi is here with me. She is not old enough yet to wear me out, but I know the day is coming! And I am actually looking forward to it!

Years ago, I read in a church bulletin, "Do all the good you can, by all the means you can, in all the places you can, at all the times you can, to all the people you can, as long as you can!"

When I think back over my life and consider all the good that has been done for me, I want to pay it forward! Not just by babysitting my grandchildren, but in every way I can. In Galatians 6:7, the Bible says, "Whatsoever a man soweth, that shall he also reap." Go out and do some good today. Pay forward some of the good that has been done for you. The rewards are eternal.

Jesus, help me to sow "good" everywhere I go today. Amen

JANUARY 28th *A MISERABLE MOTHER*

"And, ye fathers provoke not your children to wrath: but bring them up in the nurture and admonition of the Lord." Ephesians 6:4

Grandchildren are simply grand! I love being with them. I love listening to them. I love just watching them walk in the door! No matter how tired I am, seeing all the energy bottled up inside them energizes me. I have even heard it said that being with grandchildren helps keep Alzheimer's at bay by increasing brain function and memory!

I adore my grandchildren and have tried to be as wonderful to them as my grandmother was to me. That, however, does not erase the fact that I feel I was a miserable mother. In my early years of motherhood, I asked the older ladies at my church to teach me how to love my husband and my children properly. They thought I was joking, I guess. I wrote to a popular Bible teacher for help. I called in to a ministry's prayer line. I prayed for God to help me. I just could not seem to do mothering the way I thought it should be done.

I am guilty of being too harsh, too critical, too demanding, too quick-tempered, too you-name-it! I hated myself because I knew I was guilty of provoking them to wrath. I wish I had been so different. The good news is my children survived and all three are both loving and forgiving. Even better is seeing the two that are fathers now being so good with their own children. They surely patterned their parenting after George and not me!

My advice to young mothers would be to learn from my mistakes. Be kind. Be generous. Be honest. Be attentive. Be patient. In other words, be Christ-like. When my friend, Pat Sulka, was told working at the post office would be the hardest job she'd ever had, her reply was, "I don't think so. I've raised three kids!" Yes, mothering is a hard job, but it is the most rewarding.

Lord, help all the young mothers (and fathers) who are struggling in their roles. Amen

JANUARY 29th *PEELING POTATOES*

"In every thing give thanks: for this is the will of God in Christ Jesus concerning you." I Thessalonians 5:18

Although my grandmother passed away in 1989, every time I peeled potatoes I could still her admonish me, "Brenda, you are peeling your potatoes away!" No matter how hard I tried, I just never could seem to master those paper thin peelings she discarded from her potatoes.

I suppose I was too heavy handed. I suppose this trait not only showed up in peeling potatoes, but in all facets of my life. I needed a lighter touch. I needed less control and more relinquishment. I needed to surrender all my life's problems to the Lord.

However, I have now become more adept at peeling my potatoes. Justin bought me a potato peeler awhile back and I found that it really does the trick! I had never thought I needed one, but I found it makes this job much easier.

Know what makes dealing with life's problems easier? It is giving thanks in all things. Like a potato peeler, the Holy Spirit is the tool that helps make the troubles thinner. When we make use of the Spirit, there is not so much of ourselves wasted on trying to do it alone, trying to figure out what is best, worrying about why it happened and so on.

No one is happy when trouble comes. But when we can, by the Spirit, give thanks in the midst of the trial, it is amazing how much easier it becomes to deal with it.

Father God, thank You for the Holy Spirit who helps me in all my infirmities. Thank You for every trial which has caused me to turn my thoughts toward You. Amen

JANUARY 30ᵗʰ *FROM THE INSIDE OUT*

"For man looketh on the outward appearance, but the Lord looketh on the heart." I Samuel 16:7

God was very displeased with King Saul because of his disobedience. God sent the prophet Samuel to anoint a new king for the nation of Israel. Samuel was instructed to go to Bethlehem to the home of Jesse and his sons. God said, "Thou shalt anoint unto me him whom I name unto thee."

One by one, Jesse's sons passed before the prophet. When Samuel saw Eliab, a tall, good-looking young man, he thought surely this would be Saul's successor. But the Lord spoke to Samuel and said, "Look not on His countenance, or on the height of his stature; because I have refused him: for the Lord seeth not as man seeth; for man looketh on the outward appearance, but the Lord looketh on the heart."

After seeing each of the sons, Samuel was instructed to anoint the youngest one, David, to be the next king. David was also good looking and ruddy; however, God looked past the outward attributes and saw David's heart was after His own.

Bill Gaither and his wife Gloria wrote a song for kids entitled, "From the Inside Out." The song says: "From the inside out, God's looking at me. From the inside out, I hope He likes what He sees. From the outside I might not look so good, but you might change your mind if only you could, see me from the inside out."

It is still the same with us today as in the time of David. God is not concerned with our outward appearance as much as He is with our hearts. He wants our hearts to be tuned to His. He wants us to hide His words in our hearts. He wants our hearts to be pure and sound. In

Proverbs 4:23, the Bible says, "Keep thy heart with all diligence; for out of it are the issues of life."

I had much rather have a pure heart than a pretty face. How about you?

Jesus, you said, "Blessed are the pure in heart, for they shall see God." I want to see God. Help me keep my heart with all diligence. Amen

JANUARY 31st *MANY SINS*

"Wherefore I say unto thee, Her sins, which are many are forgiven; for she loved much:" Luke 7:47

George had a cousin who lived a very sinful life. Don't we all? But this man drank, cheated on his wife, used drugs, gambled, etc. He never seemed to care about the Lord in any way. When he passed away, his funeral was the coldest one you could imagine. The ministers even had a hard time trying to find good things to say. They focused on the goodness of Christ instead, as they should have.

Dr. Jimmy Orr said in a Bible study, "That person you can't stand? God loves him!" Every time this cousin's name was mentioned, I would have to remind myself that God loved him. I was repulsed by his lifestyle and his very name was repugnant to me! I had to remind myself Jesus died for him just as he did me.

But, truthfully, I am no different than this cousin. My sins may not be as many of the outward kind as this man's, but the sins of anger, resentment, self-centeredness, pride, selfishness, etc. were often rampant inside my heart. The Bible tells me all have sinned. All of us are less than that perfect standard which Jesus set. We all need Jesus to forgive us. I am sorry to admit, I was more like the Pharisee than the publican in regard to this cousin.

I am also sorry I have not lived a life that was more pleasing to the Lord. However, I am so grateful that God took my feet up out of the miry clay and set them on the rock. He established my goings (Psalm 40:2). Yes, my sins are many, but I am thankful I have been forgiven.

No matter what kind of lifestyle we have lived, nothing is too hard for the Lord to forgive. We may have done shameful things, but we no longer have to be ashamed. Jesus loves us everyone.

Lord Jesus, thank You for forgiving me of my many sins. Remind me often of where You brought me from and where I might have been had it not been for Your mercy and grace. Amen

FEBRUARY

FEBRUARY 1st *THE WAVE*

"For ye shall go out with joy, and be led forth with peace: the mountains and the hills shall break forth before you into singing, and all the trees of the field shall clap their hands." Isaiah 55:12

When my grandson Jake was a baby, I sometimes drove over to the Kroger on Bethelview and met his mom if she were in a hurry to get to her teaching job at Midway Elementary.

Every time I would open the door and peer into that car seat, my heart was filled with joy! Sometimes Jake was sleeping, and what is more precious than a sleeping baby? Other times, he was alert and would smile at me when I spoke to him. As he grew into a toddler, he could look out the window and see me as I approached the car. Often, he would put up his little hand and wave at me!

Jake had no idea he was such an ambassador of joy in my life. He could not have known how that simple wave made my heart sing and made me want to clap my hands! He had no way of knowing how he blessed my days.

In Isaiah, these verses are related to the salvation of the Lord. He freely gives us blessings. He generously forgives us. This promise of joy and peace is for all who will accept His pardon. I don't know about anyone else, but when I think of how God loves me and what Jesus did to accomplish my salvation that certainly makes me want to break forth with singing and clap my hands.

Maybe one day we will actually hear the hills singing and maybe we will actually see trees of the field clapping their hands. I don't know. Until then, I will try to share the joy of the Lord with others. That involves not only my words and my walk, but it also involves giving someone a smile and a friendly wave. Let's let our joy show!

Lord, Your joy is my strength. Help me share it everywhere I go. Amen

FEBRUARY 2nd *GROWTH CHARTS*

"As newborn babes, desire the sincere milk of the word, that ye may grow thereby:" I Peter 2:2

Hanging behind the door of the playroom, we have a Muppets growth chart. We have had it hanging there since 2001. The first entry is for Ryan and it is dated November 2nd of that year. He was four feet tall at the age of seven. Sadly, there is only one entry for Jackson. We measured his height at twenty-five inches on May 8, 2005. Tyler, Jake and Jada all have various markings with dates beside their names. Josi's first entry was January 30, 2016, at twenty-six inches.

It is easy to chart the growth of their physical bodies. In school, they are frequently tested to chart the increase of their knowledge. I, on the other hand, have been thinking about the way the Lord charts our spiritual growth.

Peter tells us to desire the sincere milk of the word. Paul said to the Corinthians, "I have fed you with milk, and not with meat: for hitherto ye were not able to bear it.(I Corinthians 3:2)." The writer of Hebrews says everyone that uses milk is unskillful in the word of righteousness and that strong meat belongs to them that, who by reason of use, have their senses exercised to discern both good and evil (5:13, 14).

Just as newborn babies start out with milk, so do newborn babes in Christ. We first need the simple truths and basic tenets of the gospel. As we grow in grace, we need the strong meat. The writer to the Hebrews says our senses are exercised BY REASON OF USE (emphasis mine). So, the more we walk in commitment to Christ, the easier it is to discern both good and evil.

The *Life Application Study Bible* says our spiritual growth determines our capacity to feast on the deeper knowledge of God. In other words, we reach the point where we need to stop going over the basics and press on to maturity in our understanding. When we abide in the vine, the fruit of the Spirit also becomes evident in our lives.

I hope the Lord is pleased with the way I have grown in my walk with Him. I hope there is much evidence I am pressing on to maturity. Just as Ryan is too tall now for the Muppets growth chart, I hope to reach the top of the chart in my spiritual growth.

Lord Jesus, help me continue to grow in grace and in Your knowledge. Amen

"And I said, Oh that I had wings like a dove! For then would I fly away, and be at rest." Psalm 55:6

My church took part in a mission trip to Kentucky a few years ago. I was very excited about being able to go along. I had to get up at 3:40 that morning in order to catch a ride with some friends. I rode with one of our deacons, Nathan, and his wife Susan. A few other ladies also rode in the car with us.

We met other folks from our church at the Publix parking lot on Highway 20 West. Craig Richard, our pastor at that time, led us in prayer and asked God to help us let our lights shine. Just as he finished praying the lights in the parking lot came on, illuminating us all with their glow! We took that as a sign of God's favor on the trip!

When we arrived, the first order of business was washing dishes. I washed until my arms ached. Jamie also washed for about an hour. Others rinsed, dried and stacked. After lunch, we worked in the food pantry. We organized, unloaded boxes and stacked groceries on shelves for hours. Later, we moved boxes of clothing and cleaning supplies to the proper areas and unpacked them. Finally, it was time for a meal and time for rest.

The next morning, we were all awakened when a new group of volunteers arrived at two o'clock! By the time they all got settled, it was almost time to get up again! After breakfast, we sorted through box after box and bag after bag of clothing. We sorted them by men's, women's and children's and then boxed them up again so we could move them out of the way. By this time, my back was "killing" me. I asked Craig, "Which Psalm says, 'if I had the wings of a dove, I would fly away and be at rest'?" He told me it was in Psalm 55:6. We all got a good laugh.

But, truthfully, I had never been so pleased with being so tired. I was thankful I could go and help that mission with the work that so desperately needed to be done. The needy of that community would have been unable to find the food and clothing in that building without the organization done by all the volunteers. And while I did not witness personally to anyone, some of our men were able to do so.

Working for the Lord may be physically exhausting. But the sheer satisfaction of being helpful to the less fortunate in His kingdom was worth every sore muscle and worth every hour of lost sleep!

Jesus, you said, "Inasmuch as ye have done it unto one of the least of these my brethren, ye have done it unto me." Thank You for the opportunity to serve You. Amen

FEBRUARY 4TH   A TOTE FULL OF TREASURES

"Then said he unto them, Therefore every scribe which is instructed unto the kingdom of heaven is like unto a man that is an householder, which bringeth forth out of his treasure things new and old."
Matthew 13: 52

Because I am so sentimental, I tend to hang on to things that have special meanings for me. I recently went through a very large, Rubbermaid tote. It contained not only my baby book and all my report cards from grammar school, but ticket stubs, cards, drawings the boys and the grandchildren made in school, award pins for Sunday School, and love notes from George.

One very special item I found inside was the little book, *Tie My Shoe.* It was one of the first books I ever read to Kevin. I had the book memorized and can still recite some of it forty-plus years later! But, this is not the original book we owned. In fact, I have no idea what happened to Kevin's copy. Maybe I donated it to someone or maybe it was thrown away in a move. Perhaps it was torn or colored in and beyond readability.

I had searched for a copy of the book for years. I looked in every book store and antique shop I entered. It simply was not to be found.
That is, not until Justin helped me find a "like new" copy on Amazon a few years ago. The day it was delivered, I was ecstatic. This is the book I chose when I volunteered to read to Jake's class! Maybe I will be able to read it to Josi's class one day.

However, my real treasure cannot be contained in a tote. My salvation is the greatest treasure I have and God's word is my all time favorite book to read. The Bible may be an old book, but it offers new insights for living every time I read it.

Lord, thank You for treasures such as salvation and Your Word. Amen

FEBRUARY 5th *YOU GET WHAT YOU NEED*

"But my God shall supply all your need according to his riches in glory by Christ Jesus." Philippians 4:19

In 1969, the Rolling Stones released an album that included the song, "You Can't Always Get What You Want." This song became known as the 100th greatest song of all time. The lyrics tell us we just might find we get what we need.

The Bible told us that, centuries before Mick Jagger did. In the letter to the Philippians, the apostle Paul promised us God would supply all our need. I have wanted many things I did not get. Not material things, necessarily, but more important things. For instance, I prayed and prayed for my marriage to be restored. I prayed and prayed for my aunt to be healed of cancer. Neither request was granted.

Maybe my prayers were not answered because I did not exercise enough faith. After all, Jesus said if our faith is as a grain of mustard seed, we can ask and mountains will be moved. I do believe I have a great deal of faith; I believe, however, that God's will supersedes my desires. Even Jesus prayed three times for the cup of death to pass from Him, yet He said, "not my will, but thine, be done (Luke 22:42)."

When we do not see our prayers answered the way we hoped, we can trust that God has something better in mind. Yes, my aunt passed from this life, but she is totally healed now. My divorce gave way to the marriage of my dreams. I am sure we all, like Garth Brooks, have examples of being thankful for unanswered prayers!

God is omniscient and knows what we need in every circumstance of our lives. All we can see is the here and now, but God sees our future. He knows what is best and will act accordingly.

God, even when it isn't exactly what I may want, thank You for supplying all my need. Amen

FEBRUARY 6th *ATTITUDE OF GRATITUDE*

"Giving thanks always for all things unto God and the Father in the name of our Lord Jesus Christ;" Ephesians 5:20

I have some pet peeves. One of those is ungratefulness. I want to hear a person say, "Thanks" when I give a gift or offer help of some kind. It is not that I want a person to think what I have done or given is the greatest, I just want the act to be acknowledged.

As children, we often get so excited, or dejected, over a gift that we momentarily forget our manners. My mother would not put up with ingratitude. She would prompt us with, "What do you say?" I have often wanted to prompt adults in the same manner!

I can't help but think God feels the same way. The Bible teaches us to be thankful. In the verse above, we are told to be thankful FOR all things (Emphasis added). God hears us say "please" so many times, but I wonder how often we remember to thank Him for answering our prayers.

We need to keep an attitude of gratitude as we go through each day. We need to be alert to all the blessings God bestows on us and let Him know how much we appreciate Him. I know it may be impossible to count *all* our blessings for there are so many. Nevertheless, let's try to be more grateful and remember to thank God even when we aren't begging Him for something. An attitude of gratitude can make your life a beatitude!

God, please help me remember how much gratitude means to You and to others. Amen

FEBRUARY 7th   LOST!

"For the Son of man is come to seek and to save that which was lost." Luke 19:10

From 2004 until 2010, there was a television series about a group of passengers who survived the crash of a commercial jet. Their flight was between Sydney and Los Angeles but they ended up on a tropical island somewhere in the South Pacific. I personally never watched the show, *Lost,* but I can identify with being lost and with some of my family members being lost for a short time.

On a trip out west, we temporarily lost our sons Kevin and Joel. We were driving in two cars and became separated in Jackson Hole, Wyoming. About three hours later, we were reunited in Idaho Falls, Idaho. That was very frightening.

We had another experience when we lost our son Justin. He was having surgery at the local hospital. We remained in the waiting room until we received word from the doctor Justin's surgery had gone well and he was in recovery. We were given a room number for him and were told we could go to that room and wait for him to be rolled in.

We waited and waited. After about an hour, I called the nurse's desk. I was told he would be there shortly. After waiting awhile longer, I went to the desk and demanded to know what was going on. I was told he was in a different room and had been there for over an hour! This wasn't so much frightening as it was aggravating.

In both these situations, we went seeking our sons who were lost. But, Jesus came to seek and to save those whose souls were lost, or separated, from God because of sin. He died on the cross and rose from the tomb so that we could be saved, or reconciled to God.

When our sons were lost, they were not hiding from us. Being separated from us was not something they chose. However, men and women have been trying to hide from God since the Garden of Eden. Today, I ask you not to try and hide from the Lord. He is seeking you this very moment. He wants a relationship with you. Surrender your heart to Jesus.

Lord, I am so thankful You came to seek and to save me. I pray for those who do not yet know You. Amen

FEBRUARY 8th *RESPIRATORY THERAPY*

"Thou hast heard my voice: hide not thine ear at my breathing, at my cry." Lamentations 3:56

When Joel was either four or five years old, he had an episode of difficulty in breathing. I am no longer certain what actually caused the attack. It was probably croup. I distinctly remember hearing Joel's harsh barking cough which made him sound like a seal!

In the middle of the night, we rushed Joel to the emergency room because of his breathing issues. He spent two days as an inpatient and most of that time was inside an oxygen tent. We were so thankful for Dr. Mize and our respiratory therapists, Candy Hammond and Mike Findley. They knew just what to do to help our son. However, we give all the glory to God for the healing.

The prophet Jeremiah was left to die at the bottom of a well. There was no water in it, just mire. One of the eunuchs spoke to the king and asked for Jeremiah's deliverance. The king ordered that Jeremiah be rescued before he died. In Lamentations, Jeremiah referred to his time of being in the well. He remembered the way God had delivered him and he asked God to continue to hear his breathing and his cries.

George and I heard Joel's noisy, labored breathing and his cries. We asked our King to deliver him and Joel's life was spared. We continue to ask God to hear us when we cry out. When it seems our breath is almost gone the Lord is still near us. He is still, we might say, breathing the breath of life into our nostrils.

Lord, thank You for hearing our voices when we call to You. Thank You that Your ear is not dull of hearing and Your hand is not shortened that it cannot save. Amen

FEBRUARY 9th *INNER STRENGTH*

"I can do all things through Christ which strengtheneth me." Philippians 4:13

In the movie, *Steel Magnolias,* Clairee Belcher said, "That which does not kill us, makes us stronger." Have there been times in your life that you thought something was so difficult, so painful you thought you would not survive it? Only after going through the ordeal did you find you not only endured but came out stronger?

I have been through some of those trials. I know I only survived some of them because I have the Lord living within me. I know I could not have survived on my own strength. When I use the word *survive,* I am not just talking about living. I mean surviving with my sanity and my emotions intact! (George questions the sanity part sometimes!)

First season winner of *American Idol,* Kelly Clarkson, recorded a song on her fifth album which became her third number one hit. The song was "Stronger (What Doesn't Kill You)." In this song, she says what doesn't kill you makes you stand a little taller, it makes you a fighter and makes your footsteps even lighter.

Kelly was only seven when *Steel Magnolias* was released, so I am not sure just where she got her inspiration for the song, but I know my assurance of inner strength comes from the Word of God. The strength

I get from the Lord helps me stand taller and makes my footsteps lighter. I can fight against the enemy because the weapons of my warfare aren't carnal, but mighty through God to the pulling down of strongholds. With Christ to strengthen me, a hurting experience leads to inner strength and to victory.

Jesus, I thank You for the strength You give me to stand in the midst of trials and to come out stronger. Amen

FEBRUARY 10th *TERMINATED TEARS*

"And God shall wipe away all tears from their eyes; and there shall be no more death, neither sorrow, nor crying, neither shall there be any more pain: for the former things are passed away." Revelation 21:4

I am not a crier. I do cry occasionally, but my tears do not fall easily. I like to tell people I cried so much when I was younger my tears have been used up! I am not callous or cold; I care very deeply about people. Yet I seldom cry.

Nevertheless, I am looking forward to the day when ALL tears will be wiped away. When we reach the New Jerusalem, there will be nothing that will cause us to cry. It is hard for me to even imagine a place without sorrow, death or pain, but I know I will see it for myself one day.

Robert Sterling Arnold was also certain about seeing a place where there would be no tears. In 1935, he wrote the song, "No Tears in Heaven," and it is still one of the more popular hymns today. It has been published in many hymnals and has been recorded by many gospel quartets and other artists. The song tells us in Heaven there will be no sadness, all will be gladness and there will be no sorrow that can dismay.

Won't it be wonderful when we reach that happy place? That place where we will see our Savior and be with Him forever? That place where we will cease to ponder over things of this life? That place where sorrow and pain will all have flown? That place where all will be made new? I am looking forward to it. I hope you are as well.

Even so, come Lord Jesus. Amen

FEBRUARY 11th *SELF DEFENSE?*

"Bear ye one another's burdens, and so fulfil the law of Christ." Galatians 6:2

My sister is still mad. She wanted to take karate lessons, but my brother Johnny was the one chosen for that privilege. She still talks about how he took a few lessons and quit when it was time to start breaking boards.(Johnny probably tells the tale differently!) She, on the other hand, was not allowed to participate. I know she would have been good at it, too! She is good at everything she does.

Maybe Mom thought Cathy was already well advanced in self defense. She thought I was. She always said she did not worry about me because I could take care of myself. I assure you, I am no Rowdy Ronda Rousey and I have never been in a fight in my life. Her thoughts are not accurate. I am weak in many ways. I need the strong back, the strong arms, the strong resolve of my husband George to help me make it through many of life's trials.

I once read this thought in a church bulletin, "Our job is not to see through one another, but to see one another through." The Bible says it this way: bear one another's burdens. George has a big job helping bear mine. There is another friend of mine, though, who not only bears my burdens, He is also my defender. His name is Jesus.

In karate, you get a different color belt for different levels of progress. A black belt is the highest and there is even a tenth degree black belt one may attain. When Jesus returns, I do not know what color His belt may be. I only know He has this on his clothing and on His thigh, "King of Kings and Lord of Lords"! He is the one who defends me and He is the grandest of masters!

Jesus, thank You for being my advocate. Amen

FEBRUARY 12th *PERFECT VISION*

"The light of the body is the eye: if therefore thine eye be single, thy whole body shall be full of light." Matthew 6: 22

My cousin, Gary Stanford, once shot me in the corner of my eye with his BB gun. I am not sure whether he was aiming for the center of my eye or the center of my forehead, but he came close, painfully close, to either target. (Is anyone thinking of Ralphie in *A Christmas Story?* If so, I might just mention Gary's middle name is Ralph!) Praise the Lord, I had no lasting problems with my vision.

I cannot imagine life without my vision. I know there are many who have never seen the blue of the sky or the face of a loved one. Despite their handicap, many have become very talented and successful in their respective fields of endeavor. I salute each and every one who goes through life without the gift of sight.

I believe in Matthew, chapter 6, Jesus was speaking about spiritual vision. He was saying a single, or clear, eye is one that is focused on God and not on things of the world such as earthly treasures. When we focus on wealth, our spiritual vision becomes cloudy. Jesus said we cannot serve God and mammon (money).

The *KJV Study Bible* tells us a good eye, to the Jews, indicated a generous attitude, whereas a bad eye was the sign of a miserly attitude. The bad eye represented an internal darkness and a moral blindness. We must, therefore, focus on God and serve Him alone. That is the only way to have perfect vision.

Lord, I want to focus my eyes on You so that my vision will be clear. Amen

FEBRUARY 13th *THE DOORKEEPER*

"I had rather be a doorkeeper in the house of my God, than to dwell in the tents of wickedness." Psalm 84:10b

In large cities, you will usually find a doorman stationed in front of the luxury hotels and high-rise apartments. His job is to offer courtesy and security to those entering the building. I can recall having a doorman at the Hotel Washington where we once stayed when we visited the D. C. area.

One year at church camp, I stood and held the door for our group as the people entered one of the buildings. As someone thanked me for my kindness, I quoted this verse from Psalms!

The psalmist who penned these words would rather stand and perform a menial task than to dwell comfortably in a tent with wicked people. But, keep in mind, when we are serving God, no job is to be considered menial. If we are doing a routine task and we feel unnoticed and unappreciated, we need to remind ourselves God is aware of every job we do.

Also, in Colossians, we are exhorted to do everything heartily as to the Lord and not as to men (3:23). Whether you turn on the heat and the lights at your church, scrub the bathrooms or empty the trash, all jobs are to be done for HIS glory. We may not receive accolades from our fellowmen, but God will reward us. His praise is more desirable by far than any honor we might receive from our peers.

Lord God, help me do everything for Your glory, especially routine tasks that earn me no recognition. Amen

FEBRUARY 14th *ETERNAL LOVE*

"Beloved, let us love one another: for love is of God; and every one that loveth is born of God, and knoweth God." I John 4:7

I am a card-aholic. I cannot stand shopping unless it is for cards! I had thought I might like to own a card store one day, but God allowed me to work part-time at Heavenly Dove instead. The Dove has Christian books and gifts, so I got all the benefits of displaying and reading the cards when they arrived without the headaches and responsibilities of being the owner. A win-win situation!

As soon as the cards come out for the next occasion, you will find me standing in front of the racks perusing each card for the perfect one. It is a very rare thing indeed if I do not have a card readily available for each special day. I love to send cards and I love to get cards. In fact, I would almost rather have a card than a present.

There is one drawback, however. I tend to keep the ones I am given. I have recently thrown away tons of cards I had received through the years. It was a painful, but necessary process. In my tossing, it was only the cards that had to go. The love represented by each one will remain in my heart forever.

John, a disciple of Jesus, told us to love one another because love is of God. Love is not a feeling, but a choice; a deliberate act of our will. I am not saying there is no feeling to love, but it is more than that. Love is of God and is, therefore, sacrificial. Love is giving your best for the betterment of others. Isn't that what Jesus did for us?

On this day we have set aside to express our love to our Valentine, let us keep in mind that true love is sacrificial, patient and kind. True love is not jealous, not boastful, not rude, not irritable, not demanding and keeps no record of wrongs. True love never gives up and endures through every circumstance. True love is eternal.

When compared to the Biblical standard, how does your love measure up? I believe I need to deliberately make better choices much of the time. I believe I will start today.

Jesus, You showed us the meaning of unconditional, eternal love. Help me to love others just as You have loved me. Amen

FEBRUARY 15th *THE SOWER*

"I have planted, Apollos watered; but God gave the increase. So then, neither is he that planteth any thing, neither he that watereth; but God that giveth the increase." I Corinthians 3:6, 7

In his retirement, my husband George has taken up gardening. When he was still working, he did have a few tomato plants, but never a garden. Our backyard is not big enough for more than a few rows which is all George, with his health issues, can handle anyway.

The first year there was so much rain, the garden did not do very well. Then, there was a lack of rain coupled with watering restrictions. Last year, we had more tomatoes "than Carter had liver pills" as my mother used to say! Even though I had taken a couple of canning classes with the county extension service, we chose to give away a lot of the bounty rather than preserve it for ourselves.

I read a poem about sowing and growing that spoke not to our gardening, but to our everyday living. Did you know you sow seeds every day? Seeds of kindness, seeds of joy and seeds of love are all like our tomato plants. They grow abundantly and are best when shared with not only your own family but others as well. Seeds of bitterness, seeds of hate or seeds of anger are like the weeds that choke the healthy plants and hinder their growth. They must be eliminated.

Yes, we sow the seeds, but God is the grower who gives the increase. Paul, in I Corinthians, was saying the sower is not as important as the grower. Whenever we do something that is beneficial to others, we must be careful to give the praise and glory to God. He should receive all the credit. When we honor Him, we reap a healthy and holy soul.

Father God, help me sow the right seeds in my garden of life and to praise You for the increase. Amen

FEBRUARY 16th *THE BREAD OF LIFE*

"And Jesus said unto them, I am the bread of life: he that cometh to me shall never hunger; and he that believeth on me shall never thirst." John 6:35

Bread fills our stomachs. It is known as a comfort food which provides consolation or a sense of well being. Comfort foods have a high sugar or carbohydrate content and remind us of home.

When I was growing up, bread was a staple. We would have never sat down at the table without a pan of biscuits or a pone of cornbread. Yes, for lunch we did have sandwiches from time to time and everyone knows it takes bread (preferably a loaf of Sunbeam) to make a sandwich.

Jesus did not say I am the red velvet cake of life, the fried potatoes of life or even the pot roast of life. He said he is the *bread* of life. The basic, daily food source. When we come to Him we never hunger and when we believe on Him we never thirst. Jesus was not saying our physical bodies would never need food or drink, He was saying our souls would be satisfied and sustained only through a relationship with Him.

Although I do not eat very much bread, I do love spending time with the Bread of Life. I like to feast on the Word daily. The junk food of worldly pursuits can never satisfy me, but Jesus sustains and nourishes my soul.

Jesus, thank You for being my daily bread. Amen

FEBRUARY 17th *NEW CAR*

"Blessed be the Lord, who daily loadeth us with benefits, even the God of our salvation." Psalm 68:19

My family was frequently letting me know I needed a new car. They were partially correct. My car was about seventeen years old and the check engine light stayed on almost constantly. But it was such a comfortable, dependable car. I hated to let it go. It was in great shape inside and out. I also hated the thought of having a car payment again after so many years of debt free driving.

A couple of years ago, George let me know he also thought it was time to say goodbye to "the old grey mare." I balked again. I pointed out to him that we had just had the emissions tested and gotten a new tag. I said I wanted to drive it a little longer. But other plans were in my near future.

While working at Heavenly Dove with my friend Kristi, there was an accident in the parking lot. Kristi yelled, "Bren, somebody just hit your car!" I had not seen nor heard the crash because I was in the back of the store. I went out to investigate. The lady who had caused the accident seemed to be in need of attention, so I yelled for Kristi to call the police.

As it turned out, my car was totaled and so was another car parked beside mine. I believe the car belonging to the at-fault driver was also totaled, but I'm not sure about that. So, contrary to my wishes, I had to get a new car. Our son Justin, formerly an automobile salesman, had connections and found a car for me. Buying it was painless and the payments were manageable.

While I was driving my old car, we got a new truck for George, welcomed two daughters-in-law, rejoiced in the births of four grandchildren, enjoyed multiple vacations and I retired from the Postal Service. God blessed us in many big, milestone ways. But he also gave us blessings in ordinary, everyday ways, too, such as the changing of the seasons, the ability to read, food, shelter and the list is endless.

What is sometimes challenging is to count your blessings when the unexpected happens. Like having to purchase a new car!

Lord, I am so thankful You daily load us with benefits. Help me see the good in everything. Amen

FEBRUARY 18th *SAVED BY THE BLOOD*

"And the blood shall be to you for a token upon the houses where ye are: and when I see the blood, I will pass over you, and the plague shall not be upon you to destroy you, when I smite the land of Egypt." Exodus 12:13

In 1994, George was admitted to ICU with chest pains and stayed in the hospital two days. A couple of days after his discharge, he was sent to St. Joseph's for a heart catheterization. The procedure showed no blockages or other signs of heart problems.

That should have meant all was well. But, there was one not so minor complication. George started to hemorrhage from the insertion site. This went undetected, due to the bandages and bed covers, until I moved the covers and saw the blood. I asked the nurse to check George and she sprang into action. Nurses and doctors came running. A little longer before the blood was noticed and George could have been the victim of exsanguination!

This reminded me of the passage from Exodus when the Lord was about to bring the children of Israel out of Egyptian bondage. He had his people kill a lamb (without spot or blemish) and put blood over the door and on each side of it. When the Lord came to destroy all the firstborn, the blood around the door was the token of salvation to all those inside.

Likewise, when we are saved, the blood of Jesus is our token of salvation. Jesus was the unspotted, unblemished Lamb whose blood was shed for the remission of our sins. The Lord God sees the blood and no longer looks at us as worthy of death. We are forgiven because the blood has been applied to our hearts.

George's life was spared because I saw the blood and called for the nurse. But, better yet, we have eternal life because of Jesus' blood.

Father God, thank You for seeing the blood when You look at me. Amen

FEBRUARY 19th *USE YOUR GIFTS!*

"Wherefore, I put thee in remembrance that thou stir up the gift of God, which is in thee by the putting on of my hands." I Timothy 1:6

If you are like me, you hate it if a person does not use the gifts you have given. It makes me feel that my gift is worthless. Sometimes, it makes *me* feel worthless. I may have saved a gift for a special occasion, but I try to make use of every gift I have been given. If a gift isn't used, the receiver's life may be less comfortable. The receiver may miss out on remembering the giver with each occasion of use.

First, we must consider the most important gift of all: the gift of salvation Jesus extended to us by His death on the cross. Why would anyone not make full use of this gift? When we reject it we are rejecting the very Son of God. Our eternity will certainly be more comfortable if we accept His offer of salvation! And every time I stop to consider what this gift cost my Lord, it makes me all the more grateful. I wonder how Jesus must feel when He sees his gift not used by so many.

I wonder how God feels when other gifts He has given us are not used. The spiritual gifts of helps, wisdom, faith and so on, of course, but what about the gifts of teaching, singing, encouraging, etc? When we sit back and "let someone else do it," what are we saying to Him? Your gift is worthless? You are worthless?

The best way we can honor a giver is to make full use of the gift and to use it joyfully!

Lord, thank You for all the gifts You have given me, especially the gift of salvation. Help me make full use of each one. Amen

FEBRUARY 20th *ALMOST ARRESTED!*

"While they promise them liberty, they themselves are the servants of corruption: for of whom a man is overcome of the same is he brought in bondage." 2 Peter2:19

I have never been arrested in my life. I did get a speeding ticket once when I was in high school. My cousin Gene gave me the money to pay my ticket so no one else found out about it! However, I did come close to getting arrested in Auburn, California, while on a family vacation. And I wasn't alone. George was in trouble with me. Our crime? Having our clothes in a dryer in the laundromat after closing time. Oops.

The attendant was outside in the parking lot and we thought we would have them out by the time she came back. We didn't and she called the police. Two female officers came and kindly directed us to a facility with later hours. They said "Welcome to California!" That was not the kind of welcome I was hoping for!

We were almost brought into bondage for simply trying to dry a few clothes. The bondage Peter wrote about in his second epistle was a different kind of bondage. False teachers were promising liberty, but instead, they were leading their followers into corruption and spiritual slavery. Peter was saying you are a slave to whatever controls you.

In order to avoid false doctrine, it is imperative to know the truth. We can only know it by studying the Word. My friend Linda retired from the Federal Reserve Bank. She was once interviewed on the evening news. The reporter asked her about counterfeit currency. She said the bank employees study not the fakes but the real bills. They become so familiar with legitimate dollars anything false is easily detected.

When we spend time studying the Bible, false teachings will be easily discerned. Do not be deceived and brought into bondage of false doctrine. Jesus said, "And ye shall know the truth, and the truth shall make you free" (John 8:32).

Jesus, keep me from being brought into bondage by believing false doctrines. Help me know the truth. Amen

FEBRUARY 21st *GOOD TRAINERS*

'Train up a child in the way he should go: and when he is old, he will not depart from it." Proverbs 22:6

In the Hebrew, the word translated "train" is *chanak*. It means figuratively to initiate or discipline. To initiate is to begin, or it is to introduce knowledge. Discipline is not necessarily punishment, but rather it is rules or methods for regulating the conduct.

I have been through some initiations in my time. For the Beta Club, I had to eat a pickled pork brain. Disgusting! I also had to do the limbo with a goldfish in my mouth. Thankfully, I did not swallow it! I would not say there was very much knowledge to be gained from these bizarre antics, but I learned I did not want to do either ever again!

When I think of discipline, I do think of punishment sometimes. But I also think of learning rules and regulations for suitable behavior. I think of coaches for each type of sport. I think of men and women who set aside time each week for training young boys and girls in the fundamentals.

When my sons were growing up, they played for many different coaches. I think back to the hours spent by men such as James Smith, Ronnie Shoemake, Stevie Shoemake, Hoyt Frix, Richard Gill and many more who tried their best to train young minds and young bodies to perform a certain way. Men who taught them the value of hard work and fair play. Men who mentored and inspired my sons.

Of course this verse in Proverbs speaks to parents. But, I believe, it also speaks to other figures of authority who work with our children. From the classroom to the ball field to the church. All who work with young people should strive to train them up in the way they should go. One of the best ways to do that is by being a good example.

Lord, I cherish the legacies of great parents and great coaches. Help me be a good example to young people who look to me for direction. Amen

FEBRUARY 22nd *THE PRESIDENT & THE POET*

"The fear of the Lord is the instruction of wisdom; and before honour is humility." Proverbs 15:33

Phillis Wheatley was a little girl who arrived in Boston, unclothed and toothless, on board a slave ship. She was purchased by a couple who taught her to read and write. Later, they set her free. Phillis wrote poems and sent one of them to George Washington. The future president invited Phillis to visit his headquarters and she accepted.

She had no way of knowing this man would soon become the first president of the United States. Washington had no way of knowing she would become the first African American to publish a book of poems. They were just two people who admired each other. Theirs was a friendship with no regard for rank, appearance or race.

Maya Angelou, who read one of her own poems at the inauguration of President Bill Clinton, received over thirty honorary degrees from colleges and universities all over the world. She is perhaps the best

49

known African American poet of our day. She is quoted as saying, "As a child of God, it is my duty to recognize that everyone else is also a child of God."

At the heart of humility is the ability to see people without regard to status, color or national origin. Bias has no place in the heart of a child of God. Every one we meet has value to the creator and, therefore, should have value to us as well. George Washington's meeting with Phillis Wheatley is just one example of humility.

Lord Jesus, help me value humility above honor. Amen

FEBRUARY 23rd *GOD'S REPORT CARDS*

"So then every one of us shall give account of himself to God." Romans 14:12

I was always a good student who loved learning. I was constantly striving to make the honor roll. From the seventh grade through the twelfth, I made straight A's. As I looked at some of my old report cards recently, I began to think about what grades I would get if God handed out report cards. I have to admit, I do not think I would do so well.

How does God feel about the way I am conducting myself? Am I doing as Jesus did, or doing my own thing? In elementary school, the teacher would sometimes write, "Brenda has talked a lot this six weeks." My grade for conduct would be a B or an A minus. Yes, I still love to talk, but would God grade me for talking too much and not following through with what I say? Would God say when I pray I do not listen closely to His instruction? Is my conversation seasoned with salt?

Would God grade me poorly in reading? How would I be graded for my comprehension of his word? In arithmetic, would God say I add too much to myself and not subtract enough to share with others? Am I multiplying joy and dividing sorrows? In history, would God grade me for remembering dates and details of wars with others? How am I doing in geography? Am I witnessing for Him wherever I go?

In the song, "I'm Going That Way," James Rowe wrote in the third verse, *And O I believe that when we meet, "well done" He will say.* At our spring revival, I could not sing those words. I just feel I have failed the Lord so many times, there is no way He could ever say those words to me. The sermon Clint Smith preached that night was about regret. I have a lot of regret in my life, but I am striving to make better choices daily.

My goal is to make God's honor roll. He knows I can never be perfect, but He grades "on the curve." He does credit the righteousness of Jesus to my test scores. Without that, I would certainly be a failure every time.

Jesus, I am so thankful for the extra credit You give me. My report card looks so much better because of You. Amen

FEBRUARY 24th *MUSICAL INSTRUMENTS*

"Let them praise his name in the dance: let them sing praises unto him with the timbrel and harp." Psalm 149:3

I am not sure why we do not dance before the Lord these days. This psalm clearly tells us to praise him in dancing. We have become too reserved. We are stoic on Sunday mornings. I admit, I am guilty, too.

I do own a timbrel, or tambourine, that I enjoy playing from time to time. For a short while Shannon Loudermilk played it at our church when the choir sang. Recently, Lori Tipton played it for us. However, it is not something we hear very often.

My friend, Cathy Smith, plays the harp beautifully. She has a CD that I love to listen to. The music is so calming and peaceful. Every time I read in the Bible about a harp, I think of my friend. God has given her such an amazing talent that is a great blessing to others.

Some churches do not even have a piano. The voices of the members are the only "instruments." Some have guitars, some don't. Some churches have drums while others frown on them. Some of our larger churches have full orchestras.

How does this all tie together? I believe we can praise God with dancing, shouting and clapping. I believe we can praise him with all kinds of musical instruments: noisy ones like cymbals and tambourines, and with quieter ones like the harp. The focus should be on praising God regardless of our style of worship.

As we come before our Mighty Maker, let's worship Him in Spirit and in truth. Let's worship Him without condemning those whose style may be a little different. And if the Spirit bids us to dance, I hope we will do just that!

Father, I worship You in the beauty of holiness. I want to always be mindful to give You the glory due your name. Amen

FEBRUARY 25th *A LIVING FAITH*

"Even so faith, if it hath not works, is dead, being alone" James 2:17

When I was a young girl, my mother was a chauffeur. Not the kind who drives a big, fancy car and has the passenger sit in the back. She was just a good Samaritan who drove sick friends to doctor appointments, cancer treatments, the pharmacy or grocery store. She never charged them one cent for gas, either. She was just happy to be of help.

When I was a much younger lady, I had a friend named Olive who did the same things for people in her church. No matter where a person needed to go, it was never too much of a bother for Olive. She had her trusty blue Toyota there at their beck and call.

Neither of these ladies expected a thing in return. They were just helping for the sake of helping. In other words, they were putting their faith into action. James, the Lord's brother, tells us faith without works is dead. We are saved by grace through faith, but works prove our faith is genuine.

The British Baptist preacher, Charles Spurgeon, once said, "A little faith will bring your soul to Heaven, but great faith will bring Heaven to your soul." My mom and Olive were demonstrating the great faith they have. Spurgeon also said, "A good character is the best tombstone. Carve your name on hearts, not on marble."

Only the Lord knows how many hearts have names like Joyce and Olive carved on them.

Lord Jesus, help me carve my name on hearts by putting my faith into action, too. Amen

FEBRUARY 26th *A CARING PHYSICIAN*

"Luke the beloved physician, and Demas, greet you." Colossians 4:14

I do not know of anyone who schedules a doctor's appointment just to say hello. Every time we go to see our doctor, it is because we are sick or it is time for some routine annual test.

In 2012 and 2013, George was in the office of Dr. Mize so often, we thought of making one of the exam rooms George's personal space. When he wasn't in the doctor's office, George was in the hospital or the urgent care facility. At no time did Dr. Mize give any indication he was tired of seeing us. At no time did he ever say, "Take two aspirin and call me in the morning."

Every time we go into his office, Dr. Mize takes time to hear us out about what is hurting or what symptoms we have. He never seems as if he is in a hurry to get on to the next patient. When he does not recognize immediately what our problem might be, he either sends us for tests or he refers us to a specialist.

He is compassionate and caring, consistently helpful, and completely dedicated to his profession. I imagine he is a lot like Luke, the beloved physician who accompanied Paul on his journeys.

As much as we think of our doctor, we have an even greater Physician whose name is Jesus. He has the power to heal us from any disease, especially the disease called sin. In fact, Jesus has a monopoly on the remedy for sin; you cannot get it anywhere else. Sure, there are a few "quacks" who claim to be able to free you from that dreaded disease, but do not believe them. Only Jesus can, and He will if you but ask.

Lord Jesus, You are the Great Physician. Thank You for dying that I might live. Amen

FEBRUARY 27th *SEATED WITH FRIENDS*

"Now therefore ye are no more strangers and foreigners but fellowcitizens with the saints, and of the household of God."
Ephesians 2:19

When I was the Director of the Hightower Baptist Association's Women's Missionary Union, I had to travel out of town to various training events. I arrived quite early to one such meeting and, being alone, picked out a spot and sat down. Soon, the room began to fill up with groups of ladies.

No one came to my table for so long I began to feel ostracized. At last, four women who needed seats together came in and sat with me. I noticed one of them had on a tag with the name of a certain church on it. I asked if she lived in that town. She said she did not; she just attended church there. I explained that I had a cousin who lived in the town and was just wondering if she might know her. As it turned out, all four of the ladies were great friends with Deenie!

Needless to say, we hit it off big time because we all love my cousin! No longer were we strangers, but friends. I thought about the body of Christ. Isn't that the way it is? When we all love Jesus, we have a common bond which makes us love one another. In fact, Jesus said, "By this shall all men know that ye are my disciples, if ye have love one to another" (John 13:34).

Love is the characteristic that sets us apart from unbelievers. You might say love is our "birthmark." How precious and peaceful to know we are all marked by the same Savior.

Lord, thank You for the love of Your saints and for Your unfailing love. Amen

FEBRUARY 28th *THE RIVER OF LIFE*

"And he shewed me a pure river of water of life, clear as crystal, proceeding out of the throne of God and of the Lamb."
Revelation 22:1

In the early nineties, Brad Pitt starred in the movie *A River Runs Through It*. He was the rebellious son of a stern minister. While spending the mornings in religious study, his afternoons were consumed with fly fishing in the Blackfoot River in Montana.

This movie was about a family who endured what every family endures, I suppose: happy times, sorrow, anger, yearning for days gone by. Woven into the story of the clashes between the family members was the stunning Montana landscape. The thought you are left with is, "all things merge into one and a river runs through it."

I cannot help but think of a river that will run through that city described in the latter chapters of Revelation. This river will be a pure river, clear as crystal. This river does not proceed out of the mountains of Montana, but out of the throne of God and the Lamb. This river is the water of life.

The river is often used in the scriptures as a symbol of the Holy Spirit and of eternal life. Jesus said in John 7:38, "He that believeth on me, as the scripture hath said, out of his belly shall flow rivers of living water." Believing on Jesus is having a river run through you, too!

You have all heard, I am sure, the Chinese proverb that says if you give a man a fish, you have fed him for a day, but if you teach a man to fish, you have fed him for a lifetime. Teaching a man about Jesus is also feeding him for a lifetime, if he accepts or "catches" the gospel message. In fly fishing, the lure is artificial bait, but the lure of the good news is the unadulterated truth of God's word. That truth is, of course, we are all sinners but Jesus died to set us free.

I have never been fly fishing, but I have a river that runs through me; the Holy Spirit of God. What about you?

Jesus, I am so thankful for the river of living water. Amen

MARCH

MARCH 1st *ASH WEDNESDAY*

"Then I proclaimed a fast there, at the river of Ahava, that we might afflict ourselves before our God, to seek of him a right way for us, and for our little ones, and for all our substance." Ezra 8:21

Although I am ashamed to admit it, I do not believe I had ever even heard of Ash Wednesday until I started my first public job. As you know, Baptists do not typically observe Ash Wednesday or the season of Lent. When I began to see people coming into the office with black smudges in the form of a cross on their foreheads, I began seeking the reason for this ritual.

Jesus fasted in the wilderness for forty days and endured temptations by Satan before beginning His public ministry. Lent began as a way to mirror His ordeal in preparation for Easter. The duration of Lent is actually forty-six days. However, since Sundays are considered to be commemorative of the Resurrection, fasting is inappropriate on those days. Observers of Lent fast from Wednesday through Saturday the first week and Monday through Saturday for six weeks.

Jesus made His triumphal entry into Jerusalem on what is known today as Palm Sunday. Some denominations burn the palm branches and save the ashes for the following year's Ash Wednesday service. The cross on the forehead is a visible reminder of man's sinfulness and mortality.

It is typical for an observer to give up something for this period. A way of denying oneself is to fast from meat or some other favorite food. Since I learned what Lent is all about, I have given up Cokes, tea, chocolate and ice cream. I think I even fasted from potatoes one year. Then, too, you could give up a favorite activity, like television watching or abstaining from Facebook! Or, one year, I committed to calling to check on someone every day during this period. That was significant as I do not normally like to chat on the phone!

Regardless of whether we chose to observe Lent, every day should be a day of repentance and sacrificing ourselves for the Lord. Paul told us in Romans, chapter 12, we should present our bodies a living sacrifice. He said that is our reasonable service. The sign of the cross on our foreheads is not necessary if our very lives show unmistakable signs that we belong to the Lord. And, finally, as we wait for the celebration of the glorious resurrection, let us all be mindful of what the Lord Jesus gave up for us.

Jesus, I know I am a sinner and I will return to dust one day. Thank You for giving up Your life so that I could be counted righteous before God. Amen

MARCH 2nd *NEVER SAY NEVER*

"To every thing there is a season, and a time to every purpose under the heaven:" Ecclesiastes 3:1

There is currently a television commercial for State Farm which gives me great enjoyment every time I see it. It starts off with a young man at a pool party with friends. He says, "I'm never getting married." Then it shows him at a jewelry store purchasing a diamond ring.

He and his wife are shown on an airplane. You can hear a baby crying loudly. He says, "We're never having kids." She concurs. The next scene shows them in the hospital with his pregnant wife in great pain. He is coaching her and saying, "Breathe!" After this, they are living in a loft apartment with the city skyline showing outside the window. Their baby is in a high chair and the wife is telling the husband she loves it there. He says they are never moving to the suburbs.

Guess what? The next scene is their home in the suburbs. They are doing yard work and you can clearly see their sports car in the driveway. An SUV drives by and the husband says they are never getting one of those. But, suddenly, he is shown soaping up his own SUV. He is then shown in the floor trying to scrub crayon marks off the wall. He tells his wife they are never having another child. The wife heads up the stairs with a basket of laundry and tells him she is pregnant! Finally, the entire family is shown snuggling together on the couch and the husband says, "I'm never letting go." I love it!

State Farm's message is to "make the most of life's nevers." We make rash statements about things we will never do, yet so often what we said we would not do is the very thing we will do. We are guilty of thinking our lives will go a certain way, but we are constantly having to deal with adjustments to our agenda.

When faced with unexpected alterations, we can recall the words of today's verse. There is a season and a purpose under heaven for everything. When we are disappointed with life, here is a new way to look at things. Replace the "d" with an "h" and you have His appointed. Everything that comes our way is filtered through God's fingers of love. He is in control and works all things together for good if we love Him and are called according to His purpose. So, don't let life's nevers throw you for a loop! Make the most of them.

Lord Jesus, thank You for all the nevers You have changed to evers in my life. Amen

MARCH 3rd *THE BIRTHDAY SONG*

"For this is the message that ye heard from the beginning, that we should love one another." I John 3:11

Elmer Anderson, a newspaper man and former governor of Minnesota, wrote the book, *Views From the Publishers Desk.* He told of being at a party where all the people were asked to guess the world's most popular song. No one came up with the correct answer which is "Happy Birthday to You." This is a song sung countless times every day!

Mildred Hill, a school teacher from Kentucky wrote the music and her sister, Patty Hill, wrote the lyrics. This simple little song has touched many lives with its message of well wishes.

While most people enjoy hearing the song sung to them, even if they are not happy about the age they have attained, I know of one little boy who never liked the song. In fact, he would cry and put his hands over his ears when anyone started singing the song to him. That little boy is my grandson Tyler!

He is almost grown now and doesn't mind the song, but when he was younger he hated it! Maybe he was embarrassed about the attention that was focused on him. Maybe he did not understand how happy his family was as we all tried to help him celebrate. Whatever his reasoning, he did not want to hear the world's most popular song.

It is sweet to think about those wishes of happiness going out to many someones every day, isn't it? Jesus wants us to love one another, and not just feel love but to show it. Sometimes, the love we try to show is not appreciated or accepted. If we are persistent, though, we just may succeed in winning someone over. Just as Tyler eventually came to accept and appreciate our rendition of "Happy Birthday to You."

Lord Jesus, help me show love to others even if, at first, they are not receptive. Amen

MARCH 4th *MARCH FORTH!*

"O God, when thou wentest forth before thy people, when thou didst march through the wilderness; Selah:" Psalm 68:7

There is only one day of the year that can be classified as a command. That day is "March forth!" Yet, God has given us a command to march forth every day.

The dictionary defines the word "march" as walking in time with steps of the same length; walking in a stately manner; walking or proceeding steadily and also as a long, hard walk. As Christians, our walk on this earth would fit either definition.

We are called to be united, to agree, to live in harmony. That is walking in time with others. Our steps are to be above reproach; we are to walk as Jesus walked. That is walking in a stately manner. We are told to grow in grace and in the knowledge of our Lord and Savior. As we mature, we are steadily proceeding in our walk. This life is full of troubles and trials which draw us closer to God. We were never promised the Christian walk would be easy, but we were told His strength is sufficient for us. In other words, our march down here is a long, hard walk.

The good news is a reward is waiting at the end of our march. Paul wrote in II Timothy, "there is laid up for me a crown of righteousness, which the Lord, the righteous judge, shall give me at that day: and not to me only, but unto all them also that love his appearing (4:8)."

Just as soldiers look forward to the end of a march when they can lay down their equipment, rest and receive refreshment, we will also lay down our heavy burdens, rest from our labors and be refreshed in eternity with our Lord. The more we march, the closer we are to the end of our journey. So, March forth!

Lord Jesus, sometimes my feet get weary. Sometimes my burdens seem too heavy. Help me to march on. Amen

MARCH 5th *DANCING LESSONS*

"And he said unto another, Follow me." Luke 9:59

On *The Waltons,* Joe Conley played the part of storekeeper, Ike Godsey. Ronnie Claire Edwards played the part of his wife, Corabeth. When first seen on the show, Corabeth is drab and seems downtrodden. Soon after marrying Ike, she begins to be quite pretentious. She has knowledge of fine arts and etiquette not seen in most women of the area.

To surprise Corabeth on their anniversary, Ike takes some dancing lessons from Rose Burton over at John and Olivia's house. With two left feet, it takes Ike some doing to learn the slow, slow, quick, quick, slow movements. Coordination and rhythm were not Ike's strong points, but he becomes quite proficient. Of course there were ins and outs to the plot, but Ike and Corabeth are shown doing the tango at the end of this episode.

The lesson I see in this show is do not give up. Keep on keeping on. Even if we are somewhat awkward when doing whatever the Lord has called us to do, persistence is key. What God asks us to do, He will give us the ability to carry it through. It is up to us to hold on. As Kay Arthur said, 'Hangeth thou in there, baby!"

Ike did not learn to dance overnight. He had to follow Rose's instructions one step at a time. We will not learn overnight all we need to know about the Christian life either. It is a step by step process. We must keep "practicing" daily to perfectly follow Christ, our leader.

Lord, help me follow Your lead. Amen

MARCH 6th *BLOOM HERE AND NOW!*

"Israel shall blossom and bud, and fill the face of the world with fruit." Isaiah 27:6b

I have often heard someone say, "Bloom where you are planted." I know exactly what that means. The speaker is saying we should make the best of a bad situation. We cannot choose the cards life deals us, but we can play the hand. Even if we are not exactly where we want to be, we can't give up. We can not only tolerate the present circumstances, we can thrive in them.

This phase in life will prepare us for the next one. We can choose to feel sorry for ourselves, or we can choose to be happy and keep walking towards our goals. Instead of complaining, we can look for ways to be a blessing to those around us. Instead of hoping others will change, we can change. Even if we are underneath what seems like concrete, we can be like the flower that somehow pushes through it.

John Hand was a mailman in the Los Altos Hills of California. The landscape on his route was bare and drab. He began to throw out seeds along the route as he delivered the mail. Soon, flowers sprang up and made the way beautiful. John Hand was the catalyst for change. A missionary to Peru, Vince Mortimer, said, "I don't mind God using someone else instead of me, but I don't want Him using someone else *because* of me."

In planning for the future, we should not forget about today! We should fully live in each moment because there is no promise that tomorrow will come. In other words, we should bloom where we are planted! We may just be the blossom that brightens the world for another.

Lord, help me make the most of my life's circumstances. I want to bloom where I am planted. I want to bless others and bear fruit for Your kingdom. Amen

MARCH 7th *MY PIANO*

"And he shall be unto thee a restorer of thy life, and a nourisher of thine old age:" Ruth 4:15a

In the early seventies, I bought myself a piano. I saw it at Rich's and just had to have it. It was an upright piano. It had been restored and I liked the way it looked. It was bright red! It had a mirror across the upper front panel and the pedals were gold. The bench had a white padded seat. I even opened a charge account with the store in order to purchase this prize. (I am not recommending this practice, by the way!)

A few years passed and I was moving to a new place with no room for my favorite possession. I sold it to my cousin Barbara with one stipulation. If she ever wanted to sell it, I was to get first chance to buy it. She kept the piano for many years, but the day came when she got a new one for her daughter Lisa. She kept the bargain we had made and gave me the opportunity to purchase it for the same price she had paid me all those years ago.

George has had to move this heavy piano several times and he says never again. If we ever sell this house, he says the piano goes with it! I will admit I do not play it very often. My playing ability was never as great as my desire anyway. However, the restored instrument has been such a delight to me and my grandchildren. I have it willed to my granddaughter Jada. Hopefully, if we should move, George will change his mind about leaving it in the house!

It took someone a lot of time and effort to restore this piano, but the result was all worthwhile. I am reminded of the work God has done with my life. He took me and made a new creation out of me. Not only that, He restores my soul as well! I sure hope He feels His work with me was all worthwhile.

Father, thank You for making me new. I hope the music I am making for You is beautiful to Your ears. Amen

MARCH 8th *RECIPES FOR LIFE*

"And these words, which I command thee this day, shall be in thine heart: And thou shalt teach them diligently unto thy children, and shalt talk of them when thou sittest in thine house, and when thou walkest by the way, and when thou liest down, and when thou risest up."
Deuteronomy 6: 6, 7

In early 1975, some of my cousins surprised me with a baby shower for my second child. It had been seven years since my first baby and I needed lots of things! Everything I received that day has long since been discarded, but I do have one keepsake I have held on to all these decades. It is a recipe for chocolate pudding written by Diane, wife of my cousin Charles. She jotted it down for me after the shower.

I have kept another recipe from the seventies written by my aunt, Bodie. I also have one dated 1986, written for me by Jeanne Marie Cowdrey. I have kept these recipes (even though I may have them memorized) because they hold a special place in my heart. When I fix these dishes, I recall the special people who took the time to record the instructions for me. Of course I have many other treasured ones, but these are some of the oldest.

These recipes remind me of the words given to the children of Israel. God gave Moses the instructions to speak in their hearing. God said the words were to be in their hearts and they were to be taught to their children. God said to talk of them as they went about their daily routines. I am so thankful these instructions were written down and they serve as a token of remembrance for us today.

The best recipe for life is to be mindful of God. We need to keep His words in our hearts and we need to teach them to our children. We need to use our daily routines to tell others about what the Lord has done for us. Like Moses, we could also write down our special encounters with God, specific instructions he has given us and our words of praise to him. These special "recipes" could be handed down to our children and grandchildren. I can only imagine the delight they might bring to future generations. Why not start today?

Lord God, thank You for the words given to Your servant Moses. Thank You for preserving these words for us today, because Your instructions are truly our recipe for life. Amen

MARCH 9th *WHAT IFS?*

"Finally, brethren, whatsoever things are true, whatsoever things are honest, whatsoever things are just, whatsoever things are pure, whatsoever things are lovely, whatsoever things are of good report; if there be any virtue, and if there be any praise, think on these things." Philippians 4:8

My what-if thoughts get me into trouble emotionally. *What if this test shows a real problem? What if George doesn't mean what he says? What if I had made a better decision?* Etc. Once these kinds of thoughts creep in, they wreak havoc with me. I dwell on the endless possibilities too often instead of thinking on the things of God.

Marion Bond West once wrote about a mental picture she uses to keep these thoughts at bay. She imagines a truck backing up to her mind and taking away all the garbage. Next, a mesh-like dome is placed over her mind. This dome has G shaped slits in it and only the thoughts from God can get in! I like this illustration.

I also have a mental picture I use. I picture myself boxing up all my hurts, failures, worries and tormenting thoughts. I then toss this box to Jesus. He catches it and keeps it. In the Bible we are taught to cast all our care on Him for He cares for us. Today, I am going to practice only thinking God shaped thoughts.

Jesus, help me think on the things that are of good report. Help me box up all other thoughts and give them to You. Amen

MARCH 10th *BLINDED EYES*

"He answered and said, Whether he be a sinner or no, I know not: one thing I know, that, whereas I was blind, now I see." John 9:25

The ninth chapter of John is one of my favorites. I love the account of Jesus healing the blind man and the Pharisees' questioning that man about his healing. The Pharisees were angry because Jesus healed the man on the Sabbath day. They said only a sinner would break the laws of the Sabbath. The verse above shows the healed man's response to their accusations!

The man was born blind, so he had never seen Jesus before this encounter. He did not even know who Jesus was. The Bible does not tell us the man asked Jesus to heal him, it simply says Jesus passed by, saw the man and healed him. After repeated questioning by the Pharisees, the man then begins to be sarcastic when answering them. I find his answers quite amusing. Why not read the chapter right now and see for yourself.

Pulitzer Prize winner and Poet Laureate of the United States, the late Robert Penn Warren, had dreamed of attending the United States Naval Academy and becoming a career naval officer. However, those dreams were shattered when he was accidently hit in the eye by a lump of coal. His injury created a new vision for his life's work. He began to write, his talent emerged and the rest is history.

God is able to create order out of chaos. Scott Walker, author of *The Edge of Terror,* said God can bring resurrection from our most agonizing crucifixions. Therefore, when our vision dims, we can trust God to give us new dreams. Whether we are physically healed of blindness, as was our friend Jonathan Haight, or given visions to pursue new paths, God can and will turn tragedy into triumph. Our job is to trust Him.

Father God, open my blinded eyes that I may see clearly the path You have prepared for me. Amen

MARCH 11ᵗʰ   *HALTED ON THE HIGHWAY*

"And an highway shall be there, and a way and it shall be called The way of holiness; the unclean shall not pass over it; but it shall be for those: the wayfaring men, though fools, shall not err therein."
Isaiah 35:8

In 2001, George and I planned to spend our anniversary in Branson. We chose to go through Alabama, up to Memphis and then over to Little Rock. We crossed the Arkansas line about eight o'clock and then made a stop at nine-thirty to gas up, get snacks and call home. When we got back in the car, we switched places and I began driving.

We were about an hour away from our hotel when disaster struck. We came to a screeching halt on I-40. We had no idea what had taken place. We inched along and stopped, inched along and stopped. Stayed stopped. Inched some more. For four straight hours! (Now that I am writing about it, I am thinking of the snow jam we had not long ago when folks were stranded on the highways for two to three times that!)

Even though we were going crazy, we had a drink, snacks and a full tank of gas. That was more than we could say for a lot of our fellow travelers. When we got stopped beside an eighteen-wheeler, we asked the driver what was going on. He told us there had been an accident up ahead. However, there was no place to exit the expressway. All traffic was stopped on both sides of the interstate between exits 161 and 169. We finally learned that a big rig had hit a
bridge and the structure was unsafe for anyone to pass under or over it.

What a nightmare! We were re-routed eventually and we stopped just outside of North Little Rock at two in the morning. We were so tired, aggravated, hungry, thirsty, low of fuel and just plain ill! By the time we got into our room at four o'clock, we had been up for twenty-two hours. Not the best way to begin a trip.

I doubt anyone stuck in traffic that night would have called the highway the way of Holiness. Neither the clean nor unclean could have crossed the bridge. Though there were plenty of wayfaring men and women, it is impossible to say how many were fools. Maybe all of us for being on that stretch of highway at that particular time!

Like the land of Israel, Arkansas was difficult to cross that night. But Isaiah was writing of a highway he saw that would lead to God. He was saying the unclean couldn't travel that road since it was leading to the holy God; but by repenting, they would be permitted on this road. And even a fool could travel the road without getting lost.

We had inched along, slowly but surely. We did not know what was ahead, but we knew where we wanted to go. We kept going in spite of difficulty. That is exactly the way we walk the road to God. We get started on our journey the moment we are saved. The going may be agonizingly slow at times, but we must keep traveling. We may have times when trouble snarls our plans, but the key is knowing where we want to go and continuing to travel in that direction.

When halted on the highway, stay focused on the destination ahead.

Lord, keep me focused on my eternal destination as I travel life's road. When I encounter problems, help me to keep pressing on. Amen

MARCH 12th *GOD-GIVEN TALENTS*

"And he hath filled him with the spirit of God, in wisdom, in understanding, and in knowledge, and in all manner of workmanship;" Exodus 35: 31

In the late sixties, psychobiologist and Nobel Prize winner Roger Sperry discovered the human brain has two very different ways of thinking. The left side of the brain is the verbal one. Characteristics of the left brain are logic, language, facts, words of songs and thinking in words. The characteristics of the right brain are the more creative ones and this side focuses on visuals. The right hemisphere is where arts, rhythm and tunes to songs originate.

When I think of a multi-talented person, I always think of my cousin Denise. She has so many talents, I cannot even name them all. Denise seems to be using all her brain power in both halves! First, she is very intelligent. She is a reader, a writer and speaks three languages. She remembers facts and uses logic.

She is an accomplished piano player. She has taken lessons, but she also plays by "ear." She can hear a song and be playing it in minutes. I could ask her to play a song I wrote twenty years ago and she would play it flawlessly, even though she had not heard it in as many years. She is also able to transpose a song into any key whenever necessary.

She not only plays music, she is able to knit, crochet and paint! She does beautiful calligraphy. All of these talents require her to sit and be still; however, she was a "mean" second baseman when she played softball. (Several years ago she tore her plantar fascia and is no longer able to display her talent on the ballfield.)

Denise reminds me of Bezaleel, son of Uri, from the tribe of Judah. God had given him the talent to devise curious works, to work in gold, silver and brass. God enabled him to cut stones, to set them and to also carve wood. In addition, God put in his heart the ability to teach.

When the children of Israel were building the tabernacle, God gave Moses the pattern for everything which was to be constructed. Moses was not chosen to do all the work, however. God gave some men very special talents so the work could be completed.

I am more like Moses than Bezaleel or Denise. I do not possess all these talents, but I do have a heart for God. I want to use the abilities He has given me to serve Him and worship Him. I do not waste time wondering why God did not give me as many talents as someone else. I am just thankful He chose me to be a part of His family. If you have ever felt you have nothing to offer, I encourage you to ask God to show you His purpose for you. Our lives are all meaningful.

It just might be that you (or I) have not spent enough time honing the skills God intended us to use. Maybe we cannot all play a musical instrument. Maybe we cannot all paint or sew. But each and every one of us can pray for others, we can be a witness for Him and we can all make a joyful noise in praising His name. If you can't be a Bezaleel, be a Moses, a Caleb or a Joshua. We are all looking toward the same Promised Land!

Lord Jesus, help me use the talents You have given me to further Your kingdom. Amen

MARCH 13th *DAFFODILS*

'For the sun is no sooner risen with a burning heat, but it withereth the grass, and the flower thereof falleth, and the grace of the fashion of it perisheth:" James 1:11

When we see the daffodils blooming, we realize cold weather is just about over and spring is coming. These beautiful yellow flowers are the first to poke their heads up out of the cold, winter hardened soil. I have read daffodils are symbolic of friendship. They have been among the most popular flowers to be photographed, painted or written about in poems.

A couple of years ago, George and I visited Gibbs Gardens to see the largest display of daffodils in the nation. There are over twenty million daffodils planted in these gardens with over one hundred different varieties. There are about eight different colors as well. If you haven't visited, I would suggest you take a trip there this year. It is too beautiful to adequately describe. The only downside is the short growing season. Daffodils do not last very long.

Considering the short span of these flowers reminded me of the brevity of all life. James, brother of our Lord Jesus, said our lives are like a vapor. It quickly fades away. It is rare for someone to live to the age of one hundred; even if one does, that is a very short period of time when compared to the years of mankind on the earth.

What can we learn from the daffodils? Our time here is short. We should not assume we have many years in which to serve the Lord. We need to let our love for our family be known today as there is no promise of tomorrow. Make the most of every day for it very well could be your last. Start each day praising God and go about doing good. End each day being thankful. This is the way to lie down in peace.

Dear Jesus, help me make each day count because I realize my time on earth is short. Amen

MARCH 14th *PERSISTENCE*

"Yet, because this widow troubleth me, I will avenge her, lest by her continual coming she weary me." Luke 18:5

When I was a young girl, I can recall my mother telling my dad the automakers should put wipers on the rear windows of cars just as they did on the windshield. My dad, who worked at General Motors, told her the idea was ludicrous. Who had ever heard of such a thing and who would ever go for it? She never mentioned it again as far as I know.

After doing some recent searching on Wikipedia, I found the first rear window wipers were actually offered in the forties. But, I doubt my parents had ever seen them. Especially here in the "backwoods" of north Georgia. Rear wipers became popular in the seventies after being offered on certain Porsche and Volvo models in the sixties. You will normally see the rear wipers on SUVs, hatchbacks and mini-vans.

My mother's idea reminds me of the unjust judge in the book of Luke. A widow in a certain city came repeatedly to the judge and asked him to avenge her of her adversary. He would not for a while because he did not fear God or regard man. But, her persistence paid off. The judge said she troubled him with her coming again and again, so he agreed to avenge her.

Jesus used this parable to show God avenges His own elect, who cry day and night to Him, even though He is forbearing. Our tendency is to give up and quit praying if we do not see an answer right away.
The *Women of Faith Study Bible* says persistent prayer is tenacious, constant, even insistent. Jesus encourages us to ask again and again. God, unlike the lackadaisical judge, will respond eagerly to our persistence.

But, I wonder about those wipers. What would have happened had my mother pursued her vision? I wonder if she could have gotten a patent on her rear window wiper? What would her life be like today had she been the one to sell the idea to the major automobile makers?
We will never know. Neither can we know just how things might work out if we keep our requests before God. So, keep praying and expect God to answer!

Jesus, I know You did not mean for us to engage in endless repetition. But I know You expect us to keep on asking, seeking and knocking. I want to persist in my pursuit of God. Help me, I pray. Amen

MARCH 15th   *HEARING AIDS*

"Son of man, thou dwellest in the midst of a rebellious house, which have eyes to see, and see not; they have ears to hear, and hear not: for they are a rebellious house." Ezekiel 12:2

George's hearing capacity was suddenly diminished. He was in the backyard when he noticed he could no longer hear as well as he had just minutes before. After a test by an audiologist and an exam by an otolaryngologist, we were told he needed hearing aids. Glory to God, our insurance paid one hundred percent of the cost!

George had to remember to remove his hearing devices when cutting grass or operating any loud equipment. One day, he put the aids in his shirt pocket and failed to remove them before placing the shirt in the laundry. What do you suppose happened? Yes, I did. I washed and dried them! Uh-oh. But, Glory to God, they still worked! We were ecstatic.

Thinking of his hearing aids reminded me of the many times in the Bible God spoke of people who had ears but did not hear. He wasn't saying they literally did not hear His words, He was saying they did not heed His words. God called these non-hearers rebellious. He said they were disobedient. The book of James tells us to be doers of the word and not hearers only.

Our willingness to *believe and obey* makes us true hearers. God has so graciously provided some hearing aids for all who desire to hear. We have the Bible and we have the Holy Spirit. They are readily available, but will do us no good unless we USE them. Today, I want to make full use of my hearing aids. How about you?

Lord, help me be a true hearer of Your word. Amen

MARCH 16th   *REJECTING LIES*

"Jesus saith unto him, Thomas, because thou hast seen me, thou hast believed: blessed are they that have not seen, and yet have believed." John 20:29

Have you ever listened to the lies of the enemy? I know I have and still do sometimes. Lies such as: *You are worthless. No one cares*

about you. You cannot do anything right. You might as well give up.
Etc. When I focus on these lies, instead of the truths of God's words, they seem to echo louder and louder inside me. Pretty soon I become so discouraged, these lies seem more real to me than God's promises.

Until 2008, I had never really noticed the word LIE is right there in the middle of the word "believe." What an eye-opener! When I get discouraged, I can focus on the LIE, or I can BELIEVE God. The truth is, God has chosen me as His daughter. The truth is, He loves me with an unconditional, everlasting love. The truth is, He knows what I need before I ask. The truth is, He will never leave me nor forsake me. The truth is, He promises me hope regardless of circumstances that seem so hopeless.

Thomas (known as "Doubting Thomas") wanted to literally see the nail prints in Jesus' hands. He wanted to touch the prints and he also wanted to thrust his hand into Jesus' side before he would believe in Jesus' resurrection. Often, we are like Thomas. We become doubters, too, when we cannot see the physical proof. However, God's Word says we can believe without seeing because His Word is the truth.

Rather than being fixated on the lies of the enemy, we need to guard our minds. We need to make a conscious effort to put on our helmet of salvation every day. The adversary knows our actions are controlled by our thoughts. If he can get our thoughts turned away from the truth, he knows we are more susceptible to disobeying God in our actions. Therefore, it is imperative we BELIEVE God and see the enemy's LIES for what they really are.

Jesus, help me start each day by putting on my helmet of salvation so my mind is guarded from the lies of the enemy. Amen

MARCH 17th *TELESCOPIC PHILANTHROPY*

"But if any provide not for his own, and specially for those of his own house, he hath denied the faith and is worse than an infidel."
I Timothy 5:8

In Charles Dickens' novel, *Bleak House,* Mrs. Jellyby is called a "telescopic philanthropist." She is obsessed with a little known, far away African tribe, but does not consider the notion "charity begins at home." It is thought Dickens based his character on female activist of the time, Caroline Chisholm. Ms. Chisholm was involved with the female immigrant welfare in Australia.

I began to question my own telescopic philanthropy. Am I not eager to write a check when I hear of earthquakes in Haiti, a tsunami in Indonesia, starving children in Ethiopia and so on? What about flooding in the Midwest, a hurricane that hits Louisiana or a town in Alabama leveled by a tornado?

Writing a check is easy. Getting involved and actually helping in a physical way is more challenging. I confess, I am not often found doing much. But, sometimes, I am up for the task. I might take dinner to a family, give money to someone in need or run an errand for someone. I thoroughly enjoy volunteering at the local food bank and I try to be there at my post every month.

Telescopic philanthropy is certainly necessary. But, servanthood should also be nearby and neighborly. Caring for those close by, and especially in our own homes, is a spiritual responsibility we should not take lightly. Families should care for their own. I do not want the Lord to consider me worse than an unbeliever. Do you?

I read somewhere (possibly in *Our Daily Bread*), "Life is like a game of tennis: The player who serves well seldom loses!" In the hymn "I Must Tell Jesus," we are told He ever loves and cares for His own. We must do the same.

Lord Jesus, help me care for those close by as well as those far away. Amen

MARCH 18th *LIFE'S SWEETENERS*

"The memory of the just is blessed: but the name of the wicked shall rot." Proverbs 10:7

When we visited Vermont, we went to a sugar house to see how syrup is made. Vermont is the nation's leading producer of maple syrup and produces over 1.3 million gallons every year.

As the ground thaws from the cold winter, the sap is drawn up to give new life to the branches. The sap is collected in buckets and then boiled down to make the syrup. Maple syrup is quite tasty on pancakes, but it is also used in making candy and in baking pies and cakes. Syrup adds sweetness to food and drinks.

I thought of people who have added sweetness to my life. Their love and care flowed into my soul like the sap from the maple tree flowed into the bucket. They were the hands and heart of the Lord on this earth and I am so grateful for their memory. I thought of my dad's parents who cared for me until the day they died. I thought of my aunt who treated me as her own daughter. I thought of great-aunts, great-uncles and teachers. I thought of friends such as Louise Nix. She was old enough to be my mother, but she was such a special friend.

Of course, there are many people today who are still loving me and caring for me. Without their influence, I would not be where I am now in my walk with the Lord. It is my heart's desire to impact others for good just as these blessed ones have done for me. I hope my memory will add sweetness to the lives of others for many years to come. I want to be a life shaper and a blessing.

Lord, I want to be just so that my memory will be a blessing to others. I hope my name does not rot because I am considered wicked. Help me, I pray. Amen

MARCH 19th *BLOOD DONOR*

"For this is my blood of the new testament, which is shed for many for the remission of sins." Matthew 26:28

My dad was a blood donor for years. He had given gallons by the time he passed away. Every time he got a new pin from the Red Cross showing his latest achievement, I was so proud of him. I wanted to do the same sacrificial deed when I got old enough.

An average adult may donate blood every fifty-six days. A pint is taken from the donor and the entire process lasts about one hour and fifteen minutes, although the actual blood donation is usually around ten minutes. Afterward, you get juice and cookies!

Although I wanted to be a blood donor, there was just one problem. A donor must weigh one hundred and ten pounds! When I married, I weighed less than one hundred. Until I was in my thirties, I had only gone above that mark three times in my life during pregnancies. I kept waiting for the day when I could go to the blood drive and be accepted as a donor.

Finally, the day arrived. It had taken me years and years to reach the acceptable weight, but I could finally donate and hope my blood could be used to save a life. I was able to donate many more times afterwards. Some experiences were more pleasant than others, but it was always satisfying to know I had helped in my small way.

Of course, donating blood makes me think of Jesus. He shed His blood once, and His donation was sufficient to save the life of every person who has ever or will ever live. Isn't that amazing? He died on the cross for all who will believe in Him and accept Him as their Savior. It is that simple.

If you do not know Jesus as your personal Lord and Savior, why not ask Him to save you today? He is just waiting for you to ask. The process is painless and it is quick. There is no weight limit nor age limit. Furthermore, the satisfaction of knowing you have eternal life is much better than a cup of juice and a few cookies. Accept Jesus while there is time!

Jesus, thank You for shedding Your blood for my sins. Amen

MARCH 20th *THE DEEP PLACES*

"In his hand are the deep places of the earth: the strength of the hills is his also." Psalm 95:4

Neither my mother nor I can remember why we did not see the Grand Canyon as we moved to California and then back home again. But we did not stop there, and I really wanted to see it. In 1988, on our first long road trip, my family made certain we had this stop on our itinerary.

There was just one slight miscalculation. My brother Randy and I were the trusty navigators and map readers on this trip. We decided we would bypass US 180, and we would take a less traveled road a little farther west. Little did we know, there was no visitor center farther west and we had traveled about one hundred miles out of the way. So much for our great plans.

I told George we would just forget about it and keep going, but he knew my heart was set on seeing this natural attraction. So, we turned around and rode the one hundred miles back. It seemed my hopes for a wonderful trip were just meant to be dashed. We ate in the cafeteria at the park and the food was terrible. Also, my camera would not work and I did not get the first picture!

Nevertheless, I stood in awe of the canyon. I was amazed by the colors of the sandstone and limestone cliffs. The Colorado River, which cuts through the canyon, is calm in places and turbulent in others. The canyon is 277 miles long, up to eighteen miles wide and at least a mile deep. Had my camera been working perfectly, there is no way I could have adequately captured the beauty and majesty of God's creation.

Like the Grand Canyon, God's thoughts are very deep and very wide. His works are great (Psalm 92:5). He holds the deep places of the earth in His hands. And they are too wonderful for description. The geologists say the canyon is billions of years old. I don't know about that. But one thing is certain: "Before the mountains were brought forth, or ever thou hadst formed the earth and the world, even from everlasting to everlasting, thou art God (Psalm 90:2)."

I experienced God's everlasting power while viewing the South Rim of the Grand Canyon. Several years after my trip, my friend Mary Evelyn gave me copies of some beautiful pictures she had taken there, and I was pleased to put them in my photo album. However, I am so thankful I got to see the canyon for myself and have the memories to cherish.

O, the depth of the riches both of Your wisdom and knowledge, Father God. How unsearchable are Your judgments and Your ways past finding out. Amen

MARCH 21st   FINDERS KEEPERS?

"Thou shalt not see thy brother's ox or his sheep go astray, and hide thyself from them: thou shalt in any case bring them again unto thy brother. And if thy brother be not nigh unto thee, or if thou know him not, then thou shalt bring it unto thine own house, and it shall be with thee until thy brother seek after it, and thou shalt restore it to him again." Deuteronomy 22: 1, 2

I have often heard the expression, "Finders Keepers." I have also heard it said possession is nine-tenths of the law. So, I have found money, disposable cameras and various items I have kept because I had no way of knowing to whom the items belonged.

On the other hand, I lost my digital camera and someone turned it in to Lost and Found at Disney World. What a blessing! George left his Hurrycane in the shopping cart at Home Depot and someone turned it in. In both cases, the finder had no way of knowing to whom the items belonged, yet knew the rightful owner would want these items back.

When Joel was a teenager, he found three hundred dollars outside a restaurant here in town. He was so excited to have found such a large amount of cash. Even though it was very tempting to "take the money and run" (as Steve Miller sang), it was not the right thing to do. He learned from Jim and Denise Owings (parents of a friend) a waitress had lost the money and he should give it back. And he did.

Sometimes, we are tempted to keep things that are not rightfully ours. God's plan is for us to return those things whenever we can. When we know what God expects of us, we are less likely to be overcome with greed or dishonesty.

George, the waitress and I were all so thankful there are still honest people in the world. The next time you find an item, remember these verses from Deuteronomy and return it to the owner if at all possible. You will be glad you did and so will the one who accidently dropped the item or left it behind. Furthermore, your honesty will be pleasing to God.

Father, help me to remember Your words when I am tempted in any way. Amen

MARCH 22nd *PRESENTING THE CANDIDATE*

"Then said I, Ah, Lord God! behold,I cannot speak....But the Lord said unto me, whatsoever I command thee thou shalt speak. Be not afraid of their faces: for I am with thee...saith the Lord."
Jeremiah 1:6-8

Calvin Bailey, our friend and fellow church member, was called to pastor Free Spirit Baptist Church. It was his responsibility to select a man who would present him to the presbytery at his ordination. He chose George.

George has never been one to speak in front of a crowd of people. Mr. Elrod, one of his former teachers, tried to convince George it was no big deal. Finally, he gave up trying and told George to forget about it. Even when we married, George had his back to the congregation but was still so nervous his voice cannot be heard on the recording of the ceremony! Needless to say, he was quite anxious about the upcoming service.

George had never been to an ordination before and had no idea how it was to be carried out. He prayed about what to say. The main thing he did was trust God. He did not make any notes for his first public "speech." When he stepped into the pulpit and began to speak, he said all the fear left him. I know I am biased, but I thought George did an amazing job. I was so proud of him.

When we feel we are incapable of doing something, when we are called to step outside our comfort zones, when we have never attempted a certain thing before, we just need to depend on the Lord. Just as the Lord promised He would be with Jeremiah, He will be with us. He will give us the words to say. There is no need to be afraid of the faces you see in front of you. The Lord will be your helper. Just ask George.

Lord God, thank you for being with us and giving us the words to say when we feel incapable of speaking. Amen

MARCH 23rd *BLOTTED OUT!*

"I, even I, am he that blotteth out thy transgressions for mine own sake, and will not remember thy sins." Isaiah 43:25

I know how George felt about stepping outside his comfort zone. I experienced the same thing when God called me to write a devotional book. Angie McKinney originally presented the idea to me, but of course I said I needed to pray about it. My arguments were many. I do not know how to write. I do not know one thing about a computer. I do not know that many things to write about, etc. God convinced me it was His will.

Even though I had made a little notebook for the month of January and had given one to several people for Christmas, I had already deleted those devotions from my computer! I had no idea how to set up a PDF and had to get my friend, Jonathan, to do that. Then, I made a HUGE mistake.

I was trying to skip a certain day and write about it later, so I was trying to copy and paste other entries when I discovered I could no longer go back to "Desktop." I thought I needed to "x" out of the window. The screen asked if I wanted to save the changes and I clicked yes. Then I discovered all the work I had done had disappeared. I could not restore it! I did not know how. I literally sobbed and sobbed. George thought someone had died because I was crying so hard.

I can see all you computer whizzes laughing at my ignorance, but I am okay with that. Now, I can laugh, too. At the time though, it was very, very traumatic. I felt I just simply could not start over. Several days later, I met with Jonathan again and with a few clicks of keys, he had all my devotions back for me.

This experience reminded me of how God blots out our sins when we are converted. He promised to remove them from us as far as the east is from the west. He said He will remember our sins no more. Once we accept Jesus as our Savior, our sins are gone! Someone said God throws them into the sea of forgetfulness and puts up a "No Fishing" sign. Whether you like that picture or not, the main point is God sees the righteousness of Jesus when He looks at a Christian. No clicks of any keys will ever restore our sins to our record. Hallelujah!

God, thank You for blotting out all my many sins. Amen

MARCH 24th *A TIME FOR PRUNING*

"Every branch in me that beareth not fruit he taketh away: and every branch that beareth fruit, he purgeth it, that it may bring forth more fruit." John 15:2

Spring is the time for pruning trees. Well, most of them. Pruning should be done when the coldest part of the winter has passed. Pruning rids a tree of dead or diseased branches which, in turn, protects the tree from insects or other organisms invading the tree. So, pruning benefits the tree by making it healthier.

George takes care of the pruning at our house. Every time he does it, I am inclined to think the trees are ruined! Pruning makes me sad. I can say the sadness doesn't last long. Once the deadwood is cut away, the trees begin to grow strong and healthy, I am then thankful George knows just what to do and when to do it.

I, like our trees, also need pruning. A spiritual pruning. Deadwood that hinders the stronger growth of my faith needs to be cut away. Doubt needs to go. So do self-righteousness, anger, resentment, pride, anxiety and so on. It is time for everything that might cause decay in me to be taken away. It is time to be made healthier.

Even though it may be painful for a time, pruning helps bring forth the most luscious fruit. Jesus said, "He that abideth in me, and I in him, the same bringeth forth much fruit: for without me ye can do nothing (verse 5)." I want to be pruned so that I can bring forth much fruit for my Lord. Don't you?

Lord Jesus, take away everything in me that causes decay and make me fruitful for Your kingdom. Amen

MARCH 25th *BREAKING THE LAW*

"If the Son therefore shall make you free, ye shall be free indeed."
John 8:36

I've already said I have never been arrested. I have never been locked away because of some crime. However, on many different occasions I have visited various people who were behind bars. I am currently sending cards to several inmates and I pray almost every day for people who are incarcerated. Nothing is too hard for the Lord to forgive, so I pray especially for those who have committed the most heinous crimes.

I am telling you this because I have been thinking of all the crimes I have committed. I have broken God's laws and yet I am walking around free. James tells us if we have broken one law we are guilty of all (2:10). He also says, "Therefore to him that knoweth to do good, and doeth it not, to him it is sin (4:17)."

If God doled out punishment as does our legal system, I would be on death row I suppose. Or, I would be locked up for life. Thankfully, I can go free because Jesus set me free. He paid the price for my sins when he died on Calvary's cross. He took the punishment I deserved. I am free indeed!

Yes, I have been behind the walls topped with the razor wire and the searchlights. I have heard the CLANG of the metal doors. I have been through the security checkpoints. I have been locked in; but only for a brief visit. I have been able to walk out again. I have felt the relief of being freed from those places.

That relief is nothing when compared to the relief of not being held accountable to God for all His laws I have broken. I am what the law would call a habitual offender. Yet, my record has been wiped clean. I am so grateful for the freedom Jesus afforded me. If you are still held in prison because of your sins, ask Jesus to forgive you today.

Lord, thank you for dying for me and taking the punishment I deserved. Amen

MARCH 26th *SWINE FLU!*

"...for I am the Lord that healeth thee." Exodus 15:26b

In 2012, our son Joel contracted the swine flu. He had not been feeling well for a couple of days, but no one thought he was *that* sick. One morning, I woke up at 3:30 with a weird feeling. I can't explain it, but just felt like something was wrong. I began to pray for everybody I could think of and finally went back to sleep. A few hours later, Jessica called and said she was taking Joel to the doctor. In a while, she called and said he was being admitted to the hospital.

Joel was severely dehydrated, so we thought he would get some fluids and be out shortly. Wrong! When I went to see him, I had to put on a mask to go in. The next morning he was told of his diagnosis. I prayed his babies would not get it!

Meanwhile, the door to his room had to stay closed. Everyone, including all the hospital staff, had to put on gowns, masks and gloves to enter his room. We quickly found out that staff members do not want to be bothered with all that garb, so they try to avoid the patient if at all possible. One night, he did not ever get his supper tray in spite of repeated requests. At least he did not have much of an appetite.

Although deaths from H1N1 occur mostly in young children and the elderly, death can occur from respiratory failure, pneumonia, dehydration, electrolyte imbalance or kidney failure. The good news is

Joel was out of the hospital in a few days. When he came home, he still had to wear a mask to prevent spreading the disease to his family.

We praise the Lord for healing Joel. We are also thankful no one else in the family caught it. Yes, God can heal all manner of diseases, but I am most thankful that I am healed of the ravages of sin.

Jesus, You were wounded for our transgressions, You were bruised for our iniquities: the chastisement of our peace was upon You: and with Your stripes we are healed. Thank You.

MARCH 27th *LAMININ*

"And he is before all things and by him all things consist."
Colossians 1:17

I have never been a science "nerd." In fact I hated science. So, I have no idea why I joined the Science Club when I was in school. I suppose it was to get my picture in our annual as many times as possible! The hardest class I ever took was a tenth grade biology class taught by Mr. Douglas Frederick. I was bewildered when my cousin, Gina Tate Thompson, became a science teacher. Of all the subjects!

So, why did I become so fascinated when I heard of laminin? It is because laminin is shaped like a cross. I cannot explain all there is to know about it. You can look it up on the internet for yourself. But, it basically glues cells to a foundation of connective tissues. Or something like that!

Louie Giglio used laminin in a sermon as "proof" that God holds all things together. All of us who believe the Bible as the infallible word of God do not need scientific proof He holds it all together. I am, as Pastor Louie, just amazed that even the basic components inside our bodies reflect God's plan of salvation by way of a cross.

Think about it this way. Before Adam breathed his first breath, he carried inside his body the shape of a cross. The very image that would bridge the gap between sinful man and a Holy God.

Yes, God was before all things and He does hold it all together. God is the Creator and the Sustainer of life. When your world seems to be falling apart, just remember laminin. The cross is a reminder of God's mercy and grace.

I just wonder how many other "signs" there are in our world around us that we do not recognize or that we take for granted?

Lord, thank You for the sign of the cross inside our bodies. Thank You for holding us together. Amen

MARCH 28th *SIGNS IN THE SUN*

"And there shall be signs in the sun and in the moon, and in the stars; and upon the earth distress of nations with perplexity; the sea and the waves roaring;" Luke 21:25

On March 11, 2012, a planet sized ball was seen attached to the sun by a dark "thread." A burst of light could be seen leaving the sun's surface and then the ball detached and shot out into space.

People who saw this pictured on YouTube thought it might be a UFO or the birth of a new planet. The way NASA scientists explained it is way over my head, but they called the "thread" a prominence. The Solar Physics Laboratory project scientist, Joseph Gurman, said a prominence that extends over the edge of the sun is one that is about to erupt. He says this is a common occurrence. Not as exciting as a UFO or a new planet, but the truth.

Every eleven years, sun spots and solar flares reach peak activity. When this happens, the energy released sometimes wreaks havoc on the earth. It can disrupt communications, destroy satellites and cause issues with the magnetic fields. My niece's husband, Jimmy Payne, took us out on his carport that day and showed us how a metal broom could stand straight up by itself! Amazing.

Also on this date, something extremely funny happened to George out in the backyard. Well, he did not think it was funny, but I sure did. Something fell from the sky and hit him in the head. It was a piece of CHICKEN! I told him chicken would be the death of him yet! I am not saying this was because of the sun burst. I suppose a hawk or some other bird dropped it from a tree. But it was ironic this happened on the same day.

Jesus said one day there will be signs in the heavens. Cosmic signs of desolation and destruction. The world will be perplexed and anxious when these things come to pass. Men's hearts will fail them for fear. The powers of heaven shall be shaken. However, Jesus told believers to lift up our heads for our redemption is drawing nigh.

No one knows the day or the hour of Jesus' return. But, we must be ready. We must put our faith and our trust in Him. Then, when these signs in the heavens do occur, there will be no cause to fear.

Jesus, we await Your return. Help us to be watchful without being distressed or perplexed. Amen

MARCH 29th *MY LIGHT AND MY SALVATION*

"The Lord is my light and my salvation; whom shall I fear? The Lord is the strength of my life; of whom shall I be afraid?" Psalm 27:1

I love this verse. Several years ago, my cousin Denise wrote it out for me in calligraphy and painted beautiful purple (my favorite color) flowers as a border. I have her artwork hanging in one bedroom.

This verse reminds me to put my trust in the Lord. He is my light and my salvation. He is my strength. There is no need to be afraid. Whom should I fear? No one! The Lord is mightier than all others. He is the One who will rescue me from danger.

David wrote this psalm. As a shepherd, he was constantly exposed to danger. Roaming the hills were ferocious animals. Marauding bands were out to steal his flock of sheep. Also, David was without much protection from the elements. Was he afraid? No! He knew the Lord would take care of him.

Even as a young man, David was able to give an account of the Lord's protection. David told King Saul a lion and a bear came and took a lamb from his flock. He told about going after that lamb and smiting both the lion and the bear! Furthermore, David stood up to Goliath when all Israel cowered in fear. David slew that giant in the name of the Lord.

We may not face literal lions, bears or giants these days. But, we have problems that loom large over us like these would. Just remember, we must come against all our giants in the name of the Lord. He will be our strength and will give us the victory if we trust in Him. Don't be afraid. Call upon the name of Jesus.

Lord, You are in control. There is nothing to fear because You are always near us. Thank you for Your constant protection. Amen

MARCH 30th *WONDER WOMAN*

"I am as a wonder unto many; but thou art my strong refuge."
Psalm 71:7

A superhero is a fictional character that has superhuman powers, works to defend the public and is morally upright. I cannot name every one, but we are all familiar with Superman, Captain America, Spiderman, Batman, and the Green Lantern. In the fifties, female superheroes Batwoman and Supergirl were introduced. Wonder Woman was first introduced in DC Comics in 1941, but became very popular in the sixties as the first female in the Justice League.

All of our children have, no doubt, pretended to be a superhero at one time or another. All of us older folks probably have, or had, our favorite, too, I suppose my favorite was Captain America, but I could probably identify more with "Wonder" Woman. Not because I am anything like Lynda Carter who portrayed the character on television, but because I do things that will make you wonder about me!

I often cause myself to wonder why I have said or done certain things. I often wonder how God can be so forgiving and merciful to someone like me. I wonder how Jesus could stand the pain of the cross and why He endured it for me. I wonder if I am too much like the Pharisees. I wonder if I will live to see my grandchildren saved. I also wonder why I don't trust and obey like I should.

The writer of this Psalm says he is a wonder unto many. I believe he is saying God has been his protection and strength, and regardless of what the future holds, God will continue to be his helper. I wonder as I ponder all these things.

In his book, *The Treasury of David,* Charles Spurgeon wrote: "The saints are men wondered at; the believer is a riddle, an enigma puzzling the unspiritual; he is a prodigy; a wonder gazed at, feared, and, by-and-by, contemptuously derided. Few understand us, many are surprised at us." But, our strength is from God.

I think "Wonder Woman" is a good title for a Christian lady. Yes, we wonder about ourselves. And yes, others wonder about us. Few understand how we stand strong in our trials and many are surprised when we do not fall. The psalmist said God is our strong refuge. We should share the unfailing love of God and His marvelous grace with as many as we can while we can. Let's not leave them wondering, let's give them the reason for the hope that is in us.

Father, thank You for being my strong refuge. I never have to wonder if You will be there for me because Your promises never fail. Amen

MARCH 31st *PB&Js TO PANHANDLERS*

"And the King shall answer and say unto them, Verily I say unto you, Inasmuch as ye have done it unto one of the least of these my brethren, ye have done it unto me." Matthew 25:40

My first public job was at an insurance company in downtown Atlanta. After I had been with the company a few years, a new boss was hired in my department. His name was Michael Pollard and he was a Catholic. I had never actually met a Catholic before, even though I was born at St. Joseph's Hospital on Courtland Street in Atlanta.

Michael went to Mass every day at lunch and we had interesting conversations about our faith. One day, he invited me to go along and observe this worship service. I went with him several times even though the readings were in Latin and I did not understand a word of them.

One thing I did understand, though, was what Michael did on his way to church. He carried with him a paper bag filled with peanut butter and jelly sandwiches. When we passed the beggars on the street, Michael would tell them he did not have money, but he was happy to give them something to eat! He was obeying the command from Jesus in Matthew 25.

In this passage, Jesus tells His disciples about the separating of the sheep and goats. Those who treat others well have essentially done it for Jesus Himself. Likewise, those who have mistreated others have mistreated Jesus. The *Life Application Study Bible* says, "The point is not the *who* but the *what;* the importance of serving where service is needed. Such love for others glorifies God by reflecting our love for Him."

Not only did Michael's actions speak loudly to my heart, I also was blessed in knowing his wife Rhoda would make these sandwiches for him to bring along every day. This was a joint effort by this couple to serve Jesus by serving others.

Instead of judging Michael's style of worship, I observed his obedience to the Lord by the way he conducted his life. No, we did not agree on all points of our faith, but I could not argue with giving lunch to the less fortunate.

Lord, help me live out my faith by serving others. Amen

APRIL

APRIL 1st *BLESSED, NOT STRESSED*

"Be careful for nothing; but in everything by prayer and supplication with thanksgiving let your requests be made known unto God."
Philippians 4:6

Every time I ask John Roden how he is doing, he says, "I am blessed." Great answer! I tell myself that should be my answer as well. But it never fails, I end up saying, "Fine. How are you?" Sure, that lets the person know I am well, but it says nothing about the Lord.

While I was employed at the Post Office, I had a co-worker who gave an answer similar to John's. Wayne Leonard would say, "I am too blessed to be stressed." He went a little farther sometimes and would add, "too anointed to be disappointed!"

How many times every day do we pass up opportunities to mention the Lord or His blessings? How many times every day do we become stressed over our circumstances? How often do we forget our anointing and become disappointed over things that do not go our way?

Paul wrote to the Philippians from prison in Rome. Paul, who had every reason to be careful (or anxious), encouraged the saints in Philippi to pray rather than to worry. Did you notice what else Paul said? He encouraged them to be thankful as they let their requests be made known to God.

God is definitely in control. He's got this! Not only does He lead us, He has our back and is beside us as well. So why should we be stressed? We are told, in verse 7, the peace of God passes all understanding. His peace will keep our hearts and minds through Christ Jesus. So, why worry and be stressed? We are blessed and anointed! Why not say so? Let others know.

Jesus, thank You for Your blessings. Thank You for the anointing of the Holy Spirit. Help me not to get stressed. Amen

APRIL 2nd *LETTERS TO JACKSON*

"Before I formed thee in the belly I knew thee;" Jeremiah 1:5

When my children came along, you had no way of knowing whether the baby would be a boy or a girl until the day of delivery. Of course, there were all kinds of tricks to try and determine the baby's sex, but those were very fallible. An expectant mother always ended up with a lot of pink or blue items she could not use.

By the time my grandchildren came along, there were tests that could be done to determine whether a baby boy or a baby girl was on the way. When we found out Joel and Jessica were expecting a baby boy, I began writing letters to him. They started out, "Dear Baby," but once a name had been selected, the letters were addressed, "Dear Jackson."

I told Jackson how excited we all were about his upcoming birth. I told him how much I already loved him and I told him of things I was planning for us to do together as he grew. I wrote a letter every time his mom went to the doctor for a check-up and we learned different things about his development.

I had always thought we would present the letters to him on his birthday when he was older, or when he graduated from high school. Sadly, we never got the chance to do either. Jackson succumbed to SIDS at the age of five months. We placed most of the letters in his little coffin with him.

None of us knew what was in store for this precious child. None of us could see that he would never reach any of those milestones I was already writing about. In his eulogy, Steve Jones, former pastor of Arbor Hill, read from Job 13 where the Bible says, "thou settest a print upon the heels of my feet." He said God already knew the days that were ordained for our little one and God loved him.

Yes, God knew Jackson before he was ever conceived. Even before the mountains and seas were created, God already knew each one of us. Before our ancestors were born, God prepared a way for us to share eternal life with Him. He wrote letters telling of His love for us and His plans for our future. These letters from God are called the *Bible.*

If you are feeling insignificant or unloved today, why not pick up God's love letter to you and read it? It will comfort your heart and will assure you God has the future securely in His hands.

Father God, thank You for knowing me and loving me even before I was formed. Amen

APRIL 3rd *NO CONFUSION*

"For God is not the author of confusion, but of peace, as in all churches of the saints." I Corinthians 14:33

Paul's writings often cause confusion in our churches. There are disagreements about using gifts of the Spirit, about women speaking, about head coverings, about the proper way to administer church discipline and even about the resurrection. Actually, it is not Paul's writings that cause the confusion, but our interpretation and application of those writings.

Paul wrote this letter to the Corinthians because there were problems in the church! There will always be problems of some kind in our churches because churches are made up of sinful people. I once heard Charles Stanley say there is no perfect church but if you should find one and join it, you will mess it up! That is because we still have a sinful nature even after we are redeemed. We have the power to overcome temptation (I John 4:4), but too often we give in.

In his letter to the church at Corinth, Paul wanted to remind the believers the Lord is the ultimate authority. When problems arise, we should submit to the Lord rather than turn on one another and do battle with our brothers and sisters in Christ. Joe Hulsey, a former pastor of mine, always said," If we disagree, either I'm wrong, you're wrong, or we're *both* wrong."

When we do have confusion we need to come before the Lord and seek His answers. We need to speak the truth in love rather than condemn and complain about one another. We need to seek reconciliation. Paul wrote in Romans 12:18, "If it be possible, as much as lieth in you, live peaceably with all men." That's a good rule for life inside the church as well as outside it.

Lord, help me not to cause confusion. Help me to live peaceably with my brothers and sisters. Amen

APRIL 4th *KALEIDOSCOPES*

"But we all, with open face beholding as in a glass the glory of the Lord, are changed into the same image from glory to glory, even as by the Spirit of the Lord." II Corinthians 3:18

Oh, the joys of a simple kaleidoscope! I am not sure if children today even know what one is, but when I was a child it was a toy that fascinated me. Kaleidoscope comes from the Greek words *kalos,* which means "beautiful," *eidos, meaning* "form," and *scopos,* which means "to look at."

I can remember putting the kaleidoscope to my eye and twisting the bottom. Doing so would cause bits of colored glass to move around and form various shapes and patterns. All beautiful, I might add. There were always new sights; no patterns ever seemed to be repeated.

Life, like the kaleidoscope I looked through, is forever changing. Sometimes I want to hold on to the way things are, even though they were shaped by changes in the past. What I should be looking at is the future where things will be different and exciting.

Paul wrote we are being changed from glory to glory into the same image by the Spirit of the Lord. In other words, once we believe in the Lord and the veil is removed, we can see and reflect the Lord's glory. It is an on-going process, a constant changing. As we walk in faith, we are being molded and shaped into His image and others can see the transformation.

Unlike the glory that shone on the face of Moses when he came down from Mount Sinai, our glory does not fade. In fact, it will continue to increase. Oh, the joy when we see Jesus at His return and our change is complete.

Jesus, thank You for the changes You are making in me. I want to be a good reflection of Your glory. Amen

APRIL 5th *HANDICAPPED BY LIFE*

"Be strong and of a good courage:" Joshua 1:6

Many years ago, I read the story of Paul Wittgenstein. He loved music and wanted to become a concert pianist. Born in Vienna, Austria, his home was the place where great musicians gathered. Paul studied under Joseph Labor who was a blind organist and composer. At the age of twenty-six, Paul's first concert was a huge success.

Sadly, World War I exploded and he joined the Austrian Army. A bullet tore through Paul's right arm and it was amputated. He became a prisoner of war when captured on the Russian front. Despite his circumstances, Paul vowed the piano would be his life. After a prisoner-of-war exchange, he returned home and practiced the piano seven hours a day. Soon, by using the foot pedal and his one hand so skillfully, the music sounded as if he were using two hands.

After his first left-handed concert, composers hurried to write some original pieces for Paul. Eventually, he moved to New York where he performed concerts and taught piano lessons. Many of his pupils had only one arm!

Paul could have sat back and felt sorry for himself. He could have given up on life and wasted his. However, even though he had a physical handicap, he held on to his dreams, his courage, his hard work and his determination. He never lost hope and he never gave up.

There are so many others we could name that have persevered in spite of limitations. Beethoven was deaf. Helen Keller, Ray Charles and Stevie Wonder were all blind. Read the stories of Baxter Humby, Oz Sanchez or Melissa Stockwell. There are countless others.

My question is, why do I want to give up when life's circumstances are difficult? Where is my courage when things do not go according to plan? Where is my hope? Is not God still God? Does He not still have a plan for me?

In the book *Home Run,* John Maxwell tells the story about a high school home run hitter who was at spring training with a major-league team. He wrote letters to his mom telling how easy it was to hit against the pitchers. The third week he wrote, "They started throwing curveballs today. Will be home tomorrow."

When life throws us a curve, we have to hang tough and keep trying. We cannot let it take us out of the game. We cannot allow ourselves to be handicapped by circumstances when God has given us all the tools we need to succeed.

Lord, help me persevere despite my circumstances. Amen

APRIL 6th *YEARNING FOR YESTERDAY*

"Say not thou, What is the cause that the former days were better than these? for thou dost not inquire wisely concerning this."
Ecclesiastes 7:10

How often have you said, "Those were the good ole days!"? How often have you longed for days gone by? Why do we spend so much time looking back when we should be looking forward?

Unfortunately, every time we watch the news programs we are just bombarded with the evil that abounds in our world. Murders, rapes, terrorist attacks and such dominate the headlines. We yearn for days when these were the exception rather than the norm. We see the crime rate increasing and tend to become very pessimistic. Yet, God's word tells us it is not wise to ask why the old days were better.

I can understand why older people long for days when their bodies were healthy and strong. I can understand why mothers long for the days when their children were young and therefore dependent upon them. I can understand why men who have retired miss the routine of going to work. Yet, there are many blessings for us each and every day.

Someone recently pointed out to me the rearview mirror in our car is very small but the windshield is very large. That's because we need to see what is ahead more than we need to see what is behind us! Each day is a good day to count our blessings and give thanks to God. As Matthew Henry so wisely noted, "God has been always good, and men always bad; and if, in some respects, the times are now worse than they have been, perhaps in other respects they are better."

Dear God, help me not to long for days gone by. Help me be thankful every day. Amen

APRIL 7th *NO COMPARISON*

"But let every man prove his own work, and then shall he have rejoicing in himself alone, and not in another." Galatians 6:4

I don't know about you, but, too often, I compare myself with others. In my mind, I always fall short. I'm a competitive person, too. I feel so inferior, yet I strive to be better. I like to win!

Some people have natural talents and abilities I don't have. That is an established fact. What I should strive for is not to worry about what I can't do, but do my absolute best in those things I can do! (Even as I type these words my mind is asking, "What's that?")

John Wooden was the legendary basketball coach for UCLA. He led the school to ten NCAA championships. One reporter asked the coach how he motivated his players. Wooden said, "I tell them, 'Don't try to be better than someone else. Be the best you can be. Nobody's better than that.'"

So, if that worked for college basketball players, surely I can learn from them and apply that same principle to my life. Instead of jumping through hoops trying to be as good as someone else, I just need to be the best *I* can be. That's more productive than beating myself up because I can't measure up to *you!* Or vice versa. The US Army says, 'Be all you can be.' Good advice.

The apostle Paul gave us this advice long before the Army or Coach Wooden. Comparing myself with others only causes misery. If I feel better, I am easily overcome with pride. If I feel I am worse than the other person, my self-esteem is shattered. And you know what? Neither option glorifies God.

To bring Him glory, I must focus on my own responsibility and live faithfully for God. I must live up to my own potential. That's the way to be at peace with myself.

Jesus, forgive me for comparing myself to others. Amen

APRIL 8th *WHAT'S YOUR TEMPERATURE?*

"I know thy works, that thou art neither cold nor hot: I would thou wert cold or hot. So then because thou art lukewarm, and neither cold nor hot, I will spue thee out of my mouth." Revelation 3:15,16

The hypothalamus in the brain regulates the body's temperature. Our temperature is what measures the body's ability to generate and rid itself of heat. The normal temperature of a human body is about 98.6F, and it is considered to be high when it reaches 99.5F. An elevation of body temperature is called a fever. A fever is the result of an underlying illness, usually an infection.

When a child has an extremely high temperature, there is a chance seizures will occur. This happened to my cousin Denise when she was just a baby. She contracted chickenpox, her fever went too high and she was admitted to the hospital due to seizures. Our friend Jonathan recently had a fever of 105.6F! On the other hand, when the body's temperature is 95F or below, it is called hypothermia. This is a result of the body's losing heat faster than it can produce heat. Either case is a medical emergency.

But, what about our spiritual temperatures? Jesus said He would rather we be hot or cold. He said He would spew us out of His mouth if we were lukewarm. So, I need to keep a check on my temperature. Have I grown cool towards the Lord? Has my zeal for Him waned? Have I lost my desire to read His word, sing His praise or share Him with others? I need to keep my temperature high for Him. I need to have fervor for the task He called me to do. I need a passion for exalting Him.

When we become lukewarm, simply going through the motions of serving Him, we are distasteful to the Lord. We must be on guard so that we are not overcome by apathy, complacency or self-sufficiency. The Holy Spirit is our spiritual hypothalamus. He regulates our temperature. We must let Him work in us every day to generate the heat we need to serve the Lord in a pleasing manner.

I do not want to be spewed out. Do you?

Holy Spirit, keep me on fire for the Lord. Never let me become lukewarm. Amen

APRIL 9th *SEE ROCK CITY!*

"Lead me to the rock that is higher than I." Psalm 61:2

On our various road trips in my childhood, I observed many barns with three words painted on the roof tops: See Rock City. My mother has pictures of my family visiting the place from time to time. George and I took our own children there, and now we have taken some of the grandchildren as well.

In 1823, Reverend Daniel Butrick, a missionary to the Indians in the area, described "a citadel of rocks atop the mountain." He was in awe of the immense boulders and amazed they were arranged in such a way "as to afford streets and lanes." During the civil war, both a Union officer and a Confederate nurse noted you could see seven states from the top of the massive rock formations.

In 1935, the Rock City ads began to be painted in white-on-black on barn roofs as far west as Texas and as far north as Michigan. The ads were ubiquitous until the sixties, when LBJ's billboard banning legislation required the removal of many of them.

At Rock City, there is also a swinging bridge, lover's leap area, fat man's squeeze, Fairyland Caverns and Mother Goose village. Jake loved it so much he frequently said, "Let's go to Rock City!"

Going to Rock City reminds me of King David. In his psalms, he frequently referred to the Lord as his Rock. He said the Lord had set his feet upon a rock. When pursued by Saul, David often hid in the rocks where God protected him from the enemy.

A rock is a symbol of stability and, certainly, God is the stabilizing force in our lives. Paul tells us Christ is the Rock from which the children of Israel drank as they journeyed (I Corinthians 10:4). So, when I see Rock City on a barn or when I visit it personally, I think of my Rock and my Fortress, Jesus Christ.

Lord Jesus, You are the Rock that is higher than I. Lead me home to You. Amen

APRIL 10th *LET ME DRIVE*

"Remember now thy Creator in the days of thy youth, while the evil days come not, nor the years draw nigh." Ecclesiastes 12:1

Once upon a time, George was driving me around my mail route for some reason. We were riding in Eagle Creek which, at that time, had unpaved roads. Trying to be helpful to him, I was cautioning him to watch out for every bump and telling him where every hole in the road was located. Finally, he was so exasperated with me, he said, "Just let me drive!"

Isn't that how we all feel when someone else is trying to tell us how to live? We do not want advice. We want to make all the decisions for ourselves. Often, we bounce from one mistake to another. Parents (and grandparents) try desperately to warn the younger generation of the hidden dangers they are sure to face. Yet, they do not want to listen.

We would love to steer them clear of the rocks, the obstacles or the pitfalls that surely lie ahead, but they must choose the way themselves. As much as we want to, we cannot shield them from every heartache or disaster. What we can do is cover them with prayer and teach them to seek the Lord while they are young.

Probably all of us wasted our time with meaningless pursuits when we were younger. Too often young people get caught up in the pleasures of the world instead of focusing on the eternal. The best time to begin seeking God, though, is while we are young. When God is leading the way, we will have a much smoother journey. Let Him take the wheel.

Lord, help us all learn from our own mistakes as well as from those of others. Amen

APRIL 11th *AUTOGRAPHS*

"Him that overcometh will I make a pillar in the temple of my God, and he shall go no more out: and I will write upon him the name of my God, and the name of the city of my God, which is new Jerusalem, which cometh down out of heaven from my God: and I will write upon him my new name." Revelation 3:12

Unless you are visiting Disney World, an autograph book is almost obsolete these days. However, they were very popular when my mother was growing up. Not only did they contain signatures but also brief notes or bits of wisdom. These books helped them remember special people and special events.

I have collected quite a few autographs of famous (or once famous) people over the years. I have autographs from Luke Appling, Willie Nelson, R.C Thielmann, Ricky Scaggs, all members of the Atlanta Rhythm Section band, many Atlanta Crackers players and of course our local celebrity, Junior Samples! Just to name a few.

But Jesus writes His name, too. Not with pen and paper, though. He writes of His serenity in the moon-bathed waters of Lake Lanier. He writes of his majesty in sunrises and sunsets. He writes of His glory in the changing seasons. If we just look about, His signature is all around us.

Best of all, Jesus writes His name on our hearts when we accept Him as our Savior. He doesn't use ink, but His blood covering our sins is the autograph God sees when He looks at us. If you do not have His autograph, why not collect it today? Jesus will not turn you away. He is never too busy for you. Isn't it amazing that we can carry within our body, the very signature of the Lord Jesus?

Jesus, thank You for signing my autograph book when You saved my soul. Amen

APRIL 12th *WATCH YOUR WAYS*

"Wherefore let him that thinketh he standeth take heed lest he fall."
I Corinthians 10:12

The closest I have ever been to the Masters golf tournament was the year my sister Cathy and I bowled in the Ladies State Bowling Championship in Augusta, Georgia. We drove by the Augusta National Golf Club. That's it. We did not even see a green jacket!

However, my friend, Robert Harrison, was at the Masters in April of 1997, when Tiger Woods became the youngest player to win the tournament, the first man of color to win and the man to win by the highest margin. In fact, Robert had positioned himself at the eighteenth hole and appeared on the cover of Sports Illustrated with Tiger! I will admit you might have to look rather closely to pick him out, but he is there!

Tiger Woods is the name that changed golf. Tiger made golf cool for a new generation. Golf became fun and entertaining when Tiger stepped onto the green. When he played, tournament attendance increased and so did the television coverage. Everything about Tiger defied convention in the sport.

His slogan was "win early and often." And that is just what he did. He has won fourteen major championships and seventy-nine PGA Tour titles. He was the youngest to win the Career Grand Slam as well. It seemed Tiger could do no wrong.

Then came Thanksgiving of 2009. Tiger's wife found out he was being unfaithful to her and she chased him out of their house with, of all things, a golf club! He smashed their car and then the whole story became front page news.

What happened to Tiger could easily happen to anyone who does not watch his ways. We must put on the whole armor of God so that we do not fall for Satan's schemes to distract us from our walk. Sure, temptation is all around us, but we have the strength to overcome it. It takes being obedient to the Holy Spirit's leading.

Let us all be watchful today and always. We need to take heed. Remember, we must take a stand for Christ, or we may fall for anything!

Lord Jesus, help me to watch my ways at all times. Amen

APRIL 13th *MAUNDY THURSDAY*

"The sacrifices of God are a broken spirit: a broken and a contrite heart, O God, thou wilt not despise." Psalm 51:17

It was the night of the Passover. After sharing the meal with His disciples, Jesus took a towel, girded himself and washed the disciples' feet. The Master, showing His humility, took on the role of a servant.

Jesus told the men one of them would betray Him. They began to inquire among themselves which of them it was that should do this thing. They also had strife among themselves about which of them should be the greatest. Jesus' final hours on this earth were drawing to a close and His dear friends, His closest followers, were oblivious to what was ahead. They were arguing about who was the best! No humility there!

When Jesus told Peter, "Satan hath desired to have you that he may sift you as wheat: But I have prayed for thee," Peter asserted his loyalty. He told Jesus, "Lord I am ready to go with thee, both into prison and to death." Ha! Jesus said to Peter, "The cock shall not crow this day before that thou shalt thrice deny that thou knowest me (Luke 22:23-34)."

Of course everything happened just as Jesus had said. After Peter's third denial, the rooster crowed. Jesus turned and looked at Peter. Then Peter remembered what Jesus said. He went out and he wept bitterly.

How often have I vowed a vow to the Lord and then failed Him? Have I pretended everything was fine so I did not have to face my own failures? Or, have I gone out and wept bitterly over my weakness and my humiliation?

The Bible says a broken and contrite heart will not be despised by God. He will forgive us if we but ask. Even though, like Peter, we may have miserably failed to follow through for the Lord, there is hope for us yet! We need to not only weep over our sins, but we also need to accept His forgiveness.

Yes, Peter was a coward, a denier and a liar, but after the Lord's resurrection, Peter became a powerful preacher. After facing his own darkness, Peter became the rock Jesus had called him to be. And so can we. Don't give up on yourself because you may have failed. Face the darkness and overcome it through the resurrected Lord.

Oh, God, I confess all my failures. Forgive me, lift me up and make me useful for Your kingdom. Amen

APRIL 14th *GOOD FRIDAY*

"Wherefore he saith, When he ascended up on high, he led captivity captive, and gave gifts unto men. He that descended is the same also that ascended up far above all heavens, that he might fill all things."
Ephesians 4:8, 10

On April 14, 1964, Lake Sidney Lanier reached its highest recorded level of 1,077.15 feet. That is a good six feet above "full summer pool." On December 26, 2007, the lake reached its lowest level which was 1,050.79 feet. This was due, in part, to the 2005 installation of a new gauge that had not been properly calibrated. This faulty measurement resulted in excess water being released. Also, there was a drought across the southeast that year due to lower rainfall.

Thinking of the highs and lows of the lake reminds me of the highs and lows of our Lord Jesus. He came down to us from Heaven when He was born of a virgin in Bethlehem. He left the highest estate and came down to live among fallen men.

He was lifted up above the earth when He was crucified for our sins. Verse nine of this chapter says Jesus also descended into the lower parts of the earth. Although Bible scholars disagree as to the exact meaning of the verse (as well as the meaning of 1 Peter 3:19), we know for a fact Jesus descended. He said He would be three days and three nights in the heart of the earth (Matthew 12:40). Much like the levels of Lake Lanier, Jesus has been both up and down.

After His resurrection, Jesus ascended back to the Father in Heaven. One day He will call us up to meet Him in the clouds and we will ever be with the Lord. This would not be possible apart from His crucifixion. Had He not died on the cross, taking the punishment for our sins, there could have been no reconciliation between the Holy God and sinful humanity.

Jesus experienced both highs and lows in order to secure our salvation. On this day, as we remember His sacrificial death, let us be sure to give Him the thanks He so deserves. Let's exalt His name together

Jesus, I cannot thank You enough for dying for me. I praise Your name. Amen

APRIL 15th *SLEEPING IN*

"Six days shalt thou labour, and do all thy work: But the seventh day is the sabbath of the Lord thy God: in it thou shalt not do any work...."
Exodus 20:9, 10

When I was in school, I always looked forward to sleeping in on Saturday. During the week, my bus was one of the first to arrive at the school, which meant I had to get up early to be ready when James Garner's bus (#14) came lumbering up the road.

When I began to work, I had to get up early. My first public job was in Atlanta, and my aunt and I normally left Cumming shortly after six o'clock. I looked forward to sleeping in on Saturday morning.

When I began to work for the postal service, we had to report to the office at six o'clock. The day after a holiday, we reported at five instead! I looked forward to a Saturday off so I could sleep in.

On our calendar, Saturday is the seventh day of the week. By our calendar, Friday night sundown to Saturday night sundown would be the Jewish Sabbath. While I cannot say for sure exactly where the "soul" of Jesus was on this day, nor can I say with certainty exactly what He was doing on this day, I know without a doubt what His body was doing. The body of Jesus was resting in the tomb and keeping the Sabbath!

Although Peter, James and John (and probably the other disciples) were sleeping while Jesus prayed in the Garden of Gethsemane, I wonder if they were able to sleep after His crucifixion? I wonder if they were up early on this morning. I wonder if they were distraught, discouraged? I wonder if they felt defenseless now that the Lord was dead?

I cannot help but believe they did not enjoy their sleep. While their bodies may have rested on the Sabbath, I cannot help but believe their spirits were anything but restful. Little did they know what the next morning would hold.

Reverend Jackie Martin preached at Pine Crest not too long ago and his message was "It's not as bad as it seems." When things in our lives seem to be at the absolute worst, just remember these words from Psalm 30:5: "Weeping may endure for a night, but joy cometh in the morning."

Jesus, when I am feeling distraught, discouraged and defenseless, help me remember it is not as bad as it seems. I may weep for a night, but with You, joy comes in the morning. Amen

APRIL 16th *RESURRECTION DAY!*

"He is not here: for he is risen, as he said. Come, see the place where the Lord lay." Matthew 28:6

Several years ago, Joel participated in a passion play at Arbor Hill Baptist Church. He played the part of the unrepentant thief. With the black wig he wore, he really looked the part, too. I was thankful my son was just playing a role. I couldn't imagine how the mothers of the actual thieves must have felt on that day so long ago. Or how Mary the mother of Jesus felt.

But, Jesus was mindful of the pain and suffering of those around Him. He made arrangements for the care of His mother, He healed the soul of the thief who repented and He also prayed for His enemies. In spite of His own physical pain, Jesus was not indifferent to others. Not then, not ever.

The Bible tells us, as it began to dawn toward the first day of the week, some women come to the tomb, bringing spices, so that they might anoint the body of Jesus. Imagine their surprise when they see the stone is rolled back and an angel tells them the Lord has risen!

The Bible says the women depart quickly from the tomb with fear and great joy and run to tell the disciples. As they are on the way, Jesus meets them. All the sorrow, the weeping, and the uncertainty is gone. Jesus lives! They fall at His feet and worship Him. He tells them, "Be not afraid: Go tell my brethren that they go into Galilee, and there shall they see me."

The women were afraid, but Jesus calmed their fears. The brethren had not believed Jesus could be raised from the dead, but He assured them when He saw them in Galilee. Later, Jesus invited Thomas to touch His body in order to prove His identity.

As we celebrate the resurrection today, let us all be more like Jesus. Let us be mindful of the pain of others. Let's do what we can to alleviate their suffering. Let us also be like the women who ran to tell the good news. There is no place for indifference in the life of any believer. Pray for others! Share the joy! Our Lord lives!

Jesus, You are the risen Savior. You are the Hope of all who seek You and the Help of all who find You. Amen and Amen

APRIL 17th *LISTEN WITH YOUR EYES!*

"And he shall go before him in the spirit and power of Elias to turn the hearts of the fathers to the children..." Luke 1:17

I had a good relationship with my dad, I suppose. He did not ever mistreat me. I can't recall a time he actually fussed at me. But we did not have a loving relationship. He never, as far as I can remember, told me he loved me nor was he affectionate towards me. The only time I can remember sharing a hug with him was when my aunt died. I was a twenty-five year old at that time!

I never "felt" loved by my dad. Then, Steve and Annie Chapman's song, "Love Was Spoken," opened my eyes! The song reminded me my Dad rolled out of bed and went to work. He spent the money he made to buy my food and clothing. He worked on the house whenever repairs were needed. My dad did not take us to church as the dad they sang about, but he did not forbid me from going.

I specifically recall a time when I was very sick and he carried me to the emergency room. I remember my dad liked to sit around and read the encyclopedias. He often shared some new-found knowledge with me. Also, he loved sports and I often watched televised events with him. So, even though my earthly dad rarely used words to say he loved me, love *was* spoken to me.

Because some earthly fathers forsake their families or abuse their children, some people have a hard time relating to the heavenly Father's love. I had been one of those people, not because of neglect or abuse, but because I was not listening properly. As the song says, "Cause we could hear him say he loved us when we'd listen with our eyes."

As for the love of the heavenly Father, I also need to "listen with my eyes" by reading His word. The Bible tells me God loves me with an unfailing love. He loved me before the foundation of the world and made a way whereby I could spend eternity with Him. He promised He will never forsake me. He promised nothing could separate me from His love. And He promised to supply my every need. That is so much more than any earthly father could ever do.

Even if your eyes are saying your earthly dad does not love you, your heavenly Father does. Get into the word and learn of His great love for you.

Father God, I am so grateful for Your love. Amen

APRIL 18th *THINGS MONEY CAN'T BUY*

"Ho, every one that thirsteth, come ye to the waters, and he that hath no money; come ye, buy, and eat; yea, come, buy wine and milk without money and without price." Isaiah 55:1

"A Satisfied Mind" is an old country hit. I had better be careful with the use of the word *old* because the song became popular the same year George was born, 1955! The lyrics tell us it is hard to find one rich man in ten with a satisfied mind. Also, the wealthiest person is a pauper at times, compared to the man with a satisfied mind. I am sure this is true although I have never been wealthy and, most likely, never will be in terms of worldly wealth.

Not too long ago, Rocky Dodd preached a sermon at Pine Crest that reminded me of this song. Rocky told us money can buy a house, but not a home. Money can buy a companion, but not love. Money can buy a bed, but not a good night's sleep. The song goes on to say, "But one thing's for certain, when it comes my time, I'll leave this old world with a satisfied mind."

Rocky's mother, Martha, is full of wisdom. She is always sharing little bits of that wisdom. She says, "What we acquire in this world is going to be left in this world." What a good thought to help us stay focused on the eternal.

It is tempting to get caught up in the "gotta have it" mode. But, really, we need to stop and ask if the latest and greatest is really all that necessary. Our possessions do not define who we are. They just show what we have. Mostly, I tend to think they show what folks are in debt for! Jesus said, "Ye cannot serve God and mammon" (which is money).

A satisfied mind is possible through the Lord Jesus Christ. If we have been saved, His peace will keep our hearts and our minds. In Isaiah, God is saying the richest of fare is found in Him alone. He is the source of deep satisfaction for our souls. The *Women of Faith Study Bible* says, "When we seek God first, provision, and even prosperity, can follow in a way that satisfies, rather than saps, us."

Don't be sapped. Be satisfied in the Lord.

Jesus, keep me focused on the eternal and not the temporal. Amen

APRIL 19th *THE SOUND OF MUSIC*

"And David spake to the chief of the Levites to appoint their brethren to be the singers with instruments of musick, psalteries and harps and cymbals, sounding, by lifting up the voice with joy."
I Chronicles 15:16

The Sound of Music is my all-time favorite movie. It was released in 1965, starring Julie Andrews and Christopher Plummer. The movie won five Academy Awards. Based on the memoirs of Maria von Trapp, it is the story of a young postulant who becomes a governess to a family of seven children while she ponders whether to become a nun.

The movie played in Atlanta at the Martin's Rialto theatre for eighteen months. I attended the big celebration at the first anniversary. My Aunt Barbara accompanied me. We were given small vials of perfume and an orchid corsage. There were refreshments served as well. I had the time of my fifteen year old life!

In 2015, the AMC theatre at the Collection, held a showing of this wonderful movie to celebrate its fiftieth year. Susan Waters, a friend from church, invited me to go with her and her daughters, Sadie and Sari, to the event. What a pleasure it was to view the movie with others who love it as I do! We had such a grand time. For Susan and the girls, it was also a time to look for sights they had seen while on a trip to Europe.

I do love *The Sound of Music.* Over the years, I collected the soundtrack on a record album, an eight track tape and a compact disc. I have the twenty-fifth anniversary edition of the movie on a DVD.

I also love the sound of music in general. So did King David and so does God. The Bible is filled with many references to singing and music. The psalmist wrote, "O, come let us sing unto the Lord: let us make a joyful noise to the rock of our salvation (95:1)."

Even if you think you couldn't "carry a tune in a bucket," you can still lift up your voice and make a joyful noise to the Lord. I am certain it will be pleasing to His ears. Let us sing praises to God for He has done marvelous things.

Lord, I want to sing praise unto You as long as I live. Amen

APRIL 20th *NEW YORK CITY*

"For God, who commanded the light to shine out of darkness, hath shined in our hearts, to give the light of the knowledge of the glory of God in the face of Jesus Christ." II Corinthians 4:6

We took a family trip up the East coast in 1992. This trip included a stop in New York City. Our motel was actually in New Jersey, but Kevin suggested we drive into the city that Sunday night. "While there isn't so much traffic," he said. As you know, New York City is known as "the city that never sleeps." And I don't believe it does!

The city was ablaze with lights. Times Square is the most brightly lit area with its billboards and advertisements. All building owners are required to display illuminated signs. Times Square is the only place in the city where there is a minimum lighting requirement instead of a maximum.

From the sixties to the nineties, this area became dark and desperate. In 1984, there were over two thousand crimes reported in the block of 42nd Street between 7th and 8th Avenues. About one fifth was rape or murder. In the mid-nineties, Mayor Rudy Guiliani began a clean-up effort. Security was increased and more tourist-friendly attractions were opened. Once again, the area is thriving.

Times Square reminds me of my own heart. Once dark and desperate, God shined His light in it to give me the knowledge of His glory in Christ. Now my heart is ablaze through the power of the Holy Spirit. Also, the Holy Spirit provides security so the enemy cannot come in and take over. Now I am thriving.

God has called us out of darkness into His marvelous light. He has called us to be a holy nation, a peculiar people, a royal priesthood. Like the lights in Times Square, we are to shine for Him and show forth His praises. Get glowing!

Lord, help me let my light shine brightly for You. Amen

APRIL 21ˢᵗ *GOOD DIRECTIONS*

"In all thy ways acknowledge him, and he shall direct thy paths."
Proverbs 3:6

Shortly before my retirement from the Postal Service, I was sent to Crown Road in Atlanta for a class. I did not feel I should have had to attend but, nevertheless, I went. I had asked my acting supervisor for directions. I told him I was not going unless I got specific instructions. So, he wrote them down for me.

There was only one problem. The directions he gave me were faulty. He said I was to exit I-285 at a certain road and there was no such place from my direction. I was so mad! I was like Pasqual Perez who went completely around the perimeter looking for his destination. I had to stop and make a call to the Post Office for clarification, but did not get anyone on the phone who could help. I got another number and tried again. By this time, I was late for class. I was fuming! A GPS would have been a life-saver, but I did not have one in the car at that time.

How often do we set out, thinking we know the way to go, and end up like I did: lost, angry and confused? How many times have our best laid plans caused us more trouble in the end? How often have we wished we had someone who could just lead us the right way? Someone who knew exactly where we needed to go and exactly how to get us there? I am not only referring to auto travel, but to life as well.

The Bible tells us the answer for life. Proverbs says to acknowledge God in all our ways and He will direct our paths. We are not to lean on our own understanding, but to trust in Him with all our heart. He will get us where we need to go and all the specific instructions for travel are written in His word.

We can try to get through life on our own and we are sure to make a mess of it. But, if we follow God, He will steer us in the right direction and will never lead us astray.

God, help me acknowledge You in all my ways. I need You to direct my paths. Amen

APRIL 22nd   *THE WAY TO A MAN'S HEART*

"So David received of her hand that which she had brought him, and said unto her, Go up in peace to thine house; see, I have hearkened to thy voice, and have accepted thy person." I Samuel 25:35

I have often heard it said, "The way to a man's heart is through his stomach." Newspaper columnist Fanny Fern is credited with coining this phrase in the eighteen hundreds. In other words, a woman can make a man love her by cooking him good meals.

I hope it wasn't my meals that won George's love, but I did cook for him occasionally while we were dating. He was especially fond of my fried chicken. My sister and her boyfriend often ate with us. Once, her friend turned over his tea and splatterd all of us and all our food!

And speaking of tea, Joel's friend Lou had an affinity for mine. It seemed every time he came by, his first words to me were, "Mrs. Sams, do you have any sweet tea?" That sweetness satisfied his thirst.

Joel loves it when I make chicken casserole, Justin is partial to my beef stew and Kevin likes meatloaf and fried potatoes. My family knows I do not cook gourmet meals, but I enjoy making dishes that satisfy their hunger.

In the Bible we learn of a woman who found her way into the heart of soon-to-be King David by bringing food for him and his men. David had been on the run because King Saul was trying to kill him. The men were very hungry and hoped Nabal would allow them to eat with his shearers. Nabal refused and David became very angry. He and his band of followers strapped on their swords and went to battle this churlish and evil man.

The Bible says Abigail, Nabal's wife, was a woman of good understanding. When she learned of her husband's refusal to give food to David and his men, she gathered bread, wine, meat, corn and fruit. She loaded the food on donkeys and hurried to meet David. She apologized for her husband's actions and entreated David for mercy.

David willingly and gladly accepted the food Abigail brought and he extended mercy to her household as well. Within a fortnight, the Lord smote Nabal and he died. Abigail then became David's wife.

Who knows? Maybe Fanny Fern coined her phrase because she knew the story of David and Abigail?

Lord, I was hungry and You filled my soul. Thank You for inviting me to your banquet. Amen

APRIL 23ʳᵈ *ANGELS' FOOD OR DEVIL'S FOOD?*

"Man did eat angels' food: he sent them meat to the full." Psalm 78:25

When I am in the bakery department of the grocery store, I often see Angel Food cakes as well as Devil's Food cakes. Since I am crazy about chocolate, the devil's food cake is more tempting. The Angel Food cake is better for me, though, because it is practically fat-free. It is light and it tastes heavenly. The choice I have to make reminds me of the children of Israel.

After four hundred and thirty years, the children of Israel left the land of Egypt for the land God promised them. The water had barely settled back in place after drowning Pharaoh's army when the people started their constant complaining. First, the water was bitter. Then they longed for the flesh pots and bread. They accused Moses of bringing them into the wilderness to kill them with hunger.

God said He would send bread from Heaven for the people. Please remember this was a sizable group to feed. There were over half a million men, not even counting the women and children. But God is able and the bread was sent. Not just for a day or a week, but for the entire forty years they wandered about, there was the bread. They were to gather it six days per week and rest on the seventh, but God sent enough on the sixth day to carry them through the Sabbath.

The people called this bread 'manna.' That literally means, "What is it?" It wasn't long before they were complaining about their provision. In one place the Bible says the Israelites lusted for the fish, the cucumbers, the melons, the leeks, the onions and the garlick they had so enjoyed in Egypt. They said their souls were dried away and they had nothing but "this manna." They longed for more than what the Lord God had given them.

Does that sound familiar to anyone? These people had been slaves in Egypt, yet they longed to go back so they could be satisfied there. They began to think of what God had given as undesirable. When we are slaves to some sin, we desire the satisfaction it temporarily brings. We tend to think of God's way as bad and the devil's way as good.

Too often we had rather partake of the devil's food than angels' food. It may taste sweeter for the moment, but the consequences are bitter for much longer.

Father God, help me choose correctly today and always. Forgive me when I long for the devil's food. Amen

APRIL 24th   *FLINTSTONES OR JETSONS?*

"But thou, O Daniel, shut up the words, and seal the book, even to the time of the end: many shall run to and fro, and knowledge shall be increased." Daniel 12:4

Several months ago, I read *Life Is a Wheel* by Bruce Weber. The book details Weber's bike ride across America. One quote from the book that I especially liked was, "One day you're a Flintstone, the next day a Jetson." I feel all of us baby-boomers can relate.

When I was nine years old, the first prime time cartoon series was broadcast on television. The program was *The Flintstones.* It was about the misadventures of a stone-age man named Fred, his family and his neighbors. The show included dinosaurs yet the Flintstones and the Rubbles played records, ate at restaurants and drove cars, albeit all quite different than the ones of our day.

A mere two years later, *The Jetsons* made their debut. This was the space-age counterpart to *The Flintstones.* Rather than dinosaurs, this show featured robots, aliens and computers. I, for one, thought living in the space-age would be lots better than living in the stone-age. It would be so much easier to travel and knowledge was certainly increased.

While a captive in Babylon, Daniel wrote about the time of the end. He said people would run to and fro and knowledge would be increased. All you need to do is try to drive anywhere in Forsyth County to see that people are definitely running to and fro. Knowledge has increased many times over in the few short (!) years since these cartoons debuted on television.

Is this the time of the end? I don't know. Only the Father in Heaven knows the day and the hour of the end. One thing is certain. The time of the end is a lot closer than it has ever been before. Are you ready? Should this be the last day, are you prepared to meet the Lord? If not, why not confess your sins and ask Jesus into your heart? It is not His will that any should perish, but that all should come to repentance. He gave His life that you might be saved. Call out to Him today.

Jesus, I pray for all those who are not prepared for the time of the end. Convict them and draw them, I pray. Amen

APRIL 25th *SAVING THE FLAG*

"Thou has given a banner to them that fear thee, that it may be displayed because of the truth. Selah." Psalm 60:4

Forty-one years ago today, Rick Monday saved the flag! Let me refresh your memory.

Monday was a center fielder for the Chicago Cubs. During a game in Los Angeles at Dodger stadium, two protesters tried to set fire to an American flag. It was just after the bottom of the fourth inning started. These protesters ran into left-center field and knelt to start the fire. However, Monday rushed over, grabbed the flag, ran through the infield towards the Dodger dugout and handed the flag off to a Dodger pitcher.

When Monday came up to bat in the top of the fifth, the crowd gave him a standing ovation. The big message board flashed "Rick Monday, You Made a Great Play." Later Monday said, "If you are going to burn the flag, don't do it around me. I've been to too many veterans' hospitals and seen too many broken bodies of guys who tried to protect it."

Monday still has that flag. The flag was presented to him by a Dodgers' organization executive on "Rick Monday Day," May 4, 1976, at Wrigley Field. He has been offered up to a million dollars for it, but has refused to sell it.

The pair of would-be-burners were arrested and taken into custody. They were a father and son team and the son was just eleven years old. Isn't that sad? The father was later fined, charged with trespassing and put on probation. I wonder if the son ever again tried to burn the flag?

While burning the flag is considered "freedom of speech" and is protected by the First Amendment, I frown on the practice myself. I, like Monday, think of all the men who have protected the flag. I think of what it stands for: life, liberty and the pursuit of happiness. I think of what it once was to our enemies: a symbol of might and truth.

I think of God's banner over us the same way. His banner is one of might. It is a banner of truth, a banner of love and a banner of freedom. God's banner keeps us aware that He is fighting for us. If He is for us, who can stand against us? His banner reminds us of His protection.

As we remember Rick Monday's heroic deed today, let us also remember our Jehovah-Nissi.

Lord, thank You for being a banner of love over me. Amen

APRIL 26th *FINDING THE PRIZE*

"I press toward the mark for the prize of the high calling of God in Christ Jesus." Philippians 3:14

For many, many years George was a collector of John Wayne memorabilia. When the building of a museum was begun in Winterset, Iowa, Wayne's birthplace, I bought a brick for George that was inscribed, 'From your biggest fan.'

George had pictures, plates, tin signs, books, movies, cardboard statues, playing cards and almost anything you can imagine with John Wayne on it. His most treasured items, though, were the Case knives. George had found the white, the black and the brown handled knives, but the one with the red handle was not to be found. Today, we could just search the internet, but when we were on the hunt for this elusive treasure the internet was not as well known.

One year, we took a vacation with Eddie and Connie Hitt. We were going to Branson. Eddie wanted to see the home of outlaw Jesse James in St. Joseph, and the letter written by Frank James on the wall of the Farris Truck Stop in Faucett. Connie and I wanted to visit the home of Laura Ingalls Wilder in Mansfield. We were having a grand time.

Eddie had the hammer down as we headed south on US 65. He flew past a place called Pickle Gap Village, but Connie really wanted to stop there. She asked Eddie to turn around. When we entered the first shop, George walked over to one case and there it was! The knife with the red handle! He was ecstatic.

In Philippians, Paul wrote about pressing toward the mark for the prize. The prize he referred to is not an object or a trophy. It is, rather, a life lived for the Lord Jesus which will result in our ascension to Him. When we are together for eternity, we will know true ecstasy! Keep pressing onward. The prize is just ahead.

Lord, help me as I press toward the prize. Amen

APRIL 27th *NO ROOM FOR IDOLS*

"Thou shalt have no other gods before me." Exodus 20:3

Jefferson Bethke of the spoken word video *Why I Hate Religion but Love Jesus* says, "When we get our satisfaction, worth and identity from another, we make them an idol. When we make another person an idol, we end up squeezing the life out of them."

When I think about squeezing the life out of a person, I tend to think of a snake, namely the boa constrictor. Scientists now say the boa does not suffocate its prey but causes circulatory arrest. Either way, the prey dies. Does anyone find it fitting that the enemy of our souls, the devil himself, was portrayed as a serpent in the Garden of Eden?

The enemy will do anything to squeeze the life out of us. Even if it means having someone set us up in his heart as an idol! God knew before the foundation of the world what turmoil would be caused if a person worshipped a creature more than the Creator. That is why He so adamantly stated we were to have no other gods before Him.

Our satisfaction, worth and identity is found in Jesus. In Jesus alone. He can meet each and every need we have whether that need is emotional, mental or physical. Blaise Pascal, mathematician and philosopher said, "There is a God shaped vacuum in the heart of every man which cannot be filled by any created thing, but only by God the Creator made known through Jesus." No other human is capable of fulfilling us completely. And it is impossible for us to fulfill ourselves.

I know we need others. After all, God Himself made Eve to be a helpmeet for Adam. Humans are made to interact with others, to love one another and to help each other. But we were not made to worship one another. Our worship must go to the Lord God only.

God, help me to have no other gods before You. Amen

APRIL 28th *JAKE'S PITCHING*

"Therefore, my beloved brethren, be ye stedfast, unmoveable, always abounding in the work of the Lord, forasmuch as ye know that your labour is not in vain in the Lord." I Corinthians 15:58

Our nine-year-old grandson Jake is a lefty. He plays first base with his ball team. He also pitches. He has a good record on the mound, but he does walk a batter sometimes and he has hit a batter. He enjoys picking off a runner at first as much as he does striking out a batter. It is good to get an out either way!

Sometimes, those outs are hard to come by. It is tough when he falls behind, then gets a full count but the next pitch is called a ball. It is tough when there are errors in the field which allow runs to score. It is tough when Jake makes an error himself. Do you know what Jake does? He just keeps throwing the ball. He does not quit.

I can learn from Jake how to handle life. I must not quit. I must keep on keeping on. Of course there will be calls that do not go my way. Of course there will be errors by myself and others around me. Of course I will get brushed back or knocked down. But at those times I can be strengthened by the power of God. He does not promise me a perfect game, but He does promise to be beside me when I just "keep throwing the ball."

Jesus, give me the courage and strength to follow through and finish the game. Amen

APRIL 29th *DELIVERANCE*

"And the Lord shall deliver me from every evil work, and will preserve me unto his heavenly kingdom: to whom be glory for ever and ever. Amen." II Timothy 4:18

Deliverance is not always granted just at the time we want it. Deliverance does not always look the way we want it to look. I can give you many examples from the Bible.

Moses was placed in the Nile River, but he was rescued by the daughter of Pharaoh. The three Hebrew children were thrown into the fiery furnace. Yet, they were delivered. They did not even smell like smoke when they came out. Daniel was thrown into the lions' den, but God closed the mouths of the lions. Peter began to sink in the waves. Jesus stretched out His hand and caught Peter, but Peter was already afraid and wet! Jesus Himself prayed to be spared the death on the cross, but God allowed Him to die. Deliverance came three days later when Jesus was resurrected.

Can you think of examples from your own life when deliverance was not exactly how you expected it to be? The best example from my life occurred in 1975. My marriage was on the rocks. I begged God for deliverance from the trial. Deliverance was not given the way I hoped. Instead, the marriage ended in the spring of 1976. Deliverance came in the form of a new relationship that has now lasted forty years!

I encourage everyone to hold tightly to God, trust Him even when you are hurting and when His ways do not make sense. In Romans, chapter 11, Paul wrote these words, "O the depth of the riches both of the wisdom and knowledge of God! How unsearchable are his judgments, and his ways past finding out! For who hath known the mind of the lord? or who hath been his counsellor?" The prophet Isaiah told us the Lord said, "For as the heavens are higher than the earth, so are my ways higher than your ways, and my thoughts than your thoughts (55:9)."

When you do not understand God's ways, just remember His are so much higher. Deliverance will come in His way and in His time.

Lord, remind me how limited my wisdom is and how great Yours. Amen

APRIL 30th *OUR DIFFERENCES*

"And he answered and said unto them, Have ye not read, that he which made them at the beginning made them male and female. And said, For this cause shall a man leave father and mother, and shall cleave to his wife: and they twain shall be one flesh?" Matthew 19:4, 5

My husband, George, and I are as different as two people could be. I am mostly introspective and could be alone for hours without any problem. He thrives on being around people. I am a lot older than my siblings, but George is the baby of his family. I am a night owl, but George is a morning person. I love music; George not so much. I love to read. He doesn't. He loves action movies. Not me. George likes to work in the garden. I like to keep my hands clean. The list goes on.

We love each other and can accept each other's weaknesses and strengths. For the most part. At times, we get frustrated with each other. For instance, when I want to go for a ride, but George wants to sit in the recliner and flip the remote. Or, I want to watch *Jeopardy!* but George wants to engage me in conversation.(Thankfully, we have a DVR.)

We have learned to give and take. We don't always see eye-to-eye, but we always work things out. Someone once said if both partners were just alike, there would be no need for one of them. I agree.

A marriage takes a lot of work from both partners. The grass is not greener on the other side of the fence. The grass is greener where it is watered. Today would be a good day to begin watering the grass of your marriage. Spend time with the one you love doing something of his or her choice. Show your spouse how much you care. You may be surprised how much love will come to you in return.

Lord, thank You for the differences that make our marriage interesting. Amen

MAY

"A time to get, and a time to lose; a time to keep, and a time to cast away;" Ecclesiastes 3: 6

From talking with many senior citizens, I have found most people spend their younger years accumulating things and the latter years of their lives getting rid of them. I myself have the urge to purge!

The writer Malcolm Muggeridge and his wife Kitty lived in a mansion, but decided to give away most all their possessions and move into a small cottage. They began to eat simpler meals which meant fewer dishes to wash. Forgetting about fashion saved the time they once spent on shopping. I like their way of thinking!

Last year, my sister had to face a mountain of casting away. She had moved many years ago and had put into storage everything that was not absolutely essential. Like three years worth of *TV Guides*. She wanted to one day work the crossword puzzles in them! For years she paid the rent on the storage building every month. Her son and I kept hounding her to clean it out and get rid of stuff. Finally the day arrived.

George and I tried our best to help. Even though it was painful for her, emotionally, almost everything in the building was carried to the landfill and discarded. She posted a long tribute to her belongings on Facebook and said her entire life was now in the dump!

Although it is often hard to let go because so many things have sentimental value associated with them, as our lives draw closer to the end, we tend to want to lighten the load. And we need to cast away more than tangible items. We need to rid ourselves of jealousy, anger, resentment, coveting, fear and all that other garbage.

It is high time we quit "paying rent" to store that spiritual baggage. We will feel so much freer once it has been cast away!

Lord, help me get rid of any items or attitudes that keep me from being free. Amen

MAY 2nd *CLASS REUNION*

"He hath put my brethren far from me, and mine acquaintance are verily estranged from me." Job 19:13

In 2015, my graduating class had a picnic at Poole's Mill. I had not attended a reunion in about twenty years, but decided to go to this small venue and renew old acquaintance. We all told each other we had not changed a bit! We mostly talked about health issues and our wonderful grandchildren. We took the proverbial class picture and all who have a Facebook page posted our smiling faces.

Yes, most of us had been estranged from each other for decades, but once we saw one another, it was as though no time had really passed. We were laughing and talking just like we did when we walked the halls of Forsyth County High.

I think of all my friends and loved ones who have gone on to Glory. I feel certain our reunion will be similar to the one I had with my classmates. I believe we will recognize each other and I can't help but believe when we meet it will seem as though no time has passed.

Just thinking about that glad reunion day makes me happy. I am looking forward to seeing Jesus most of all, but I want to see my little grandson Jackson. I do not know what "age" we will be in that land, but I believe I'll know him and he will know me. There are so many others I look forward to seeing again as well.

When I get there, no one will be talking about any health issues! No pain and no sickness will be found in that place. There will be no tears. No death will ever again separate us from our friends because there is no death there. The Lord God has planned a perfect reunion for us. I hope you are planning to attend!

Jesus, what a day that will be when I see You face to face. What a day when I am reunited with those I love. Amen

MAY 3rd *REBUKE AND REPENTENCE*

"As many as I love, I rebuke and chasten: be zealous therefore, and repent." Revelation 3:19

"Why did I let him do that?" "Why in the world didn't I speak up?" "I should have asked him to leave my yard!" These words have made their rounds in my mind for years. I wish I had handled the day very differently.

When our sons were growing up, other boys from the neighborhood would come over to play basketball in our driveway. One day a father from up the street came into our yard and began to berate a couple of the guys who were visiting. I am not sure what had happened. I can't recall exactly why he was so upset.

All I know is I did not like it one bit. But George was at work and I did not say anything to this man. I just stood there in silence. Yet, I kept wishing I could go back and say, "Please leave my property. You can take this up with them at their houses, not mine." Or something similar.

I don't know if I ever apologized to the boys. Mark and Allen most likely don't even remember the day, but I do. I do not know if this dad ever regretted his actions. I just know I regretted my inaction.

Maybe you readers disagree with me, but I think our guests should have been able to feel safe when visiting our home. I know whatever the situation, it was some minor issue between his sons and these young men. It was nothing that could not have waited until they were back at home. Then he could have taken the matter up with their dads!

I am not saying the rebuke was unfounded. I am just saying it should have been in the proper place and at the proper time. I am just saying I should not have allowed him to come chasten them on my watch. Rebuke is never pleasant no matter where it takes place. And chastening should not be done in anger. (You know anger is just one letter short of danger!)

Jesus said He rebukes and chastens those He *loves*. When the Lord corrects us, His intentions are to shape us into His likeness. He doesn't punish us as we deserve because He knows we are but dust (Psalm 103:14). The Lord is slow to anger and plenteous in mercy, so His discipline is restrained. It is never done out of malice. When the Lord rebukes us, it causes in us a desire to repent. After all, love reduces friction to a fraction!

Lord, Your word says there is a time to keep silence, and a time to speak. Help me know when to do which. Amen

MAY 4th *NATIONAL DAY OF PRAYER*

"If my people, which are called by my name, shall humble themselves, and pray, and seek my face, and turn from their wicked ways; then will I hear from heaven, and will forgive their sin, and will heal their land." II Chronicles 7:14

Each spring, the people of the United States are called to "turn to God in prayer and meditation." The Second Continental Congress established a day of fasting and prayer, but through the years, the date was often changed or ignored.

During the Korean War, the Reverend Billy Graham expressed a desire for a united national prayer. In 1952, President Harry Truman signed a proclamation for a National Day of Prayer with the date to be decided by each subsequent president. In 1988, the law was amended to set aside the first Thursday in May for this purpose.

Today, people will gather in homes, in churches and in front of courthouses to pray with civic and government leaders. Prayers will be offered for communities, states, the nation and all the leaders. I feel certain the verse above will be quoted in many of these gatherings.

Although this prayer was offered by Solomon when the temple was dedicated, the principle is still appropriate today. All Christian people should humble themselves before the Almighty God. We should pray and seek God's face. We should turn from our wicked ways if we want God to bless us!

I think we all agree that forgiveness and healing are needed in our hearts and in our land today. Won't you join me in praying?

Jesus, I come humbly before You. I ask You to help me turn from every wicked way to seek Your face. I pray that You would hear all the prayers offered for our nation today. Forgive us, Lord, and heal our land. Amen

MAY 5th *KING OF THE COURSE*

"After these things, and the establishment thereof, Sennacherib king of Assyria came, and entered into Judah, and encamped against the fenced cities, and thought to win them for himself." II Chronicles 32:1

My Uncle Linton was an avid golfer. To the best of my knowledge, he was the only golfer in my family. As a child, I never did understand what was so interesting about hitting a little white ball into the distance and then walking so far just to hit it again! I did not understand all the challenges and mental toughness of the game. I still don't because I do not play golf. Except for putt-putt, better known as miniature golf.

Back in the day, there was a miniature course across the road from the Brunswick Roswell Bowling Center. We went there frequently. We've also played in many states while on vacation. My brother Randy was a demon on the putt-putt course. He won every game we ever played, except one. When I finally beat him, he was just furious with himself (and me!).

George never cared that much for the game, but he was a good sport and played with us most of the time. He and I played a game in Panama City a couple of years ago and he beat me! It was his first win, too! I am just waiting for the re-match.

Winning brings out the pride in us, doesn't it? No one likes to lose, but winning often causes us to feel superior. We can become haughty and look down on others. We also can become too self confident. When that happens, we are setting ourselves up for a fall. Just like King Sennacherib.

This king of Assyria was a great builder and conqueror. His intentions were to capture the cities of Judah. He felt confident that he could do so because he was accustomed to winning all the battles.

He sent his servants to King Hezekiah of Judah and to all the people to warn them of the impending destruction. The servants said, "Who was there among all the gods of those nations that my fathers utterly destroyed, that could deliver his people out of mine hand, that your God should be able to deliver you out of mine hand?"

What Sennacherib failed to realize was these were no gods at all, whereas Judah was protected by the God of Heaven. That night the Lord sent an angel who destroyed 185,000 Assyrians and their king returned home with shame on his face. His sons killed him with a sword as he worshipped in the house of his god.

We can learn some great lessons from the life of this king. We must never put our confidence in our own ability because even the mightiest can be brought down. When we fail to recognize God as the Almighty and take the glory for ourselves, there are dire consequences. The Bible tells us pride goes before destruction and a haughty spirit before a fall. I do not want to allow myself to become like King Sennacherib. Not in miniature golf and certainly not in life.

Lord, I pray for humility. You must increase but I must decrease. Amen

"Now at the end of the days that the king had said he should bring them in, then the prince of the eunuchs brought them in before Nebuchadnezzar." Daniel 1:18

On this day in 2010, Tyler literally brought them in. His baseball team was tied with the opponent at the end of regulation play and they went into "sudden death" overtime. In this overtime period, each team gets a runner on second base and has two outs on the board.

The visiting team scored a run. It was do-or-die time. The first batter for Tyler's team was able to reach first. Two on, two out. Tyler stepped into the batter's box. The pitcher threw two balls. Tyler swung and missed the third pitch. Kevin said, "Man, I hope he doesn't make the last out." We were hoping he would walk. Why were we willing to settle for that? On the next pitch, Tyler ripped the ball through the infield and it went nearly to the fence for a game winning home run!

Tyler's "bringing them in" won the game. His face was glowing. (So was mine.) His "bringing them in" was different from the king's but the results were similar.

Daniel and his friends were captives in Babylon. They requested they be allowed to forego eating the king's food so as not to defile themselves before God. Daniel asked they be given pulse to eat and water to drink for ten days. After that, the king's servant was to compare their faces to the faces of those who did eat the king's food.

When the ten days were completed, the king's servant found the faces of Daniel and his friends to be fairer and fatter than the faces of the others. You might say their faces were glowing. God had taken care of them because they wanted to honor Him.

There is a song in the *Church Hymnal* entitled "Bring Them In." It was written by Alexcenah Thomas. The song encourages us to go find the lost and bring them in to Jesus. When we bring in our friends, the Lord makes them winners in the game of life. What a great way to honor Him. Also, seeing a friend, or even a stranger, accept Jesus will make your face glow. Go, share the gospel today and bring someone in to His fold.

Jesus, use me to bring someone in before it is too late. Amen

"Pray without ceasing." I Thessalonians 5:17

Since I retired, I felt my prayer life had "suffered." Of course I still prayed, but I no longer had four or five hours each day alone with the Lord. I found it much harder to carve out a niche of time to concentrate the way I once did.

When I delivered mail, I could pray all the way around the route if I wanted to. I did not have contact with that many of my six hundred customers, so there were not many interruptions. You may be thinking what I did was not really praying because I was not bowed down with my eyes closed and I was busy doing a job all the while. All I can say is the Lord was with me and we communed while I worked.

When I came to a house where I knew there was sickness, I prayed for the one who needed healing or help with managing the pain. If a family had lost a loved one, I prayed for comfort, peace and hope. If there was an expectant mother, I prayed for a healthy baby and a safe delivery. While delivering in a new subdivision, I would pray for the workers atop the houses. There were so many needs along the way!

Then, I realized, the Lord and I still commune while I work. I talk to Him during the day while I am taking care of my grandchildren, preparing meals, ironing or cleaning the house. There are so many things to be thankful for!

When I see the plants growing in George's garden, I thank God for giving George the strength to tend the garden. While I cook or wash dishes, I thank God for our food and ask Him to help the hungry. When I get in the car, I thank Him for it and for the ability to drive. When I hear it raining, I thank God for the shelter we have and ask Him to help the homeless. When I iron, I thank Him for our clothing. You get the picture.

George and I pray together before we eat our meals. We pray together before we go to sleep. Often, we pray the moment we wake up. The Bible says, "Where two or three are gathered together in my name, there am I in the midst of them (Matthew 18:20)." Now I have a partner in prayer! I don't have to be alone. I am still talking with the Lord and I am not limited to a time frame either.

We *can* pray without ceasing. We do not have to pray for a certain amount of time each day. We just have to pray frequently and persistently.

Lord, thank You for giving me all the time I need to praise You, thank You and to pray for others. Amen

MAY 8th *THE REST OF THE STORY*

"...not one thing hath failed of all the good things which the Lord your God spake concerning you; all are come to pass unto you, and not one thing hath failed thereof." Joshua 23:14

We are all familiar, I'm sure, with radio broadcaster, Paul Harvey. He was best known in his later years for his series, The Rest of the Story, which was part mystery and part history. These stories were written by his son Paul, Jr.

I can't help but think of "the rest of the story" from the Bible. Were Paul Harvey narrating about it today, I am sure he would talk about God's people being slaves in Egypt. Surely his story would end with these words spoken by Joshua shortly before his death.

I can imagine Harvey telling the story of Samson. He would mention the killing of the lion and the eating of the honey. He would tell of the riddle posed by Samson to the Philistines. He would tell of Delilah's trickery to gain knowledge of Samson's source of strength. His story would end with Samson's pulling down the house on himself and all the Philistines gathered there that day.

Let's skip to the New Testament. We would hear the story of the virgin birth of the Lord Jesus. We would hear of Herod's plot to kill Jesus. We would hear of His crucifixion. But the rest of the story would be the resurrection.

Harvey would tell of the end times. He would probably describe the battle between good and evil, but the rest of the story would be the final victory of the Lamb. As the Reverend Billy Graham once said, "We know how it ends. We win."

Were Paul Harvey telling about your life, how would your story end? Would he be able to tell how you came to know the Lord in the forgiveness of sin? Would your story include working for the Lord?

My life's story doesn't contain much mystery. My history is not even very interesting. But I was saved and set free by the blood of the Lamb. In spite of all my many sins, I will live with the Lord in eternity. Like Paul Harvey, I could say at the end, "Now you know the rest of the story."

Lord, You made the rest of my story good. Thank You for all You have done in my life. Amen

MAY 9th *HABITS OF BIRDS*

"Behold the fowls of the air: for they sow not, neither do they reap, nor gather into barns; yet your heavenly Father feedeth them. Are ye not much better than they?" Matthew 6:26

We have a dogwood tree in front of our kitchen window. I can look out that window in the spring and often see a nest a bird has built in the branches. Since the branches extend over the porch railing, I can usually see the eggs inside the nest. I have never been able to actually see them hatch, but I have seen the little birds with their hungry mouths opened, just waiting for Mother Bird to bring their meals.

I enjoy pointing out the nest to the children. It is hard to resist getting close enough to inspect it. The turquoise eggs are so pretty they seem to beckon little hands to pick them up. When the baby birds are hatched, we want to see them begging for food and hear their hungry cries. But, we do not want to frighten Mother Bird and cause her to abandon the nest or the nestlings. So, we keep our distance and watch from behind the storm door.

But recently, I read those abandonment stories are unfounded for most birds. They do not have a strong sense of smell, so the scent of humans will not deter them from taking care of their young. Once the eggs are hatched, the mother bird is pretty tenacious about caring for her own.

Did you know the father bird also feeds and guards the babies? This was news to me. But God is like a Father Bird, and I am not just talking about His relationship to the feathered, flying birds. He also feeds us and watches over us every moment of the day. God has promised to supply our need. He has promised to never leave or forsake us. He is tenacious about caring for His own.

The verse from Matthew asks if we are not better than the fowls of the air. If God will so lovingly care for them, we can rest assured He is going to hover over us and keep us as well. Jesus said not one sparrow falls to the ground without the Father and we are of more value than many sparrows (Matthew 10:29-31).

If you feel you are being pushed out of the nest, just remember, God will either catch you or teach you to fly! He will not abandon you.

Father God, thank You for valuing me above sparrows even when I feel lower than the worms. Amen

MAY 10th *WHAT DOUBLEMINT MEANT TO ME*

"Whoso keepeth his mouth and his tongue keepeth his soul from troubles." Proverbs 21:23

After serving many years as the environmental manager, the father of our daughter-in-law DeAnn retired from the Wrigley Company. I can't help but wonder if she grew up loving gum as much as I did. I have some special memories associated with Wrigley's products.

My grandmother's favorite flavor was Doublemint. Launched in 1914, the flavor was the third one introduced. The name came from the double distillation process for the mint and it was packaged with a distinctive green wrapper. Grandmother carried a package of the gum in her purse at all times.

This gum was especially helpful during the church services on Sunday mornings. If I began talking or became restless, she would pull out the gum and hand me a stick of it. Not only did I enjoy chewing the gum, I loved watching her make a tiny, silver cup out of the inner wrapper.

Even though Juicy Fruit gum is the oldest brand in the Wrigley family, it did not become my favorite until much later. For many years, I chewed Doublemint because my grandmother did. As I said, this kept my mouth and tongue from trouble during "preaching."

If Wrigley's helped me then, maybe it could help me today. Maybe I should carry a package of gum in my purse at all times. Each time I am tempted to say something unkind or hurtful I could quickly slip a stick in my mouth and busy my tongue with keeping my soul from trouble. I would literally be doubling my pleasure by doing so.

Oh, that it were really that simple and a stick of gum would help me as much today! The book of James tells us no one can tame the tongue. I will admit, I still find it hard to do even though I have grown older and, hopefully, wiser. James says the tongue is an unruly evil, full of deadly poison. We must constantly guard the words that come from our lips if we want to keep our souls from trouble.

Even though my grandmother has passed through this life to the next, I appreciate the kindness she afforded me as she shared her gum. Her small gift was a stick of grace I can savor still.

Lord, help me remember to keep my soul from troubles by controlling my tongue. Amen

MAY 11th   *THE ANCHOR HOLDS*

"Which hope we have as an anchor of the soul, both sure and stedfast, which entereth into that within the veil;" Hebrews 6:19

On a bowling team, the last person listed on the line up is called the anchor. This is normally the strongest bowler on the team. I had a chance to try out the anchor position when I substituted for a few weeks in a mixed league. My nephew Dustin had broken his ankle at the American Ninja Warrior course in Norcross and asked me to bowl in his spot until his foot was mended.

The first week, game one came down to the wire. All I needed in the tenth frame was nineteen pins. I got a spare, but on the next ball I threw a seven, causing us to lose by one pin! Would you believe the second game was the same exact scenario? I needed nineteen pins, but after the spare I threw a six and we lost by two. Dustin wasn't very happy with me. He told me they had only lost two games up to that point and, with me bowling, they had lost all four games that night to the last place team! Oh, dear.

They were in dire straits for someone to bowl, so they kept me on. I was able to redeem myself, somewhat, a couple of weeks down the road. In the tenth frame, I threw two strikes and a nine count. I turned around and asked, "Is that what an anchor does?" The team agreed it definitely was what an anchor does. I ended my stint on the team with a 202 game. But, for the most part, I had failed them miserably.

In the physical sense, an anchor is a heavy object of metal which is used to hold a ship in place. Though the ship may be battered by the winds and waves, the anchor will keep it from drifting.

The anchor we have for our souls is Jesus Christ. When we see the word *hope* in this verse, it is not referring to a wish but to a confident expectation. Jesus is sure and He is steadfast. He will never fail us. He entered one time into the veil and He is our High Priest forever.

Jesus is working to bring about His perfect will in our lives even when we are going through some rough storms. The old hymn, "In Times Like These," tells us we need an anchor and Jesus is the only One. So, I encourage you to be very sure your anchor holds and grips the solid Rock.

Jesus, I am very sure my anchor holds because I trust in You alone. Amen

MAY 12th *HE KNOWS MY NAME*

"And when Jesus came to the place, he looked up, and saw him, and said unto him, Zacchaeus, make haste, and come down; for today I must abide at thy house." Luke 19:5

I have never been a coach for any youth sports team, but our sons Kevin and Joel have. The toughest part is probably making sure every child plays. It might be easy to forget about one or two players, still sitting on the bench, waiting for their names to be called. When practice starts for the new season, it might even be difficult to remember each child's name.

Francesca Battistelli's song, "He Knows My Name," says, "I wouldn't choose me first if I was looking for a champion, In fact I'd understand if You picked everyone before me." Sometimes, we may feel we are the least important and the Coach doesn't even know our name. We may feel we will never be called to participate in the game.

Zacchaeus was little of stature. I am sure, on occasion, he had been overlooked. One day, Zacchaeus was in a sycamore tree, waiting for Jesus to pass by. He had no clue Jesus even knew him. Can you imagine his surprise when Jesus stopped and called him by name? Not only did Jesus know who Zacchaeus was, Jesus said He was going to abide that day with Zacchaeus at his house.

This encounter changed the life of Zacchaeus. On this particular day, he was not left out and forgotten. His name was called by the very Son of God. Formerly hated by the people because he was a tax collector, Zacchaeus was called to participate in the kingdom of God. He hastened, joyfully, to do as Jesus said.

Like Zacchaeus, we need to get as close to Jesus as we can and we need to be listening when He calls us by name.

Jesus, I am so thankful You know my name. When You call my name, help me joyfully respond. Amen

MAY 13th *PUTTING DOWN ROOTS*

"That Christ may dwell in your hearts by faith; that ye, being rooted and grounded in love, May be able to comprehend with all saints, what is the breadth, and length, and depth, and height;" Ephesians 3:17, 18

We have been rooted and grounded in this home for thirty years now. Sure, there have been discussions of selling and buying a new place, but we are still here. This place is full of our family's memories.

And I mean literally full. Our basement is the storage place for our sons' team trophies, hunting equipment, books, etc. It is also where George and I have stocked countless items. Moving would be such a job!

Moving to a new church or to a new job would also be hard. When you are firmly established in a place, it is hard to pick up and move on. The same is true for a new relationship. When your memories are all tied to one person, the thoughts of finding someone new are painful.

Nevertheless, when we are uprooted and planted in a new place, we can live again. Our roots can be firmly embedded in new soil and our limbs can be full of new growth. God will help us grow strong and secure once more.

When delivering mail for over two decades, I noticed people were being uprooted and replanted right here in our own community. They were not just moving from place to place within the county. They were coming here from all fifty states and from many foreign countries as well. I know they were all searching for a new start, something better.

No matter where we live, our something better is found in Jesus Christ. Our faith in Him will take root downward and bear fruit upward. His love is the soil that helps us grow to maturity.

If your roots are not in Him, why not ask Him to transplant you to the right place where you can be rooted and grounded in His love?

131

Lord Jesus, You dwell in my heart by faith. Help my roots to go deeper in Your love. Amen

MAY 14th *A MOTHER'S INFLUENCE*

◆————————————————————————————◆

"And Adam called his wife's name Eve; because she was the mother of all living." Genesis 3:20

A mother has a profound effect on her children whether for good or bad. The Bible gives us some examples of both kinds of mothers.

Rebekah was the answer to a prayer of Abraham's servant, yet she taught her son Jacob to be a schemer and a deceiver. Jacob deceived his own father and later his father-in-law.

In the days when kings ruled the land, we read of Ahaziah, grandson of Omri. The Bible tells us his mother Athaliah was his counseller to do wickedly!

In the New Testament, we find Herodias. She was the wife of the tetrarch, Herod. She instructed her daughter to ask for the head of John the Baptist on a charger.

On the other hand, we have mothers like Jochebed, the mother of Moses. We have Hannah who gave her son Samuel to the Lord. We have the mother who was willing to give up her child to save his life when King Solomon offered to cut the child in half. We have the mother of Lemuel who taught him prophecy.

Of course, there is Mary, mother of Jesus. She became pregnant by the Holy Ghost while she was not married. She did not seek to destroy her child because He would be an inconvenience or a cause for gossip. She was there by Him even unto His death and was one of the first to the tomb the following day.

And let's not forget about Eunice, the mother of Timothy. Paul said Timothy's unfeigned faith had first dwelt in his mother as well as his grandmother.

A good mother will train her child up in the nurture and admonition of the Lord. A mother who leads her child astray will answer to God. But, regardless of the kind of mothering we have had, we have to be responsible for our own choices. Ultimately, we will answer to God for the ones we have made whether good or bad.

The Bible instructs us to honor our mothers. Make the right choice today and honor yours. Give her a call. Say, "I love you." Pray for her.

Forgive her for the times she failed you. If she has passed away, visit her grave site or share a memory of her with someone.

Most importantly, if you are a mother, share your faith with your children and lead them to the Lord.

Lord, thank You for mothers who influence their children for good by sharing their faith in You. Amen

MAY 15th *A GOOD STEWARD*

"If therefore ye have not been faithful in the unrighteous mammon, who will commit to your trust the true riches?" Luke 16:11

God expects us to be good stewards of what He has given us. Not just our time and our talents but our money as well. Many Christians are quick to give God credit, but reluctant to give Him cash! Why is that?

I would venture to say it is because we are too selfish. We want to spend our money on what we want and give God the few dollars that are left over. I know how that is. I was once a reluctant giver. That was not going very well, so I persuaded George we needed to up our giving.

We have found we cannot out-give God. He has taken care of us through everything we have encountered. He has opened the windows of Heaven and poured us out many blessings. Some way, somehow, God has always provided for us. Maybe a bill was less than I had budgeted or maybe an unexpected check came in the mail. The funds we have needed have always come in.

In Luke 16, Jesus is teaching about an unjust steward. He says we cannot be trusted with much until we prove we can be trusted with a little. In other words, our use of worldly wealth is a good indicator of the way we would handle eternal riches.

Ask yourself these questions. Am I a good steward? Am I using my resources to further God's kingdom? If not, why not? How can I make the necessary changes?

Once you step out in faith, God will help you. We know from our own experience this is true.

Father God, I know I still need to reassess my efforts from time to time. Help me be faithful in giving. Amen

MAY 16th *BECAUSE SOMEONE CARED*

"Because thou shalt forget thy misery, and remember it as waters that pass away." Job 11:16

I don't remember what trial had brought me down, but I remember my friend noticing right away. When I walked into church she asked, "What's wrong?" I didn't realize anyone could tell, but she said she knew by looking at me that I was not myself. Even though my face carried a smile, my eyes carried the sadness.

How observant have I been with others? How often had I overlooked a little sign they were hurting? Maybe a tone of voice, a look in the eye, or sagging shoulders? A lot of people walk by me with their silent struggles while I am oblivious to their pain. I need to notice!

Inez Franck wrote the poem, *Because.* It says, "Because somebody cared today I knew God's love was strong; I found new hope to bear my cross and courage for my song. My neighbor's heart conveyed the love I needed for my pain; And happily I felt the faith To dream and smile again."

It has been said Christians are to be the hands and feet of Jesus. We are to be "Jesus with skin on." It is our duty to bear one another's burdens. Yet, often I am too busy with my own issues to notice the burdens another carries. That is not pleasing to the Lord. I need to be aware of those around me who are hurting. And I need to try to help if I can.

Just knowing my friend cared helped me forget my misery. Today I want to show someone I care. I want to see others through the caring, compassionate eyes of Jesus.

Lord Jesus, help me be a noticer today and extend Your love to those who are hurting. Amen

MAY 17th   *LITTLE THINGS*

"And they say unto him, We have here but five loaves, and two fishes." Matthew 14:17

The people were hungry. The disciples had no food to share. One young boy had five loaves and two fishes. But Andrew asked, "What are they among so many?" Jesus answered him by feeding over five thousand men with that small amount and there were twelve baskets full left over! Little things mean a lot.

Often I pop into the dollar store for an item or two and when I get to the register I have a basket full of things! I wonder how I spent so much money in a place where things are so inexpensive. It is by taking one item at a time. Little by little. It all adds up.

Whether it is overspending or overeating, it happens little by little. A bowl of ice cream here, a few cookies there and before you know it, a few extra pounds are added!

But what about the *good* little things we do? A smile here, a note sent there, a hand offered, a prayer said. Little things can mean so much to someone who is hungry, physically or spiritually.

One of our Dove customers, Mary G., would always ask us how she might pray for us. She prayed right then and there, too. Her little acts of kindness brightened my days.

My church choir sings "Little Is Much When God Is In It." One verse of the song asks, "Does the place you're called to labor, seem so small and little known?" Then the words assure us it is great if God is in it and He will not forget His own.

If you feel that your part is too small to matter, just remember God sees and remembers every effort you make to share His love. Little by little, you can gain a great reward.

Dear God, help me do what little I can; then use what good I do to further Your kingdom. Amen

MAY 18th   *THE SMELL OF SOAP*

"And walk in love, as Christ also hath loved us, and hath given himself for us an offering and a sacrifice to God for a sweetsmelling savour." Ephesians 5:2

I grew up in a small church. Most of the people who belonged to the church were my kinfolks. My cousin Louie Hansard often led the singing and his wife Hazel played the piano. My grandmother did not sing, but her sisters had beautiful alto voices. My uncle Early Day was the pastor for many years. It was a close knit church.

During revival, I can remember being especially close to those about me. In a day when central air was not common, I could smell the scent of soap on the person squeezed into the pew beside me. The Ingram Funeral Home fans people gently waved back and forth just made the smell even more noticeable. What a sweet memory.

Rather than the smell of soap, God was pleased with the sweet scent of worship and praise. I believe He looked down and saw concern for lost souls. He heard the fervent prayers and was pleased when one walked down the aisle and accepted His Son as Savior. I believe the fragrance of obedience was pleasing in His nostrils.

Under the old covenant, God smelled the blood of lambs, rams, goats and oxen. Incense was offered up daily for a sweet smelling sacrifice. When the people continued to sin willfully, God became sick of the smells. He said their incense was an abomination to Him. He could no longer tolerate their sacrifices.

However, the blood of Christ was a sweet smell to the Father. He was pleased with the obedience and sacrifice of His only Son. Since the vicarious death of Jesus was a once-for-all event, the smell still lingers throughout the ages.

The smell of Lifebouy or Dial was sweet to me at one time, but Christ's sacrifice will never lose its fragrance.

Father God, thank You for the sacrificial death of Your Son. How sweet it is. Amen

MAY 19th *SO LONG, FAREWELL*

"The eternal God is thy refuge, and underneath are the everlasting arms:" Deuteronomy 33:27a

When I was a young girl, we had vinyl records: 78s, 33s and 45s. If we wanted to record our voices, we had those big reel-to-reel tapes. Records were replaced in popularity by the eight-track tapes and later those were replaced by cassette tapes. I collected hundreds of the cassettes. (After my car was totaled, I donated most of them to my coworker Patience). Then the compact disc came along.

We no longer have slide projectors, 8mm home movies, cameras that use drop-in film cartridges, floppy disks and so on. Our first television showed a black and white picture. I was thrilled when I could see *Walt Disney's Wonderful World of Color* in color! Back then, tv sets were big and bulky. Most people I knew had the cabinet models called consoles. Now the sets are slim and lightweight.

When I was in school, I had a typing class using a manual typewriter. I used my meager skills in my first job at Coastal States Life. The typewriter of my choice was an Underwood electric model.

Most homes have central heat and air. When I was young, we had a coal furnace in the basement and a fan in the window. Putizer Prize winner Rick Bragg said they put a man on the moon before he had a window (air conditioning) unit. He said they put a man on the moon before we had GPS, cell phones, internet, etc. He said they put a man on the moon before they put wheels on suitcases!

We have seen so many changes in our lives. We wonder if anything is permanent. When something is old, we seldom have it fixed these days; we toss it out and buy a new item. It is goodbye and good riddance.

God, however, is from the beginning, but He is never obsolete. His kingship, love, strength and righteousness are all everlasting. We can always rely on Him for protection. That is very assuring to me.

Eternal God, I am so thankful You are my refuge. I have no cause to fear for Your everlasting arms are beneath me. Amen

MAY 20th *FIRST IN FLIGHT*

"That we henceforth be no more children, tossed to and fro, and carried about with every wind of doctrine by the sleight of men, and cunning craftiness...." Ephesians 4:14

Several times we spent our family vacation on the Outer Banks of North Carolina. We visited Ocracoke, Nag's Head and Cape Hatteras. When the boys were younger, they enjoyed riding the ferry. We rented bicycles once when the "greenheads" were abundant. Bad mistake.

137

Joel stopped his bike in the middle of the road because he was too busy swatting the flies to ride!

We have visited Kitty Hawk. Four miles south of there is Kill Devil Hills where, in 1903, the Wright brothers made the first powered airplane flight. Their first flight lasted just twelve seconds. The record flight of the day lasted fifty-nine seconds and covered a distance of 852 feet.

Although the brothers were from Ohio, they chose the North Carolina beach for their experiment because of the constant wind which would add lift for their flight. Orville and Wilbur Wright changed the course of history from this very spot, although one paper's headline was "Flyers or Liars?"

Their efforts were challenged by what is called "adverse yaw." I am not able to adequately explain this, but there is a facsimile of the wind tunnel they designed and built to study this effect. Their tunnel was slightly flawed, though. Their plane crashed after that record flight and the front rudder was damaged.

Like the Wrights, we are sometimes tossed about by the winds. We may encounter cunning craftiness at the hands of false teachers. We must be prepared to face the adverse yaw the devil throws at us. The best line of defense is to know the truth. As babes in Christ, we are easily misled. As we mature in Christ, we gain discernment.

The Wrights kept trying to perfect their flying machine and we must keep trying to grow to a new level of maturity. We should spend time in prayer, in Bible study, in fasting and in fellowship with other believers.

Let's be on guard so we are not blown about by contrary winds.

Jesus, I want to grow in grace and in knowledge. Help me, I pray. Amen

MAY 21ˢᵗ *NO STRINGS ATTACHED*

"Then said he also to him that bade him, When thou makest a dinner or a supper, call not thy friends, nor thy brethren, neither thy kinsmen, nor thy rich neighbours; lest they also bid thee again, and a recompence be made thee." Luke 14:12

I enjoy staying at hotels where there are candies on the pillows and complimentary toiletries by the sink. I liked it when our new car was filled with gasoline before we drove away in it. I think it is great to get free pie at O'Charley's on Wednesdays. I love a discount from Belk.

All of these are wonderful ways to thank the customers for spending money. These perks are ways to entice the customer to come back and spend more! But shouldn't we be giving just for the sake of giving?

So often we give because we expect something in return. Jesus said to give even when you know the other person can never repay you. He told His host to invite those who could never reciprocate the invitation to dinner. Jesus died for us, expecting nothing in return. He knew we could never return the favor or repay Him. All He wants is for us to accept His love.

Other than invite someone to dinner, there are countless ways we can brighten the day for another. Let a driver go ahead of you. Pay for the person in line behind you. Give someone with a frown one of your smiles. How about a thumbs up to someone doing a good deed? Wink at your spouse. High-five a kid at church! We miss a lot because too often we neglect doing the little things. We can and should give with no strings attached.

Like a driver I saw at the intersection of Highways 9 and 20. A car had stalled and traffic was backing up more than usual. I saw a young man in a truck jump out, run over and help push the vehicle out of the way. He hurried back to his truck, got in and sped off. No strings attached for his good deed. He expected nothing in return. It warmed my heart and blessed MY day even though it was not my car that had stalled.

Be on the lookout for some small way you can bless the life of a loved one or even a stranger. Give with no strings attached. It is what Jesus would do.

Lord, help me do good deeds today with no strings attached. Amen

MAY 22nd   HEAVY BURDENS

"So shall it be easier for thyself, and they shall bear the burden with thee." Exodus 18:22

George was once a very strong man. He had big muscles and could lift heavy objects with no problems. He has carried a washing machine out of the house by himself. George was the one everybody called when they needed some lifting done. Those days are gone. Now he can barely lift our granddaughter!

He has carried heavy emotional burdens as well. Two of the heaviest were his mother's declining health and her death, as well as the death of our grandson. Recently we had a discussion about all the burdens George has shouldered.

Some required great physical strength but the heavier emotional ones required much prayer and exertion of faith. While he is no longer the man to call when you need a sofa moved, he is surely the one to call when you need a mountain moved. He is a praying man with unstoppable faith. He considers it an honor to pray for his friends and his family.

The Bible tells us to bear one another's burdens. We are assured that will make it easier for us. Even though George's shoulders are not able to lift heavy loads anymore, he is willing and able to help carry the toughest spiritual loads.

We all need someone to care about us when we are hurting. We want others to intercede for us. One song in the *Church Hymnal* says, "I want my friends to pray for me and lift me up on wings of faith." George will gladly do this kind of lifting for anyone who asks. How about you? Help bear the burden for someone today.

Lord, help me always be willing to lift the burdens of another. Amen

MAY 23rd   *MONEY FROM A STRANGER*

"Love ye therefore the stranger: for ye were strangers in the land of Egypt." Deuteronomy 10:19

For many years, our grandson Tyler spent the night with us on Thursday nights. Every Friday morning, I fixed his breakfast and I drove him to Dawsonville to his school.

One morning, I needed gas before I returned home. I stopped at the Kroger store at the intersection of Highways 53 and 400. I was busy pumping my gas when a young lady approached me. She handed me some folded bills. She said, "Ma'am, I am supposed to give you this. I know it might seem weird, but I have to obey the Holy Spirit."

Although I thought she probably needed the money more than I did, I was certainly not going to argue with the Holy Spirit. I accepted the money and thanked her very much. I asked God what I should do with the cash.

Later that morning, while I was at the landfill, I paid the dumping fee for a lady who was short of funds. Then, George and I saw a man with an oxygen tank begging in the Home Depot parking lot. We stopped and gave him part of the money. I don't know if he really needed help, but God knew. I also donated ten percent to my church.

Both the lady and I tried to be obedient to the prompting of the Holy Spirit. She made my day and I think I helped make the day a little brighter for two others.

No matter how weird the command may seem, when the Holy Spirit bids us to do something, we should obey. The act of obedience is like throwing a rock into a pool of water. The ripples spread out in a widening circle. In other words, the good we do will multiply and have far reaching effects. Don't hesitate when the Spirit says, "Do."

Jesus, help me be obedient whenever I feel the Holy Spirit telling me to act. Amen

MAY 24th *THE SPLINTER*

"They pierced my hands and my feet." Psalm 22:16b

Theodore Samuel "Ted" Williams was a major league baseball player. He spent his entire career playing left field for the Boston Red Sox. Considered one of the greatest hitters in the history of the game, Williams was known by several nicknames. One of which was "The Splendid Splinter." But my story is about a not-so-splendid splinter.

One spring, George was doing some project around the house and needed my help lifting some pressure treated boards. I happened to get a splinter in my hand just below my little finger. I tried to use my grandmother's method of getting the splinter out with a needle. But my hand did not heal. Every time I closed my hand the site became more irritated. Sometimes it would bleed.

I could tell that it was infected, and finally George insisted I go to urgent care. The diagnosis was cellulitis. I got a tetanus shot and two different antibiotics. Soon, the healing was complete. I learned a valuable lesson. Now, I never handle treated lumber without work gloves!

Jesus' hands were pierced with nails, not splinters. His scars never healed because, after the resurrection, He showed them to Thomas to prove His identity. I know how much pain was caused by a very small sliver of wood. I cannot imagine what Jesus endured with the nails through His hands.

What I do know is that He endured the cross, despising the shame and is set down at the right hand of the throne of God. Out of His great love, He did this for you and for me. Have you accepted His love as payment for your sins? If not, ask Him to forgive you and save you today.

Lord Jesus, thank You for enduring the nails for me. Amen

MAY 25th *TRIPLE D*

"Nay, in all these things we are more than conquerors through him that loved us." Romans 8:37

Kevin, Tyler and I enjoy watching *Diners, Drive-Ins and Dives* on the Food Network. The show is often referred to as Triple D. Host Guy Fieri travels around looking for the best "greasy spoon" restaurants. He samples the specialties of each place he visits.

One such place was the Westside Drive In located in Boise, Idaho. Finger steaks are the favorite menu item. On our last trip out west, we found the place and enjoyed a meal there. We ate outside even though the temperature that day was 109 degrees!

The other night, I began thinking about the triple Ds of my life. I often feel defeated, depleted and even deleted in some instances. The enemy of my soul tortures me with such thoughts.

This verse from Romans assures me I am more than a conqueror through Christ. There is no reason to ever feel beaten, used up or destroyed. I have power over the devil because the One in me is greater than the one in the world.

Ephesians, chapter six, tells me to put on the helmet of salvation.

When I am wearing the helmet, my thinking is like that of Christ. When I do not wear all the pieces of my armor, I am susceptible to the attacks of Satan. He wages a full, frontal assault on Christians every day.

It is my job to be on guard against him. Jesus quoted Scriptures to the devil when tempted in the wilderness and I can do the same. I need to remind myself I am more than a conqueror. I am declared righteous, I am defended by the Lord, I am delivered through the blood of the Lamb. Those are the triple Ds I need to focus on.

Lord, Your Word is what I need to feast on daily. Help me to sample the specialties of each book. Amen

MAY 26th *GIVE A BLESSING*

"And this is it that their father spake unto them, and blessed them; every one according to his blessing he blessed them." Genesis 49:28

I recently read in the *Forsyth County News* about a service at a local church for the specific purpose of blessing the dogs. While I did not attend the service, I found it very interesting.

People want their babies blessed, their marriages blessed and a new home blessed. We also want our food blessed. At our recent class picnic a gentleman was asked to bless the food. He said only God could bless the food, but he would pray. Amen to that.

The *Thorndike-Barnhart Comprehensive Desk Dictionary* lists one definition of blessing as anything that makes one happy or contented. We might also say *anyone* who makes us happy or contented; anyone who has the ability to bless those around him or her.

Like my grandmother or Bodie, my aunt. When George asked me what some of my favorite childhood memories were, I spoke of times spent with these ladies. Their small acts of faith and love were blessings to me.

We all have it within our reach to be a blessing to others. Kind words, prayers, smiles, gratitude, a listening ear or genuine interest in the other person are all ways to be a blessing. Not just to those in our homes but to all those who cross our paths.

A person who is a blessing is also someone we can turn to when we are battered by the storms of life. A someone we can trust to help us find love and peace in the midst of the turmoil. If you know people like this, tell them today what a blessing they are to you!

Jesus, help me be a blessing to all I come in contact with today. Amen

MAY 27th *SELFISH OR SELFLESS?*

"Let nothing be done through strife or vainglory; but in lowliness of mind let each esteem other better than themselves. Look not every man on his own things, but every man also on the things of others."
Philippians 2:3, 4

No one has to teach a child to be selfish. It seems they all know, so instinctively, how to say, "Mine!" They refuse to share their toys or their snacks. I began to wonder if any of us ever grow completely out of that behavior.

Whether a parking place or a piece of cake, we want what's ours. When we hear of a person in need, do we often complain about his misuse of funds and talk about how hard we work for ours? When a person calls and needs to talk to us, do we grumble about the time we have "wasted" when we could have been doing something else? I am certainly guilty of all kinds of selfishness.

Yet the Bible tells me to esteem others better than myself. In other words, I need to put my needs last. Jesus was a servant who washed the feet of His disciples. Can I do any less?

I realize Jesus took time to be alone with the Father and to pray. I am not suggesting we need no boundaries. I am not talking about enabling others in their bad habits or unwise choices. I am saying I need to follow the leadership of the Lord in serving others.

I like the commercial where the mom tells one child, "You get to cut but he gets to choose." That makes the cutter more careful about making the slices as even as possible. Our basic desire would be to get the bigger slice as our own!

In everything we do, we need to esteem ourselves less than our brothers and our sisters. Instead of being pushy and demanding, we need more humility and more giving. This would be a good day to start being more selfless and less selfish.

Jesus, help me follow in Your steps as I seek to serve You unselfishly. Amen

MAY 28th   *LAMBERT'S CAFÉ*

"And I will fetch a morsel of bread, and comfort ye your hearts; after that ye shall pass on." Genesis 18:5

In 2002, George and I took my mother on a trip out west. She had always wanted to see the Little Bighorn area where General Custer made his last stand.

On the way home, we stopped in Sikeston, Missouri, at Lambert's Café, the home of the "throwed" rolls. There was a thirty minute wait, but it was well worth it. Ragtime piano music was playing. There were old license plates covering the walls and flags hanging from the ceiling. A very eclectic décor.

I had first heard about the place from my supervisor Ed. He said we should stop at the restaurant if we were anywhere near it. The roll throwing started in the late seventies. There was such a big crowd, it wasn't possible to get around to everyone with fresh rolls, so someone yelled, "Throw 'em." That is just what Norman Lambert did and the rolls have been thrown to customers since.

The food is served from big dishpans with dippers, but you have to catch your roll. Even though she once was a mighty force to be reckoned with on the softball field, it took my mother three tries to catch hers! George and I kept teasing her about it!

After comforting ourselves with the food, we passed on out of town and drove almost to Paducah, Kentucky, where we spent the night.

In Genesis, chapter 18, Abraham played host to the Lord and two others. Abraham asked them to stay and rest, to wash their feet and to share a meal. He said they could pass on after their hearts were comforted.

As it turned out, Abraham's heart was the most comforted. Little did Abraham know the Lord would promise him a son in his old age. Sarah laughed when she heard the Lord's promise. She knew she was past child-bearing age and thought having a baby was impossible. I wonder if she was tempted to throw the rolls at the visitors to her café that day? But, nothing is too hard for the Lord. Isaac was born when Abraham was one hundred years old and Sarah was ninety.

We never know how our hearts might be comforted when we share a morsel of bread.

Lord, I know all things are possible with You. Help my unbelief. Amen

MAY 29th *PATRICK'S CAFÉ*

"Repent ye therefore, and be converted, that your sins may be blotted out, when the times of refreshing shall come from the presence of the Lord;" Acts 3:19

Please indulge me for a moment and allow me to share one more restaurant story with you. Another story from our trip to Montana with my mother.

We had just spent part of the day with my brother's two children at their mom's house in Billings, Montana. We had not seen Brittany and Zach in awhile and the reunion was wonderful. But now it was time to head on out. We stopped in a small town at Patrick's Café. It turned out to be one of the most refreshing stops we made.

The waitress brought our menu. They were out of everything we tried to order! Finally, George told the lady, "Just bring us whatever you have." So, first up was the salad. When the bowl was placed on the table, the greens looked like weeds the waitress had pulled from the side of the road. George told her he now knew how a horse feels!

We kept her laughing and she kept us laughing as well. Before we left, our server gave us all free desserts and the owner gave my mother a glass and a cup as souvenirs of our visit. We asked the ladies if we could make a picture of them for our photo album and they gladly obliged.

We were weary from a long road trip, but one little stop put us all in a great mood as we faced the miles ahead. Surely this time of our refreshing came from the Lord.

If we have been converted, we are on a long road trip toward Heaven as we travel this weary life here. But the Lord sends us times of refreshing as we joy in His presence. Psalm 126:2 says, "Then was our mouth filled with laughter, and our tongue with singing; then said they among the heathen, The Lord hath done great things for them."

The Lord has done great things for us; not only here at home, but in all fifty states as well. He knows just what we need and how to supply it. Even if it means sharing a laugh with strangers in a café.

Oh, Lord, thank You for blotting out my sins. And thank You for the times of refreshing that come from being in Your presence. Amen

MAY 30th *THE THIRD DEGREE*

"But sanctify the Lord God in your hearts: and be ready always to give an answer to every man that asketh you a reason of the hope that is in you with meekness and fear." I Peter 3:15

School is now out for the summer and many high school grads will be preparing to head off to college in a few weeks. Depending on the chosen field a student wants to pursue, there are four degrees one might earn: an associate, a bachelor's, a master's and a doctoral. Both of my daughters-in-law have earned Master's degrees. (They also both earned something extra. A specialist's degree.)

I went to work the day after I graduated from high school and have never stepped foot in a college. Unless you count the time I visited the planetarium at North Georgia, or the times I have gone to different events at Lanier Tech.

However, I did not let this stop me from getting a degree. No, Sir. I actually got the third degree and I am not referring to a master's. I am referring to the third degree I always got from my mother! I had to offer up reasons for much of my behavior during my young years.

But Peter tells us to always be ready to give an answer when we are asked about the hope that is within us. It is up to us to give our personal testimony about how the Lord has worked in our lives. We have no way of knowing how the Lord will use our words to affect the life of another.

Whether you are getting the third degree from an unbeliever or discussing theology with your Sunday School teacher, we are all called to be ready with an answer when asked. No, we will never have ALL the answers, but we can be ready with *The Answer*, which is Christ Jesus. Thankfully, that requires no degree at all.

Jesus, direct my conversations to include You. Help me be ready with an answer when questioned about my hope. Amen

MAY 31ˢᵗ *GO TO THE SOURCE*

"He that believeth on me, as the scripture hath said, out of his belly shall flow rivers of living water." John 7:38

Although they are now obsolete, when I was a girl no respectable family would have been caught without a good set of encyclopedias. *World Book, Encyclopaedia Britannica* and *Collier's* are three popular ones that come to mind.

My dad often sat and read from these books. He was always asking my mother or me if we knew certain facts. He would phrase his query this way, "Hey, Bren, I bet you don't know (whatever)." Mostly I did not. But, I recall his asking my mother if she knew where the headwaters of the Mississippi River were located. She sure surprised him when she said, "Minnesota." He asked her how she knew!

The "Mighty Mississippi" begins in Lake Itasca. A Chippewa chief led Henry Schoolcraft to the place in 1832. For centuries men had been searching for the hidden forested spot from which the river flows about twenty-five hundred miles to the Gulf of Mexico.

I have hiked to the headwaters of the Chattahoochee, but have never seen the source of the Mississippi. I have read there is a rock walkway, nine steps in length, where clear water springs from the lake to form a small creek. In its travels the river expands to more than a mile wide.

We can compare our lives to this mighty river. We may begin with just a mere trickle. We may feel we will never accomplish anything or be any good. But, the scriptures tell us when we believe on Jesus, rivers of living water flow out of us. Of course, this refers to the Holy Spirit. The Spirit can use our trust in Him to make us a channel of His blessings for others. Our part is to trust and obey.

Lord Jesus, our Source of Living Water, when I feel mere, make me mighty for You. Amen

JUNE

JUNE 1st *DIRT BIKE WRECK!*

"A man's heart deviseth his way: but the Lord directeth his steps."
Proverbs 16:9

We were planning a big vacation to the western portion of our nation. Kevin and I had been watching the computer for inexpensive flights. The first morning of June, my grandson Tyler and I searched again. No deals. But later that night Kevin found a great price and we booked it! Tyler and I made a packing list and he actually packed up some of his clothes.

Two days later the accident occurred. Kevin and Tyler had gone to ride their dirt bikes. While I was on the phone with Justin giving him our flight number from Denver to Salt Lake City, Kevin came limping in. He had wrecked the bike and broken both ankles. Then he had to drive a stick shift all the way from above Jasper back to Cumming!

We were not sure what would happen about the trip. Our flights were non-refundable. We decided we would make the best of it even if Kevin had to go in a wheelchair! As it turned out, he only had to ride in a wheelchair through the airport. He only had a boot on one foot by the departure date, he used his crutches and we had a wonderful trip.

Isn't that the way it goes in life? We spend so much time devising and then, suddenly, everything goes awry when we least expect it. The Bible tells us the Lord directs our steps. He knows in advance all that will happen to us. He has everything under control even when it seems our whole world is completely out of control!

Our job is to trust the directing to the Lord. That is so hard for us because we want to be in charge of our own steps. When we try to be in charge, we will usually take one step forward and two back. When the Lord is the director, He leads us on the right path. He takes our feet up out of the miry clay and sets them on a solid rock.

I would much rather follow the Leader. How about you?

Lord, lead me in the way I should go. Amen

JUNE 2nd *CALIFORNIA DREAMING*

"For the kingdom of heaven is as a man travelling into a far country."
Matthew 25:14

"California Dreamin'" sang the Mamas and the Papas in 1965. The song was written by John and Michelle Phillips. It tells of the narrator's longing for the warmth of L. A. during the cold New York winter. John actually dreamed about the song and woke Michelle for her help with writing the lyrics. This song became the number one single in 1966.

Although I was just fifteen at the time, I also dreamed of returning to California one day. That day finally arrived when I was quite a bit older. I would hear the song played on Fox 97, and I would feel the excitement as the day of our departure drew nearer. It was going to be such a fabulous trip! Or so I thought.

It turned out to be, probably, the worst vacation of our lives. And it was all my fault I suppose. I just figured four days out, four days back, eight days to sightsee! It did not turn out to be so easy. I had too many sightseeing stops included in the four days of drive time! We were behind schedule before we crossed Texas!

George was ill because he was so tired by the time we finally stopped each night. Every time we reached a new time zone, I would cheer because that meant one more hour he could drive! And some of the time, he got quite hungry before we reached a restaurant.

Actually, we did so many exciting things on our journey to this far "country." It was a vacation we will never forget, that's for sure. And I learned a great lesson. I had to quit making so many stops for all the "attractions" along the way. I had to make sure there were timely stops for meals. I learned George could only drive a certain number of miles per day. I had to stop pushing us to go farther. We were all much happier when we were well fed and well rested.

In the parable of the stewardship of talents, Jesus is the One doing the travelling. He has gone away for a good while until the time of His second coming. Meanwhile, He expects us to be good stewards of the talents he has given us. In this case, a talent is a coin, but it could also represent our time, our gifts and our opportunities as well as our money. In other words, Jesus expects us to use His gifts wisely.

He does not want us to make too many stops by the wayside. He expects us to stay focused as we "travel" and not be sidetracked by the enemy's allurements. Jesus knows we become better travelers when we feed on His word and when we rest in Him. We are to use well what we have been given.

Don't be like I was! Be wise on your "trip." Use what the Lord has given you to advance His kingdom, not your own agenda.

Jesus, forgive me for failing You. Help me wisely use what You have given me. Amen

JUNE 3rd *THE RIGHTEOUS WILL SHINE*

"And they that be wise shall shine as the brightness of the firmament; and they that turn many to righteousness as the stars for ever and ever." Daniel 12:3

Have you ever wanted to be a "star?" Glitz and glamour, fame and fortune? Paparazzi and autograph hounds following you everywhere you go? Not me. On a tour of Memphis, we learned when Elvis wanted to see a movie he rented out the entire theatre. To me, that is no kind of life at all.

Daniel was a Hebrew captive in the land of Babylon. He tells us all how to be a star. First, we must be wise. How do we obtain wisdom? The Bible says to ask God. He will liberally give us wisdom and will never upbraid us for asking.

Next, we must turn many to righteousness. A little more difficult, perhaps, because this part involves the free moral choice of another. We do know, however, that nothing is impossible with God. We know it is not His will that any should perish, but that all should come to repentance.

So, we must be willing to talk with others about our Lord. We must be an apologist which is one who gives a reasoned defense for his beliefs. We must pray for the Holy Spirit to bring the convicting, drawing power. We must trust the Lord to use our words in reaching a lost soul.

We must also be mindful of our behavior. People are always watching to see if our walk matches our talk. The apostle Paul urged people to follow his example. Too often our philosophy is, "Do as I say, not as I do." Yet the Bible tells us to walk as Jesus walked.

I will never be a star in this life. I am perfectly okay with that. I would rather shine like the sun because I am wise. I would rather shine like the stars because I have turned many to righteousness. Would you agree?

Lord, give me wisdom, I pray, and the right words to say. Amen

JUNE 4th *TEASING JADA*

"Then I commended mirth, because a man hath no better thing under the sun, than to eat, and to drink, and to be merry: for that shall abide with him of his labour the days of his life, which God giveth him under the sun." Ecclesiastes 8:15

A couple of years ago, Joel and his family went to Pigeon Forge for vacation. On Facebook, he posted a picture of Jake and Jada in some astronaut suits. Actually, they had their heads stuck through a cut-out to make it look like they were wearing astronaut suits.

When Jada called me, I asked her if she went to the moon. She asked, "What moon?" I said the moon in the sky. She replied they did not go there. So I told her I had seen their pictures in the astronaut suits and thought they went to the moon. She yelled, "Mom, Grandmom thinks we went to the moon!"

How funny. I am not a natural born teaser, but Jada, at six years old, was gullible enough to believe me! I have been gullible enough to believe the devil from time to time. He tries to make me believe God does not love me, or that God will not forgive me for certain things.

When he tries his old schemes, I need to laugh at him. I know the truth. God loves me unconditionally and will forgive me for all my sins if I confess and repent. Instead of taking the enemy so seriously, I need to realize he is "teasing" me with foolishness.

Solomon encourages us to have fun and enjoy life. We are not to fret over evil because there will always be evil in this world. We must not let it bring us down so that we do not relish what God has given us. We have a choice. We can live with despair or we can have joy in spite of all the unfairness, the evil or the difficulties of life.

God is good all the time. We can trust Him to settle all accounts at His own pace. Meanwhile, let's have some mirth as we go about our day-to-day activities. Have some fun today!

Jesus, thank You for the gift of laughter. Help me not to take things so seriously all the time. Amen

JUNE 5th *WHAT GOD IS LIKE*

"And Jesus said unto him, Why callest thou me good? There is none good but one, that is, God." Mark 10:18

When Murphy's Law seems to reign supreme at our household, I have to remind myself that God is love and He is working all things together for good in my life because I love Him and am called according to his purpose.

I am sure you have all probably seen this before, but I would like to share it once again.

God is like Coke—He's the real thing.

God is like Ford—He has a better idea.

God is like General Electric—He lights your path.

God is like Bayer Aspirin—He takes the pain away.

God is like Hallmark—He cared enough to send the very best.

God is like American Express—Don't leave home without Him.

God is like Frosted Flakes—He's Grrrreat!

When everything seems to be going wrong, we need to remind ourselves He is in control. He filters everything through His fingers of love. When the stress is almost too much to bear, grab a box of Frosted Flakes and remember how grrreat God is! Or drink a Coke and recall God is the real thing.

Even though neither the cereal nor the drink will change your life's circumstances, either one will help you focus on Him who is in control. Sometimes, we just need to stop and think. We can compare ourselves to Timex. We can take a lickin' and keep on tickin.' We can bear whatever comes our way, because His strength is made perfect in our weakness.

God, Your goodness and Your love are indescribable. I am so thankful I know You. Amen

JUNE 6th *LOCKED IN SADNESS*

"Wherefore the king said unto me, Why is thy countenance sad, seeing thou art not sick? This is nothing else but sorrow of heart."
Nehemiah 2:2a

I have experienced sorrow of heart. When my marriage failed, I was home with no job and no one to help me raise two children. I felt as though I were locked in a prison of sadness. I wished I could just die and escape. I was finally able to get a job at Coastal States where I had worked previously. Things were looking up.

154

My story reminds me of the rebuilding Nehemiah did in the city of Jerusalem. The walls of the city were broken down and the gates were burned with fire. When he heard the news, Nehemiah wept over the destruction. He was a captive in Persia and was cupbearer to the king.

The king noticed Nehemiah's sad face and inquired as to the reason for it. Nehemiah was afraid and he prayed. He then asked permission to go rebuild and the king was pleased to grant his request. Not only did the king give Nehemiah the time off, he also provided military protection and supplies. Nehemiah encountered fierce opposition, but his people had a mind to work and the wall was completed in fifty-two days.

When I met George, he was like Nehemiah. He did not realize the extent of my brokenness but was ready to take on the rebuilding process. Once George and I were engaged, our marriage took place in just fifty-four days! Yes, there was some opposition. Yes, our marriage has taken some work. But God supplied all that was needed for my rebuilding. George and I both had a mind to work on it together.

Sorrow of heart can give way to satisfaction of the soul. Though I was once sad, disappointed with myself, weary and self-doubting, I was given a new lease on life. I was afraid and I prayed, just like Nehemiah did. God granted my request and my rebuilding is complete. Hallelujah!

God, I am so thankful for the life You have given me. Amen

JUNE 7th *NEW BEGINNINGS*

"Therefore if any man be in Christ, he is a new creature: old things are passed away; behold, all things are become new." II Corinthians 5:17

I call it the year of good-byes. It was 1992, and so many changes were taking place. I left the church I had attended for forty-one years of my life. That meant I was no longer teaching Sunday School. And my days as the Regular Carrier on Route 13 also ended.

It seemed to be too much in too short a period of time. I felt as if my identity were tied to all these things. But, I found out differently. *Who* I was had not changed, just *where* I was had.

Soon I was attending a new church. Before long I was in the rotation to teach a new Sunday School class once a month. I was studying the Bible with new friends and new teachers. I was learning to sing new songs with a new choir. I was in a new missions group.

And I loved my new route. Route 6 was out in the country. No more mobile home parks, office complexes nor schools! No more cluster boxes. Yippee!

I realized, once again, that many of life's endings are just new times of beginning. Looking a little farther ahead and trusting God gives me courage to let go of the old and embrace the new.

When we place our trust in Jesus, we are a new creature. The Bible says old things are passed away and all things are become new. I am thrilled to know the old habits, thoughts and hang-ups are now gone. I am thrilled to know I am a new creature in Christ. What was once so familiar has been replaced with something better.

Don't waste time longing for everything to remain status quo. Embrace the changes God sends your way. They bring excitement and freshness where once were the same old dull routines. Remember, God knows the thoughts He thinks toward us, thoughts of peace and not evil, to give us an expected end (Jeremiah 29:11).

Lord, thank You for all the new beginnings in my life. Amen

JUNE 8th   *THE MATH OF MARRIAGE*

"And the Lord God said, it is not good that the man should be alone; I will make him an help meet for him." Genesis 2:18

It was God Himself who said man should not be alone. It was God Himself who made Adam a helper, a woman named Eve. So, when Eve sinned by eating of the forbidden fruit and Adam also ate of it, Adam blamed God. He said, "The woman whom thou gavest to be with me, she gave me of the tree, and I did eat." Men have been blaming women ever since for things that go wrong.

But, before anyone gets in an uproar over that last sentence, let me also add that women have blamed men as well. We always want to pass the blame to someone else. We do not want to take responsibility for our actions. We do not want to suffer the consequences.

Remember Sarah was the one who suggested Abraham have a child with her handmaiden. After Ishmael was conceived, Hagar despised

Sarah and Sarah blamed Abraham. Zipporah blamed Moses and Delilah blamed Samson. Those are just a few examples.

In *Down Home Wit and Wisdom,* Steve Chapman wrote, "To *sum* up, in marriage if you *multiply* kindness, *subtract* judgment, *divide* the work, and *add* humor, you'll reap the *dividend* of happiness." I love it.

Both husbands and wives should practice kindness to one another every day. Neither one should be judgmental. Both should divide the work. Adding a little humor makes the spirit lighter.

George loves to see me smile, so he is constantly joking around. I think of James and Jamie from my church. They always seem to be laughing together. Jamie also tells about James playing with the kids when he came home from work. When our boys were little, George would either wash the supper dishes or give the kids a bath for me. We divided the work. He took turns getting up in the night to feed Joel, too.

If your marriage is lacking in happiness, try following Steve Chapman's advice. Show kindness, withhold judgment, divide the work and laugh together. The dividends are very rewarding!

Lord, thank You for a recipe for a better marriage. Help all couples to put it to use in their homes. Amen

JUNE 9th *ALLERGIC TO ALMONDS*

"Moreover the word of the Lord came unto me, saying, Jeremiah, what seest thou? And I said, I see a rod of an almond tree." Jeremiah 1:11

Almonds are good for your health. Even though they are high in fat, it is the same fat found in olive oil that is known to reduce a person's risk of heart disease. We are encouraged to eat a handful daily.

George and I were happy to oblige. We ate almonds as snacks and we added almonds to our salads. We were nuts about this nut. Until the day George became allergic to them.

At first, we were not certain that is what caused his throat to swell. We told the doctor he had always eaten them with no problem. After the second visit to the urgent care center, he was told to never eat them again. Ah, man.

George unknowingly ate something that was wrong for his body. He suffered life-threatening consequences. This caused me to think of how often we knowingly partake of sin. We know sin has life-threatening consequences, too, yet we go right ahead and indulge ourselves.

I have always heard people say, "You can't do wrong and get by." The Bible phrases it this way, "Be not deceived; God is not mocked: for whatsoever a man soweth, that shall he also reap (Galatians 6:7)." You may have also heard, "If you play with fire, you will get burned."

It all boils down to this known fact: the wages of sin is death. A sinner needs Jesus as his Savior. We are all born into sin, yet we can be free from its penalty by confessing our sins, repenting and asking Jesus to save us. It is His will that everyone accept His forgiveness and then turn from living a sinful lifestyle.

If you have not asked Jesus to save you, ask Him today. Tomorrow may never come.

Jesus, I thank You for being the antidote I need for sin. Amen

JUNE 10th WHAT IS A FRIEND?

"A friend loveth at all times, and a brother is born for adversity." Proverbs 17:17

In 2016, our friend Myles Goss passed away. I had delivered his mail for many years and George had worked with him at Tyson Foods for many years.

Reverends Jerry Orr, Jerry McCormick and Rex Byrd conducted the funeral. They all had wonderful words of tribute to Myles, but here is what Reverend Orr shared with us.

He said Myles was his F. R. I. E. N. D. The words in this acrostic are faithful, real, interesting, encouraging, noble and dependable. He talked about how each word described Myles. That is the kind of friend I want to be.

A true friend will be faithful. A true friend will not desert you in your time of need. A true friend will not pretend to be something he or she is not, but will be real. A true friend will be interesting to talk with and will also be interested in you. A true friend encourages you and doesn't tear you down. A true friend is honorable and is high in character. A true friend is one who keeps his or her word and one you can count on.

I have friends on this earth who are described by this acrostic, but the best example of a Friend is the Lord Jesus. He certainly is all the things Reverend Orr talked about, but His friendship goes higher than that. Jesus laid down His life for our sins. The apostle Paul wrote in his epistle to the Romans, "For scarcely for a righteous man will one die: yet peradventure for a good man some would even dare to die. But God commended His love toward us, in that, while we were yet sinners, Christ died for us (5:7 & 8)."

Jesus did not die for pretty-good, church-going folks, but for all us miserable, rotten sinners. And He was not confused about what we were when He died. He knew exactly how depraved we all are and He died anyway. How then shall we neglect so great (a) salvation?

Not only do I want to be like Myles in being a F. R. I. E. N. D. to my earthly companions, but I want to be a F.R. I. E. N. D. to Jesus as well. Don't you?

Lord Jesus, I want to spend my life for You and be Your friend until my years shall end. Amen

JUNE 11th *LICKING THE BOWL*

"And they shall be filled like bowls, and as the corners of the altar."
Zechariah 9:15

When I was a girl, neither my mother nor my grandmother would make cakes very often. My mother mostly made puddings. My grandmother also made puddings, plus she made pies and teacakes. But whenever there was a bowl with some sweet concoction in it, I was allowed to "lick the bowl." And not just the bowl, but the egg beater as well.

This is very much frowned upon today because of the danger of the Salmonella bacteria one is likely to get from the raw eggs. Back then, I don't think I had ever heard of Salmonella. I would wait impatiently for the bowl to be pushed in my direction. I sometimes used a spoon and sometimes my finger to get the last of the batter out of the bowl. But I always licked the egg beater. One of my favorite pictures is one of Kevin and Justin doing the same thing when I made a cake.

Fast forward to the next generation. My grandson Tyler was here one day when I was making a cake. I asked him if he wanted to lick the bowl and he said, "Sure." I handed it to him and turned around to put the pans in the oven. When I looked back, Tyler had his head down in the bowl! He had chocolate all over his face as well as his hair! It was hilarious. I learned I have to explain some things or else he will take my words literally!

In Zechariah, the Lord God is promising to protect His people. He promises they will defeat their enemies. This is figuratively speaking of the final victory of God's people over evil. In the fullness of their joy, they will be like a bowl full of sacrifices for His altar.

When making a dessert, my mother, grandmother and even my aunt would sacrifice a little of their batter to give me a special treat. Just as the sacrifices were sweet to the Lord God under the old covenant, the sacrifices when I was allowed to "lick the bowl" were sweet offerings to this little girl. I would venture to say you have some special memories like mine. Sweet memories.

Lord God, I want my life to be a sweet sacrifice for You. Amen

JUNE 12th *THE RED SEA PLACE*

"By faith they passed through the Red sea as by dry land: which the Egyptians assaying to do were drowned." Hebrews 11:29

On Antioch Road, we lived a few doors down from a retired teacher. Her name was Lydia Thome. She was quite elderly by the time we met her, but her mind was as sharp as a tack. She shared with me a book of some treasured poems.

One I especially liked was entitled *The Red Sea Place.* It said:
When you come to the Red Sea place in your life,
Where, in spite of all you can do,
There's no way round, there's no way back,
There's no other way but through.
So trust in the Lord with a soul serene
Til the dark and the storm are gone,
He will calm the winds, He will still the waves
When He says to your soul, "Go on!

Later I found out she was not the original poet, but had copied the poem written by Annie Johnson Flint.

When the children of Israel came to the Red Sea, they were sore afraid. They cried out to the Lord and they also cried out against Moses. They accused him of bringing them out to the wilderness to die.

Moses told them to stand still and see the salvation of the Lord, but the Lord said unto Moses, "Speak unto the children of Israel, that they go forward." In other words, get moving!

There is a popular saying these days, "If God brings you to it, He will bring you through it." That thought is based on Isaiah 58:11. It is a fact that we will experience times of hardship and fear, but God is in control and He will lead us onward.

We may want to sit down and cry and feel sorry for ourselves, but God said to go on! He will make a way where there seems to be no way. We just have to trust Him.

If you are experiencing a Red Sea place in your life, don't waste time wringing your hands and worrying. Trust God and go forward.

Lord, help me to trust You in the darkest places of my life. Amen

JUNE 13th *WHAT SHAPES MY LIFE?*

"Behold, I was shapen in iniquity; and in sin did my mother conceive me." Psalm 51:5

Anyone who is about my age will probably remember the music of the T-Bones from 1965. They had a hit record with the instrumental "No Matter What Shape (Your Stomach's In)." I guess, even now, your mind is flashing back to the television commercial in which the music was popular. The camera focused on the stomachs of people as they walked down the street, exercised, danced and so on. Alka-Seltzer was touted as the remedy, regardless of the problem.

Thinking of the music, I am reminded of those little flowers that are handed out at weddings. The flowers are made of satin or maybe netting and filled with birdseed. The birdseed gives the flower its shape. Once released, the seed is nourishing and sustaining to the birds, whereas the traditional rice expands in their stomachs and kills them.

And what about the shape of my life, not just my stomach? What gives me my shape? Am I full of nourishing, sustaining traits or full of things that would be detrimental to the receiver? Often I have been more like the destructive rice. I have been rejecting, snobbish, unloving, unkind and unwilling to take the remedy.

Sure, we were all shapen in iniquity, but we do not have to remain in that shape! There is a remedy. First and foremost, we need to accept Jesus as our Savior. Then we need the good seed of God's love to provide the continuing balm for our souls.

I want to grow in grace. I want to be like Jesus and grow in favor with God and man. I want my shape to be just right!

Lord, I want the seed of Your love to be what shapes my life. Forgive me for being like the rice. Amen

JUNE 14th *AN OLDER GLORY*

"Now unto the King eternal, immortal, invisible, the only wise God, be honour and glory for ever and ever. Amen." I Timothy 1:17

Our American flag is often referred to as "Old Glory." Most historians say the title was given by William Driver, a nineteenth century sea captain. The flag is flown twenty-four hours a day above his grave in Nashville.

When I was in school, we started our mornings by pledging our allegiance to the flag. We would stand, place our right hands over our hearts and recite the pledge in unison. No horseplay or other nonsense was allowed during the pledge. No one was ever offended by the words, "under God," although they had not been added, officially, until Flag Day of 1954, when President Eisenhower signed the bill into law.

In his speech, the president said, "In this way we are reaffirming the transcendence of religious faith in America's heritage and future; in this way we shall constantly strengthen those spiritual weapons which forever will be our country's most powerful resource in peace or in war."

Many lawsuits have been filed in recent years in an attempt to have "under God" removed from the pledge. Children are no longer required to recite the pledge. We have come a long way and I, personally, do not feel we have chosen the right way.

Pledging allegiance to the flag itself is not what bothers me so much. I am more concerned with the fact our allegiance to God has shifted away from Him.

In his book, *Onward,* Russell Moore stated, "There's coming a day when 'Old Glory' yields to an older glory." One day every knee shall bow to Jesus and every tongue shall confess Him as Lord. Before that day comes, I pray many people will place themselves "under God," by accepting Jesus as their Savior.

Jesus, I count it a privilege to kneel before You and call You my Lord. Amen

JUNE 15th *MESS-UPS*

"Do not err, my beloved brethren." James 1:16

I enjoy reading biographies about sports figures. One book I read several years ago was *Yogi Berra: Eternal Yankee* by Allen Barra. Yogi was a major league catcher and played with the New York Yankees. In addition to his athletic abilities, Yogi was known for his euphemisms.

Of his top fifty, number two was, "You can observe a lot by just watching." Unfortunately, we probably spend too much time watching others when we should be watching ourselves. We are quick to spot errors made by those around us while we are blind to our own.

Number three on Yogi's list was, "It ain't over til it's over." What great news for us. When we do err, we have an advocate with the Father. Jesus is our advocate and if confess our sin, He will forgive us and cleanse us of all unrighteousness.

Fourth on the list was, "It's like déjà-vu all over again." I know just what Yogi meant by this one. I have made some of the same mistakes over and over again. I do try to learn from my mistakes and change my ways, but some pesky little sins keep popping up again and again. One fruit of the Spirit is temperance (or, self-control), so I must be mindful to walk in the Spirit.

Number nine was, "We made too many wrong mistakes." To that I say, "Amen, brother." We have all sinned and come short of the glory of God. I would also say every mistake we have ever made has been a wrong one!

Number forty-nine was, "If the world were perfect, it wouldn't be." The world started out as perfect, but in the Garden of Eden, Adam and Eve sinned. The world has been imperfect ever since.

One day there will be a new heaven and a new earth. Satan will be cast into the lake of fire to be tormented for ever and ever. The tabernacle of God will be with men and no sin will ever be known again.

I am so glad Yogi reminded us, "it ain't over til it's over." I know how the game of life ends. Those who have been saved by the blood of Jesus are the winners. I am so glad I am on Jesus' team. He is our manager and coach. There is always room for one more on His roster. Would you like to be a part of the team? Get signed up today. Ask Jesus to save you.

Jesus, thank You for forgiving all my sins. Amen

JUNE 16th *WHO'S THE GREATEST?*

◆————————————————————————————————————◆

"And when the Philistine looked about, and saw David, he disdained him." I Samuel 17:42

One year ago this month, Muhammad Ali passed into eternity. Born Cassius Clay, his name was changed to Ali when he converted to Islam in order to avoid serving in the war in Viet Nam. Ali famously declared himself to be the greatest. He even said he was the king of the world.

When Ali fought George Foreman in Zaire, the fight was known as the "Rumble in the Jungle." Foreman was the heavyweight champion and Ali's goal was to win back that title. He made himself a "citizen" and portrayed Foreman as an interloper. He asked a witch doctor to put a spell on Foreman.

He was known to taunt his opponents. This match was no exception. During the fight, Ali goaded Foreman with remarks such as, "That all you got, George?" and "They told me you could punch, George!" Ali wore Foreman down and won the bout in the eighth round.

This reminds me of another fight between a man who thought himself the greatest in the world and a younger opponent. That battle ended quite differently, though. It took place in the valley of Elah. The Philistine champion, Goliath, taunted the Israelites. His sheer size and appearance struck fear into the hearts of all the men. But David volunteered to fight him.

When Goliath saw David, he cursed David by his gods. He threatened David, but David did not back down. He told the champion, "I come to you in the name of the Lord of hosts, the God of the armies of Israel, whom thou hast defied." David then smote the giant in the forehead with one smooth stone and cut off Goliath's head with the Philistine's own sword. The younger, smaller opponent had won.

David declared his victory before he ever removed a stone from his bag. He told Goliath, "This day will the Lord deliver thee into mine hand; and I will smite thee, and take thine head from thee." That is exactly what happened. Unlike Ali, David did not try to avoid a battle. He did not change his name. He simply trusted in the Lord and he emerged victorious.

Sometimes even a champion needs a little redirection. I realize Ali was a great boxer. I am not trying to take anything away from his skill in the ring nor from his mental abilities to overcome his opponents. I just feel his trust, like that of Goliath's, was sadly misplaced. When we think of ourselves as the greatest, God has His own way of showing us differently. Our trust should be in Him alone at all times.

Lord, forgive us for our pride. Let our boasting be in You. Amen

JUNE 17th *DON'T WORRY, BE HAPPY*

"And whoso trusteth in the Lord, happy is he." Proverbs 16:20

When you read the title for today, did your mind automatically go to the little tune of the same name by Bobby McFerrin? Did you start whistling? I find it increasingly harder to actually whistle anymore, but I can still hum the tune.

The renowned psychiatrist, the late Dr. Smiley Blanton, wrote in his book *Now or Never,* all people are fighting a demon. He says the demon is worry. Some people have learned to live with it, some have learned to control it, but no one has been able to eliminate it.

I consider myself a person who worries very little. My trust is in the Lord. I do not feel that I am ever stressed out much about anything. That is one reason I was so surprised when I was diagnosed with shingles. I know they are caused by the chicken pox virus, but I have read they are exacerbated by stress.

I have an acquaintance, though, who worries about everything. She worries about driving, about the weather, about her grandson, about her job, about taking medication, about almost anything you could name. She is a complete worry-wart! And I feel so bad for her.

When we realize just Who is in control, we can stop feeling so anxious about the circumstances of life. Worrying cannot prevent any trouble from occurring. It just robs today of its happiness. Maybe, as Dr. Blanton said, the demon can't be eliminated. But, with the Lord, it can be overcome by placing our trust and faith in Him.

Bobby McFerrin sang, "In every life we have some trouble, But when you worry you make it double. Don't worry, be happy." I urge you to lay your worries at Jesus' feet. Peter wrote in his first epistle, "Casting all your care upon Him; for He careth for you (5:7)."

Here is a small poem that will help us focus on how the Lord works for us. It was written by Gordon Thomas. "Each morning brings its promise, Of good things yet to be. And nightfall will affirm again, That God is good to me." That should make us all want to whistle a little tune.

Lord, forgive us all for worrying instead of placing our trust and faith in You. Amen

JUNE 18th *FATHER'S DAY*

"Behold, what manner of love the Father hath bestowed upon us, that we should be called the sons of God." I John 3:1

I was working in my little cubicle at Coastal States Life Insurance Company when the call came. Suddenly, I could hear my aunt's voice on the other side of the divider. She was talking with someone about a person who had just died. Bits and pieces of the conversation made me realize this death was not that of one of our customers. It was the death of her brother, my dad.

I rose from my chair and walked into her office to listen. I learned my dad had passed away while driving down Highway 141. His car had left the road and travelled across a large field. A man who was bush-hogging saw this take place and called the police. The rest of the day is mostly a blur, but we learned he had suffered a heart attack.

I remember my aunt's boss, Don May, drove us both back to Cumming. I remember relatives coming to console us. Mostly, I recall being numb. My mother and grandmother could not deal with some of the funeral home business, so as the oldest child, I was the one to make some decisions and answer questions. My dad was buried on my aunt's birthday. He was forty-four years old.

I have already written I never "felt" loved by my dad. Now I am wondering whether he ever felt loved by me. Did I ever tell him I loved him? Did I ever ask his advice? Did I buy cards for him on his birthday or give him gifts? I honestly do not know. Did I ever try to make Father's Day special for him? I can't say. I wish I had just one memory of doing something loving for my dad, but I don't.

If your father is still living, I urge you to make a fuss over him today. Give him a hug, tell him you love him, buy him a card. You may never get another chance.

Regardless of the relationship with your earthly father, you can have a loving relationship with the heavenly Father. He bestowed the greatest love upon us by giving us the opportunity to become his sons and daughters. He provided the means whereby we could be forgiven for all our sins and made righteous in Him. This reconciliation came through the death of His son, Jesus Christ.

I can't think of a better decision to make on Father's Day. Become a child of God. Ask Jesus to save you.

Father God, I love You and I am so thankful I am Your child. Amen

JUNE 19th BE *A LIGHT FOR JESUS*

"Also, Jonathan David's uncle was a counseller, a wise man, and a scribe:" I Chronicles 27:32

For most of my childhood I lived within walking distance of my Aunt Grace and my Uncle Herbert. They were actually my dad's aunt and uncle and my "great" ones. I did consider them great, to be sure.

Uncle Herbert led the singing at Roanoke Baptist Church for quite some time. Before going to our Sunday School classes, Uncle Herbert would lead us in some old hymn like "Be a Light For Jesus." During the worship service, he often led "I've Been a Waitin.'" One of his favorites to lead for the invitation was "Come Unto Me." Those are some precious memories.

I would describe my uncle as a barrel-chested man. He had a broad chest, a round torso and was very strong. He was in the pulpwood business for years but was also a deputy sheriff at one time and the owner of a small store on Buford Dam Road.

I would place Uncle Herbert in the same category as Jonathan, David's uncle: a counselor, a wise man and a scribe. The Hebrew word for scribe means to enumerate or to recount. It can also mean talk or tell. My uncle was a great talker. His mind was sharp and he had a great memory. I was amazed at all the stories he could tell and the facts he remembered.

Mostly, I remember him for being a man of God. He was faithful to his family and to his church. Even though he has been gone for many years, I am thinking of him today because it is his birthday. I am thanking God for all my aunts and uncles who set a good example for me.

My desire is to also be a good example for those who are looking to me for direction. I truly want to "Be a Light for Jesus." Just as Uncle Herbert encouraged me to be as he led that song so long ago.

Lord Jesus, I do want to be a light for You. Help me keep my lamp trimmed and burning so that all may see You. Amen

JUNE 20th GRIZZLIES IN THE GRANDS

"And there came forth two she bears out of the wood." II Kings 2:24

I had always wanted to see a grizzly bear. Not up close and personal, understand, but just from a nice, safe distance. When we were in Yellowstone National Park, areas of the park were closed due to bear activity, but we saw no bears. Neither did we see any when we were in Montana or Idaho. When we were in Alaska, the only sighting of one was at a store called Grizzly's and that was a huge fake bear above their outdoor sign.

In 2012, when we once again travelled west, I was hoping to see one of these elusive creatures. The grizzly is a subspecies of the brown bear and was actually given the name by explorers Lewis and Clark. In 1815, naturalist George Ord classified the grizzly as Ursus Horribilis, which means "terrifying bear."

As Kevin drove us along, Tyler and I were peering steadily out the windows in our attempt to spot one. We saw several antelope, some cows, a huge flock of sheep, but no bears. The second day, we were headed toward the Grand Tetons and saw more antelope and a couple of buffalo. Shortly after entering the national park, traffic suddenly came to a halt. We asked some of our fellow tourists about the delay. We were told a mama grizzly and two cubs were feeding up ahead!

Of course, traffic was backed up like 400 in rush hour and I had no idea we would actually get to see the bears. But, a trusty park ranger came along and made everyone get in their cars and get moving. So, as we inched along, those of us who were far back in the line slowed enough for a good look as we passed the little family. I was able to snap a couple of pictures even though the bears were quite a distance off the roadway.

Thanks to the zoom lens, I do have a treasured photo of my one and only encounter with grizzly bears. My experience was quite different from those who encountered the bears in II Kings.

The prophet Elisha was bald. As Elisha travelled toward Bethel, a group of children made fun of him. Elisha cursed them in the name of the Lord and two she bears came out of the woods taring forty-two children! The word tare can mean rip, open or cleave, so we can assume the children were mauled by the bears and not killed. If so, I am sure they learned to never again make fun of a servant chosen by God!

Today the Lord might not literally send a bear to wound us, but He still expects us to treat our fellow man with kindness and love. We should be careful to honor those who serve the Lord and treat them with respect. The Bible commands us to esteem others better than ourselves. Let's not be "unbearable" in our dealings with others.

Lord, Your word tells me charity (or, love) bears all things. Fill me with Your love. Amen

JUNE 21st *LETTER WRITING*

'Ye see how large a letter I have written unto you with mine own hand." Galatians 6:11

Being a mail carrier was a perfect job for me. I have always enjoyed both sending and receiving mail. Even today, I never toss out a piece of bulk business mail (what my grandmother called "junk mail") without looking over it!

When I was in elementary school, a few of my classmates and I wrote letters back and forth during the summer break. Not all of us had telephones at the time. After their college graduation, my friend Judy Austin was in Europe while her husband was stationed there. I couldn't wait to get one of her letters in my mailbox. We corresponded as they were moved all over the United States as well.

A few years ago, Judy and I decided to be pen-pals again because our lives are busy and we never chat on the phone. I admit the letters are infrequent, but every time I open the mailbox and see her very distinctive handwriting, I am thrilled.

Even though I do not have a Facebook page, I am frequently on the computer checking my sister's page for news from friends and family. I look to see if anyone has sent a thought or a question by way of cyber-space.

Often I look in my Bible for a "letter" from God. I want to see what special words He has addressed to me for the day. It may come in the form of a passage I've read countless times, but He gives me new insight about the meaning. He may speak to me through a verse I have never even thought about before.

The apostle Paul had Tertius write the book of Romans for him, but he said he had written Galatians with his own hand. Even though the Bible is not written by the actual "hand" of God, it is all God-breathed. It is all given that I may learn of His love for me and understand more about Him.

Do you pick up the Bible and eagerly read it like a letter from a dear friend? You should, you know.

Lord, I am so grateful for Your letters to me. Thank You for assuring me of Your love and revealing Yourself to me through them. Amen

"Charity suffereth long, and is kind;" I Corinthians 13:4a

Katie is the daughter of my first cousin Denise. When she was a young girl, Katie and her family lived across the road from us. She came over and stayed here in the afternoons until her mom arrived home from work.

Katie was the quietest little girl I had ever known. You could not get her to say a word. She would listen to the rest of us jabber, and she would smile that beautiful, shy smile but getting her to talk was like getting blood out of a turnip.

Grown up now with a family of her own, Katie has overcome her timidity. She has taken leadership roles in the workplace as well as at her church. She was in charge of putting together the 100th anniversary celebration for Roanoke Baptist. That certainly required a lot of talking!

Recently, I needed to make a CD for a special occasion. I had asked Denise to play the piano for me and she was willing to oblige. Due to unforeseen circumstances, the sound man (Sid Bramblett) could not be there that night. Who was willing to step up and fill in for him? Katie! At the last minute, on a Friday night, Katie, her husband Kevin and their youngest son Joseph all came right over and spent about two hours helping me out.

Just what cousins do, you might say. But Katie was just a few days away from having a cardiac ablation. She has an atrial flutter which causes the upper chambers of her heart to beat too fast. This, in turn, makes the muscles contract too fast and be out of sync with the lower chambers.

Some of the symptoms of her condition are heart palpitations, shortness of breath, chest pain and dizziness or fainting. If left untreated, the side effects of an atrial flutter can be life-threatening.

In spite of the seriousness of her issues, Katie was willing to be there to help me with a fun, light-hearted project. Her assistance was really appreciated.

But, I ask myself, how kind is my heart? Am I willing to do for others when I have the slightest sniffle or pain? Am I willing to put myself out for my family or friends? I confess, too often, I retreat into my own little shell and let someone else do it.

What would Jesus do? You and I know the answer to that question, don't we? He laid down His very life for His friends. He was willing to put aside His own comfort for our eternal good.

I realize there is only one Savior. His work has been done. I cannot die for anyone's sins. But I can be like Katie. I can put aside my wants and needs to help another. So can you!

Lord, help me be kind today and every day. Show me how I may serve You by serving others. Amen

JUNE 23rd *WORK AND LOVE*

"Shew me thy ways, O Lord; teach me thy paths." Psalm 25:4

My mother was an avid reader. She, you might say, introduced me to the love of books. Once I learned to read, there was no stopping me. I read road signs as we travelled. I read while I ate. I sat in my bed, with a flashlight, reading after the lights were out.

I helped Nancy Drew solve all her mysteries. I lived in the big woods, on the prairie and by the shores of the lake with Laura Ingalls Wilder. I was Anne Shirley, hitting Gilbert on the head with a slate. There were so many adventures to share in the pages of a book.

I soon decided I would love to become an English teacher. I could help others learn the parts of speech. I could teach them to diagram a sentence. I could introduce them to good books. We could discuss the plots and the characters. Life would be so good!

My dream collapsed. I became a claims examiner at an insurance company. My reading on the job consisted of hospital records and autopsy reports. Later, I read prescriptions at the pharmacy and doctor's notes on medical charts at the hospital. When I became a mail carrier, I read names and addresses on countless letters and magazines.

The late Dr. Karl Menninger, the noted psychiatrist, said everyone needs two things to be whole, fulfilled and healthy-minded. Those two things are work and love. He said we need work to do that we consider important. And, we need someone to love who loves us in return.

Although I never became an English teacher, I did have work which I considered important. I never expected to serve God by being a claims examiner, a pharmacy tech or a mail carrier, but He used me in all those jobs. And He called me to teach His word instead of the words of others. There is no better book to discuss than the Bible!

In the Bible, God called men to serve Him in ways they did not expect. He called them to serve in ways they didn't even want! God called Moses from leading sheep to leading people. He sent Jonah to Ninevah to preach an eight word sermon. Peter, James and John were called from being fishermen to become fishers of men. He called Saul from being the persecuting Pharisee to become Paul the preacher of the gospel. How has He called you to serve?

And what about love? First and foremost God loves me. When I was saved, I learned about the unconditional love of Jesus. As a young woman, I never dreamed I would marry someone four years my junior. But God knew just the kind of man I needed in my life and He sent George to rescue me.

No, neither my work nor my love turned out the way I had imagined. But God, in His infinite wisdom, gave me just what I needed in both my career and in my family.

Lord God, thank You that my dreams were changed because You had something better in mind for my life. Amen

JUNE 24th   *ROSE COLORED GLASSES*

"That I may see the good of thy chosen, that I may rejoice in the gladness of thy nation, that I may glory with thine inheritance."
Psalm 106:5

Have you heard the term "rose colored glasses?" One is said to be wearing them when one holds a cheerful or optimistic view. Having "rose colored glasses" means one thinks of situations as better than they really are.

My Aunt Iris constantly wore "rose colored glasses." Her lenses were not literally rosy, but her outlook sure was. My aunt saw more than most people through her glasses. She saw the good in people when everyone else saw the bad. She could see what a person meant to do, even when he didn't do it. She always had a defense for anyone who was guilty of doing bad things.

My aunt was a lot like Pollyanna. You will recall Pollyanna was the heroine of the book by the same name. "Pollyanna" suggests a person who is irrepressibly optimistic, someone who sees the bright side of things. Author Eleanor Hodgman Porter never denied the presence of evil or pain in the world; but she focused on the positive things regardless of how unclear or simple they may be.

Isn't that what we should be doing? Looking for the good in others? Focusing on all the blessings God sends our way instead of making a mountain out of a mole hill? Instead of being like a buzzard that dwells on the rotten and ugly, shouldn't we be more like a butterfly that looks for what is beautiful and sweet?

In 1978, country recording artist John Conlee released a song he had co-written called "Rose Colored Glasses." The narrator is deluding himself about the woman he loves. The "rose colored glasses" show only the beauty because they hide all the truth. Or so he says.

Our "rose colored glasses" may not hide all the truth, but they can help us see the best parts of life. Sure, situations may be bad, but we can trust the Lord to bring us through and work things out for our good. Choose carefully which glasses you put on today.

Lord, help me see the good. I want to always look with optimism as I trust in You. Amen

JUNE 25th *GOOD LOOKS*

"Talk no more so exceeding proudly; let not arrogancy come out of your mouth: for the Lord is a God of knowledge, and by him actions are weighed." I Samuel 2:3

When I look in the mirror, I have never seen beauty staring back at me! I see a pointed nose. I see a once scrawny body which now has succumbed to middle-age (or, old-age!) spread. I see wrinkles and age spots and gray hair! Oh, my!

But, I remind myself, God designed me. He had a purpose when He put all my genes together just so. He knew I would need to be loved for who I am, not for the way I look.

Had I been a raving beauty, who knows? I might have been arrogant, selfish and thoughtless. Who knows what paths I might have followed in my quest to flaunt that beauty? Who knows where pride might have led me?

All my imperfections remind me God knows the number of hairs on my head. He formed me in the womb. He knew what my stature would be before I was born. Nothing about the way I look surprises Him.

Are good looks important to God? I don't think so. In I Peter 3, the Bible says, "Whose adorning let it not be that outward adorning of plaiting the hair, and of wearing of gold, or of putting on of apparel; But let it be the hidden man of the heart, in that which is not corruptible, even the ornament of a meek and quiet spirit, which is in the sight of God of great price."

In 1966, the Temptations released the song, "Beauty's Only Skin Deep." The lyrics tell us not to judge a book by its cover because a girl could be fine on the outside but so untrue on the inside. Possessing a pretty face is not as important as tenderness and a pleasing personality.

Doesn't the Bible tell us God looks on the heart? He is interested more in the condition of my spirit than on my facial features. Yours, too. If you feel you are lacking in the looks department, try looking at yourself through the eyes of Christ. Does He see a meek, quiet spirit within you? Are you abiding in Him? Are you sharing His love with those around you?

If so, there is none more beautiful.

Lord, I am thankful for all my imperfections which draw me away from my mirror and closer to You. Amen

JUNE 26th *THE SCULPTOR*

"Shall the clay say to him that fashioneth it, What makest thou? Or thy work, He hath no hands?" Isaiah 45:9

As you know, Michelangelo was one of the most renowned artists of the Italian Renaissance period. His famous works include "David" and "Pieta." He also painted the ceiling of the Sistine Chapel. Michelangelo is noted for saying, "I saw the angel in the marble and carved until I set him free." I have never seen any sculpture by Michelangelo except in pictures.

However, my grandson Tyler and I have seen some pieces by the French sculptor, Auguste Rodin. Several years ago, North Georgia College and State University displayed some posthumous pieces which were on loan from the gallery of Erin Wertenberger in Atlanta. We saw "The Kiss," "The Hand of the Great Thinker," and "The Age of Bronze," among other pieces.

I must admit, every time I think of "The Thinker," I am reminded of the television series, *The Many Loves of Dobie Gillis.* Baby boomers will recall the reproduction of the sculpture in Central City Park where Dobie would sit, his head resting on his fist, as he mulled over his problem of the week!

I am like a block of marble or a piece of bronze in the hand of God. He is working on me, fashioning me into the person He wants me to become. He is carving away all the things that do not look like Christ. My character is taking shape slowly, but steadily. I have no right to question God as He forms me. He is the One who holds the chisel.

In another place, Isaiah says we are the clay and God is the potter. He says we are all the work of God's hand. In Romans, Paul wrote, "Hath not the potter power over the clay, of the same lump to make one vessel unto honour, and another unto dishonor?" In other words, God makes us into whatever it takes to fulfill His purposes.

I may not be like the Venus de Milo. I may appear to be more like Medusa. But God is still working on me. He is not finished with me yet. Nor is He finished with you. As long as we are at home on this earth, we are a work in progress. We can trust the Sculptor to make us what He wants us to be.

Father God, mold me and make me after thy will as I yield to You. Amen

JUNE 27th   *MY SON GROWS UP*

"For I was my father's son, tender and only beloved in the sight of my mother." Proverbs 4:3

In 1986, Alice E. Chase wrote the poem "To My Grown-Up Son." In the poem, she is reminiscing about her son's childhood days when she was too busy with daily duties to indulge in activities with the boy.

I bought a copy of the poem and hung it on the wall in a son's bedroom. When one son read the poem, he started to cry. I asked him why he was crying and he said, "That is just so sad." Yes, it certainly is.

The fourth stanza begins with, "For life is short, and years rush past, A little boy grows up so fast." I know all mothers can relate to this. It seems our children grow up in the blink of any eye. One minute, your child is in diapers and the next thing you know, he is in a cap and gown. One minute, he is riding a tricycle and the next he is behind the wheel of a car. One minute he hates girls, the next minute, he is married. Where does the time go?

Now our house is empty except when the grandchildren visit. There is no one to slam the door, stomp down the stairs, tie up the telephone for hours or beg for one more cookie. That all belongs to yesteryear.

One thing has not changed. We still pray for our sons and commit them to the Master. We know God loves them even more than we do and He is concerned for their spiritual well-being. He will never lead them astray. He has promised to work all things together for their good if they love Him and are called according to His purpose.

We cannot go back and do all the little things our sons asked us to do. Missed opportunities are forever gone whether we are raising our children or serving the Lord. We need to be about the Father's business while we can. If someone is asking for your help today, let the chores go and help that person. Or, if God is bidding you to speak to someone about Him, do it right then. You do not want the chance to slip by and then spend a lifetime regretting your silence or inactivity.

Redeem the time because the days are evil. Use your days wisely because they will be gone, like childhood, in the blink of an eye.

Lord, our lives truly are like a vapor which appears for a little time and then vanishes away. Help us make the best use of the time You have given us. Amen

JUNE 28th *A BUG IN THE BED*

"Then was our mouth filled with laughter, and our tongue with singing: then said they among the heathen, The Lord hath done great things for them." Psalm 126:2

Laughter is the best medicine. I have heard that all my life, but now studies at leading universities have proven it. An experiment at the Loma Linda University in California showed laughter improved recall ability and reduced levels of the stress hormone cortisol. A study done by the University of Maryland found laughter can reduce the risk of heart disease.

Proverbs 17:22 says, "A merry heart doeth good like a medicine: but a broken spirit drieth the bones." God knew the importance of laughter years before the scientific research began.

George loves to tease me and tell outlandish tales. All my brothers and my sister have a wonderful sense of humor. I am not quick-witted like they are, but I do love to laugh.

I recently read a story of a lady who put a rubber chicken under the mattress. When her husband sat on the bed, the chicken squawked! I imagine he was pretty surprised, but he moved it to her side before she came to bed and the joke was on her.

That story reminded me of my Uncle Albert. The last time he went to Texas with us to visit Aunt Delores, we bought a plastic bug and put it under the covers in his bed. That was just one of the pranks we played on him, but he was such a good sport and provided us with many laughs along the journey.

Laughter is said to lighten our burdens, inspire hope, connect us to others, keep us grounded and keep our relationships fresh and exciting. There is no reason to go around with a frown on our faces when we can smile. Smiling takes less effort than frowning anyway.

If your day is not going well, try a little laughter. Sing a funny song. Play a harmless prank on someone you love. You might be surprised by how much better you will feel. And laughing may cause others to realize the great things God has done for you!

Lord, forgive me when I go around with a frown. Give me a merry heart today, I pray. Amen

JUNE 29th *NAVIGATING THE CURRENT*

"When thou passeth through the waters, I will be with thee; and through the rivers, they shall not overflow thee: when thou walkest through the fire, thou shalt not be burned; neither shall the flame kindle upon thee." Isaiah 43:2

Since I almost drowned when I was a young girl, I have not cared at all for the water. George and the boys always loved it, though. That is why I wanted them to float down the Colorado through the Grand

Canyon. It seemed like a marvelous experience for them. Just enough rapids for an occasional adrenaline rush and plenty of calm water for enjoying the canyon itself. For some reason, that dream never materialized.

When Tyler was just a toddler, Kevin bought his family a boat. He loved speeding along on Lake Lanier, creating his own turbulent waters. He made sharp turns which brought one side of the boat too close to the lake to suit me. Kevin pulled Ryan and Tyler behind the boat on a float shaped like an inner tube. They loved bouncing along and squealed with delight.

But sometimes, other boats came too close and created big waves which frightened them. Sometimes they were pitched around and wanted back in the boat with their captain where it was safe.

Isn't that what we all want? Safety? When facing a "white-knuckle" situation, here are some tips to help us. First we must realize there comes a time when we will launch out into the unknown. When we do, we can ask our friends for advice and help. We can expect to encounter others who make waves for us, but we must hold a steady course. Last, but not least, remember our Captain can be trusted and He will help us navigate when the going is tough.

As you set out today I wish you a bon voyage.

Lord, You are my navigator and I trust You to guide me safely through the dangerous currents. Amen

JUNE 30th *CLOSE ENCOUNTER*

"Go thy way, eat thy bread with joy." Ecclesiastes 9:7

At one family gathering we had the most unusual experience. We were outside on the deck while Kevin was grilling our dinner on his Big Green Egg. Suddenly, we heard talking coming from somewhere above us and we heard a loud *Whoosh!*

When we looked up, we saw a hot air balloon just slightly above the treetops in our backyard. We could not believe how low it was. We could see the folks inside the gondola and we yelled up to them. I ran inside to get my camera and capture the magnificent sight.

The beautiful stripes of the balloon glistened in the sunlight. But then, just as suddenly, there was a plume of flame which shot up into the balloon, it lifted a little higher and drifted away. We watched until it was completely lost from our view.

The encounter lasted a few minutes at most, but afterward, we ate our meal with joy! Our spirits were lifted as high as the balloon. This event was completely unexpected, but how it brightened our day!

Although I do not own a hot air balloon, I can still look for ways to unexpectedly brighten someone's day. A visit to a shut-in, a call to a friend, a helping hand to someone at the store or letting someone out in traffic are all ways to put a smile on the face of another. Spreading joy costs little or nothing, yet it may mean the world to someone who is down and out.

Look for some small way to lift someone else's spirit. I believe it will bring joy to your heart as well.

Lord, thank You for all the unexpected events that bring joy to my life. Help me watch for ways I can pass that joy along to others. Amen

JULY

JULY 1ˢᵗ *THE CONVENIENCE STORE*

""And he said, Behold, I have heard that there is corn in Egypt: get you down thither, and buy for us from thence; that we may live, and not die." Genesis 42:2

When I was a young girl, my Uncle Herbert built a store on Buford Dam Road. It was the last chance to buy any supplies before reaching the lake. At this store you could buy soft drinks, gas, picnic items and bait. The store was a very short walk from my house.

My Aunt Grace ran the store. I can remember seeing her do her ironing between customers. She was always glad to have someone come in and chat awhile, even though it might be just one of us youngsters. When we needed something from the store, no money was necessary at the time of purchase. We just asked Aunt Grace to "put it on our ticket."

My favorite thing in the store was the hand-dipped ice cream. Aunt Grace kept the scoop in a jar of water. This was no Baskin-Robbins and the only flavors were the basic chocolate, strawberry and vanilla. I also loved that old coke cooler. The glass bottles sat down in a bath of icy water that dripped on your feet when you lifted your drink out of the chest.

One place I didn't like was the bait area. As you walked into the store, there was a porch off to the left where the minnows and spring lizards were kept. I was scared of those spring lizards, but at times I would briefly watch the minnows swimming around in their cement tank.

Later, the store was sold to my cousin Jody and her husband Bill. I thought it was hilarious when Bill would count out our change in some foreign language. He was stationed in Europe while he was in the service, so maybe he was counting in German. All I knew was it surely sounded funny.

Having the store close by was a life saver on many occasions. When we needed a loaf of bread, or maybe some milk or sugar, it was so handy to be able to get it there and not have to make a trip to Cumming.

I was thinking of the long trek Joseph's brothers had to make to get corn from the storehouses in Egypt. Due to the severe famine in the land, going to Egypt was the last chance to get supplied with food. When they got there, the brothers had to pay upfront for the corn.

Joseph spoke to them through an interpreter so I am sure he sounded funny to them. The storehouses of Egypt were not convenient for Israel's sons, but if they wanted to eat, that is where they had to go.

When his brothers sold Joseph into slavery, they had no idea he would be responsible for helping to save their lives. Years later, God used Joseph to put a plan into place whereby all the people could come and buy grain. What the brothers meant for evil, God meant for good. Joseph finally revealed himself to his family. He spoke kindly to them and comforted them. He put aside any grudges he had held against them and he provided for them.

I love the story of Joseph. It shows us God is at work even when everything seems to be going wrong. (And it reminds me of going to the store in my own neighborhood so many years ago!)

Lord, thank You for turning evil motives into good results! Amen

JULY 2nd *FILLINGS*

"I am the Lord thy God which brought thee out of the land of Egypt: open thy mouth wide, and I will fill it." Psalm 81:10

When Justin was a small boy, he received a Play-doh Doctor Drill and Fill set for his birthday. The set included a plastic head (the "patient"), electric drill, tweezers, a dentist tool, a mirror, a toothbrush and three containers of Play Doh. Using the modeling compound for the patient's teeth, he could use the electric drill to fill the cavities.

While Justin enjoyed playing dentist, I enjoyed looking at the picture I had made of him with his gift. Justin was smiling ear to ear. With his blonde, almost white, hair and his big blue eyes, he looked an awful lot like the patient out of the box!

A dentist fills a tooth when we have cavities. We get those because of the bacteria that make acids which eat away the enamel, or outer portion, of a tooth. Even after we get the filling, it is necessary to take care of our teeth. We must brush at least twice a day, avoid sugary snacks and drinks, use dental floss and see the dentist for regular check-ups.

We could liken sin to those acids. Sin eats away at us. Sin causes us to need a filling from God. God does His restoration when He saves our souls. Once saved, we need to take care of ourselves by praying and reading the Bible. We need to avoid the sweet tasting sin which so easily besets us. We need to go to God for regular check-ups to make sure no sin is taking over any area of our lives.

Seeing Dr. Drill and Fill (Justin) beside his patient, reminded me of this verse from the Psalms. All God wants is to be number one in our lives. When we seek to put Him first, He welcomes our deep hunger and promises to fill us. We can open our hearts and our souls to Him and expect Him to provide. We never have to be ashamed of our neediness. God is delighted to fill us with Himself.

In return, our mouths should be filled with His praise and His honor all the day (Psalm 71:8).

Lord, thank You for filling me with Your goodness and love. I want my mouth to be filled with Your praise and honor always. Amen

JULY 3rd *MAKING MUSIC*

"and all the people of the land rejoiced, and sounded with trumpets also the singers with instruments of musick, and such as taught to sing praise." II Chronicles 23:13

When I was a young girl, there were not a lot of things to do around Cumming for entertainment. So, people visited their friends and their relatives. They made homemade ice cream or cut a watermelon to share. Children played outside games like Kick the Can, Hide and Go Seek, Red Rover or Dodge Ball.

One of my family's favorite pastimes was "making music" at the home of friends. Bodie and Clifford, my aunt and uncle, both played guitar and sang. My mother and daddy sang and my mother also played the spoons! My grandpa played the banjo and sang bass.

Clifford's friends, Frank and his son Norman, also joined us from time to time. Frank played banjo and Norman played the guitar. Then there were Joyce and Burma Roland. I don't recall the women playing instruments, but I do recall their singing. My mother had a friend, Martha Haney, who played the upright bass.

You can see we had a variety of instruments and voices for four part harmony. We were our own version of a Gaither Homecoming concert! We would sit on the porch, weather permitting, and sing far into the night. What wonderful memories of long ago.

I don't hear much of folks "making music" anymore. Several years ago, some of us met at the home of Phyllis Samples to do just that. Our friends Robert and Kathey Quimby came. Phyllis' brother Michael Stone and his wife Marion, friends from the Post Office, were there. Hoyt Estes came, too. All the men except George played guitars and most of us women sang. At "intermission," we enjoyed sweet treats Phyllis and Marion had made. We had the grandest time.

Did you know Christians need to be "making music" to the Lord all the time? Ephesians 5:19 says, "Speaking to yourselves in psalms and hymns and spiritual songs, singing and making melody in your heart to the Lord." With the Spirit inside us, we need to be praising the Lord for all He has done for us.

Jeremiah said, "But his word was in mine heart as a burning fire shut up in my bones, and I was weary with forbearing, and I could not stay (20:9)." That is how I feel about singing. Words of praise are as a fire in my bones and I can't stop myself!

I urge you to make music to the Lord today. Even if you think you are not a singer, go ahead and try singing by letter. That means open up and "let 'er" fly. It will be pleasing to the Lord and will lift your burdens. Try it. You'll see how much better it makes you feel!

Lord, I want to praise You continually with my heart as well as my voice. Amen

JULY 4th   FIREWORKS ON THE FOURTH

"Ye shall celebrate it in the seventh month." Leviticus 23:41

Cumming celebrates Independence Day by hosting the Thomas-Mashburn Steam Engine Parade. People come from miles around to watch and to hopefully take home a sack full of candy or other prizes thrown from the floats. If I am not mistaken, this is the sixtieth year for the popular parade.

When our sons were young, we were a part of the festivities every year. We have been several times with the grandchildren, but George and I prefer to stay out of the heat these days.

In 2003, we were in Virginia on the Fourth of July. We were on a vacation to Williamsburg with our son Joel and his wife Jessica. They were wed just a few months prior to this trip. We were having a great time exploring the colonial town, mainly because Jessica had never been there before. The highlight of the trip, though, was seeing the fireworks that night.

I have seen fireworks in many states at various events, but none can compare to those we saw in Williamsburg. These burst into such vivid colors and seemed to touch the sky above us! Everyone around us was oohing and aahing over the display. It was finished much too soon.

Parades, fireworks and vacations are all so nice on the Fourth, but let's not get so caught up in them we forget what this day is all about. It is about the signing of the Declaration of Independence signifying the thirteen original colonies were a new nation. We were no longer under the rule of the British. Richard Henry Lee of Virginia is the man who proposed the resolution for independence. Thomas Jefferson was the principal author of the declaration.

Just as the Fourth of July is considered our day of deliverance from tyrannical rule, Christians can celebrate for another reason as well. When we are saved by the Lord Jesus, we are delivered from the penalty of sin. We are new creatures in Christ. Old things have passed away and all things are become new.

The apostle Paul wrote, "Stand fast therefore in the liberty wherewith Christ hath made us free, and be not entangled again with the yoke of bondage (Galatians 5:1)." Just as America no longer wants to be under bondage to another country, we no longer desire to be under bondage to sin. Satan no longer controls our lives when we stand fast in the liberty of Christ.

Now that is a special reason for celebrating!

Lord Jesus, thank You for setting me free from the law of sin and death. Amen

JULY 5th *LONG SHOT ROOKIE*

"Know ye not that they which run in a race run all, but one receiveth the prize? So run that ye may obtain." I Corinthians 9:24

Alexander Rossi. The first rookie in fifteen years to win the Indy 500, and he did it on fumes!

At age 14, Rossi became the youngest winner of the Skip Barber National Championships, placing third overall. He is the only

American to hold an F1A Super License. After being in Europe's Formula One contests for the past seven years, Rossi raced on an oval track for just the second time when competing in the 100th running of the Indy Car Series race in 2016. (The first time was on a one mile oval at the Phoenix Grand Prix.)

At one time Rossi was in last place. Despite multiple lead changes, accidents and a sudden rain shower, the twenty-four year old went a record thirty-six laps between fuel stops to win the race. After crossing the finish line, his car completely stopped and had to be helped to victory lane. Speaking of the win, the rookie said, "I have no idea how we pulled that off."

I often feel like a long shot rookie. Even though I have been in the race for many years, I often feel that I am in last place with very little hope. Often I feel I am running out of fuel to keep going. That is when I have to tell the enemy of my soul to get behind me and I have to take the lead. That is when I ask the Holy Spirit to fill me again and help me get going!

I am more than a conqueror through Jesus. I will win the race and I will receive the crown. The devil may slow me down at times, but he can never stop me. I may experience lead changes, accidents and sudden showers but nothing can separate me from the love of God which is in Christ Jesus (Romans 8:39).

I am on my way to the finish line and Jesus Himself will help me get there. There is no sweeter victory than the one awaiting the follower of Christ.

Jesus, You made me a winner when You saved my soul. I want to do my best as I near the finish line. Help me, I pray. Amen

JULY 6th *THE TEACUP LADY*

"I will take the cup of salvation, and call upon the name of the Lord." Psalm 116:13

About ten years ago, my friend Kathey Quimby invited me to take part in a special ministry. She told me of a place that helped women who were going through difficult circumstances and in need of spiritual direction. This place was having a retreat for some of the ladies. It would be a time of Bible study, prayer, mentoring and caring.

At the retreat, the ladies would be presented a special gift from a prayer warrior. The woman who donated the teacup and saucer committed to pray daily for one of the unnamed ladies for one year. I agreed to do this.

We met at Kathey's home to hear about the ministry and to write letters to the one who would receive our teacup set. Although most of the other women chose dainty, delicate cups, the one I chose was a thicker, more substantial cup. I explained my choice in the letter I wrote.

I told the lady I felt dainty, delicate cups were easily broken. They did not hold up well under the daily rigors of life. I wrote about her cup being able to go through hot water. While a teacup is for special occasions, the cup I chose was for use every day.

I said her life was like the cup. She may have felt easily broken, but with the Lord as her Guide, she could hold up under daily challenges. She could endure hard times with the help of the Holy Spirit. I also said the Lord wanted to use her every day in the work of His kingdom. I told her I would be praying for her to be strong.

To this day, I have no idea who received my cup and my letter. The Lord knows. I don't know if she appreciated the words I wrote, but I feel the Lord spoke to me as well as to her. I can make it though any challenge with the Lord's help. The Lord wants me to be strong in Him and in the power of His might. He wants to use me for His glory.

Whether dainty and delicate or strong and sturdy, the Lord has a purpose for each of us. Think about His purpose for you the next time you reach for a cup.

Dear God, help me fulfill my purpose for You. Amen

JULY 7th *MOTHER, DON'T SMOTHER*

"How often would I have gathered thy children together, as a hen doth gather her brood under her wings, and ye would not!" Luke 13:34

The current description of a parent who hovers over a child too much is "helicopter parent." I don't think I was ever that kind of mom. I went in the other direction and gave my children too much freedom for their own good. Just as my mom did in raising me.

I can remember the night when one of my sons came in and woke me up. Something had happened and he needed to talk to me. He said, "Mom, I need you." I told him I had no idea what to do about the situation. He said that didn't matter, he needed me! At least when the chips were down, he knew he could come to me about the problem. I could and did pray about it.

A man I worked with asked me once why we allowed one of our sons to have his hair so long. I told him we picked our battles. I said the son made good grades, worked, saved his money and the length of his hair was not an issue to us. Our home was not a military base. We allowed our children some freedom of expression.

Thinking of parenting reminded me of what Jesus said about the city of Jerusalem. He said He would have gathered her children together as a hen gathers her brood under her wings, but they would not allow Him to do so.

Jerusalem had been known for rejecting the prophets and for killing them. Jesus knew He would be rejected also and He knew His death was imminent. Yet Jesus loved His people. He wanted to protect them and shelter them from harm.

However, getting His people from where they were to where they needed to be would require suffering. Both on the part of Jesus as well as on the part of His followers. Jesus would go to the cross and die for their sins and those who chose to follow Him would suffer persecution.

He allowed them to make their own choices. Even if they made the wrong ones, He allowed them to suffer the consequences of their decisions. In fact, He has made all of us free moral agents. We can choose to accept Christ or to reject Him. It is up to us. He will never smother us into submission.

Jesus, I thank You for allowing me the opportunity to choose You. Even though You are always with me, You just guide me in the way I should go and You never smother me. Amen

JULY 8th   *WELCOME TO OUR WORLD*

"For unto us a child is born." Isaiah 9:6

We thought Joel and Jessica's family was complete. I had given away all the baby items that had been a part of my household for several years. There was no longer a high chair in the kitchen. No car seat in my vehicle. No diapers no toys, no pacifiers.

And then we heard the news. A baby was on the way once again! I was shocked but excited. The months dragged by. Finally Jessica called and said to be on stand-by because she might go to the hospital. And she did, but the baby was in no hurry to make an appearance.

After a seven hour wait, Josi Faith entered the world! She had a little fluid on her lungs and an air bubble in her tummy so she was in the NICU for a few hours and had to get an IV. But, unlike Mary Poppins, to us she *was* perfect in every way.

Today we are celebrating Josi's second birthday. What a joy and a blessing she has been to our family. Each new stage in her development is a delight. We are praying for her to accept Jesus as her Savior when she is older and to be committed in following Him.

Isaiah wrote about a child being born. The child he wrote about would have the government upon His shoulder. This child's name would be called Wonderful, Counsellor, the mighty God, the everlasting Father, The Prince of Peace. Of course, we know the child referred to is none other than Jesus Christ.

Isaiah's description tells us Jesus had extraordinary wisdom, He had life eternal and He would be the bringer of peace. Furthermore, the baby in Isaiah's prophecy is called the Mighty God. John the apostle wrote, "In the beginning was the Word, and the Word was with God and the Word was God (John 1:1)."

In spite of His deity, Jesus came to the world in humble beginnings. He was conceived in a young virgin, born in a stable and laid in a manger. His first known visitors were shepherds. Later, His family had to hide out in Egypt because Herod wanted to kill Him.

Several years ago, Chris Rice recorded "Welcome to Our World." It says, *Fragile finger sent to heal us, tender brow prepared for thorn, tiny heart whose blood will save us, unto us is born.* I like to imagine how Mary felt about her precious baby when He entered the world. I can't help but believe her feelings were similar to ours when Josi was born. I am sure Mary cherished those fragile fingers, tender brow and tiny heart just as we did. And still do.

Lord Jesus, Perfect Son of God, I am so thankful You wrapped our injured flesh around You and robbed our sin to make us holy. Amen

"But the Lord is my defence; and my God is the rock of my refuge."
Psalm 94:22

I have written about my personal trials. I shared the turmoil of my divorce. I wrote about the death of my dear aunt and my precious grandson. I shared about the struggle with my son. Those valleys are what helped me know my faith is real. That faith in God is the only thing that held me up and got me through.

When things were going well, I did not realize how deeply I needed the Lord. As a twenty-four year old, I took Him for granted much of the time. Then my marriage fell apart. I may have cried to my family and friends but they were really of no help. Sure, they tried their very best to say the right things and encourage me, but I had to learn my help could only come from God. He was, and still is, the only One who knew my deepest thoughts and emotional needs.

When my aunt died, despite all our prayers for her healing, I learned God is in control of all situations. He hears us pray, but the outcome is totally in His hands. His will supersedes ours.

I cannot understand why my little grandson died. It is still a puzzle to me, but I know I can trust God. I can't see how He is working this together for our good, but I know He is. My faith in Him is what caused me to bow my head in worship as we waited for the autopsy results.

I tried my best to think of some way to help my son, but I kept hitting a wall. When I finally turned it all over to God and relinquished my attempts to control the results, He showed His power in a mighty way.

We can read all the theology books, we can quote the Bible verses, we can teach Sunday school lessons and listen to great sermons, but until we have known personal pain and heartache, we are not able to fully appreciate Immanuel, God with us.

What about your personal pilgrimage? Are there specific times you can recall when it seemed all hope was lost? Those times when God made His presence so real you knew beyond any shadow of doubt He was with you? The Scottish preacher James Stewart said, "It is when you have sunk right down to rock bottom that you suddenly find you have struck the Rock of Ages."

191

My house is built on that Rock. It has a sure foundation. When the rains come and the winds blow, it will stand steadfast and sure. What about your house?

Our Lord Immanuel, thank You for being with me through all the storms of life. You are my Rock. Amen

JULY 10th *MEALS FOR MOURNERS*

"And they continued stedfastly in the apostles' doctrine and fellowship, and in breaking of bread, and in prayers." Acts 2:42

When I was growing up, the entire community came together when one of its own passed away. The women would clean the home of the deceased and cook enough food to feed an army of mourners. As a young wife and mother, I would never go to bed until everything was clean just in case I died in the night! I did not want anyone to see my house in disarray!

Back then, the funeral home was open all night and many people sat up with the dead. On this day in 1976, my cousin Jimmy Samples was one of several who sat up with us at Ingram's when my dad died. Shortly thereafter, he had an automobile accident which left him paralyzed for the remainder of his life.

Sitting up with the dead is no longer a custom. As far as I know, it is no longer customary to clean the home of the deceased either. Now I can go to bed with dishes in the sink! But people still pull out all the stops and feed the mourners. Most churches in our area provide a post-funeral meal for the family which, I know from experience, is greatly appreciated.

When my mother-in-law passed away in the mid-nineties, I can recall to this day the wonderful meal for the army of mourners prepared by Ann Jett. Ann was the wife of Marvin Jett, the father of my sister-in-law. She cooked so much food for us, the entire family was filled and there was food left over.

It was such an act of love for a family she barely knew. She did the same thing just weeks later when my brother-in-law Jack passed away. You do not forget such unselfish deeds. After praying, as we sat down and broke bread together, we ate each bite feeling loved. Not only by the Lord, but by Ann as well.

But, I ask myself, why wait until someone dies? Why don't I invite people over to break bread and share happy times as well? I have to admit, I have quit opening my home to family and friends except on holidays or special occasions. I think it is time to break out of my rut and feast on God's love while I feast with those I love. I need the fellowship with Him and them all year through.

Lord, help me to love my "neighbors" as I have been loved. Amen

JULY 11th *COMPLAINTS*

"I complained, and my spirit was overwhelmed." Psalm 77:3b

As you know, we love to travel. Like so many others who fly, we have had some issues which caused us to grumble. When Kevin and Justin flew down to meet us in Daytona Beach, they flew down on a big jet plane. Their return flight turned out to be on a prop plane!

The morning after the ValuJet crashed in the Everglades, we experienced turbulence on our flight to Atlanta. It felt like our plane dropped at least a thousand feet. You talk about scary!

On our way to Hawaii, we had a two hour delay while we sat on the tarmac in Dallas. We had to refuel before the flight could begin. George was seated next to a man who drank during the entire flight. Just smelling the alcohol on his breath was enough to make a person nauseous.

Another time, we were seated near a crying baby on a flight between Anchorage and Seattle. In Salt Lake City, our plane had some mechanical issues and our flight was cancelled. We were rerouted to Phoenix.

But, these experiences sure made for some interesting stories once they were behind us! Kevin and Justin made it home safely, our flight to Atlanta was smooth after that brief bout with turbulence, we were thankful for the refueling on the trip to Hawaii, the baby and its tired parents got off the plane in Seattle, and Tyler was on the ground in his ninth state when we flew to Phoenix. Also, we could pray for the man with the alcohol problem.

Life is sometimes like those flights. The struggles end up being blessings in disguise. When the unusual and the unexpected happen, try to look for the silver lining. When we are most tempted to complain, ask God for patience and a sense of humor as well. The stories you can share later will be opportunities to tell of God's hand at work in your life.

Oh, God, when I complain and my spirit is overwhelmed, help me turn my eyes upon You. Amen

JULY 12th *MOUNTAIN GOATS*

"The high hills are a refuge for the wild goats; and the rocks for the conies." Psalm 104:18

The mountain goat is a large hoofed mammal also known as the Rocky Mountain goat. It is very sure-footed and is often seen on cliffs and ice. Both the male and the female have beards, long black horns and short tails. Their woolly white double coats protect them from the elements. They are mostly found in Alaska, Washington, Idaho and Montana, although they have been introduced to other areas as well.

The first time we saw mountain goats was when we went to Mount Rushmore in 2002. It was about dusk as we made our way out of the park. Suddenly, we saw a few of them along the side of the road. I grabbed the video camera and started filming. Being so close to these animals was very exciting to me. Ten years later, we were able to see mountain goats again.

This time we were outside Glacier National Park. We were riding out Highway 2, headed towards Maria's Pass, when we saw a sign for "Goat Lick." We stopped and spotted a goat down by the water. Then we saw a mama and two babies on the rocks. The sign we read explained the goats descend from the high country to the Middle Fork of the Flathead River because their bodies need the salt and the minerals.

We started riding again and spotted more of them at a secondary lick. Kevin parked the car and we all jumped out to join the other tourists in gawking. Justin had to point out some of the distant ones to a couple who were having trouble seeing the goats. Tyler and Kevin, who was on crutches at the time, kept inching closer and closer as they tried to hide behind a stand of trees! Later, on the Going-to-the Sun Road, we saw goats licking salt off the highway.

How are we like the mountain goats? First, we will look at their appearance and characteristics. All humans may not look alike on the outside, but we are all made in the image of God. Even though we all have the inherent characteristic of sin, we all have a soul that needs God.

A mountain goat usually stays within a certain range. Seasonally they will travel to lower levels in search of the salt licks. Humans try to stay within their comfort zones, though God will lead us through the valleys in order to teach us, test us or to draw us closer to Him. He provides the nutrients for our souls.

Mountain goats spend most of their time grazing, which means they are mostly looking down. So often we are found looking down on ourselves or our fellowmen and around on worldly pleasures that we fail to look up to God. We need to focus on Him.

Both nanny goats and human mothers protect their offspring by leading them out of danger, standing over them when a predator is near and positioning themselves between the young and a steep slope. God also leads His own out of danger, stands by us when the enemy is closing in on us and keeps us from ultimately falling away from Him.

Finally, the goats exhibit aggressive behavior from time to time. So do humans. We want to protect our space, we want to compete to be the best and we want to dominate others. God, however, tells us to be meek and to be humble. He says we should not seek the highest honors but rather take the lower position. He says the first shall be last and the last shall be first.

Even if I never see another mountain goat, I have learned some things about myself and others by observing them.

Lord God, You are my refuge. Thank You for making my feet sure on the slippery slopes of life. Amen

JULY 13th *THE GOOD BOOK*

"Thy word have I hid in mine heart, that I might not sin against thee."
Psalm 119:11

I have always loved a good book. From the minute I learned to read the simplest books, I was hooked. I have my own library in the basement of my home. Many books are ones I want to keep, but most of the volumes are just ones I am hoping to read as time permits.

As a teenager I could be found in my room curled up with a good book. Back then I liked to read mysteries by Victoria Holt. I also loved the strange tales by Edgar Allen Poe and short stories by O. Henry. I read *Gone with the Wind* several times. I was not partial to one genre.

Later, I started to read biographies and non-fiction. Whether movie stars or sports figures, I enjoyed reading about the lives of famous people. I soon began to read only inspirational books. I would read at least one book per week.

As I have grown older, my favorite book is the Good Book! I look forward to reading God's Word every day. I can't wait to open the pages and behold wonderful things from His law (Psalm 119:18). Not only do I read devotional passages daily, I read through the Bible every year. I love marking my favorite verses and writing comments in the margins of my Bible.

Since the seventies, I have been memorizing Scriptures. My memory is not what it once was, as you might imagine, so I am thankful I learned many verses long ago. I still try to hide God's Word in my heart so that I do not sin against Him.

Inside the pages of the Bible you can find history, mystery, love stories, biographies and all the inspirational material you could hope for. It has everything in one book! If you are not currently hooked on reading the Bible, I would encourage you to start reading today.

Pray as you read and ask God to speak to you through the pages of His Word. Ask Him to open your eyes so you can behold wonderful things from the Bible. A book you once thought of as hard to understand or boring may just become your very favorite book. Just as it became mine!

Lord, thank You for the Word. Continue to open my eyes to Your truths and help me apply them to my life. Amen

JULY 14ᵗʰ   *THE TATES*

"This book of the law shall not depart out of thy mouth; but thou shalt meditate therein day and night, that thou mayest observe to do according to all that is written therein; for then thou shalt make thy way prosperous, and then thou shalt have good success." Joshua 1:8

Do you have any members of the TATE family in your church? We have had many from time to time. First, there was the patriarch, Dic TATE, who wanted to run everything. His brother Ro TATE tried to change everything. They had a sister Agi TATE who stirred up plenty of trouble with a little help from her husband Irri TATE.

No matter what new projects were suggested, Hesi TATE and his wife Vege TATE always wanted to wait until the next year. Then there was dear old Aunt Imi TATE who wanted our church to be just like all the others. Deves TATE provided the voice of doom and gloom, while Poten TATE wanted to be the big shot. Every family has that one black sheep and in this case it was Ampu TATE who completely cut himself off from the church!

But not all members of the family were so disagreeable. Brother Facili TATE was quite helpful in all church matters. And a delightful, happy member of the family was Miss Felici TATE. Her cousins, Cogi TATE and Medi TATE always thought things over and lent helpful, steady hands.

This little piece was found in a church bulletin from about thirty years ago. No offense is intended to any real Tates anywhere. If there is any resemblance to anyone in your family, it is purely coincidental! Nor is this meant to describe anyone at my own church.

Seriously, though, are you like any of the Tates? Am I? If so, I hope I am more like Facili TATE, being helpful in church matters. I would also like to be more like Medi TATE, not only thinking things over, but being more like Joshua. God told Joshua to meditate in the book of the law day and night so that he would do what it said and would become prosperous and have good success.

I do not want to hesitate or vegetate when God speaks. I do not want to irritate nor agitate others. I have no desire to dictate nor be the potentate. And I certainly do not want to amputate myself from my fellowship of believers. I need them to help me in my walk with the Lord.

Examine yourself today. Be the right TATE!

Lord, forgive me when I am not the TATE I should be. Help me as I meditate on all that is written in Your law. Amen

JULY 15th *THE WHISTLE STOP CAFE*

"For brethren, ye have been called unto liberty; only use not liberty for an occasion to the flesh, but by love serve one another."

Several years ago, my mother, my sister and I took a "girls' trip" to the Whistle Stop Café in Juliette, Georgia. The café was used in the movie *Fried Green Tomatoes.*

Near the Ocmulgee River, the café was built in 1927 and was actually a general merchandise store for forty-five years. The meat scales, the cash register, the file system, the wood heater and the safe are among the items still in the building today. The building still has the original oiled wood floors.

After the filming of the movie, Robert Williams and a friend decided to make the store into a real café. The sign on the front of the café says, Fine Food at Fair Prices. The only hint of fame is a poster of Jessica Tandy. The fried green tomatoes served here are crunchy on the outside and juicy inside, just like they should be.

While we ate, we were entertained by a gentleman who walked around the restaurant playing guitar and singing for us. He was dressed in some outlandish costume. He stopped at our table and I started singing along with him. Then he asked me to sing a song and I did.

I certainly agree with Daniel Schantz who wrote, "The Whistle Stop Café reminds me of the people I most admire: colleagues and friends who have distinguished themselves, yet have stayed true to their sense of service. They're the kind of people who will help you move a piano or mow your lawn while you're on vacation. They have the spirit of Jesus, Who left the wealth of heaven to serve the poor of Palestine. I would like to be more like them." So would I.

I can think of several who fit this category. I imagine you can, too. I will never know fame for myself, but I do want to be one who is true to a sense of service. I want to be one who will roll up my sleeves and pitch in whenever and wherever needed. Like Jesus, I want to serve my fellowman. If the very Son of God took upon Himself the role of a servant, how can I do any less?

Jesus, help me be more like You. Help me be a servant to God the Father as well as to my fellowman. Amen

JULY 16th *VISIONS IN THE NIGHT*

"For God speaketh once, yea twice, yet man perceiveth it not. In a dream, in a vision of the night, when deep sleep falleth upon men, in slumberings upon the bed." Job 33:14, 15

George has visions in the night. God speaks to him in various dreams and visions in the wee hours of the morning. This has been a part of our lives for years.

There are simple things and then there are the profound. The first time, George had a vision of a black funnel cloud. He did not understand the vision, yet he knew someone was going to die. When our neighbor perished in a fire, that black funnel cloud could be seen when the firemen forced open the door and the smoke came rushing out.

Then there was the time George wanted an old pick-up truck. We had looked all around and couldn't find one. During the night, George dreamed he could find one at a car lot in the Midway community. A blue one. Sure enough, the next morning, he headed down to the lot, and there sat Old Blue. He kept that truck for years. You might not think that was from God, but we do.

George has seen Jesus in visions multiple times. Jesus has spoken words of encouragement to George and He has asked George to do certain things. Of course, everything the Lord has spoken to him has come to pass exactly as He said. Jesus showed George the lawsuit would be settled, and it was. He told George, "I will take care of you," and He has. He instructed George to speak to someone and reconcile their differences and George obeyed.

I can't share all that has taken place, but when George tells me God has shown him something in a dream or a vision, I know I can believe it. I, on the other hand, can only remember one dream that I felt was directly from God.

I was a death claims examiner at Coastal States Life in Atlanta, and I was at home with the flu. My supervisor called about whether a policy was a participating or a non-par one. That simply indicated whether it had dividends payable. I told him it was par, but he said the print out from the computer did not show dividends. So, I gave him all the steps necessary to change the records so he could pay the claim. I then dreamed about the first print out I had pulled up when the claim was initially submitted. It plainly showed dividends.

The next morning, I called Michael and asked him to check the file for the first computer-generated description of the policy. Sure enough, there were the dividends just as I had said. Finding the facts saved the company time and money in regard to paying the claim.

I know God has spoken to me many, many times giving me words of wisdom, encouragement and instruction. But, I will never forget the vision in the night, the dream, about the dividends. Like the policy in my dream, we also are participating in the dividends of God if we know Christ as our Savior. We have been made joint-heirs with Jesus to all the riches of the Father. Now there is something to dream about!

Father God, thank You for all the dividends You have for me. Amen

JULY 17th   *REMEMBER THE RIVETS*

"In whom all the building fitly framed together growth unto an holy temple in the Lord:" Ephesians 2:21

Did you ever stop to think about this? Ships don't sink because of the water around them. They sink because of the water that gets in them! Take the ark for example. Noah built the ark according to the plan God gave him. The ark encountered more water than any vessel to date, yet it stayed upright and came to rest on Mt. Ararat.

Then we have the "unsinkable" HMS *Titanic*. A person claimed to have overheard Captain Edward John Smith say, "Even God Himself couldn't sink this ship." But we know the ship sank at 2:20 a.m. on April 15, 1912. I read scientists have discovered it was the faulty rivets, made of wrought iron rather than steel, which caused the ship's hull to open as it did after striking an iceberg.

We can learn great lessons from looking at these two examples. First, even the smallest part of a ship or a church body is important. If we feel insignificant, we must remember the rivets. It takes every part working together to make the body complete and strong.

Regardless of the turmoil going on around us, we must not let it get inside us and weigh us down. We must remain afloat by sticking to God's plan for us. That plan is to trust Him in all circumstances.

Finally, nothing is too hard for the Lord. If we think there is nothing He can do, just remember what the angel Gabriel told Mary, "For with God nothing shall be impossible (Luke 1:37)."

As you face the raging sea of life, think about the ark. Water was all around it, yet none got inside to sink it. Likewise, we are protected by the Holy Spirit of God and the devil cannot sink us!

Thank You, God, for keeping me afloat through all of life's storms. Amen

JULY 18th *ACHING FEET*

"And your feet shod with the preparation of the gospel of peace;" Ephesians 6:15

When I met George, in 1976, platform shoes were in vogue. He thought I was tall until I changed shoes! Those shoes are back in style now, but they are not the most comfortable kind. And they can be dangerous! I fell once while wearing those shoes. Justin was a baby and I had him in my arms at the time. Thank the Lord, he wasn't hurt.

I have worn other kinds of shoes that were very uncomfortable but very much in style. Take for instance those shoes with the pointy toes. Or those with the little bumps that are supposed to massage your feet while you walk. Give me a good pair of tennis shoes any day over those!

The word translated "shod" in this verse means to bind on your feet or to be fitted. Nothing is more uncomfortable than shoes that do not fit correctly. But, there is another kind of discomfort that is just as problematic. That is trying to fit ourselves into someone else's ministry.

We hear well-meaning speakers urge us to teach Sunday school, go to a foreign mission field, witness on the street corners. They make us feel guilty for not doing so, even though the Lord may not have called us to do those things. I realize everyone that has been saved is to be a witness for the Lord, but he uses us all in different ways. One size does not fit all when it comes to His work.

You have heard, "If the shoe fits, wear it." Likewise, if the shoe does not fit, don't try to wear it! You cannot share His peace when your feet are in the wrong shoes.

Put on the shoes God has for you to wear and go where He sends.

Lord, I know You have shoes just my size. Help me serve You by wearing the ones You selected just for me. Amen

JULY 19th *OUR PETITION IS GRANTED*

"For this child I prayed; and the Lord hath given me my petition which I asked of him:" I Samuel 1:27

Hannah was one of the wives of Elkanah. His other wife Peninnah had borne children, but Hannah was barren. Every year when Elkanah went to worship in Shiloh and offer sacrifices unto the Lord, he gave Peninnah and her children portions, but he gave Hannah more.

Hannah's adversary provoked her sore and made her fret because she had no offspring. This caused Hannah to weep and she was not able to eat. Elkanah tried to cheer her up. He asked, "Am I not better to thee than ten sons?"

In bitterness of soul, Hannah prayed unto the Lord and wept. She vowed a vow to the Lord and said, "O Lord of hosts, if thou wilt indeed look on the affliction of thine handmaid, and remember me, and not forget thine handmaid, but wilt give unto thine handmaid a man child, then I will give him unto the Lord all the days of his life, and there shall no rasor come upon his head."

Eli, the priest, thought Hannah was drunk! He told her to put away her wine. But once he learned the reason for her behavior, he said to her, "Go in peace: and the God of Israel grant thee thy petition that thou hast asked of him."

Hannah soon gave birth to the boy Samuel. And when he was weaned, Elkanah and Hannah presented the boy to the Lord and he lived with Eli and ministered before the Lord. After keeping her vow, the Lord gave Hannah five more children.

Every time I see my nephew Luke I think of Hannah and Samuel. My nephew Dustin is the only child of my sister Cathy. He married Jennifer in 2002. Years passed and they had no children. We began to pray for the Lord to give them a child. Nine years later, our petition was granted. They were expecting!

However, Jennifer had gestational diabetes. She and Dustin were worried about the baby. I told them not to waste their time worrying. I assured them everything would be okay. I said we had prayed too long for this baby and I did not believe the Lord would allow anything to happen now.

On July 19, 2011, Luke Bradley Frix was born. I sat with my sister all night long in the ice-cold waiting room until we felt like icicles, but our hearts were warmed when we heard Luke cry for the first time. He had a great set of lungs!

He weighed the exact same as Kevin, he has Joel's middle name and he was born on Jessica's birthday. While all of those things were special to us, none was more special than knowing this baby was an answer to prayer. He is a very special little boy.

If your prayer is not answered right away, don't give up. God will answer in His own good time. He knows what is best.

Lord, thank You for Luke today. Thank You for all the petitions You have granted for my family. Amen

JULY 20th *HEAVEN'S PEAK*

"Great is the Lord and greatly to be praised in the city of our God, in the mountain of his holiness. Beautiful for situation, the joy of the whole earth, is mount Zion on the sides of the north, the city of the great King." Psalm 48:1, 2

Really, George was too sick to travel. He was recovering from a serious bout with pneumonia and we should have stayed home. The doctor who had been treating him had cleared him for travel, though, so we packed our bags and flew away.

It was our fourth day when he almost died. Basically, he had sat silently as we drove along, feeling lethargic and watching his legs and feet swell more every day. We were in Columbia Falls, just outside Glacier National Park, where we had rented a cabin for a couple of nights when he thought the end was near!

He was feeling that he was going to die and he was in bed praying that God would spare his life until he got a new roof on the house for me. Suddenly, he began to hear the most beautiful music played on instruments he could not identify. He entered a tunnel and began his journey towards the brightest light imaginable. When he was almost to the Light, he heard a voice say, "It's not time yet. Go back." Then he got up, took a breathing treatment and some medicine and went to sleep.

The next morning, Kevin, Justin, Tyler, George and I were going to board a red bus for our Going-to-the-Sun Road trip. George did not say a word to any of us about what had taken place during the night. Justin helped the driver roll back the canvas top of the bus and Tyler was chosen to ride shotgun. We were off!

As we were riding up the mountain, a slightly cool breeze was blowing and snow was still on the ground in mid-July. Then we saw it! Heaven's Peak, the highest of four peaks in the Livingston Range which form the divide between Camas Creek and McDonald Creek at the head of Lake McDonald. At 8,987 feet tall, the snow covered mountain dominated the landscape. It was breath-taking to me, but I had no idea the effect it was having on George.

After we returned home, George was admitted to the hospital. Once again, he had pneumonia. Only after almost dying a second time, did he share what God had showed him on the mountain. He said he had heard a voice saying, "This is the last step to Heaven." In other words, the beauty of Heaven is far beyond that of the earth, but Heaven's Peak was as close as we could get to comprehending it.

Hearing that made me think of Psalm 48. The sons of Korah composed this tribute to the city of Jerusalem, the capital of not only their nation, but of their religion as well. The city was home of their king, the Lord God. Korah's sons said the mountain was beautiful for where it was situated and was the joy of the whole earth. It was called the mountain of holiness because God's presence dwelt there in the temple.

I will most likely never see the earthly Jerusalem. Even if I do, the temple has been destroyed and God's presence now abides in those who believe in His Son Jesus Christ. But, because I am a believer, I will be able to see the new Jerusalem one day. After I have taken my last step to Heaven.

Lord, thank You for the assurance that one day I will see You and praise You in Your great city, in the mountain of Your holiness. Amen

"Be ye angry, and sin not: let not the sun go down upon your wrath:"
Ephesians 4:26

At one of our Women on Mission meetings, our director Shannon Loudermilk presented a program that really spoke to my heart. I would like to share with you some of what she said.

Anger. We don't know how to handle it, so it often turns into actions or harsh words we later regret. Romans 13:8, tells us to owe no man anything but to love one another. We should not feel we owe the person who made us angry any retribution. The Bible tells us, "Vengeance is mine; I will repay, saith the Lord (Romans 12:19)."

The popular ad asks the question, "Got milk?" We all know milk is good for our bones and our teeth. But milk can turn sour. Just like the little things that bother us. If they are not dealt with quickly, they can turn sour. Ignoring them, like ignoring a container of milk, does not keep the sourness away, it only grows worse.

If we add ketchup to the glass of sour milk, that doesn't help one bit. Sure, it turned the milk a different color, but the sourness is still there. Neither can we hide our deep feelings of anger for long. They will show up.

If we add vinegar to the glass, it doesn't change the appearance of our sour milk, but it does add sharpness to the mixture. Anger also adds sharpness to our disposition when it controls us. This sharpness is beneath the surface and it shows up at the worst possible times.

If we add tuna to our glass of milk, ketchup and vinegar, it then becomes downright repulsive. The tuna represents our contempt or hate for those who have angered us. We begin to see them as less than ourselves. When we reject them, we reject the Lord's plan for the world. It is His desire that we work together and help one another.

The key to finding our way out of this pit of anger is to use our GPS. *G*o to the person and be honest with him. Confess your part of the problem and try to resolve it. *P*ray for the Lord's forgiveness. *S*eek forgiveness from the person at whom you have been angry. *GPS.*

In Matthew 5, the Bible teaches us whoever is angry with his brother without a cause shall be in danger of the judgment. It also says if we bring a gift to God and remember a brother has something against us, we are to leave our gift and be reconciled with the brother before offering the gift. Heavy stuff, I know.

You might say, "But you don't know what happened." No, I don't, but God does. He knows who is right and who is wrong. I will admit, I have been on both sides of the anger. I have been falsely accused and misunderstood, and I have been angry when I shouldn't have. Some issues are hard to resolve, but God is able.

If you have anger issues today, get out your GPS and find your way home. Home to God and home to the offender as well.

God, help me deal with anger in the right away. Help me not to sin when I am angry and help me resolve the issues quickly. Amen

JULY 22nd   TUNE-UP SPECIAL

"Thou hast loved righteousness, and hated iniquity; therefore God, even thy God, hath anointed thee with the oil of gladness above thy fellows." Hebrews 1:9

This is the vacation season. Every summer I read articles in the newspaper and in various magazines about preparing your automobile before embarking on a road trip. There are many things that need to be checked out to insure a safe journey. Many of the things could also relate to our spiritual walk. I will share ten of those.

First, we must **adjust** our lights so that others may see our good works (Matthew 5:16). We must **set** our timing so as to be in church on time (Hebrews 10:25). We need to make sure the **brakes** on our tongues are in good working order. (Read James, chapter 3, to see how much trouble the tongue can cause.) We must **tune-up** our hearts and have the peace that passeth understanding (Philippians 4:7).

We must **align** our direction so that we may be able to steer ourselves up the straight and narrow road of life without a wreck (see Matthew 7:13). We must **tune** our minds so as to think on pure, holy, noble things (Philippians 4:8). For a **quick start** and a sure victory, be ready always to do the Lord's will and then do it (Ephesians 5:17)!

Also, we must **anti-freeze** our hearts, being fervent in spirit, serving God (Romans 12:11). We need to **lubricate** our spirits with the oil of gladness, rejoicing always, giving thanks in everything (see Psalm 45:7, Philippians 4:4 and I Thessalonians 5:18). Finally, if we do all the maintenance, we should **re-tire** with full assurance of eternal life (John 3:16).

This piece was submitted by Michael Nix for publication in our church bulletin nearly thirty years ago. I do not know the identity of the original author, but I believe the advice given.

As you get your car readied for summer travel, remember to check out your spiritual life and see where any tune-ups might be needed.

Jesus, help me be in tune with Your will in every season of my life. Amen

JULY 23rd *COMMUNION ON THE MOON*

"If I beheld the sun when it shined, or the moon walking in brightness;" Job 31:26

Can you remember what you were doing on July 20, 1969? That was when the Apollo 11's Lunar Module, carrying Neil Armstrong and Buzz Aldrin, touched down in the Sea of Tranquility on the surface of the moon at 4:17 p.m., Eastern daylight time.

I was awake for the landing. However, I fell asleep and missed the actual first step on the moon, which occurred six hours later at 10:56 p.m., EDT. I had missed the most climactic moment in the history of the space program! Just like something I would do.

Buzz Aldrin asked everyone listening in to pause and give thanks. He then took communion. Aldrin was an elder in the Presbyterian church and his pastor prepared the communion kit for him. Webster Presbyterian has the chalice used on the moon and every year on the Sunday closest to July 20th the church commemorates the event.

In a phone call to the astronauts, President Nixon said all the people on Earth are "one in our prayers that you will return safely to Earth." In a televised broadcast the last night before splashdown, Aldrin also had this to say: "Personally, in reflecting on the events of the past several days, a verse from Psalms comes to mind. 'When I consider the heavens, the work of Thy fingers, the moon and the stars, what is man that Thou art mindful of him?'"

When I heard about Aldrin taking communion, I was thankful we had a man acquainted with God on the mission. He did not publicly mention the communion, though, because NASA was fighting a lawsuit at the time with the infamous atheist Madalyn Murray O'Hair.

She did not want the astronauts broadcasting religious activities while in space.

Yet, even the lawsuit did not stop Aldrin from quoting a Bible passage. It did not stop the president from saying the people are one in praying for a safe return. Before splashdown, Armstrong concluded his own remarks with, "God bless you. Good night from Apollo 11."

I do not know if being on the moon made Aldrin feel closer to God as he took communion. I imagine it might have. Yet, I feel close to God anytime I take communion. As I remember the sacrifice of the Lord's body for my sins and I remember His blood that was shed for a new covenant, I feel drawn to Him in a special way. Most of the churches in our area only have communion twice a year. But, I ask you today to remember what communion is all about. And thank God that He is mindful of man whether we are on the moon or on the earth.

Lord Jesus, thank You for communion which we do in remembrance of Your sacrifice for us. Amen

JULY 24th *JESUS SAVES*

"This is a faithful saying, and worthy of all acceptation, that Christ Jesus came into the world to save sinners; of whom I am chief."
I Timothy 1:15

Marcus Waters was what I would call a "character." Although I had gone to school with Linda and Jimmy, two of his children, I did not meet Marcus until the nineties. He was painting the house next door and our dog ran away with his paint brush! He came right over to let us know about it!

I never dreamed we would end up going to church with this man. He was always teasing me and would ask me what I was going to "preach" about that day. That is because I am outspoken and unafraid to voice my opinions, I suppose. Hopefully, though, it was because he enjoyed hearing me testify about the goodness of the Lord.

When he passed away in 2011, I attended the funeral. Our pastor, Craig Richard talked about Marcus asking the Lord to grant him "one more day." Craig told us in Heaven it is eternal day, so God had granted Marcus' request.

John Roden also had a part in the funeral. John is a home preacher at Pine Crest and was a close friend to Marcus. John told us Marcus had asked him to have a part in the funeral and had actually written down on a slip of paper what he wanted John to say when the time came.

I was expecting some joke or some story about hunting or fishing. Marcus was a funny man who enjoyed making people laugh, so I did not expect him to write such a profound statement as he had. John said when he unfolded the paper, there were just two words written on it. Those two words were "Jesus Saves."

I cannot think of two words any more powerful than those. That is the message all Christians should be proclaiming daily, with our words and with our lives. Like Marcus did.

Jesus, the only begotten Son of God, came to earth to redeem fallen man. He lived a sinless life, He died a vicarious death on the cross of Calvary to pay the penalty for our sins, He was sealed in a borrowed tomb, He rose the third day and appeared to many, He ascended back to Heaven and He will return one day to gather His children and put an end to Satan and sin once and for all.

Marcus summed all that up in two words. Jesus saves.

Lord, I thank You for saving me. I pray for those who do not yet know You. Amen

JULY 25th *THE INVISIBLE GOD*

"Who is the image of the invisible God, the firstborn of every creature:" Colossians 1:15

In 1897, H. G. Wells published his science fiction novel, *The Invisible Man*. The story was about a scientist who learned to make himself invisible by changing the body's refractive index to that of air, so that it would not absorb or reflect light. The only problem was once he had become invisible, it was impossible for him to reverse the process!

In 1933, Universal Pictures produced the film of the same name and there were many spin-offs from the film. These shows were basically unrelated to the original story by Wells. There was even an

Abbott and Costello Meet the Invisible Man. In the late fifties, there was a television series about an invisible man that centered on espionage.

Are you wondering what this has to do with God? I believe a lot of people think of God as "the man upstairs." I believe they think of Him as "out of sight and out of mind." I believe too often people forget to focus on the supreme holiness and the majesty of God.

Paternus, in *Advice to a Son,* wrote, "First of all, my child, think magnificently of God. Magnify His providence; adore His power, pray to him frequently and incessantly. Bear Him always in your mind. Teach your thoughts to reverence Him in every place for there is no place where He is not. Therefore, my child, fear and worship and love God; first and last, think magnificently of Him!"

This ancient advice is still right on target for today. Although we are God's children and are urged to come boldly to His throne, we should hold Him in the highest regard with awe and reverence. We should not treat Him with too much familiarity.

Walter Chalmers Smith was a Scottish pastor who wrote the words to the song, "Immortal, Invisible." The first verse describes God this way, "Immortal, invisible, God only wise, in light inaccessible hid from our eyes, most blessed, most glorious, the Ancient of Days, Almighty, victorious—Thy great name we praise." I like the third verse, too. It says, "we blossom and flourish as leaves on the tree, and wither and perish--but naught changes Thee."

In I John, 4:12, the Bible says, "No man hath seen God at any time." Yet, John also wrote in 3:2, "Beloved, now are we the sons of God, and it doth not yet appear what we shall be: but we know that, when he shall appear, we shall be like him; for we shall see him as he is."

Job said, "And though after my skin worms destroy this body, yet in my flesh shall I see God: Whom I shall see for myself, and mine eyes shall behold, and not another (19:26, 27)." God may be invisible to us now, but one day we shall see Him as He is. Oh, glorious day!

Lord God, One day You will not be invisible and my eyes shall see You as You are. What a day that will be! Amen

"Charge them that are rich in this world, that they be not highminded, nor trust in uncertain riches, but in the living God, who giveth us richly all things to enjoy." I Timothy 6:17

Before there was on-line shopping, there were mail-order catalogs. In 1845, Tiffany's sent out the first mail-order catalog in the United States. Later, there were the Montgomery Ward catalogs, followed shortly by those from Sears. As a child, my favorite catalog was the Sears "Wishbook." I would pour over its pages, picking out exactly what I wanted for Christmas each year.

When I started working for the Postal Service, I was thrilled to see how many mail-order choices were available. I found out you could order almost anything through the mail. From chickens to clothing and from bees to trees, you could have it all without having to leave your property. I ordered from some of the catalogs every week or two.

Although the glossy, colorful pages made the merchandise seem to be just what I had been needing, after awhile they started to be too much. Mailing lists are sold to other companies, and my name began appearing on catalogs for things I would never even think of buying. I realized all I really needed could be found in a "catalog" of a different sort.

The Bible may not be a "Wishbook" like the one from Sears, but in its pages I could find how to "order" with no money involved at all. The best "item" is, of course, everlasting life through Jesus Christ (John 3:16). Also, "items" such as joy (John 16:24), peace (Philippians 4:7) and laughter (Job 8:21) are available.

As much as I enjoy receiving the mail, it isn't the mail carrier that can bring true enjoyment. It is God. I need to store up, not mail-order treasures, but treasures of the spiritual kind. Treasures from God's Word. Mary Lou Carney once said, "He always gets the order right."

God, You know what I need even before I ask. Help me store up the true treasures that come from Your Word. Amen

"The voice of thy thunder was in the heaven: the lightnings lightened the world: the earth trembled and shook." Psalm 77:18

March 12, 1993, was a cold day and the weatherman was predicting snow during the night. I hoped and prayed they were wrong. I hated delivering mail with snow on the road. Although the day was cold, I had seen a beautiful bluebird and had noticed the Bradford Pear trees and the Forsythias were blooming. Spring was on its way.

About dark, the rains began. At five o'clock the next morning, it was still only rain, but changed to snow just before I got to work. It kept coming down and about 7:30, I called George and asked him to come put the chains on my car. While he was still outside trying to do this task, the postmaster told us mail delivery was cancelled for the day. The first time, in my ten years employment, delivery had ever been suspended.

This snowstorm was actually a blizzard. Power was out for hours, trees fell on houses, there were multiple accidents and the wind chill factor was ten below zero! But, the roads were clear in a few days and we carried on with our normal routines.

In 2011, we had Snowpocalypse and in 2014, we had Snowmageddon. I was, thankfully, retired before these storms hit our area. But, today, I want to tell you about another storm I dubbed The Storm of the Century. This was in the summer of 2011.

George called me from work and said he was about to come home so he could clean up and go to Gainesville. A team member had passed away and he was going to the funeral home. I decided to go with him. While George was getting ready, the hail started. (The first time my grandson Tyler saw hail he said, "Grandmom, it's raining ICE!") It was also lightning like crazy and I did not want to leave the house until the storm blew over.

As we started up the road, we saw a tree down across some power lines and we saw an ambulance and firetruck at a house nearby. We saw two wrecks on Highway 369, and a tree had fallen at Little Mill Road. When we arrived at the funeral home, I opted to remain in the car.

When we began our trip home, George stopped for gas. Just as we turned into the driveway of the station, there was a loud pop of thunder that shook the ground and a huge flash of lightning. Then the power went out. In a few minutes the power came back on and George was out pumping gas in the worst lightning I had ever seen. I was praying he would not be struck by it. Also, it was raining so hard, he could barely see how to drive. I wished we had not gone, but there we were.

God brought us home safely and I can tell you I was thankful to be back inside. I have been through many summer storms but this was the worst one, with no tornado activity, I had ever experienced!

As Asaph wrote in Psalm 77, the clouds poured out water; the skies sent out a sound (verse 17). The voice of God's thunder was in the heaven. The lightning lightened the world. The earth truly did tremble and shake. It was frightening. Yet God is in control over all the forces of nature. Whether winter storms or summer storms, He has His hand on us.

He is also in control of all life's spiritual storms we may encounter. We can trust Him to bring us through. Hollis Dinsmore liked to lead page 68, in the church hymnal. That song is "He'll Take Me Through." The words of the song tell us Jesus will be with us to the end, comforting us with His power. It also reminds us He will be our closest friend in death's dark hour. What a wonderful promise!

Jesus, my Redeemer, I know You will lead me safely through. Either safely through the storm on the earth, or safely home to You. Amen

JULY 28th *PEACE IN PICTURES*

"Then ye shall drive out all the inhabitants of the land from before you, and destroy all their pictures, and destroy all their molten images, and quite pluck down all their high places:" Numbers 33:52

I believe I have already mentioned that I have enjoyed photography from a young age. I couldn't wait for the envelope from Jack Rabbit to arrive in the mailbox. Jack Rabbit was the name of the place my mother sent our film to be developed. What a thrill to open up the envelope and see how the pictures turned out. Back then, you had no way of knowing until the developing was done. There were no retakes!

I have always stressed one thing to my family. I always said if the house catches on fire and you can get out, grab some of the pictures to take out with you! You can replace almost all material things, but not the pictures. We have an L-shaped hall and I once had pictures hanging the entire length of the hall. My brother Randy called it my "Hall of Shame."

George nicknamed Kevin's son, Tyler, "Jack Rabbit." It had nothing at all to do with the picture place, but it could have. Tyler loved looking at pictures as much as I did. After I started scrapbooking, he would get out the books every time he came over and see what photos I had added. There was another place he loved to go to look at the pictures. That place was Sawnee View Gardens!

I am not sure how he got interested in doing so. I just remember every time we went there, he wanted me to walk all over the cemetery with him as he lifted cover after cover to see the pictures encased in glass on the headstones. We would talk about how the deceased looked and wonder how they died. Some pictures were of elderly people and some were of tiny babies. Some pictures were of people I knew, and I could tell Tyler about their lives and deaths.

This may seem morbid to a lot of people, but we did not think so. It gave my young grandson an accurate picture of how death can come to the young and old alike. It gave us a chance to talk about going to be with Jesus when death overtakes us. Or the alternative.

Even though we do not have a picture holder on the marker we bought for our plots, one day, in God's own time, someone may come across my headstone and wonder about my life. But today, I am fully alive and thankful for the world in which I live. When God calls me home, I know I will be so peaceful in the arms of God. I can only hope pictures of me, living my life, will help bring back fond memories and will offer sweet peace to my family.

Lord God, thank You for the years You have granted me. Help me to be a picture of Your peace every day of my life. Amen

JULY 29ᵗʰ *MARK'S SACRIFICE*

"Greater love hath no man than this, that a man lay down his life for his friends." John 15:13

For many years I have admired Mark Nix. He is my cousin and his family lived near me for a time. He has amazing talents. He is a singer, songwriter and guitar player. I also hear he is a wonderful husband, father, son, brother, in-law, etc.

Last summer, Mark and his family were vacationing in Florida. It was while he was there, he almost fulfilled the verse from John! There were riptides prevalent in the ocean that day. They may be prevalent every day, I don't know about that. But they are strong, narrow currents of water that pull objects away from the shore and out to sea.

As I understand the situation, a little girl got caught in a riptide and almost drowned. Mark hurried to rescue her. He was able to get her to safety, but that is when he was taken out himself. The riptide threw him back into the ocean. People thought he was gone! His wife, Caymon, said, "By the sheer grace of God, my husband made it back."

Paramedics checked Mark and worked with him to get his oxygen levels stabilized. Mark had saved the little girl but he was almost lost in the process. One friend wrote on Facebook, "God sure does use people as other people's angels at the right time."

Jesus said laying down your life for a friend is the greatest kind of love. This little girl was a stranger to Mark, yet he gave no thought for his own safety as he hurried to her rescue. That is the MARK of a true hero, don't you think? That is Christ-like.

Jesus willingly laid down His life for us. We were separated from Him, not by ocean waves, but by our sin. Satan, like the riptide, tried to pull Jesus away from God's plan for our redemption. He offered Jesus all the kingdoms of the world if Jesus would fall down and worship him instead. Jesus' rebuttal was the Word of God.

Mark did not call for the paramedics to come to his rescue, but after the ordeal, they came. Neither did Jesus call for legions of angels to rescue Him from crucifixion. He endured the cross, despising the shame, so that believers could have eternal life.

While Mark saved the little girl from drowning, he could not die for her sins. Only Jesus could do that. Jesus is the only One who is able to be the perfect sacrifice, because He is the only One who never sinned. He was in all points tempted as we are, yet He was without sin. I am so thankful Jesus died for me and has called me His friend.

Jesus, I am thankful for the heroic actions of my cousin Mark. However, I am most thankful for You, my real Hero. Amen

"Who, when he came, and had seen the grace of God, was glad, and exhorted them all, that with purpose of heart they would cleave unto the Lord." Acts 11:23

In Acts, we learn of a man named Joses. He was a Levite from Cyprus. He sold some land, then brought the money and laid it at the apostles' feet. The apostles gave him the surname Barnabas, which means "the son of consolation (or encouragement)." He was a good man who was full of the Holy Ghost and of faith.

After Stephen was martyred, believers were persecuted and were scattered abroad. Saul had been one who persecuted believers. We know the account of Saul's conversion on the road to Damascus. Needless to say, when the apostles heard of the conversion, they were skeptical. But Barnabas took Saul, now Paul, to the apostles and vouched for his sincerity.

Later, they sent Barnabas to Antioch to seek Saul. For one full year, Barnabas and Saul stayed in Antioch teaching about the Lord. Many people became believers as a result of their ministry. Barnabas went on missionary journeys with Paul. He interceded for John Mark and befriended him when Paul refused to take John Mark with them on one of the journeys.

You can see from these accounts how Barnabas was an encourager. He was there to lend a helping hand for the apostles, he supported Paul and he took John Mark with him on a mission trip. All of us need an encourager in our lives. All of us need to encourage others as well.

Thinking of Barnabas reminded me of my granddaughter Jada. She loves to swing in our backyard, but I have to give her a little push to get her started. Sometimes, others need a little push to get them moving. Let's try to be a Barnabas to someone today. Encourage someone by giving them a little "push" in the right direction.

Lord, help me to be an encourager. Use me to gently push someone forward in their walk with You. Amen

"For we are labourers together with God: ye are God's husbandry, ye are God's building." I Corinthians 3:9

In 2010, Kevin had some problems with his truck. I can't remember just what had happened, but I do know it was going to take some time to get it fixed. Meanwhile, he needed a mode of transportation. Justin was working as a car salesman at the time, and he brought home a very inexpensive car that Kevin could drive until he had his truck going again.

As you might expect, the car needed to be cleaned thoroughly and needed some things adjusted or repaired. George, Kevin and Justin all pitched in to get the car shined and running smoothly. It was so nice to see them working together on this family project.

Paul told the Corinthians we are workers together with God. In other words, we are His partners. It is our job on this earth to be God's hands and feet, so to speak. We are a part of His building and we are to work so others come to realize they need to be a part of it as well. We are to use the skills and talents God has given us to build up His kingdom and support His followers.

As we work for the Lord, we should not strive to gain any glory for ourselves. This is a team effort. Unlike James and John (Matthew 20: 20-24), we must not seek the highest positions, but humbly do what the Lord asks of us as individuals. We must leave the line-up to Him.

Working together divides the labor and no one is overwhelmed with the tasks. As we work together, we can accomplish so much more than one person could do alone. Are you part of the workforce today? Be a laborer together with God.

Lord, I want to labor for You. Help me do my part without grumbling or seeking the glory for myself. Amen

AUGUST

AUGUST 1st *TYLER'S BURN*

"And at the ninth hour Jesus cried with a loud voice, saying, Eloi, Eloi, la-ma sa-bach-tha-ni? Which is, being interpreted, My God, my God, why hast thou forsaken me?" Mark 15:34

Our grandson Tyler has been involved in many accidents. When he was about two, he pulled the birdbath over on himself. He has cut his head, broken his bones, had his hand closed up in the car door and suffered many scrapes and bruises from various injuries. He has also been the victim of a couple of serious burns.

Several years ago, Tyler burned his calf on the muffler of a motorcycle. It fell my lot to take him to the doctor a few days later for debridement of the wound. Debridement is the removing of dead tissue from burns and other wounds to speed the healing process. The doctor took a brush, like you might use to clean vegetables, and scrubbed the wound. OUCH!

I know it may have been necessary, to keep Tyler from getting an infection, but watching the process was too painful for me. I had to turn away. Tyler was crying out as his doctor worked vigorously on the leg, but the doctor was oblivious to Tyler's cries. Thankfully, after a time, the wound healed completely.

As Jesus was dying on the cross, He cried out to the Father. Bible scholars say the Father turned his back on Jesus just long enough for Him to pay the penalty for our sins. The crucifixion was painful for our Lord, but completely necessary for our healing. Had the Father not allowed the suffering of His Son, we would all be doomed.

Isaiah tells us, "But he was wounded for our transgressions, he was bruised for our iniquities: the chastisement of our peace was upon him; and with his stripes we are healed (53:5)." Healing sometimes involves pain, but, in time, we are thankful for the result.

Father, thank You for turning away while Jesus died for me. Thank You, Jesus, for enduring the cross that I might have eternal life. Amen

AUGUST 2nd *JUDGING THE JOURNEY*

"And he said, Let us take our journey, and let us go, and I will go before thee." Genesis 33:12

In 2011, I decided to join a book club at the library. The staff selected a book for the members to read; then we would meet and discuss the selection. One month, the book chosen for us was *Eat, Pray, Love.* I will just say I did not like the book nor approve of it at all. Most of America disagreed with me I guess, as the book stayed on the *New York Times* bestseller list for 187 weeks!

One woman berated me for judging the author's spiritual journey. I told her I wasn't trying to "judge," but I was simply talking about it based on what the Bible says. I was trying to state the Biblical truths in a Christ-like way with wisdom and meekness, but I think I failed.

I think I came away from the meeting being labeled an ultra-conservative wacko! Sometimes, it is difficult and unpopular to stand up for what we know to be right. People with other beliefs do not want to listen to the gospel. That is, they do not want to listen until the Holy Spirit woos them and convicts them of their sin.

Until that time, we must continue to be a witness for our Lord in all situations. We never know when the Spirit may be working on the other party. Or on someone else who may be listening to the conversation.

In the book of Genesis, the verse above was part of a conversation between Jacob and his older brother Esau. Esau offered to go before Jacob to lead the way back to their homeland. Going ahead also meant he would provide protection for Jacob's family and flocks. Jacob declined the offer.

Others may also decline our effort to lead them in the right way. All we can do is offer them the truth and leave the results in God's hands. He promised His word would not return to Him void, but would accomplish His purpose wherever He sends it. So, keep spreading the Good News on every journey you take. Taste and see the Lord is good. Pray often. Love everyone. That is the way to a well balanced life.

Jesus, help me be bold enough to share Your truths with others even if those truths are not well received. Amen

AUGUST 3rd *AUNT VIOLA'S LAMP*

"Thy word is a lamp unto my feet, and a light unto my path."
Psalm 119:105

My paternal grandmother came from a large family. There were eight children, six girls and two boys. My Aunt Viola was the baby of the family. For a good number of my years, we lived on Hitt Road, just up the hill from her house on Buford Dam Road.

Aunt Viola was the "fun" aunt. I loved all my aunts dearly and they all had their own special qualities, but I always thought of her as the one for fun. I loved to see her smile and hear her laugh.

She liked to fish, although I didn't. She liked to go places. She was a great cook, as were all her sisters. She had a beautiful alto voice and I loved sitting near her in the church services and trying to sing along with her. My grandmother did not sing, she whistled. (But not in church!)

After my aunt passed away, some of her things were donated to a local charity. I happened to see an old Bible among some items and I picked it up to look at it. When I opened it, the name inside was none other than my aunt's! I asked the lady in charge if I could make a donation and take the Bible. She said I could have it, no money required.

What a treasure! I wondered how many hours my aunt had spent pouring over the pages of this Bible. I wondered what her favorite passages were. I wondered who, other than Jesus, her favorite Bible hero might have been. She did not mark in her Bible as I do. I guess most people of her generation thought that was disrespectful. But, I know she read this Bible for it was well worn.

In Psalm 119, the writer tells us the Word is a lamp for his feet and a light for his path. A light will show us where our feet must go so that we do not stumble and fall. A lamp will not shine into the distance to light up the entire pathway, but it will give us just enough light for the step we are taking.

We must trust God day by day, step by step. We know Jesus will return one day and call up all the saved to meet Him in the air. We do not know all that will transpire until that time, so we have to be guided by the Word all along the journey.

Is your Bible being used as a lamp and a light? I know Aunt Viola's was. Or is yours a dust collector? I urge everyone to make daily Bible reading a priority. Don't stumble over Satan's snares and fall into sin. Use the light you have available!

God, I am so grateful for the lamp You gave me to light my path. Amen

"And no marvel; for Satan himself is transformed into an angel of light." II Corinthians 11:14

The Lady's Slipper is a wildflower that belongs to the orchid family. I had never seen one until we moved to Hulsey Road back in the eighties. We found one growing at the edge of our property. My Aunt Polly lived next door. Being somewhat of an expert with plants, we asked her about this unusual looking flower. She dug it up and took it home with her to replant it. Whether the Lady's Slipper lived, I just can't recall.

I do remember when our friend, a Georgia Certified Nurseryman, found an unusual flower in the mountains. He dug around it carefully to make certain he had a good root ball. He gingerly placed the flower in a bucket to transport it home. He made certain he did not touch the plant itself. When he got the bucket out of the vehicle, he discovered the flower was artificial!

Our friend was deceived by the beauty of an a fake flower. In spite of his training in identifying various varieties of plants, he was duped! In the same manner, we can easily become fooled by our archenemy Satan if we are not careful.

The Bible tells us Satan makes himself look appealing by disguising himself as an angel of light. He makes himself look good so as to hide the dark and sinful consequences of choosing him. Even if we are well-trained in Christian beliefs and behaviors, we still must be on guard constantly so that we do not fall for Satan's shenanigans.

The Marlboro man made smoking look so cool, but the ads failed to reveal the lung problems that resulted from the habit. The alcohol ads make drinking seem like so much fun, but they fail to show the DUI arrests, the accidents or the cirrhoses of the livers that may follow. Our music, movies and magazines promote illicit sexual encounters, but fail to mention the STDs, the unplanned pregnancies or the divorces that are sure to follow. These are just a few examples.

Don't be deceived. Know the truth. Resist the devil and he will flee from you. Draw nigh to God and He will draw nigh to you. Remember Jesus rebuffed Satan with the Word. Hide the Word in your heart so you do not sin against God. The Bible says to try the spirits to see if they are of God. We can win against this angel of light by the power within us. Let's use this power today and every day!

Lord, help me resist Satan. Help me be on guard so that I do not fall for his lies. Help me try the spirits and follow only the Holy Spirit. Amen

AUGUST 5th *POISONED BERRIES*

"The night is far spent, the day is at hand: let us therefore cast off the works of darkness, and let us put on the armour of light."
Romans 13:12

The late Arthur Gordon of Savannah, Georgia, was a writer for the *Guideposts* magazine. He once shared a conversation he had with an old psychiatrist named Smiley Blanton. Arthur had heard people say if a mockingbird was caged, another mockingbird would come and feed the caged bird a poisoned berry to put it out of its misery. He asked Dr. Blanton if he believed the story.

The psychiatrist said he did not. But he said he had many patients who feed themselves poisoned berries! He said they keep anger, hatred, jealousy, self-pity and self-doubt locked inside. Then they wonder why they are sick.

I have been guilty of feeding myself a steady diet of poisoned berries. The berries of anger and hatred are not my favorites, but the other three I usually find pretty tasty. I have to continually remind myself these berries are from the devil, not from God. They are like the poisoned apple the queen, disguised as an old woman, tried to feed Snow White.

Every year, George has an annual physical and wellness exam by Dr. Mize. There is a questionnaire we fill out before the visit. As I was going through the questions recently, I was glad I was marking George's answers and not mine. The questions were about feelings of inferiority, worthlessness, self-blame, etc. I have also eaten my share of these poisoned berries.

In the book of Romans, Paul tells us to cast off the works of darkness. In other words, not only must we change our behavior, we must also change our diet! It is time to feed on the truth God has given us. We are loved by Him. He rejoices over us with singing. All these doom and gloom feelings have no place in the minds of God's children. He is our constant and faithful companion. Everything He has promised will be done for us.

If you are anything like me, we must stop eating the poisoned berries. They may have been a staple in our diet for years, but we must make some lifestyle changes. Believe God and not the enemy. In Colossians 1:13, we learn God has delivered us from the power of darkness and translated us into the kingdom of His dear Son.

Begin today. Throw away all the poisoned berries and begin to eat a healthy diet of God's divine truths. You and I will both feel a lot better. Guaranteed!

Father, forgive me for eating poisoned berries that rob my soul of Your joy. Help me resist when they are on the daily menu. Amen

AUGUST 6th *THE COMPASS*

"O send out thy light and thy truth: let them lead me; let them bring me unto thy holy hill, and to thy tabernacles." Psalm 43:3

A compass is an instrument used for showing directions by using a needle which points to the North Magnetic Pole. Whatever that means! I have never learned to use a compass. Give me a map and I can find my way to almost anywhere, but leave the compass to the Boy Scouts, sailors or soldiers.

I have read the compass was used by the Chinese as early as the second century B.C. It was used for navigation by the eleventh century A. D. It is a tool that has been around for many, many years and has been very helpful. However, I do not understand how it works. The only thing I know about a compass is this: it will not move if I am standing still.

God is like the compass and the Holy Spirit is like the needle which will point us in the right direction. He wants to lead us. But as long as we are standing still, we cannot make any progress. We must begin! When we step out in faith, God will show us the way. He will direct our steps.

The writer of the 43rd Psalm asks God to send out His light and His truth and let them bring him to God's holy hill. He recognized his need for guidance, as do I. Even though I cannot read a magnetic compass, I do know how to read God's word. Without His truth and His light, I would be hopelessly lost.

The book of James tells us to draw nigh to God and He will draw nigh to us. We won't get any closer to God by standing still. Let's get moving!

Lord Jesus, You are my True North. Help me to step out and move toward You. Amen

AUGUST 7th *BEEN THERE, DONE THAT*

"Forasmuch as ye are manifestly declared to be the epistle of Christ ministered by us, written not with ink, but with the Spirit of the living God; not in tables of stone, but in fleshy tables of the heart."
II Corinthians 3:3

I am sure you have heard the expression, "Been there, done that." It has been a popular saying since the seventies or eighties. It is usually meant in a negative sort of way, as in boredom with the conversation or topic of discussion. Later the phrase became, "Been there, done that, got the T-shirt."

I have shared time and again about my love of books. When I read, I feel I have been there and done that. I walked across America with Peter Jenkins. I visited China with Pearl S. Buck, I hid from the Germans with Anne Frank and I survived life in a concentration camp with Corrie ten Boom. In no way were the adventures boring. Quite the opposite.

Better still, I have parted the Red Sea with Moses, I have crossed the Jordan River with Joshua, I have fought Goliath with David. As Queen Esther, I saved my people from Haman. I walked along the shores of the Sea of Galilee with Jesus and the disciples, I saw the water turned to wine, I watched as He healed the sick and made blinded eyes to see.

And then, I was part of the crowd who demanded his crucifixion. I followed Peter and John to the tomb. I was there when Thomas knew, without a doubt, Jesus was the risen Lord. I was on the road to Damascus when Saul encountered Jesus. I sat on the Isle of Patmos with John as he received the revelation.

Yes, I feel I have shared all this because of the books I have read. The Bible is by far the best because its truths are for eternity. Its truths, preached by followers of the Lord, made me realize I needed my life changed by accepting Jesus as my Savior. As I read and studied its truths, and put them into practice, I became a different person. When my life began to reflect the characteristics of Jesus, I became a living "book" that others could read. My life is written by the Spirit of God.

No, I did not get the T-shirt, but I did get a robe of white which I will wear one day when I meet Jesus!

Lord God, my life is a book others are reading every day. Let it be a book which inspires them and makes them want to follow You, too. Thank You for the Spirit who convicts and the Son who saves. Amen

AUGUST 8th *THE HAIRCUT*

"Howbeit the hair of his head began to grow again after he was shaven." Judges 16:22

For many, many years, my mother got her hair done at Sandra's Beauty Shop. Sandra Williams owned and operated the little shop next to her home on Buford Dam Road. My mother was not one who wanted her hair blown dry, she preferred to have it rolled with curlers and then to sit under the old-style hood dryer.

When Sandra retired, my mother had no interest in finding another beautician. She stays in the house almost all the time, much of that time in bed, so her philosophy was, why bother? My grandson Jake said she was beginning to look like Einstein! So, George and I took her to the Great Clips near her home. A stylist named Robyn worked to make Mom look so much better! Then, like Samson's, her hair began to grow again!

Samson was the miracle child of Manoah and his wife. The angel of the Lord told the mother, "no rasor shall come on his head: for the child shall be a Nazarite unto God from the womb (Judges 13:5)." Later, Samson became a strong man who killed a lion with his bare hands and killed a thousand men with the jawbone of a donkey. He also took the doors of Gaza's city gate, and its posts, and walked away with them on his shoulders.

The Philistines enlisted the help of Delilah to determine the source of Samson's strength. He tricked her several times, but finally gave in and revealed his secret. He told Delilah, "if I be shaven, then my strength will go from me, and I shall become weak, and be like any other man (Judges 16:17)." Delilah called for a man and caused him to shave Samson's hair. Samson's strength left and the Philistines took him and put out his eyes. They put him to work in the prison house. But then his hair began to grow.

As the Philistines celebrated Samson's capture they offered a great sacrifice to Dagon, their god. They said Dagon had delivered Samson into their hands. They called for Samson's release from the prison so he could make sport, or entertain, for them. Samson asked to be allowed to feel the pillars of the house and lean on them. Then he prayed and asked God to strengthen him one more time and let him die with the enemies. He wanted revenge for the loss of his eyes.

He bowed himself with all his might, pulling down the house on the people inside. He killed more in this one feat than he had killed in his life. He did begin the work of rescuing Israel from the Philistines, even though he died without the deliverance being complete.

One haircut (or one failure) does not mean God will never use us again. One haircut (or one failure) does not mean God will close His ears to our prayers. When the razor (the enemy) comes upon our head, just remember to call on God.

Samson made many mistakes in his life, just as we all do. But God will use us for His purpose in spite of our failings. When our strength is used up, He will hear our prayer for more. He will be our strength.

Lord, when we have failed, when the enemy has prevailed against us, thank You for new growth, new strength to be an overcomer once again. Amen

AUGUST 9th *SOOTHING SOUP*

"Then Jacob gave Esau bread and pottage of lentils; and he did eat and drink, and rose up, and went his way:" Genesis 25:34

What is your favorite "comfort" food? Something that tastes just right when you feel bad? Something that soothes and warms you? Some favorites people have mentioned are chicken soup, macaroni and cheese or pancakes. I remember when potato soup comforted me.

George, my mother and I had gone to Texas to visit my aunt. The farther west we traveled, the worse I felt. We made a stop to get some over the counter meds, but I got no relief.

When we arrived at my aunt's house in Lufkin, I went to the back bedroom to lie down. I covered myself up, holding my tissues and moaning. My throat felt too swollen to swallow. Since I got no better after a couple of days, George took me to the emergency room of the local hospital.

That night, my mother cooked a big pot of old-fashioned potato soup. As I took a few bites, I could feel the warmth inside and it helped to relieve the pain. It was just a simple bowl of soup, but it did make me feel better.

Like so many times when God's word comforted me in times of pain, stress or uncertainty. Like the soup, God's word had soothed my soul and brought healing. Some of my favorite "comfort" verses are:

"I can do all things through Christ, which strengtheneth me (Philippians 4:13).

*"And we know that all things work together for good to them that love God, to them who are the called according to his purpose (*Romans 8:28).

*"The eternal God is thy refuge, and underneath are the everlasting arms: and he shall thrust out the enemy from before thee; and shall say, Destroy them (*Deuteronomy 33:27).

" ...for he hath said, I will never leave thee, nor forsake thee(Hebrews 13:5).

After "eating" and "drinking" from God's word, I am able to rise up and go my way, knowing God will do what He says. His word is certain and I can always depend on Him.

God, You are our Eternal Comforter. We need Your healing and Your help today. Amen

AUGUST 10ᵗʰ *THE FIRST DAY OF SCHOOL*

"But continue thou in the things which thou hast learned and hast been assured of, knowing of whom thou hast learned them;"
II Timothy 3:14

Most mothers dread the day they send their firstborn off to school. The child seems too little to go out into the world alone. The overly large backpack just intensifies the child's smallness. How will the child fare in a classroom full of strangers? Will he or she cry upon realizing Mommy is gone? What if he or she drops the lunch tray? Has an accident? Is made fun of or bullied?

Surely some of these thoughts were going through the mind of my friend Linda Stowers as she took her son Eddie to Cumming Elementary so many years ago. Surely she was thinking that their lives would never be the same, now that he was off to learn from someone who did not love him as she did! For at least twelve years that learning would continue to take her son away from her.

I say these thoughts must have been in her mind because she had not one, but two accidents that day! In the school parking lot, one of these accidents occurred when she backed into my aunt's car. When Bodie came out, Linda was crying and said, "I hope whoever owns this car is nice." My aunt replied, "That's my car!"

It is hard on mothers (and fathers) to release their children into the school system. I feel it is even harder sometimes to release them into the hands of our loving heavenly Father. We think we know what is best and we want to control their environment as much as we possibly can. But we don't know how He will use the circumstances of their lives for furthering His kingdom.

We must come to the realization that He loves them more than we ever could. He always knows what is best. He is always by their sides. He can cause even the worst situations to work together for good in their lives.

When we know these things and continue in them, we can rest assured our children are in good hands. There is no need to worry and fret. We must learn to trust Him with what is most precious to us.

Father God, as another school year begins, help all parents entrust their children to Your perfect care. Amen

AUGUST 11th SLOTHFULNESS

"By much slothfulness the building decayeth; and through idleness of the hands the house droppeth through." Ecclesiastes 10:18

I had a good friend years ago whose husband was not much of a handyman around the house. In fact, she had a leak at the kitchen sink which he failed to repair. Nor did he call in someone who could repair it. After a time, the water kept the cabinets so wet, they began to rot.

Being the take charge person that I am, I offered advice. I told her to call in a repairman herself! Maybe this is not the way a wife should respond. I am just saying it makes no sense to me to let the problem go unresolved until more and more damage is done.

The Bible is clear about slothfulness. God is in no way pleased with one who is slothful. For instance:

The hand of the diligent shall bear rule: but the slothful shall be under tribute. Proverbs 12:24

The slothful man roasteth not that which he took in hunting: but the substance of a diligent man is precious. Proverbs 12:27

The way of the slothful man is as an hedge of thorns: but the way of the righteous is made plain. Proverbs 15:19

He also that is slothful in his work is brother to him that is a great waster. Proverbs 18:9

His lord answered and said unto him, Thou wicked and slothful servant, thou knewest that I reap where I sowed not, and gather where I have not strawed: Matthew 25:26

Not slothful in business; fervent in spirit; serving the Lord; Romans 12:11

That ye be not slothful, but followers of them who through faith and patience inherit the promises. Hebrews 6:12

A slothful person is one who is unwilling to work or exert oneself. In other words, a lazy person. We should guard ourselves against having idle hands. Whether in our workplaces and homes on earth or in building up God's kingdom, let's be mindful to work so the "house" does not drop through. Let's get busy!

Lord, help me to guard against slothfulness. I do not want my hands to be idle, so I ask You to use them. Amen

AUGUST 12ᵗʰ   *GOD'S ANSWERS*

"And he gave them their request;" Psalm 106:15a

Jabez was a descendant of the tribe of Judah. Well, I believe he was. His name is listed smack dab in the middle of the listing of the descendents in I Chronicles, chapter 4. The Bible does not specify the name of the father of Jabez. Nor does it tell us the names of his brethren.

What it does tell us about Jabez is that he was more honorable than his brothers. What they did to be considered dishonorable, we do not know. The Bible tells us his mother named him Jabez because she bore him with sorrow. Whether that meant sorrow as in pain or sorrowful circumstances we do not know. And yet we know a great truth about this man.

I Chronicles 4:10, says, "And Jabez called on the God of Israel, saying, Oh that thou wouldest bless me indeed, and enlarge my coast, and that thine hand might be with me, and that thou wouldest keep me from evil, that it may not grieve me! And God granted him that which he requested."

The great truth is God heard the prayer of Jabez and granted his request. Jabez found favor with the Almighty God even though he was basically an unknown person. Jabez was very specific about what he asked of God and he asked for four different blessings. And God granted them all!

When we feel too small or unknown for God to hear us, we can recall Jabez and his prayer. God was intimately acquainted with him and was listening to his every word. Furthermore, God was willing to give him just what he asked.

Now, let's look at the remaining words of Psalm 106:15, "but God sent leanness into their soul." The writer of this Psalm tells us about the nation of Israel sinning repeatedly. They forgot God's works, they did not wait for His counsel, they lusted exceedingly in the wilderness and they tempted God in the desert. God listened when they prayed and gave them their request, but He sent leanness into their souls.

I had much rather be like Jabez, hadn't you? I want to be honorable before the Lord so that when my prayers are answered I do not also receive leanness in my soul. I want God's hand to be with me, not against me. Don't you?

Oh, Lord God, bless me indeed and keep me from evil. Amen

AUGUST 13th *SEEKING AND FINDING*

"And ye shall seek me, and find me, when ye shall search for me with all your heart." Jeremiah 29:13

My grandson Jake and I are experts when it comes to seeking and finding bugs. When he was a much younger boy, hunting bugs was one of our favorite things to do together.

George and I bought him one of those little bug-catching kits. You know the ones. They have a little net, a pair of tweezers and a vented bottle for holding the captured insects. Every day, weather permitting, Jake and I would go outside and begin our search.

We would dig in the dirt, turn over rocks, move pieces of wood or look in corners of the carport. We found ants, worms, spiders, ladybugs, centipedes, stinkbugs, grasshoppers, aphids, June bugs and grubs, to name a few. I know all these aren't actually "insects" but to Jake it didn't matter. He searched with his whole heart for something to put inside his collection bottle.

God said we should search for Him with all our heart. He promised when we do seek Him, we will find Him. Unlike some of the elusive insects, the Lord is not hard to find. Our hearts are the collection bottles for Him. In fact, He is the only One that fits the space exactly. Once inside, He will never try to escape. When we invite Him in, He takes up residence permanently. He will never fly away and leave us.

Please understand I am not attempting to compare God with an insect. My point is the searching and finding. Isaiah wrote, "Seek ye the Lord while he may be found, call ye upon him while he is near (55:6)." Jesus said, "Ask and it shall be given you; seek, and ye shall find; knock, and it shall be opened unto you (Matthew 7:7)." James wrote, "Draw nigh to God and he will draw nigh to you (4:8a)."

God wants to be found. He is just waiting for us to do the seeking. It is my heart's desire that everyone would seek Him today and call upon His name. Don't delay!

Lord, I am so thankful You are eager to be found by anyone who will seek You. Amen

AUGUST 14th *DEATH OF A DEMON*

"But the Lord your God ye shall fear; and he shall deliver you out of the hand of all your enemies." II Kings 17:39

If you were to ask baby-boomers where they were on November 22, 1963, I imagine most of them would know. They would know because that is the day President John F. Kennedy was assassinated in Dallas, Texas. If you asked where they were or what they were doing on July 20, 1969, they would know because that is the date Neil Armstrong walked on the moon.

Baby-boomers and their parents, Generation X and Generation Y could tell you where they were and what they were doing on the morning of September 11, 2001. You recall that is the day the twin towers of the World Trade Center in New York City were destroyed, the Pentagon was hit and a plane was crashed in a field in Pennsylvania. The master-mind behind the attacks was Osama bin Laden, founder of al-Qaeda.

For almost ten years, the United States' military had attempted to locate this demon. On Sunday night, May 1, 2011, I was in bed, groggy from taking a Benadryl for my allergies, when the ringing of the phone got my attention. It was our son Justin calling to tell us Osama bin Laden was dead!

George and I were in disbelief. We immediately flipped on the news to catch the reports. We were glued to the television set until 1:30 in the morning. However, Justin, who was in New York City at the time with his friend Adam Jones, joined the crowd down at Ground Zero. The news showed the throngs of jubilant people shouting, "USA! USA!" These revelers were also waving flags and at times singing patriotic songs.

Even though this villain is dead, the evil lives on. At the time of this writing, turmoil is taking place across America, in Turkey, in Nice, France and other locations. The devil is alive and well. He is using anyone he possibly can to steal, kill and destroy.

One day, though, we will be delivered from this enemy as well. One day, the devil will be cast into the lake of fire and tormented day and night forever and ever (Revelation 20:10). Then there will be no more sin, no more death, no more destruction nor anything that can harm or cause pain.

On that day all believers will be gathered around the throne of God. Like the New York crowds, we will all be shouting and singing. However, we will not be shouting "USA!" We will be shouting "Glory to the Lamb!" That will be the greatest gathering of jubilant people ever assembled. Will you be there?

Lord Jesus, even so, come quickly and deliver us from our enemy. Amen

"And he said, What pledge shall I give thee? And she said, Thy signet, and thy bracelets, and thy staff that is in thine hand." Genesis 38:18

The engagement ring is given at the time of a marriage proposal. It is worn by the bride-to-be to signify to the world she is taken and is committed to her partner. In our culture, it is worn on the third finger of the left hand. This custom came about because, supposedly, the Vena Amoris, or vein of love, is located in that finger and it leads straight to the heart.

Currently, there are television ads about purchasing engagement rings at various jewelry stores. One says, "He went to Jared's." One says "Every kiss begins with Kay." Most engagement rings contain at least one diamond. Most girls feel the bigger the diamond, the better. But, when George proposed to me, the carat weight of the diamond was of no concern to me.

George bought my ring at the Shane Company, which is the largest privately owned jeweler in the United States. One of their stores was conveniently located near my office in downtown Atlanta. On this date in 1976, George picked up my ring from that store. I wore it as a symbol of my love and devotion to him.

Thinking of an engagement ring brought to mind my commitment to the Lord Jesus. He has my love and my devotion. I want nothing more than to be faithful to Him. Yet, I have no outward symbol that I belong to Him. Sure, I can and do wear the Christian t-shirts. I have worn my WWJD bracelet. I have had the bumper sticker or tag on my car. But, can these things be trusted to prove I am His?

Being faithful to the Lord has to be an inward quality before the outward symbols mean anything. I must have the fruit of the Spirit in me for my behavior to be something more than self-discipline. Anyone can "act" righteously for a time, but to BE righteous is a work of the Spirit.

Just having the ring on my finger did not automatically make me a loyal, loving fiancé for George. I had to prove myself every day by my behavior. Every day, by my walk, I am trying to "prove" to the world I am a loyal, loving, faithful follower of the Lord Jesus. He has not given me a ring to wear, but He has a robe and a crown ready for me!

Lord Jesus, I want everyone to know I am Your chosen one and I am dearly loved by You. I want to be faithful so the world knows I am serious about my commitment to You as well. Amen

AUGUST 16th *THE WALKING CANE*

"Thus saith the Lord of hosts; There shall yet old men and old women dwell in the streets of Jerusalem, and every man with his staff in his hand for very age." Zechariah 8:4

George has used a walking cane for quite some time. Due to his Parkinson's disease he needs one to help him keep his balance. He has several different models. He purchased some of them and others were given to him as gifts. In May of last year, he was surprised with a new addition to his collection.

When we had some trees taken down in our backyard, we had a dumpster delivered for hauling the logs away. The truck driver who came to pick up the dumpster was a man I had known for ages, but George wasn't acquainted with him. Dennis and George had a lengthy conversation. They talked about everything from John Wayne to Jesus.

Weeks later, George received a call from Dennis. He wanted to come over because he had something he wanted to give George. We could not imagine what in the world it could be. As it turned out, Dennis had carved a walking stick for George out of a piece of wood he'd had lying around for five years!

He told us every time he had picked up the piece of wood intending to make something out of it, it just did not seem "right." However, after talking with George he knew he had to make a walking cane for George out of it.

He recounted to us part of the conversation he'd had with George on his previous stop here. Dennis said he had left here literally crying because George had witnessed to him about Jesus. Dennis said in spite of his health issues George is better off than he is himself because George has a closer walk with the Lord. So, Dennis made the walking stick to reflect George's faith as well as his own.

At the top of the stick, at the end of the handle, he carved the name "Jesus" and made three crosses with little "rays of light" radiating out from there. He carved SAMS about halfway down the stick and then put his initials at the very bottom. Dennis said he wanted Jesus to be at the highest point and he wanted to be at the lowest.

Then he told us about a real estate deal that had worked out perfectly for him after he started carving the cane for George. So, God worked things out for both of them! George has a new cane that is a great witnessing tool and Dennis was able to purchase the property he wanted. Being obedient brings blessings.

When we talk about the Lord in everyday conversation He will honor us in some way. Whether the person being spoken to is an old friend or a stranger, talk about what Jesus has done for *you*. This stick story is just one small example of how your words may touch someone's life. Let's talk about Jesus!

Jesus, I want to be willing to share what You have done for me and how You have worked in my life. Help me be obedient to the gentle nudges of the Holy Spirit, I pray. Amen

AUGUST 17th *POKEMON GO!*

"Order my steps in thy word: and let not any iniquity have dominion over me." Psalm 119:133

Thirteen months ago, Pokemon Go was released in most regions of the world. It is a location-based mobile game for Android and iOS devices. Pokemon Go allows players to capture, train and battle virtual creatures called Pokemon. They appear on the screen as though in the real world. Apple said for an app in its first week of release, it was the most downloaded one ever! After two weeks, thirty million people worldwide had downloaded it.

However, Pokemon Go has caused much havoc for people who play. It seemed every night the news was reporting accidents involving players who had walked into traffic while engrossed in the game. Or, because the player was staring down at the screen and not being attentive to the surroundings, the player was the victim of some crime!

I have seen groups of people in Cumming who appeared to be searching for Pokemon. They were walking around, looking down at their phones, at what I supposed was either a Pokestop or a Pokemon gym. If a Pokemon is captured, the player is awarded either candies or stardust!

I confess I have never played the game. I most likely never will. I have too many other things I'd rather do. I have too many real-life battles to fight, as well! And, as I do not own an Android device, my opportunities to play are severely limited!

I thought of how many people are hooked on the game. I thought of how much better it would be if thirty million people downloaded a copy of the Bible and walked around reading it instead. Please do not get me wrong. I am not condemning anyone who does play. Not at all.

I am just thinking of all the steps that could be ordered in the word of God. Wouldn't it be wonderful if a revival swept through the world and thirty million people accepted Jesus as their Savior? If the Bible were downloaded, the user would find all the tools necessary to battle the enemy of our souls. Also, there would be ways to train ourselves to do God's will and ways to bring every thought captive in obedience to Christ. Our reward for following Christ is more substantial than candies or stardust. We gain eternal life!

If you are playing Pokemon Go, I hope you reach the highest level! If you are not reading the Bible as well, I hope you will download one and reach the highest level awarded to a believer: the opportunity to spend eternity with Christ.

Lord, order my steps in Thy word and let not any iniquity have dominion over me. Amen

AUGUST 18th *PLAYING CHESS*

"The Lord shewed me, and, behold, two baskets of figs were set before the temple of the Lord, after that Nebuchadrezzar king of Babylon had carried away captive Jeconiah the son of Jehoiakim king of Judah, and the princes of Judah, with the carpenters and smiths, from Jerusalem, and had brought them to Babylon." Jeremiah 24:1

When my grandson Jake was eight years old, I taught him to play chess. I am not an expert chess player by any means, but I know how the game is played. The object is to checkmate the other player's king. You back him into a corner, so to speak, so that he can be captured no matter which way he tries to move.

Jake quickly picked up how each chess piece is allowed to move. He understands the object of the game completely. However, neither one of us are great strategists. Neither one of us likes to sit and stare at the board planning what might happen if we move any piece a certain way. Our games do not last very long. An eight year old does not have a very long attention span. Neither does a Grandmom!

But, I have been thinking of all the kings in the Bible who were checkmated. Many were killed, many had their eyes gouged out and many were carried away captive. Like Jeconiah, king of Judah.

God's prophet Jeremiah warned the people of Judah of the upcoming invasion by Babylon, but they would not heed his warning. They refused to repent and worship God alone. Jeremiah's words came true when King Nebuchadnezzar invaded the land three different times. The king of Judah turned to Egypt for help, but Egypt could not deliver them. Judah faced a seventy year exile from their homeland because of their disobedience and idolatry. And yet, God promised them a restoration.

Do you realize God still works in the same way today? Even though we may have Jesus as our Savior, we will still sin and face the unwelcome but not unwarranted consequences. When we confess our sin and turn from it, God will forgive us and cleanse us of all our unrighteousness (I John 1:9).

Our opponent in the chess game of life is the devil. He follows us around the "board" in his attempt to capture us. It is comforting to know he cannot ever say, "Checkmate," because we have God to rescue us. When it seems there is no way out of any given situation, all we have to do is call on God. He will deliver us and restore us if we but ask.

Father God, I thank You that the devil has no authority over me and his limited power is only what I allow him to have. Help me to see his every move and call on your name when I need to be rescued. Amen

AUGUST 19th *CATCHING WITH CANDY*

"Then did I eat it; and it was in my mouth as honey for sweetness."
Ezekiel 3:3b

George thoroughly enjoys taking Jake to fish in a friend's private lake. They catch bass, bluegills and catfish. They use various kinds of bait, including artificial lures. It seems the fish especially enjoy the dough balls made out of whole wheat hot dog buns! There is just no accounting for taste, right?

Not too long ago, I had dropped the guys off at the lake and I left to take my mother to see a friend. I had packed a cooler with water and snacks for them in case they got hungry before I returned. Jake, who often casts a little too aggressively, sometimes loses his dough ball off the hook before it hits the water. When he was out of bread, he began to fish with his snacks!

Instead of a fish, he caught a snapping turtle using a miniature Snickers bar! About the time he got the turtle on the bank, it let go of the candy and fell onto the grass! Jake made a hasty retreat!

I am sure you've heard a person can catch more flies with honey than vinegar. Jake and George found out you can catch more turtles with candy! Like Ezekiel, Mr. Turtle took a nibble and found the candy as honey for sweetness. But what did Ezekiel mean?

Ezekiel was a priest who was in captivity in Babylon. While he was among the captives by the river Chebar, the heavens were opened and he saw visions of God. One vision was of a hand holding a roll (or scroll) of a book. He was commanded to eat the roll and go speak to the house of Israel. He ate the roll and its taste was as honey.

The Bible tells us the roll Ezekiel ate had lamentations, mournings and woes written on the outside. God's words are sometimes words of condemnation of sin and judgment, but the sweetness comes from the fact Jesus is willing to forgive us when we ask. There is sweetness in spite of the bitterness because God promises us hope and restoration.

His words will make us stronger in our faith. When our pastor, Terry Cowart, charged the candidates after their baptizing his chief instruction to them was to read their Bibles daily. We won't know what all God has done for us, we won't know what He expects of us and we won't know how to overcome the enemy if we don't ingest the word!

Let God's word bring sweetness to your soul today. Don't be like Mr. Turtle, though. Don't let go of the goodness.

Father, my prayer is that all would taste and see that You are good. Amen

AUGUST 20th *PARADISE*

"And Jesus said unto him, Verily I say unto thee, Today shalt thou be with me in paradise." Luke 23:43

Paradise is a place of great beauty or one of great happiness. People tend to think of some tropical beach location as paradise. People say Hawaii is paradise. I agree, because it is a place of great beauty *and* great happiness. At least it was for us. When I think back to our trip there with our son Kevin and my brother Randy, I think of some things that reminded me of Bible verses.

When we went to a luau, Randy and Kevin were selected to come up and dance with the hula girls. They were told to "inhale the spirit of the girls." I don't know about that, but I do know "All scripture is given by inspiration of God, and is profitable for doctrine, for reproof, for correction, for instruction in righteousness (II Timothy 3:16)." In other words, all scripture is God-breathed!

When we went to visit the Pearl Harbor Memorial, we discovered we could have thrown our leis into the water over the *USS Arizona.* But we were not prepared. We did not bring them with us. Like the foolish virgins in Matthew, chapter 25. They brought their lamps, but had no oil in them. While they went to purchase oil, the bridegroom came, the door was shut and the foolish virgins were locked out.

Then there was the day we hiked to the top of Diamond Head. We thought it was closer to our hotel than it was. We started out walking but soon discovered it was too far away. We caught a ride with a good Samaritan, but not before we had almost croaked. This reminded me of what Jesus said about building a tower. He asked, "which of you, intending to build a tower sitteth not down first, and counteth the cost, whether he have sufficient to finish it (Luke 14:28)." We should have calculated the distance before we began the journey.

Yes, Hawaii was definitely a paradise. We thoroughly enjoyed it. We ate shaved ice at Matsumoto's, Kevin dived into the ocean from a huge rock at the North Shore, we visited Volcanoes National Park and the Dole pineapple plantation as well as many other fun places. But this earthly paradise is nothing compared to the Paradise Jesus talked about with the thief on the cross.

We were able to go to Hawaii because we made plans in advance and budgeted for it. The only way we can gain entrance to the Paradise of God, however, is by having our sins washed away by the blood of the Lamb. It is imperative that we get prepared and ask Him to save us. We must also count the cost of serving the Lord so that we do not faint on the way. Furthermore, we must study the inspired word of God to show ourselves approved unto Him.

While the thief received his forgiveness when he was near death, I urge everyone to realize NOW is the day of salvation (II Corinthians 6:2). If you have not made your plans to go to Paradise, please don't delay any longer. Jesus will come back as a thief in the night. Make sure you have the oil in your lamp when He comes.

Jesus, I thank You for the assurance I will one day be with You in Paradise. Amen

AUGUST 21st *MOVING TO IDAHO*

"Casting all your care upon him; for he careth for you." I Peter 5:7

The black Mustang left our driveway that morning, pulling a small U-haul trailer behind it. Our oldest son Kevin was moving to Idaho to become a motorcycle mechanic with Desert Mountain Cycles in the town of Mountain Home. He had recently graduated at the top of his class from the Motorcycle Mechanics Institute in Orlando, Florida.

We had a going-away party with all the family the night before. George and I were up until midnight helping Kevin load his things into the trailer. We were happy for him as he set out on a new adventure, but we knew he had four days of hard driving ahead of him. Did I mention a distance of over twenty-one hundred miles would then separate us?

Twenty-one hundred miles in a small car.....alone. I could not help but think of all the possibilities. *He drives too fast and what if a tire blows out? What if he gets mugged at a rest stop? What will he do if something happens to the car? What if? What if?* All I could do was pray and entrust him to God

When Kevin called home, he told us he did not run out of gas even though he'd had a close call. The next day he told us of having to detour due to flooding along his planned route. Water was nearly up to some of the bridges, and he'd seen a barn floating by, but he was safe. When he finally reached Idaho, he was full of stories of how things had worked out better than expected.

He found a nice place to live that was less expensive than he had thought. The deposits for utilities were not as much as he was afraid they would be. He had turned in the U-haul trailer and had money left over! I praised God as I remembered and quoted Ephesians 3:20: "Now unto him that is able to do exceeding abundantly above all that we ask or think, according to the power that worketh in us."

Yes, God had watched over our son and done exceeding abundantly above all we had asked or thought. Unto Him be the glory throughout all ages, world without end (verse 21).

When we have cares, the thing to do is get out of the way and let God do His work. He cares for us and no burden is too heavy for Him.

Lord, when I am full of what-ifs, I ask You to remind me of Your care for me and of Your omnipotence to handle every situation. Amen

AUGUST 22nd *RESCUED BY UNCLE RALPH*

"Therefore whosoever heareth these sayings of mine, and doeth them, I will liken him unto a wise man, which built his house upon a rock: And the rain descended, and the floods came, and the winds blew, and beat upon that house; and it fell not: for it was founded upon a rock." Matthew 7:24, 25

When I was growing up, my cousin Gail Stanford was my best friend. We lived either near each other or beside each other most of our lives. We were also born on the same day! We shared so many fun times and memories as young girls. One day when we were about thirteen, we shared a storm and that was no fun at all!

Back in those simpler, safer times, we were allowed to ride our bicycles all over the hills and hollows around Roanoke Baptist Church. On this particular day we had ridden from Hitt Road over to see our friend Deborah who lived on Kemp Road.

After our visit, we began our trip home. The sky had turned ominously dark and a strong wind was blowing. The thunder rolled and the lightning streaked across the sky. Just about the time we reached the bottom of the hill at the cove below H. C. Williams' house, the deluge began. The rain was pelting us so hard, it felt like bees stinging us. We got off the bikes and began to push them up the hill on the other side. We were drenched and scared of being struck by lightning.

Just about that time, we saw the most welcome sight in the world! Our Uncle Ralph's station wagon stopped just ahead of us. He hopped out, told us to get in the car and he put our bikes in the back. Then he carried us both home. What a blessing!

At that time, I am not sure I even knew the parable Jesus told about building on a firm foundation. But now, when I read that passage, I can picture a storm like the one Gail and I were caught in so long ago. Jesus said the rain could come, along with the floods, and the wind could blow and beat upon the house, but if it is founded upon a rock, the house will remain standing. If the house is built on the sand, it will fall in the storm and come down with a great crash.

Jesus is saying just using His name doesn't make you known to Him. Just because you may have prophesied in His name, performed miracles or cast out demons in His name does not make you one of His. Those in this category are like the foolish builder who built on the sand. Those who listen to His teachings and obey them are wise, like the builder who built on a rock.

At first the "houses" may look the same, but when the storms of life beat and batter the structure, only the one with the solid foundation will survive. Let us practice obedience so we will never have to hear the Lord say, "Sorry. I never knew you."

Jesus, Help me through the storms of life. I want to obey You. I would not want to come crashing down and be eternally separated from You. Amen

AUGUST 23ʳᵈ *SAVORING SIN*

"Yet his meat in his bowels is turned, it is the gall of asps within him. Surely he shall not feel quietness in his belly, he shall not save of that which he desired." Job 20: 14. 20

Savor. A word which, when used as a verb, means to taste with pleasure. It means, when used as a noun, the taste or smell of something, a pleasing flavor or aroma.

243

Did you know March is National Nutrition Month and the theme last year was "Savor the Flavor of Eating Right"? Pizza Hut also used "Savor the Flavor" as its theme a couple of years ago.

Almost everyone I know eats quickly, especially my husband. He inhales his food. I, on the other hand, like to savor my food. I enjoy taking my time and letting the flavors linger on my tongue.

Food is not the only thing people savor. Sometimes we savor sin. We enjoy partaking of it. We know it is not pleasing to God, but as a former co-worker of mine once said, "It pleases me!" And it does for a while. We are quite content to continue in whatever sin we are engaged in at the time.

In the Bible, Job's friend Zophar, the Naamathite, spoke the words in chapter 20. Zophar was one of three friends who had come to comfort Job after the loss of his children and his possessions. Zophar used the illustration of savoring food to drive home his point about those who savor sin. In verses 12 through 14 he says, "Though wickedness be sweet in his mouth, though he hide it under his tongue; Though he spare it, and forsake it not; but keep it still within his mouth: Yet his meat in his bowels is turned, it is the gall of asps within him." In other words, that which tastes so good can become harmful inside us.

The *KJV Study Bible* says, "The image of eating expresses the idea of consuming life's pleasures and delicacies and enjoying them to the fullest." Yes, that is just what we do when we aren't walking as Jesus did. We are not only consuming sinful pleasures and enjoying them. we are putting ourselves in danger of being consumed by them.

Verse 15 says, "He hath swallowed down riches, and he shall vomit them up again: God shall cast them out of his belly." The Holy Spirit is, we might say, like an emetic that forces us to vomit that sin.

Rather than savoring sin, let us make savoring the things of the Spirit a top priority. Let us lay aside every weight and the sin which does so easily beset us.

Lord, help me to savor the things of the Spirit and put away sin. Amen

AUGUST 24th *LAMPS DON'T TALK*

"That ye may be blameless and harmless, the sons of God, without rebuke, in the midst of a crooked and perverse nation, among whom ye shine as lights in the world;" Philippians 2:15

Charles Haddon Spurgeon, England's best known Baptist minister, once wrote, "Lamps do not talk, but they do shine." He also said he would not give much for religion that could not be seen. Our actions should shine out our religion.

In his letter to the Philippians, Paul the apostle said they were to shine as lights in the world in the midst of a crooked and perverse nation. But, do you know what is just before that statement? It is an exhortation to do all things without murmurings and disputings. You might say without grumbling and arguing.

Not many of us can go through the day without doing a little of both. I know I am guilty. If nothing else, we grumble about the weather! If we are truthful with ourselves, we grumble about a lot more and never take a second thought about doing so.

Isn't that what the children of Israel were so guilty of as they made the exodus from Egypt and journeyed toward the Promised Land? They grumbled because they had no water, no meat, no garlic, no onions and no leeks. They grumbled against Moses and against God. Of course they needed water and food, but they did not depend on God to supply their needs. Instead, they wanted to return to Egypt.

In I Corinthians 10, Paul wrote about their grumbling and listed it, along with idolatry, sexual immorality and tempting God, as evils which resulted in destruction. If murmurings were serious to God then, don't you think they still are? Instead of grumbling and complaining, let us be the lamps that shine brightly for the Lord Jesus.

Jesus, every time I am tempted to complain help me remember my primary function. Remind me I am to be a lamp that shines for you. Amen

AUGUST 25th *HERE COMES THE JUDGE*

"Judge not, that ye be not judged." Matthew 7:1

Comedian Flip Wilson had some famous skits on his television show. One I liked was his "Here comes the judge." He certainly knew how to make us laugh.

People today, including me, often take on the role of a judge. But what does the Bible say about judging? Jesus himself spoke the words in Matthew 7:1. Don't do it!

Between customers in the Dove, my friend Kristi and I were able to talk about many things. Shortly after a school friend of mine killed himself, we had a heart to heart talk about things that bring us down. We talked in great length about things in the past that had negatively affected our lives. Later, Kristi gave me a big hug and said she had enjoyed talking to me because I'm not judgmental.

But, you know what? Too often I am judgmental. I look on others and base my opinions on things I can see from the outside. That is not where God looks. He looks on our hearts. Unless we know what the other person is dealing with, unless we have walked a mile in his shoes, we don't really know what makes him think or act a certain way.

I should be the last person in the world who would judge someone else. The reason? I have been judged by things I have said and done and I did not like it one bit. I am willing to guess everyone can relate to my feelings. I am willing to guess you have experienced this same judging at some point in your life.

Usually, the things we condemn others for are the very same ones we have done ourselves. The things we dislike about ourselves are the very things we think others should change.

Several years ago, the late Michael Jackson recorded the song, "The Man in the Mirror." The lyrics tell us we can make the world a better place by starting with the man in the mirror. Jackson sang, *I'm asking him to change his ways. No message could have been any clearer, If you want to make the world a better place, Take a look at yourself and make a change.*

He was right, of course. No message could be clearer because it came directly from the Lord himself. If we do not judge, then we won't be judged. It all starts with the one we see in the mirror.

Lord Jesus, forgive me for judging. That is not my job, but Yours. Amen

"And the streets of the city shall be full of boys and girls playing in the streets thereof." Zechariah 8:5

When I was growing up in the vicinity of Roanoke Baptist Church, boys and girls literally could play in the streets. There was not much traffic at that time. Even if a car was traveling down the road, you could hear it coming from a mile away!

Almost all the children around the church were related. We did everything together. We played together, rode the bus together and went to church together. We were part of a close-knit community.

In the evenings after school, we gathered at someone's home to play basketball, baseball, football, kick the can, red rover or any game one of us could dream up. When we chose sides, I always liked to be on the team with my cousin Harold Hansard. He was a couple of years older than I and I looked up to him.

I can still picture us playing touch football in my grandmother's front yard. Most of the time, I got to be the quarterback and Harold would devise some play for us to execute. I remember he would whisper the details in my ear and I would try with all my might to do what he had said. Sometimes it worked, sometimes not. But he did not get mad at me. He'd just say, "Second down coming." Or third, or fourth.

When we were in high school, Harold dated one of my best friends. I was dating a guy Harold did not think was right for me. He let me know it, too! Then came the day he got drafted and was later shipped to Viet Nam. I prayed for him and wrote him letters while he was deployed to that war zone. What a blessing to see him arrive home.

All those days are far behind us now. We rarely get to see each other except when a family member passes on. Every time I do see him I think of all the fun times we had back then.

Every time I read this verse from Zechariah, I can picture young boys and girls playing in the streets as we did. Not a care on their minds. No worries about drive-by shootings or kidnappings. No thoughts of drug dealers trying to coax us into trying their wares.

Through the prophet Zechariah, God was telling His chosen people a new day was coming. He was bringing Judah home from captivity. Their nation would be restored. Jerusalem would be called a city of truth. Once again, there would be older men and women dwelling in

247

the streets. The youngsters would be safely playing. The people would be peaceful and prosperous. But God wanted more for them and from them. He wanted a renewed relationship with them. He would test them to see if they had learned the lesson. However, we know how that turned out.

As long as we are at home on this earth, there will be trouble, heartache and unrest. But God's plan of redemption and restoration has not changed. One day, He will usher in His glorious kingdom. One day, all evil will be put down forever. One day the Prince of Peace will give us eternal peace. I am just wondering if there will be children playing on the street of gold?

Jesus, I am awaiting the time when all believers will experience tranquility and prosperity in Your kingdom. Amen

AUGUST 27th *THE WHIPPING POST*

"Then released he Barabbas unto them: and when he had scourged Jesus, he delivered him to be crucified." Matthew 27:26

On August 7, 1969, at Atlantic Studios in New York City, The Allman Brothers Band recorded "Whipping Post." Gregg Allman wrote the lyrics on an ironing board cover because the lyrics came so fast, he had no time to get out the paper.

Gregg's song tells of loving someone who is doing him wrong. Because of this cruel treatment, he says he feels like he is tied to the whipping post and feels like he is dying. Every time I hear the title, I think of Jesus being scourged. While the song had nothing whatsoever to do with Jesus, there are some similarities.

Jesus also loves us in spite of our failure to love Him as we should. We do Him wrong by rejecting His love and embracing sin. I can't say for certain whether Jesus was tied to a post for His scourging, but in Mel Gibson's *The Passion of the Christ* Jesus was chained to one.

We know from history a scourging was extremely brutal. We know bits of bone or iron were tied into the leather cords at the end of the whip. Every time the whip came down, the flesh would be ripped apart. Surely this made Jesus feel like he was dying.

Whereas the narrator in the song *could* have walked away from his torturing relationship, Jesus was fully committed to giving his life for anyone who would accept Him. He not only endured the whipping post, He also willingly went to the cross and was crucified.

When I think of what the Savior endured, I wonder how anyone could say no to His offer of everlasting life.

Lord Jesus, thank You for suffering and dying in my stead. Amen

AUGUST 28th *PACK YOUR OWN CHUTE*

"For we must all appear before the judgment seat of Christ; that every one may receive the things done in his body, according to that he hath done, whether it be good or bad. " II Corinthians 5:10

When I was in my late twenties, I was promoted to Assistant Manager of the Claims Department at Coastal States Life Insurance Company in Atlanta. As part of my job, I was required to attend classes and watch training films to help me become a better manager. I have forgotten almost everything I learned in those classes, but one film still sticks in my mind. The title of it was "Pack Your Own Chute."

In the film, a lady was going sky-diving. We watched as she went through the training sessions. When it came time for her to see the parachute selection, the instructor had her to pack her own chute. In doing so, she would make certain it was done correctly because she knew her very life depended on it.

The purpose of the film was not to make a manager think he or she had to do everything, but rather to point out we had to be responsible for the decisions we made. We were not able to "pass the buck." Ultimately, the accountability landed squarely on our shoulders. As the sign on former president Harry Truman's desk said, "The buck stops here."

It is the same principle with Christianity. Each one of us has to take the responsibility for accepting or refusing Jesus. If we choose to follow the devil instead, we cannot blame our parents, our spouses, our friends or anyone else. It is a personal choice.

Jesus comes to an individual and offers Himself as the way to eternal life. Each individual has the opportunity to pack his own chute because his very life depends on his decision. The Bible says, "There is none other name under heaven given among men, whereby we must be saved (Acts 4:12)." We can bail out of hell by accepting Jesus or we can free fall all the way down with the devil. How have you packed your chute?

Jesus, You are my parachute because You are holding me up for eternity. I am so thankful I had the opportunity to make a decision to follow You. Amen

AUGUST 29th *BRAVING THE LOSING SEASONS*

"And God shall wipe away all tears from their eyes; and there shall be no more death, neither sorrow, nor crying, neither shall there be any more pain: for the former things are passed away." Revelation 21:4

Currently there are four active NFL teams that have never appeared in a Super Bowl game: the Detroit Lions, the Jacksonville Jaguars, the Houston Texans and the Cleveland Browns. I have read the Browns fans refer to their home stadium as the "Factory of Sadness."

I know my mother can relate to their disappointment. She has been a die-hard Atlanta Braves and Atlanta Falcons fan since both teams made their appearance in the capital city. The Braves were, at best, only a mediocre team from 1966 until 1991. Between 1970 and 1981, they only had two winning seasons! Yet she faithfully watched every game that she could on the television or listened to the play-by-play on WSB radio.

Likewise, the Falcons came to Atlanta and played their first season in 1966. They only won twelve games in the sixties! In 1999, the team played in the Super Bowl but lost. They'd had just four winning seasons in the twenty years prior to the 1998 season and only two in the nineties. Despite getting her hopes up several times, the Falcons always seemed to dash those hopes for greatness.

This world in which we live could also be called a "Factory of Sadness." There is a never-ending supply of disappointment. Whether caused by our own poor performance or by things beyond our control, heartache is around every bend.

And yet, we who are Christians have hope! Jesus promises to give us peace and joy. He knows we will have struggles as long as we are here, but His grace is sufficient for each one. Also, He has promised us the ultimate victory.

Nothing is too hard for the Lord. We may brave some losing seasons, but like the falcon, we should have great courage and fight! We are more than conquerors through Christ today and in all the seasons to come.

Jesus, thank You the ultimate victory is mine. Help me to keep pressing toward the goal. Amen

AUGUST 30th *SOME PEOPLE*

"O generation of vipers how can ye, being evil, speak good things? for out of the abundance of the heart the mouth speaketh." Matthew 12:34

"Some people come into our lives and quickly go. Some stay for awhile, leave footprints on our hearts, and we are never, ever the same." I'm sure most of us are familiar with this quote from artist and author, Flavia Weedn. We may have read the words countless times and yet never been aware of the woman who wrote them.

Mrs. Weedn passed away in 2015. In part, her obituary read; "Born not of money, prestige or finery, but of giving and gracious hearts. She had a unique way of embracing every moment as a miracle. She never forgot to thank God for small blessings. She understood there was no time to leave words unsaid."

I know many people like her and I am sure you do as well. First, there is my husband George. He was also born of giving and gracious hearts. He tells me multiple times every day how much he loves me and how special I am. I never tire of hearing those words!

I think of my wonderful friends and relatives who are quick to share their hearts by sending the perfect cards at the perfect times. The handwritten lines inside the cards are what make them "perfect."

Or, even if someone doesn't send many cards, but is always quick with an encouraging word, a smile or a compliment, you are well aware those come from an abundant heart.

However, Jesus wasn't complimenting the Pharisees when He spoke the words in today's verse. He was saying they were blaspheming the Holy Ghost because they said He cast out devils by the power of Satan. What we say shows what is in our hearts.

Sure the Pharisees knew the scriptures, but their hearts were corrupt. The *Life Application Study Bible* says, "You can't solve your heart problem, however, just by cleaning up your speech. You must allow the Holy Spirit to fill you with new attitudes and motives; then your speech will be cleansed at its source."

Mrs. Weedn understood there is no time to leave words unsaid. We must, however, make certain our words come from the proper source. Let us be mindful today of leaving footprints on some heart. That is much better than leaving sole prints showing we walked over someone who was down.

Lord, help me be one of those people who leave footprints on hearts. Amen

AUGUST 31st *BABY STEPS*

"Doth not he see my ways, and count all my steps?" Job 31:4

In May of 1991, the movie *What About Bob?* was released. It starred Richard Dreyfuss as a successful psychotherapist. Also starring as an OCD narcissist who tracked down the doctor and his family while they were on vacation was Bill Murray.

Dr. Leo Marvin had written the book *Baby Steps* about his theory as how to treat patients and their phobias. When Bob Wiley becomes a new patient, Dr. Marvin gives him a copy of the book and leaves for a month's rest and relaxation. When Bob shows up, he endears himself to the good doctor's family but drives Dr. Marvin berserk. So much for his theory about baby steps.

But, isn't that how our faith comes? In baby steps? None of us started out as giants in faith. We learned to trust God one step at a time. Just like a baby, we may have teetered and tottered and fallen many times. Our falls may have hurt us spiritually, emotionally and even physically. Yet, like a baby, we can't stay down, we must get up and try again.

Sometimes, a baby just needs a hand to hold in order to get balanced. So do we. When we take hold of God's hand we are well balanced and, in time, we learn to walk steadily in faith. We place our confidence in God, not ourselves. With His hand holding ours, there is no limit to what He can do through us or for us.

In his book, *Faith, Foolishness or Presumption?* Dr. Frederick Price wrote about people who say they are trusting God to heal them of cancer, yet they haven't even learned to trust Him to cure their headaches! We may find this amusing, but it reminds me of the man who came to Jesus to ask for his son's healing. The father said, "Lord, I believe; help thou mine unbelief (Mark 9:24)." Often we come to God with hope rather than faith.

True faith takes hope and makes it a sure thing. The Bible says, "Faith is the substance of things hoped for, the evidence of things not seen (Hebrews 11:1)." However, our faith grows as God proves Himself faithful. One little step at a time. Throw out doubt and trust Him with small things today. When bigger things come tomorrow, you can be fully prepared. All things are possible to those who believe.

Lord God, I do believe You can do the unbelievable! Amen

SEPTEMBER

"Purge me with hyssop, and I shall be clean: wash me, and I shall be whiter than snow." Psalm 51:7

Last year, I read a devotional in my *Daily Guideposts* about a man who had *Tabula Rasa* tattooed on his arm. When asked the meaning, the man replied, "Clean slate."

What a wonderful reminder of what Christ has done for each of us who believe in Him. He has wiped our slates clean with His blood. Because He died for our sins, we have been washed and are now, in His sight, whiter than snow. Our sins are cast from us as far as the east is from the west.

How is that possible? Why is it possible? Certainly not because we deserve anything from God, nor can we earn anything from Him by our "good behavior." Simply because God loved us before we were born and wanted us to have a relationship with Him did He send His Son, Jesus, to die on the cross for us. This miracle occurred simply by His wondrous grace.

It is so comforting to know I have a clean slate before God for all the wrongs I have done. His mercies are new every morning, His compassions never fail. No matter how I have failed Him today, if He spares my life, I can wake up in the morning with the opportunity to be better. I can't let any past or current failures rob me of future obedience and joy.

We can put behind us all the "I should haves" and the "If onlys." I realize this is easier said than done. That is because the devil himself wants to keep us distracted from doing God's will. He wants to rob us of our joy and our peace by constantly accusing us. He brings up our pasts to weigh us down and make us feel God is sick of us!

However, we know Satan is a liar and he is daily seeking whom he may devour. Don't let him devour you. When he comes around, be like Priscilla Shirer's character in *The War Room.* Open the door and tell him to get out! Tell him he cannot have your home, your marriage or your mind!

I am not encouraging anyone to get *Tabula Rasa* tattooed on your body. But I am encouraging everyone to get it tattooed on your mind.

Lord God, thank You for wiping my slate clean. Thank You that I am washed whiter than snow. Amen

"Behold, thou art fair, my love; behold, thou art fair; thou hast doves' eyes." Song of Solomon 1:15

My Aunt Grace was my aunt by marriage. She had a nephew who had a huge hemangioma on his face. A hemangioma is a birthmark made up of dilated blood capillaries and is purplish or deep red in color. I always felt sad for him because he had to go through life with that disfigurement.

I am sure he was embarrassed as a child. We all know how cruel children can be and I often wondered if he had been made fun of or called names. No matter what occurred in his younger years, he did get married. Some young lady saw him through the eyes of Christ.

My friend Louise Nix used to tell me she had seen a certain person through the eyes of Christ. In other words, she did not see the blemishes or the rough areas, she only saw this person with the eyes of love. That is the way I need to see everyone I look upon! That is the way I wish everyone could see me!

I have never thought of myself as being beautiful by any means. Consequently, I love the last two verses of Proverbs 31. These tell us, "Favor is deceitful, and beauty is vain: but a woman who fears the Lord, she shall be praised. Give her of the fruit of her hands; and let her own works praise her in the gates." My desire is to fear the Lord, not to be popular or beautiful.

As we all know, movie stars, recording artists and sports heroes (just to name a few) take great pride in their appearances. But often those who are the most highly favored are those who do not know Christ. My prayer is for them to come to the knowledge of the truth.

Our bodies, regardless of how they may look, are fragile and mortal. These bodies are just temporary containers for our souls. Acts 4:7, says, "But we have this treasure in earthen vessels, that the excellency of the power may be of God, and not of us." The *KJV Study Bible* says, "Sometimes the more humble the container, the more glorious its precious contents appear."

I am trying to see through the eyes of Christ. I am trying to look upon everyone in love. Won't you join me in this attempt?

Jesus, help me look through Your eyes and behold beauty in everyone today. Amen

SEPTEMBER 3rd *VISIBLE HEALING*

"Heal me, O Lord, and I shall be healed; save me, and I shall be saved: for thou art my praise." Jeremiah 17:14

My family and my friends are experiencing many problems. There are health issues, job issues, relationship issues, you name it. All kinds of problems plague those I love. I am helpless in solving their conundrums.

However, I can think back to a recent time when I burned my left hand on the broiler in the oven. I was reaching in to get out a pan, when I touched the red-hot element. OUCH! My mistake left about a two inch burn just behind the opening between my thumb and first finger of that hand.

Over time, it seemed I could actually *see* the healing taking place. Every day it was as if I could see the wound shrinking. I was totally amazed by the body's ability to heal itself. Of course, I still carry the scar showing where the wound once was.

So then, if God can create a body with the ability to heal itself, there is no doubt He can heal all the problems of my loved ones. All our problems can be safely left in His hands. He knows just how to "fix" each one. Sure, there may be scars left behind. We may have a visible reminder of how we once suffered, but the scar shows that the healing has taken place.

No matter what kind of problems you may be having at any given moment, just reach out to God with faith in His ability to heal. Like the prophet Jeremiah, trust in the Lord to save and heal you.

Lord God, You are the great Physician. I know I can trust You to heal me as well as those I care deeply about. Amen

SEPTEMBER 4th *BACK SURGERY*

"I gave my back to the smiters, and my cheeks to them that plucked off the hair: I hid not my face from shame and spitting." Isaiah 50:6

Last summer, George began experiencing pain in his right leg. He thought he was just having muscle cramps due to his Parkinson's disease. He tried using muscle rubs and the heating pad.

Being the trooper that he is, he went ahead with a vacation we had already planned. On the trip, he took arthritis strength acetaminophen and soaked in hot water at night. The pain persisted. When we returned home, the pain intensified daily. We tried everything we could think of to relieve it, but nothing helped.

We made a trip to the doctor's office on Monday, a trip to the emergency room on Tuesday night and George was admitted to the hospital on Wednesday. After an MRI, the diagnosis was a herniated disc. The neurosurgeon scheduled an operation right away. Meanwhile, George was getting an injection for his pain every two hours! As George was being rolled back into his room after surgery, he was thanking God for the relief he could already feel.

Prior to his admission, he had been lying in the floor, moaning and praying for the pain to subside. He heard Jesus speak to him and say, "I experienced more pain than you can imagine when I died on the cross for you and I did not cry out." What a sobering thought.

Speaking of Jesus, Isaiah 53:7 says, "He was oppressed, and he was afflicted, yet he opened not his mouth: he is brought as a lamb to the slaughter, and as a sheep before her shearers is dumb, so he openeth not his mouth."

George suffered unwillingly and vocally. Jesus, however, suffered willingly and silently to save us from our sins. We can be thankful for that relief every minute of the day.

Silently Suffering Savior, thank You for the relief You provided for me when You died for my sins. Amen

SEPTEMBER 5th *BRISTLECONE PINES*

"Before the mountains were brought forth or ever thou hadst formed the earth and the world, even from everlasting to everlasting, thou art God." Psalm 90:2

Bristlecone pines are some of the oldest living things in the world. I have read scientists believe some of them started growing around 2600 B.C. That is the time Egypt was flourishing as a nation and the pyramids were being built. The trees are sculptured by winds, arid limestone soil and the ravages of a hostile environment at a ten thousand feet elevation.

These trees have survived because they have adjusted and adapted to their environment. For instance, during droughts, they shut off some of their branches to conserve water. As the soil erodes from beneath them, they cling tenaciously by just one lifeline of their root system.

We can learn a lot from the Bristlecone pines. For instance, if we are experiencing a financial drought, we can shut off some "branches" by eating more salads and less of expensive cuts of meat. We can stay at home and read the Bible instead of going to the movies. If we are going through a time when our health seems to be eroding, we can cling tenaciously to a lifeline of prayer and faith.

Like the pines, we can adapt and adjust to any hostile environment the Lord allows for our lives. When our faith is tested, it becomes even stronger than before. The Lord can use these trying times to sculpt us into sturdy, enduring witnesses of His help in every situation.

Father God, help me adapt and adjust to the howling winds that buffet me. Help me stand strong as a witness for You. Amen

SEPTEMBER 6th *SHEPHERD OF THE SHEEP*

" Now the God of peace, that brought again from the dead our Lord Jesus, that great shepherd of the sheep, through the blood of the everlasting covenant, Make you perfect in every good work to do his will, working in you that which is well-pleasing in his sight, through Jesus Christ; to whom be glory for ever and ever. Amen.
Hebrews 13:20, 21

The year we went out west with Kevin, Justin and Tyler, we saw the largest herd of sheep you could ever imagine. We were driving through Wyoming and were amazed by the large number we saw grazing beside the highway. There were literally thousands of the little wooly creatures. While it was a thrill to see an antelope or a buffalo, I was just as enthused by the sheep.

I was wondering how many shepherds it takes to tend a herd of that size. And that made me think of all the sheep our Savior shepherds twenty four hours a day every single day! I am thankful for His great omnipotence, omniscience and omnipresence.

In Psalm 23, David wrote, "The Lord is my shepherd; I shall not want." This verse tells us he has a personal relationship with the Lord who supplies all his needs. The remaining verses tell of all the blessings from the Lord such as rest, refreshment, healing, protection, hope and security.

In John, chapter 10, Jesus said, "I am the good shepherd: the good shepherd giveth his life for the sheep (verse 11)." He also said, in verse 14, "I am the good shepherd, and know my sheep, and am known of mine." Yes, Jesus willingly gave His life for us and now we can know Him as He knows us.

The verse from Hebrews says Jesus is the great Shepherd of the sheep who brought about an everlasting covenant through His blood. In I Peter 2:25, we read that Jesus is the Shepherd and Bishop of our souls. Finally, in I Peter 5:4, the Bible says, "And when the chief Shepherd shall appear, ye shall receive a crown of glory that fadeth not away." Hallelujah!

So then, Jesus is the good Shepherd, the great Shepherd and the chief Shepherd. He is constantly tending, leading and loving us. He also continually provides for us. Unlike the hired hands that tended the sheep in Wyoming, Jesus shepherds us out of His great love for us.

Great Shepherd of the sheep, thank You for Your loving care and provision. Amen

SEPTEMBER 7th *REBUKED BY A FRIEND*

"Ointment and perfume rejoice the heart: so doth the sweetness of a man's friend by hearty counsel." Proverbs 27:9

There is no other way to say it. She "let me have it!" Only she had no idea she was letting me have it. Let me explain what happened.

One day I walked into Heavenly Dove to talk with Angie. I asked about a mutual friend who was having some issues. Angie began to tell me about her counsel to this lady. Angie had no idea every word she had said to our friend was hitting me right in the heart! I was guilty of being just as weak, depressed and unbelieving as the other lady.

But, I did not confess that to Angie. I walked out and immediately confessed it to God, though. I asked Him to forgive me and help me stand on His words. (Ok, Angie. Now you know!)

There are some hurts from years ago that keep robbing me of my joy and peace. Why? Because I do not resist the devil when he brings them to my mind. Instead, I have embraced the hurt and clutched it to myself like a security blanket. Only this blanket smothers me and it threatens to choke the life out of me at times.

I am well acquainted with verses that tell me I have been made more than a conqueror (Romans 8:37), I can do all things through Christ (Philippians 4:13), if I resist the devil he will flee from me (James 4:7) and God will give me peace that passes understanding (Philippians 4:7). The reason I am not standing victorious, the reason I am dragging around dead weights, the reason I am being bombarded by the fiery darts of the wicked one is because I am not holding up my shield of faith as I should be. I am guilty of not using my sword of the Spirit (the Word of God) as I should be doing. I am not resisting the enemy by drawing closer to God.

I have been a Christian soldier for many decades, yet sometimes this warrior is still a child. When I get into that mode, I know I have friends who will counsel me with hearty counsel and get me headed in the right direction once again. Whether or not they realize it's me who needs the counseling!

Lord, I know I have friends I can turn to when I am hurting. Help me admit my weaknesses and ask for their counsel and prayers. Amen

SEPTEMBER 8ᵗʰ   *BACK TO THE BASICS*

"Beloved, when I gave all diligence to write unto you of the common salvation, it was needful for me to write unto you, and exhort you that ye should earnestly contend for the faith which was once delivered unto the saints." Jude, verse 3

I have to confess that even as I typed the verse for today, I had to chuckle. The verse is not funny at all, but when I typed the reference, I was reminded of my friend, Tony Allen, who is always teasing me by saying he read something from the third chapter of Jude. All Bible students know Jude has only one chapter!

Recently, our teen choir sang a song recorded by Avalon called, "The Basics of Life." When I heard it, I asked their director, Susan Waters, if I could have a copy of the lyrics. She was happy to oblige.

The song tells us we have re-arranged what is right and wrong. It says we have drifted so far from the truth. The song asks, "Where are the virtues that once gave us light? Where are the morals that governed our lives?" It tells us we need to get back to a heart that is pure, a love that is blind and a faith that is fervently grounded in Christ. I couldn't agree more.

When Jude, who was the half-brother of Jesus, wrote his letter to those sanctified by God the Father, and preserved in Jesus, he was writing to warn them about false teaching that had invaded the church. Jude instructed these believers to "contend for the faith which was once delivered unto the saints."

He then says these false teachers had crept in unawares. In other words, they looked like believers and talked like believers at the first. But they turned the grace of God into lasciviousness and denied the only Lord God and our Lord Jesus Christ (verse 4).

In verses 5 through 7, Jude reminds the believers of ways God dealt with the ungodly in the past. He says these false teachers deserved God's judgment because they had corrupted themselves. He said they had run greedily after erroneous ways (verse 11). They were full of empty promises, so Jude compared them to clouds without water and fruit trees that were twice dead (verse 12).

Jude exhorts them by saying, " But ye, beloved, building up yourselves on your most holy faith, praying in the Holy Ghost, keep yourselves in the love of God, looking for the mercy of our Lord Jesus Christ unto eternal life (verses 20 & 21)."

Friends, not everyone who uses God's name is a true follower. We must guard ourselves against false doctrine and we must contend for the faith. To contend is not just a defense of the gospel, but it is also maintaining what is true. In other words, it is obedience to the basic tenets of our faith.

In Avalon's song we are told the newest rage is to reason things out, if we meditate we can overcome doubt and, after all, man is a god. But, it says, "We've let the darkness invade us too long. We've got to turn the tide. Oh, and we need the passion that burned long ago, to come and open our eyes, There's no room for compromise. We need to get back to the basics of life."

Indeed we do. Be a contender for the faith. Don't be deceived by false teaching no matter how popular it may be!

Lord, I still believe in the old rugged cross and in hope for the lost. I know the Rock of Ages will stand through the changes of time. Amen

SEPTEMBER 9th   *GETTING THE GUM OUT*

"Avoid it pass not by it, turn from it, and pass away." Proverbs 4:15

That particular Thursday had already been a trying day. Our granddaughter Jada was two years old and she had been crying about everything. Nothing we tried to do to entertain her had worked. When I picked up her brother, Jake, from preschool, he had gotten in trouble for some infraction on the playground.

When I picked up our eleven-year-old grandson Tyler from his bus stop, I became furious! Someone on the school bus had hit him right in the crown of his head with a huge wad of chewing gum. How disgusting! Tyler is a well-behaved youngster who never bothers a soul. Why anyone would do something like that to him was beyond my comprehension.

I heard, or read, the best way to remove gum from your hair is by using peanut butter. So, I got a big jar of Peter Pan and a pair of latex gloves and went to work on his head. Tyler has thick hair and, believe me, it was all matted together. The more I worked with his hair, the more I fumed. What a nasty trick to play on someone. After rolling the peanut butter around and pulling on Tyler's hair for what seemed like an eternity, I finally had it all out. Then he had to wash his hair multiple times to get the peanut butter out! It was a hassle, but his hair was clean again.

My cousin Gail once had an issue with her hair that was not so easily fixed. She had what we called strawberry-blonde hair. After being in the pool at the city park over much of the summer, the chlorine gave her hair a greenish tint. In those days, that was not a popular color for a teenager's hair! The only thing she could do to get back her beautiful shade was to stay out of the pool. And wait.

Sometimes sin is like that wad of chewing gum. Sometimes, we are so deeply entrenched in a sinful lifestyle, it takes awhile to rid ourselves of the desires for whatever it is that has us trapped. Like the peanut butter, the Holy Spirit is our Helper. He will free us from our bondage when we depend on Him.

Sin is also like the chlorine. We may not have recognized the danger of immersing ourselves into a sinful situation, nevertheless, the effects of sin show up on us and are hard to eliminate. We have to make the effort to avoid the sin. It is up to us to resist the temptation. Once we distance ourselves from it, we will be restored.

In Proverbs 4:14, we are told, "Enter not into the path of the wicked, and go not in the way of evil men." This advice sounds so simple, doesn't it? Why then are we so easily led astray? In the song, "I Must Tell Jesus," we learn the world allures us to evil and our hearts are tempted to sin. However, when we talk to Jesus, He will help us, over the world the victory to win.

Ask Jesus to help you "get the gum out" of your life. Also, do your part to avoid it!

Jesus, I'm so thankful You are faithful and just to forgive me of my sin and cleanse me of all unrighteousness. Amen

SEPTEMBER 10th   *WALL DRUG STORE*

"For I have satiated the weary soul, and I have replenished every sorrowful soul." Jeremiah 31:25

Situated near the entrance to the Badlands National Park in South Dakota is the tiny city of Wall. Wall is famous for its 76,000 square foot drug store. I've read over a million people visit Wall Drug Store every year and on a typical summer day there are up to twenty thousand visitors!

Ted Hustead opened his drug store in 1931. But, at that time, Wall, South Dakota was considered the "geographical center of nowhere." Several years later, Mr. Hustead's drug store was still tiny. The cars that passed by on Route 16-A, did just that. They passed by. Business was almost non-existent.

Dorothy Hustead, Ted's wife, suggested they put up a sign letting the travelers know they served free ice water. Since all drug stores offered free water at the time, Ted though it was a silly idea, but he put up the sign. The rest, as they say, is history.

All travelers who had driven across the hot prairie were thirsty and wanted a glass of ice-cold water. So, they came to Wall Drug and left refreshed and ready for new adventures.

In 2002, George, my mother and I visited Wall Drug. Along I-90, signs for the place bombarded us for miles and miles. They kept us apprised of the miles left before arriving at the famous oasis. We explored the entire complex and ate our lunch there. Then, we were ready to head to our next adventure with our weary souls satiated.

The founder of Wall Drug once said, "Free ice water. It brought us Husteads a long way and it taught me my greatest lesson, and that's that there's absolutely no place on God's earth that's Godforsaken. No matter where you live, you can succeed, because wherever you are, you can reach out to other people with something they need."

Getting the thirst-quenching, ice-cold water at Wall reminded me of the complaining children of Israel in the desert. They accused Moses of leading them out of Egypt just to die of thirst. But, every time, God provided what they needed. No place was forsaken by God then, nor is it now.

In Psalm 63, David said his soul longed for God in a dry and thirsty land where there was no water. Sometimes, I feel parched and dry, too. Then I remember what Jesus said to the woman at the well (John 4). He said if we drink of the water He gives, we will never thirst again because the water He gives will be a well of water, springing up into everlasting life.

God still performs miracles and He still uses us to reach out to others with something they need. Ted Hustead learned this lesson and so should we. Think about how you can reach out to others today with something they need.

Lord Jesus, I am so thankful You are the Living Water that satiates my weary soul. Amen

SEPTEMBER 11th *VANITY OF VANITIES*

"Vanity of vanities, saith the Preacher, vanity of vanities; all is vanity." Ecclesiastes 1:2

King Solomon, son of King David and Bathsheba, was probably the wisest and richest ruler that ever lived. Yet, in Ecclesiastes he wrote all is vanity. He said he had seen all the works done under the sun and all of them are vanity and vexation of spirit.

He listed various things that proved to be futile. Things like wealth, wisdom, folly, labor, wine, women, servants and animals. Solomon said he would leave everything at death to someone else. He wondered whether that person would be a wise man or a fool. He learned that trying to live out our purpose under our own power equals a futile life.

I read somewhere in the pop music world, Michael Jackson (1958-2009) was the "King," Whitney Houston (1963-2012) was the "Queen," and that Prince Rogers Nelson (1958-2016) was, of course, the "Prince." They all had fame and fortune, but their lives proved those things can't bring happiness. All three died of drug overdoses.

In 1969, Frank Sinatra released his recording of "My Way," which was written by Paul Anka. The song's lyrics tell us when the end is near and it's time for the final curtain, having done it "my way" is what matters. The final verse asks this question, "For what is a man, what has he got?" According to the song he has naught if not himself.

However, Solomon found a better answer. While he admits we should enjoy our lives under the sun, he summed up the book with these words, "Fear God, and keep his commandments: for this is the whole duty of man. For God shall bring every work into judgment, with every secret thing, whether it be good or whether it be evil."

Yes, our lives on earth are brief. Yes, when we die, we leave all we have accumulated behind. And yes, we all like doing things our own way. Better yet is to do things God's way. Let's all try to get our houses in order by fearing God and keeping His commandments.

Lord God, forgive me for putting too much importance on the futile things of the earth. Forgive me for trying to do things my way. Help me do Your will, not mine. Amen

SEPTEMBER 12th   *REPAY THE KINDNESS*

"And now the Lord shew kindness and truth unto you: and I also will requite you this kindness, because ye have done this thing."
II Samuel 2:2

Justin was just a baby when I decided to drive to Hilton Head, South Carolina. My sister Cathy, my brother Johnny and my older son Kevin would be making the journey with me. We were having a grand time until we had a flat tire. A state patrol officer stopped and changed it for us. Gratefully, we were on our way once again.

On the way home, we had stopped in Savannah to get the tire fixed. Meanwhile, we went to eat. We ordered our food and I went to the phone booth outside to call home. I discovered my wallet was missing.

I went back in and told my family not to touch the food because I had no money. But God showed me how He uses people to help one another.

The manager of the restaurant allowed me to cash a check. He said I could send a check for the food once I had gotten us all safely home. The man at the tire shop didn't charge us. Also, a female customer gave us money to buy milk for Justin's bottle! We were so thankful.

There have been many instances where people have come along at just the time I needed help. Too many to list, actually. But I will always remember the kind folks in Savannah. I will always remember Tim Hubbard who pushed my disabled mail truck out of Dr. Bramblett Road so I wouldn't get hit. I can't forget James Pruitt who helped me when I was stuck in the snow while delivering mail on Whitmire Road or Norris Bennett who stopped to change a flat tire for me once.

As I said, these are just a sampling of God's rescuers. I am grateful to each and every one who has ever helped me in my time of need. Now, my responsibility is to pass that kindness on to others who need help. These days, the saying is not "paying it back," but "paying it forward."

As we go about our daily routines, let's be one of God's rescuers if at all possible. Be on the lookout for some way you might help someone in need. Perform a random act of kindness today. You will be blessed for doing so. I guarantee it.

Jesus, thank you for all the ones You have sent my way in my time of need. Help me take advantage of opportunities to help others. Amen

SEPTEMBER 13th *THE REASON FOR GIVING*

"Every man according as he purposeth in his heart, so let him give; not grudgingly, or of necessity: for God loveth a cheerful giver."
II Corinthians 9:7

Our friend Jonathan Haight recently shared this quote with me: "I don't give because I have great excess. I give because I have learned what it's like to be in great need." I have been unable to verify exactly who first said these words. I have found several variations of them on the internet, though.

Like the apostle Paul, I know how to be abased and I know how to abound (Philippians 4).When I am in the abounding stage, I am a cheerful giver because I know the abased times are hard. I know from personal experience because there have been times I have found myself in great need.

I can remember a time while I was still in school, my aunt came to my tiny apartment, opened the cabinet doors and discovered bare shelves. She immediately went to the store and brought back groceries for me. She did it ungrudgingly, too. And that is not the only time she had to give so I could have.

Unlike Paul, however, I have yet to learn how to be content in the abased stage. I much prefer the abounding stage. (Don't we all?) Paul did say the contentment is a *learned* response. When we stop striving for more and more, it is possible to be content. It becomes possible when we trust God to supply our needs. Paul said, "I can do all things through Christ which strengtheneth me."

Luke 6:38, says, "Give, and it shall be given unto you; good measure, pressed down, and shaken together, and running over, shall men give into your bosom. For with the same measure that ye mete withal it shall be measured to you again." If we are generous in our giving, we will gain generosity from others. If, however, we are stingy, that is what we will reap. Galatians 6:7, says, "for whatsoever a man soweth, that shall he also reap."

To sum it all up, I would say: Be generous when you can because that pleases God. When you have little, trust God because that also pleases Him. In either situation, learn to be content.

God, help me give cheerfully and generously. Help me learn to be content whether I am abased or abounding. Amen

SEPTEMBER 14th

"Pleasant words are as an honeycomb, sweet to the soul, and health to the bones." Proverbs 16:24

Every morning when I open my eyes, my husband George begins to speak pleasant words to me. He tells me how much he loves me and how wonderful I am in his eyes. He constantly speaks affirming words over me.

Those words are definitely sweet to my soul and health to my bones. I have had more than my share of words which were anything but pleasant. The sad truth is, I have spoken more than my share of unpleasant words as well.

James, chapter 3, tells us: "And the tongue is a fire, a world of iniquity: so is the tongue among our members, that it defileth the whole body, and setteth on fire the course of nature; and it is set on fire of hell (verse 6)." Also, in verse 8, we read, "But the tongue can no man tame; it is an unruly evil, full of deadly poison." Verse 10 says, "Out of the same mouth proceedeth blessing and cursing, My brethren these things ought not so to be."

Certainly, I have regretted many of the words I have spoken. I have not been able to keep count of all the times I have had to apologize for words spoken out of anger or hurt. Even though the person may have forgiven me, you can't un-speak unpleasant words. The damage has been done. And often it lingers for a lifetime.

If I could go back and rectify all the times I used unpleasant words in speaking to my family, friends or even my enemies, I would do it. Since that is not possible, all I can do is ask the Holy Spirit to help me guard my tongue today and in the future.

My mother told us, "If you can't say something nice, don't say anything at all." How I wish I had put those words into practice all the days of my life.

Beginning today, I am going to try to speak pleasant words to those I talk with. I want my words to be like George's: sweet to the soul and health to the bones.

Lord, Please forgive me for all the times I have hurt others with my unpleasant words. Help them to forgive me as well. Amen

SEPTEMBER 15th *USING OUR HANDS*

"They were armed with bows, and could use both the right hand and the left in hurling stones and shooting arrows out of a bow, even of Saul's brethren of Benjamin." I Chronicles 12:2

Our grandson Jake is a lefty. He eats, writes, throws and bats left-handed. Yet there are so many things he can do with either hand. My mother writes with her right hand and throws with her right hand, but she always batted from the left of the plate. When we switched from our personal vehicles to the LLVs for mail delivery, I had to learn to sort my mail with my left hand. After awhile, it became as easy as pie. But writing with my left hand is more difficult. I can do it, but it is not one bit pretty.

Studies show only ten percent of people are lefties and only one percent is truly ambidextrous. Those who are ambidextrous, are more likely to carry the LRRTM1 gene linked to schizophrenia. They are also more likely to be quick to anger. Some cross-dominant celebrities are Leonardo da Vinci, Paul McCartney, Pete Rose, Benjamin Franklin, Harry Truman and Michelle Kwan.

The Bible tells us of some men who were quite proficient with either hand when using a sling or a bow and arrows. These men were of the tribe of Benjamin, relatives of King Saul. But, they joined David in Ziklag when he was on the run from King Saul.

Saul was jealous because the people were so fond of David. They gave David more credit as a warrior than they gave the king. They said, "Saul has slain his thousands, and David his ten thousands (I Samuel 18:7)." From that day forward, Saul was suspicious of David and wanted to kill him.

These mighty warriors who joined David's army became some of his elite fighters. They were loyal to David and helped in many battles. One man, Ismaiah, was over the thirty soldiers called "David's Mighty Men."

Okay, I know not many of us can use either hand with equal ease. But, keep in mind the Bible tells us, "Whatsoever thy hand findeth to do, do it with thy might (Ecclesiastes 9:10)." Use your hands in doing good to others and in doing any work in particular that God may have for you. Be about His business, no matter which hand you use the most or the best.

Lord God, I am not ambidextrous, but I want my hands to be used for building up Your kingdom. Amen

SEPTEMBER 16th *A NEW FRIEND*

"A man that hath friends must shew himself friendly: and there is a friend that sticketh closer than a brother." Proverbs 18:24

When I began to attend Bible studies at Friendship Baptist Church I made many new friends. I have mentioned some of them in other devotional entries, but today I want to focus on my tablemate, Elaine.

In 2015, I was having some rough times. Satan was attacking me daily because I was attempting to write *Through the Year with Yahweh, Yeshua and You.* During the fall of that year, he was especially relentless because I was almost finished with the project. Sometimes, I felt I could not battle anymore.

The Bible tells us Satan is the accuser of the brethren (Revelation 12:10) and that he is a liar and the father of it (John 8:44). I know how he operates. I also know what I have to do when he comes slinking around with his accusations and lies.

I know I have to resist him and he will flee (James 4:7). I also know I must quote the word to him as Jesus did when Satan tempted Him in the wilderness (Matthew 4). I know Ephesians tells me to put on the whole armor of God so I may be able to stand against the wiles of the devil (6:11).

If I know all the actionable intel, why do I not use what I know? Romans 8:37, says I am MORE than a conqueror through Christ (emphasis mine). So, why was I not looking that enemy in the face and telling him he was wasting his time with me? I can't really say.

All I know is my newfound friend Elaine told me if I ever needed to talk about my struggles, she would be very happy to be a listening ear. She assured me nothing I might say could shock her or offend her. But, I asked myself, how can I possibly confess such stupid, ridiculous feelings to a sane human being? I thought anyone would have to be as crazy and warped up as I am to understand. So, I did not tell her what I was dealing with.

I couldn't tell her, but I could talk to Jesus about it. He is a friend that sticks closer than a brother. He will never leave me nor forsake me (Hebrews 13:5). He knows my thoughts and the desires of my heart. My friend Jesus knows all about me and He loves me anyway.

(I am sure my friend Elaine would, too!)

Jesus, You know sometimes we deal with emotions that are too complicated and too hurtful to share with our friends. We can always come to You at any time about anything. Thank You for being there. Amen

"They that trust in their wealth, and boast themselves in the multitude of their riches; none of them can by any means redeem his brother, nor give to God a ransom for him:" Psalm 49:6, 7

Dictionary.com defines "status symbol" as an object habit, etc., by which the social or economic status of the possessor may be judged. Do you own any of those objects or have any of those habits? I would venture to say most every reader might have to say a resounding yes to the question. I can remember some of the first status symbols I owned.

My first real "job" was keeping the children of Benny and Katherine Nuckolls during the summer. I was in high school and Kim, Lamar and Michael were a few years younger than I. We played board games, listened to the radio, watched television and ate everything in sight while Benny was working at Sawnee EMC and Katherine was a nurse at Forsyth County Hospital.

I saved the money I earned until I had enough to buy a John Romaine purse. It was a nut-brown tweed purse with butter soft leather trim. Writer and interior designer Pamela Terry says these purses "were the ultimate acquisition and a sure symbol of fashionable acceptance." I proudly carried my purse to school as I wore my Bobbie Brooks shirtwaist dresses and, I might add, my Bass Weejuns! I was styling and profiling as they say.

In 1984, recording artist "Weird Al" Yankovic released "Gonna Buy Me a Condo." The song tells of a man who used to live in Jamaica, but doesn't now. He can't wait to buy a Cuisinart and get T-shirts with the alligator on them! Janis Joplin sang about wanting a color tv and a Mercedes Benz!

My John Romaine purse, my Bass Weejuns, my Bobbie Brooks dresses were all easily recognizable. Just like the Izod T-shirts "Weird Al" sang about. Chaps, Tommy Hilfiger and Polo brands are popular today. So are Michael Kors and Coach purses. A Mercedes is still considered by a majority of people to be the top of the line

But, what do our status symbols really do for us? Don't they just show we are spending our money for high priced items? Aren't owning or wearing these items just a way to boast in our wealth? None of them can gain a thing for us that will last forever.

I believe my one and only status symbol would be the cross. Or, better yet, the empty tomb. Jesus died on the cross to give me eternal life and rose from the grave to prove He had accomplished His mission. What could compare with that? Furthermore, it cost me nothing! The question is, how can I show this status symbol to others? It should be by the way I live my life. People should be able to recognize Christ in me by the love I show to others.

I have to ask myself daily whether my walk matches my talk. Does yours?

Jesus, I know sometimes I fail, but my heart is toward You. Forgive me and help me, I pray. Amen

SEPTEMBER 18th   *THE LIFELINE*

"Let us therefore come boldly unto the throne of grace, that we may obtain mercy, and find grace to help in time of need." Hebrews 4:16

When we lived on Antioch Road, we had an elderly neighbor. Mrs. Thome asked me to be her "lifeline." She wanted me to call her every day to check up on her in the event she had some emergency. I readily agreed.

At the time, I was working and had three children to attend, so sometimes things in my home were hectic. I could not be counted on to call at a specific time every day. But, call I did.

One day, I had been extremely busy and did not call her until late in the evening. I got no answer, but assumed Mrs. Thome had gone to bed already. The next day, it was in the late afternoon before I called. This time I was worried when she did not answer. George and I went to investigate.

We found her screen door locked from the inside. We went around trying to peek in her windows. Then we saw her sprawled in the floor. I knew this could not be good. I wanted to break in, but was overruled and the police were called. Mrs. Thome was still alive, but very sick and probably severely dehydrated. An ambulance came to carry her to the hospital. Unfortunately, she passed away not long afterwards.

I carried the guilt for a long time. I felt I had let Mrs. Thome die. We did not know how long she had lain in the floor in that condition, but I still blamed myself. She depended on me and I had let her down. The one day she needed me in the worst way, I did not call until it was too late to help.

I failed my neighbor. However, we have Someone we can call on who will never let us down. We can have confidence in His ability to hear our cries for help and grant us mercy and grace. That Someone is the Lord Jesus. Furthermore, we can come **boldly** unto His throne.

If you need a dependable Lifeline, just call on Jesus.

Jesus, thank You for inviting me to come boldly unto Your throne. I also thank You for the promise of mercy and grace to help in my time of need. Amen

SEPTEMBER 19th *HOME RUN HITTERS*

"He that is faithful in that which is least is faithful also in much; and he that is unjust in the least is unjust also in much." Luke 16:10

Yesterday, I confessed my calls to my neighbor were not made in a timely fashion. I also confessed I did not follow through when she did not answer her phone late in the evening. I admit I wasn't faithful enough in the little thing she asked me to do. I will always regret that.

But today we turn our attention to baseball. The World Series is looming. If our favorite team doesn't stand a chance, many of us will become more interested in following those who might make the big games.

Did you know there were 3,180 home runs hit during the 1988 season? That may sound like a lot, but there were, I have read, 25,838 singles hit. Eight times more than the number of home runs. We can deduce more games are won by singles than home runs. Right?

I can tell you that I never was a home run hitter. I was a singles kind of batter. I don't think one of my singles ever won a game, though! So, it is easy to get discouraged when I consider that I have never accomplished great things. Yet, God calls me to be faithful in little things. I do "strike out" sometimes, but I am "at the plate" trying to do my part.

Babe Ruth hit 714 home runs but struck out 1,330 times. He once said, "Every strike brings me closer to the next home run." That is an attitude I can adopt. When I falter or fail, I need to stay positive and lean on the Lord. All the little things I do, day in and day out, may not be spectacular, but they add up to a winning lifestyle.

Even if I am a singles kind of person, I can still "play the game" of life with great gusto. God is keeping the score book and He is aware of each accomplishment.

If you feel insignificant because you haven't done great things, think of all the "singles" you have hit for the Lord. He sees them all.

Lord, You see every little thing I do and You keep the records. I want to be faithful in that which is least as well as that which is much. Amen

SEPTEMBER 20th *THE BIG WHEEL*

"For as the heavens are higher than the earth, so are my ways higher than your ways, and my thoughts than your thoughts." Isaiah 55:9

A couple of years ago, we joined Eddie and Connie Hitt and Connie's mom, Ann Hamby, in Pigeon Forge, Tennessee. We went to Cades Cove, we shopped, we ate and we went into museums. Typical tourist things, but we were having a grand time.

George and I wanted to ride the Great Smoky Mountain Wheel. It is a ferris wheel that stands two hundred feet high. The seats are enclosed in glass and the ride was so smooth I could have been sitting on my couch had I not been looking out. I told Eddie we could see all the way to Michigan from the top! Being at the top made me think of God's looking down on us.

John Anderson had a song entitled "Thirty Thousand Feet." He co-wrote the lyrics which say at thirty thousand feet you can't tell the difference between a race horse and a mule, a chicken and a duck, a genius and a fool or a doe and a buck. John sang that we all look the same to the "Big Man Looking Down."

In one sense he is correct. God does look down on every single one of us with love. It makes no difference to him whether we are young, old, male, female, white, brown, black or yellow. He loved us so much He sent His one and only Son to die for us. He desires a relationship with all of us.

On the other hand, John's song is totally false. God *can* discern the most minute differences between all of us because His knowledge of us is beyond our comprehension. Not only can He tell the differences between humans, he can distinguish the length of an ant's antennae and the number of feathers on a bird. He is omniscient.

Yes, His thoughts and ways are higher than ours, but His thoughts toward us are thoughts of peace and not evil. His thoughts are to give us an expected end (Jeremiah 29:11). That end is actually eternity with Him. I can almost see it from here.

O, Father God, thank You for knowing me so completely. Thank You for Your thoughts of peace toward me. Amen

SEPTEMBER 21st *THREE S TONIC*

"But the God of all grace, who hath called us unto his eternal glory by Christ Jesus, after that ye have suffered a while, make you perfect, stablish, strengthen, settle you." I Peter 5:10

How many of you can remember being forced to take a dose of Fletcher's Castoria when you were a child? Does the name Lydia Pinkham ring a bell? Or, what about Hadacol? The item I want to tell you about today is the S.S.S. Tonic.

It is marketed as a high potency iron and B vitamin supplement. It has been around since the early 1800's when it was, supposedly, an old Indian remedy for blood poison. It is reported the Creek Indians gave up their treasured remedy to Captain Irwin Dennard of Perry, Georgia, as a reward for saving the life of one of their chiefs.

Dennard later sold the formula to Charles Thomas Swift. He and his partners formed the S.S.S. Company and it became one of the richest patent medicine businesses in the country. The S.S.S. stood for Swift's Southern Specific.

When I read this verse from I Peter, I couldn't help but think of God's own "S.S.S. tonic." Notice the verse says, "after that ye have suffered a while." The original S.S.S. tonic was not a preventative, but a curative. In other words, the person who bought the tonic had been suffering, but taking the tonic would provide relief.

God promises to make us perfect after we have suffered awhile. He also promises to stablish, strengthen and settle us. I like to think of our suffering as being the conviction of our sin and our being made perfect as our salvation. After we accept Jesus as our Savior, God will make us strong, solid and steadfast.

I realize Peter was referring to suffering caused by Satan and he was admonishing the elect to be self-controlled and alert. Peter urges them to resist the enemy and to stand firm in the faith. Some of these elect would gain victory here in this life and some would do so in God's eternal glory.

Either way, I want God's S.S.S. tonic for my life. I know there is no other curative which is one hundred percent reliable. God's tonic goes down easily and has no bitter aftertaste. Would you like a dose?

Father, thank You for the remedy for my sin which also stablishes, strengthens and settles me. Amen

SEPTEMBER 22nd *BYE, BYE BOOKS*

"Brethren, I count myself not to have apprehended: but this one thing I do, forgetting those things which are behind, and reaching forth unto those things which are before," Philippians 3:13

I am a dyed-in-the-wool bibliophile. I have loved and collected books as long as I can remember. I have quite a collection and there are books in almost every room of my house.

When we moved into this house, there was one finished room in the basement which we designated Kevin's bedroom. The rest was open space. George and his brothers Mark, Roy and Jack finished another room for my books and my piano. George's friend Morgan Phillips built a bookcase all across one wall for my treasured possessions. It filled up quickly and I continued to buy books!

There came a time when I knew I had to part with some of them. This was harder than I imagined it would be because I felt like each one was an old friend. I hated to let go. But, I realized I was being selfish. It was time to bless someone else with my "friends." As I chose the ones to give away, you might say I mentally kissed them goodbye.

The apostle Paul had to mentally kiss some things goodbye. Maybe not things he treasured so much, but things he did not want to hinder his goal of knowing Christ. For instance, he had to say goodbye to his persecution of the saints. He surely had to say goodbye to the images of Stephen's stoning. He had to say goodbye to his own rejection of the gospel before he encountered Jesus on the road to Damascus.

His guilt and shame could have weighed him down and kept him from becoming the missionary and bold evangelist that he soon was. Had he not kissed them goodbye, about half of the New Testament would not have been written.

There comes a time when we all must say goodbye to the past and move on toward what lies ahead. Our angst must give way so we can be a blessing to others through our knowledge of the Lord. Don't let your past hinder you. Reach out to Jesus.

Mentally kiss the past goodbye just as I did my books.

Gracious Lord, parting with the past is not easy. Help us all as we reach forth unto those things which are before. Amen

SEPTEMBER 23rd *THE GIFT OF HELPS*

"Having then gifts differing according to the grace that is given to us...." Romans 12:6

In I Corinthians, chapter 12, Paul wrote about different gifts given by God to those in the church. He went on to tell the Corinthians they should earnestly covet the best gifts; yet, he showed them a more excellent way. That way was the way of charity, or love.

My friend, Linda Stowers, certainly has the gift of helps! If someone we know happened to be sick, I would most likely pray and send a card. Linda would organize the meals and do the laundry!

When George and I married, she volunteered her home for the wedding reception. To make way for all the guests, she and Jackie had to remove one entire room of furniture and store it in the neighbor's basement. She and her mother made the three-tiered wedding cake for us. When Joel was born two years later, Linda came and took Joel home with her one afternoon so I could simply get some rest. That is just a sampling of the things she has done for me personally.

While I do not possess the same gift as Linda, it takes all of us, working together in the body of Christ, to make the body complete. It takes all of us doing our part to make the body healthy. Without each one, the body will not thrive.

When we are working together, let's not forget the more excellent way of love. Paul wrote, "And though I have the gift of prophecy, and understand all mysteries, and all knowledge; and though I have all faith so that I could remove mountains, and have not charity, I am nothing (I Corinthians 13:2)." Linda did everything with love and that is the way I want to use the gifts God has given me.

God, thank You for the gifts You have given each one of us. My prayer is that we would use them, with love, to glorify You. Amen

SEPTEMBER 24th *BORROWING AT THE BUFFET*

"But every woman shall borrow of her neighbor…" Exodus 3:22

When I was a young girl, my great-grandparents and my Papa loved to watch wrestling. They called it "rassling." Back then there were stars such as "Classy" Freddie Blassie, Gorgeous George and Big Chief Little Eagle.

George and our sons watched it weekly on television. One year we went to the Omni on Christmas night for a series of matches. We saw, among others, the Road Warriors, Dusty Rhodes and Ric Flair. I never cared for the sport at all, but many people do because it is still very popular today. Our younger grandchildren enjoy it immensely.

A couple of years ago, our friend Robert informed us Abdullah the Butcher was going to make an appearance at Steven's Country Kitchen here in Cumming. George and I went because we wanted to get a photo of him for Jake and Jada.

Abdullah was born Lawrence Shreve and he was a Canadian. He was involved in the bloodiest and most violent of the hardcore wrestling matches. The deep scars on his head are from the blading in his career. He was also known to use some judo and karate in the ring. Shreve's gimmick was an evil Arabian.

When we arrived, we were surprised to learn there was a fee for the photo even when using your personal camera. I don't know why we were surprised, we should have been prepared. However, we usually pay with a debit card and never carry cash. Abdullah did not accept debit cards! Billy Robertson said we could get a photo and pay later but I did not want to do that.

Instead, I went over to another table where our friends Carol Best and Adell Roper were seated. I borrowed enough money from Carol to pay for the picture. Then when paying for our meal, I begged for cash back so I could repay Carol's money! It seemed all I had done was beg and borrow. At least I did not do any stealing. We left the restaurant with our meal and our picture both paid for!

Borrowing is not something I like to do. But, borrowing is what God told the Hebrew women to do before they left Egypt. The women were to ask for jewels of silver, jewels of gold and clothing. He said that is the way they would spoil the Egyptians. The Israelites would be rich as they left the land of their bondage.

It seems the Egyptians would not want their workforce to leave at all, much less leave with such material wealth, but what God says will come to pass. God, hundreds of years prior, had spoken to Abram about this very night.

God said, "Know for certain that your descendants will be strangers in a country not their own, and they will be enslaved and mistreated four hundred years. But I will punish the nation they serve as slaves, and afterward they will come out with great possessions (Genesis 15:13, 14)." Later, these items were used in the building of the tabernacle.

What God promises, He is also able to perform; even if it sometimes requires borrowing from those who are masters over you.

God, we know all Your promises are yes and amen in Christ. We give you all the glory. Amen

SEPTEMBER 25th *PUZZLING PROMISES*

"Accounting that God was able to raise him up, even from the dead; from whence also he received him in a figure." Hebrews 11:19

Pneumonoultramicroscopicsilicovolcanoconiosis. No, that is not a misprint. It is the longest word in the English language published in a dictionary. It is a word said to mean a lung disease caused by inhaling very fine ash and sand dust. If I typed it correctly, it is a forty-five letter word! I can't even pronounce it, much less memorize how to spell it! It is very puzzling.

Also very puzzling to me are words like apartment, driveway and parkway. Why do we call them a-part-ments when they are so close together? Why is it called a drive-way when all we do is park on it? Why is it called a park-way when we can't park on it at all? Sometimes, our words just don't make sense.

Sometimes, God's words don't make sense to us either. Sometimes, we are very puzzled by His commands or His promises. Abraham is a fine example. He had waited twenty-five years for his son Isaac to be born. Then, God told him to go into the land of Moriah and sacrifice the child as a burnt offering!

This made no sense to Abraham, yet he knew God could raise Isaac from the dead. The *Bible* says Abraham rose up early in the morning to begin his long trek. There is no record of his tossing and turning in the night. We do not read anywhere that he wrestled with whether to go.

Here's what we do read about Abraham: "He staggered not at the promise of God through unbelief; but was strong in faith, giving glory to God; And being fully persuaded that, what he had promised, he was able also to perform (Romans 4:20, 21)."

We know the rest of what happened. God provided himself a ram for the sacrifice and Isaac's life was spared. Isaac became one of the patriarchs of the nation of Israel.

When God's words do not make sense to us, we need to be more like Abraham. We need to have faith in Him whether or not we understand how He will accomplish what He has spoken. God is able. He can do what is impossible for us to do by our own power.

Romans 8:28, tells us: "And we know that all things work together for good to them that love God, to them who are the called according to his purpose." I know I use this verse frequently because it is one of my favorites. I may not understand how things will work out for good, but I do believe God. What He has promised, He is able to perform.

When His words do not make sense, simply trust Him!

Almighty God, I know I can trust You. I do not want to stagger at Your promises. I desire to be strong in faith like Abraham was. Amen

SEPTEMBER 26th *HURRY UP OR WAIT?*

"The Lord is not slack concerning his promise, as some men count slackness; but is long suffering to us-ward, not willing that any should perish, but that all should come to repentance." II Peter 3:9

We live in an instant society. Everything imaginable is done with a click of a button these days. We pay our bills, microwave our food, make reservations, send messages to friends, etc. We do not want to wait ten seconds at a red light, much less a full minute. Hurry, hurry, hurry is all we seem to do.

Gone are the days when almost every family planted the seeds and waited for the crops to produce. Gone are the days when letter writing was the norm. Now people call letters "snail mail." Gone are the days when preparing dinner took a good portion of the evening. We want everything NOW!

We talk about what terrible shape the world is in and we wonder why the Lord does not come back and take us out of here. We wonder what He can possible be waiting on. While it is a good thing to look forward to the coming of our Lord, Peter tells us the Lord is not slack concerning His promise. Rather, He does not want any to perish. He wants all to come to repentance.

That verse reminds me of a song we sang when I was a young girl. The song was "Wait a Little Longer, Please Jesus." It was written by Hazel Houser and Chester Smith in 1954. Houser had this to say about the song, "This song was written like a prayer. My father, a minister, raised me as a member of the Assembly of God church, and we believe in Christ's second coming. When you're a Christian, you want that day to come as soon as possible, because you'd like to be in heaven with the angels and have happier times than we have here on earth. Yet at the same time, you don't want Him to rush it, because there are others that might be lost because they're not saved. As a Christian, I was anxious to be in a better place, but at the same time, 'Wait a little longer---give these others I love so much a chance to become Christian, too, before the end of time.'"

The chorus says, "Wait a little longer, please, Jesus. There's so many still wand'ring out in sin. Just a little longer, please, Jesus. A few more days to get our loved ones in."

I am looking forward to the day Jesus calls me home. I am sure you are as well. However, I believe every one of us would want the Lord to wait just a little longer if we knew our spouse, parent, brother, sister, child or grandchild was not ready for that day.

I can be just as impatient as the next person, but sometimes, waiting is good.

Jesus, help me be a better witness for You as I wait for Your return. Amen

"For if ye forgive men their trespasses, your heavenly Father will also forgive you:" Matthew 6:14

Several years ago, I unintentionally upset one of my friends in our Sunday school class. We disagreed on the interpretation of a verse in our lesson for the day. I asked, "Do you think the *Bible* is a lie?" Of course I already knew she believes every word it says, but that is what popped out of my mouth!

When I saw how badly I had upset her, I apologized in front of the class. I told her the entire class was well aware of her knowledge and wisdom. I told her I did not mean anything by what I said, I was just being facetious.

But, we all know what it is like to be embarrassed and hurt in front of a group of people. What I said had stung her and she was still hurting. After class, I apologized again. This time, I was sobbing. I do not cry very often and when I do, it is usually just a few tears. But on this day, I was sobbing uncontrollably! I did not know I had that many tears inside me.

She told me to forget it, but I sobbed harder. The last thing I had meant to do was hurt my friend. Another friend had also stayed behind and she mediated the situation. She told my hurt friend I needed to hear her *say* she forgave me. I did not even realize at the time that is what I needed, but she knew.

Of course she forgave me and our friendship is intact, but do you see what can happen when we don't watch our words? We, especially I, need to think before we speak and be aware of how the other person may perceive what we say. When we do hurt someone, the first order of business is to apologize openly and honestly. Go to the person you have hurt with humility and tears.

If we are on the other side of the hurtful words, we need to be like my friend and forgive the one who has hurt us. Jesus said *if* we forgive, our Father in heaven will forgive us. The very next verse says if we don't forgive, neither will He forgive us.

Finally, be a mediator if God so leads. Sometimes a third party can see both sides objectively and recognize the underlying method of reconciliation much better than the ones whose emotions are raw.

King David was well aware of his sin against God. He repented with humility and tears. In Psalm 51, David wrote, "The sacrifices of

God are a broken spirit: a broken and a contrite heart, O God, thou wilt not despise (verse 17)." If God does not despise our broken and contrite hearts, how can we despise those whose hearts are broken and contrite when they have hurt us?

Forgive and you shall be forgiven.

Father God, help me be more forgiving. When I offend those I love, help me come before them with humility and tears to ask for forgiveness. Amen

SEPTEMBER 28th *WATCHING JADA GROW*

"But grow in grace, and in the knowledge of our Lord and Saviour Jesus Christ." II Peter 3:18a

Several years ago, the Women on Mission of my church decided to sponsor a Mother-Daughter Tea. Shannon Loudermilk, our director, asked me to prepare a song to sing. I chose to rewrite the lyrics to an old song from the seventies, "Watching Scotty Grow." The song was written by Mac Davis but recorded by Bobby Goldsboro.

I wrote about my granddaughter Jada. I changed the lyrics to include updated distractions such as Facebook and videos. I also used things mothers like to do such as shopping and watching television, but the sentiment was the same. I wrote about the precious little things Jada does as she is growing up.

Jada and her mom were sitting in front of me as I sang the song. When I finished, I saw tears streaming down my daughter-in-law's face. That was not a credit to my song-writing ability, but a testament to the preciousness of a little child.

Jada has her own distinct personality. She is quite independent, sassy and opinionated. Dare I say, like me? She doesn't like to wear frilly things that are "itchy." She wants her hair to be done a certain way. She is only eight, but already admits to having a "boyfriend." She is definitely growing up.

It seems like yesterday when I held her in my arms and caressed her almost bald head! Now she has a mass of red hair. Where did the days go when we watched *Dora, the Explorer?* Now she likes to play pretend games and to help me cook. Change is hard, but each stage has its own rewards.

I wonder if God looks at us as we mature in Him and thinks about how far we have come? It is not His will that we remain babes. He expects us to grow in grace and in the knowledge of Jesus. This change does not come automatically. We must deliberately draw close to Him, seek His face, pray, read His word, fellowship with other believers and put into practice what we learn.

God's will is for us to move from milk to meat. He is watching us as we grow.

God, help us embrace each stage of our growth. Help us make the most of the time You have given us. Amen

SEPTEMBER 29th   *TALKING ABOUT TRIALS*

"Who comforteth us in all our tribulation, that we may be able to comfort them which are in any trouble, by the comfort wherewith we ourselves are comforted of God." II Corinthians 1:4

George's sister Faye and I have been very close ever since we met. She has been like the older sister I never had. She has done so much for my family I couldn't begin to list all the things. We have been able to talk about almost anything and share our thoughts and feelings. One thing, however, was never really talked about. That was the death of her baby girl, Rhonda.

That changed in 2005, shortly after our grandson Jackson passed away. Faye, her husband Charles, George and I decided to go to Florida for rest and reflection. All four of us were having a hard time dealing with this loss and we thought visiting the Holy Land Experience in Orlando might help us get refocused.

While we did enjoy the theme park, that is not what made the trip worthwhile. The time we spent together talking about our losses made us all feel somewhat better. Faye and Charles could relate to Joel and Jessica's pain and suffering in the death of a baby. It helped them to finally open up about their own bereavement. Their loss gave us more insight about what Joel and Jessica were most likely going through.

The Bible tells us to bear one another's burdens and that is what we did. We came alongside each other and helped one another endure the emotional upheaval we had encountered. In his second letter to the Corinthians, Paul said believers can pass on to others the comfort they have received from God. Being comforted by God does not make our troubles go away, but rather gives us the ability to stand strong while we are in the middle of them. We experience God's compassion while we are suffering.

No suffering is pleasant. Jonathan Martin, author of *How to Survive a Shipwreck,* wrote: "There are some losses that in their way mark you forever, and some things you never get over. The shipwreck that threatened to destroy you utterly, may be the thing that saves you yet. It may not drown you; it may transfigure you."

While Jackson's death may not have exactly transfigured us, it for sure did not drown us. Yes, we have been marked forever by this loss, just as Faye and Charles are marked by their loss. We may never get *over* our losses, but by the grace of God, we have gotten *through* them.

God of all comfort, I am thankful You have sustained us through every trial. Amen

SEPTEMBER 30th *WHAT IS A CHURCH?*

"And I say also unto thee, That thou art Peter, and upon this rock I will build my church; and the gates of hell shall not prevail against it."
Matthew 16:18

This is the first verse in which the word *church* is used. Jesus spoke these words to his disciple, Simon Peter. The word *church* is translated from the Greek word *ekklesia,* which means a "calling out." Or, you might say, a popular meeting, especially a religious congregation.

On what was Jesus building His church? Not on Peter himself, even though his name meant "rock," but on Peter's recognition of Jesus as the Son of God. Certainly, Peter was very important in establishing the church, but it was Peter's declaration of faith in Jesus as the Messiah that prompted Jesus' words.

We read in the New Testament about churches in homes of the new believers. In many countries, that is still where the churches meet. Or, they may meet in a public area or by a body of water. Unlike the Jewish synagogue, there is no minimum number of men required. The Bible tells us Jesus Himself is the cornerstone of the church.

But what is the basic function of the church? Henry W. Beecher wrote, "The church is not a gallery for the exhibition of eminent

Christians, but a school for the education of imperfect ones, a nursery for the care of weak ones, a hospital for the healing of those who need assiduous care."

Our churches today seem well equipped to carry out all three of these functions. We learn through Bible studies and Sunday school classes, we care for our weaker members and we point those who are sin-sick to the Great Physician.

All members of the true church must come through faith in Jesus. Some people have their names on the church membership roll, yet have never trusted Jesus as Savior and Lord. Are you truly a member of the church? Can you say, like Peter, "Thou art the Christ, the Son of the living God."? If not, your name on the roll will not count for anything when Jesus calls his church out of this world.

If you haven't accepted Him, I urge you to do so before it is too late.

Jesus, I know You are the Christ, the Son of God. I am thankful to be a member of Your church. Amen

OCTOBER

"He that saith he abideth in him ought himself also so to walk, even as he walked." I John 2:6

The writer of I John is the disciple "whom Jesus loved." That is the way he referred to himself in the gospel of John. He is the son of Zebedee and brother of James. Before Jesus called him to be a disciple, John was a fisherman and a business partner of Simon Peter and his brother Andrew.

Although John doesn't identify himself as the writer, scholars agree three epistles were written by his hand. I John does not even identify the recipient. However, all believers today can learn from the words John penned down. We all should not only learn from them, but we should put them into practice.

In this book, the second chapter begins this way, "My little children, these things write I unto you, that you sin not." Verses three through five tell us, "And hereby we do know that we know him, if we keep his commandments. He that saith I know him, and keepeth not his commandments, is a liar, and the truth is not in him. But whoso keepeth his word, in him verily is the love of God perfected: hereby know we that we are in him."

In other words, our behavior should, at all times, be like that of Jesus Himself. Jesus obeyed God perfectly. While none of us, because of our inherent sin nature, can ever attain perfection on this earth, we should constantly strive to keep our minds and our bodies under control by submission to the Holy Spirit.

As we grow in grace and in the knowledge of Jesus, it becomes easier to deny ourselves on a more consistent basis. As young people, however, we think we know everything, we do not want to listen to our parents or teachers, we are quick to fly off the handle and we tend to experiment with sin's pleasures.

In Sunday school one morning, my friend Jamie Thompson made this statement, "I never did live it up while I was young but I never did have anything to live down, either." I sure wish I could say that. I did not get involved in a lot of things my peers did, but I sure have had to live down some things. Unfortunately, not all of them were done as a young person.

I have no excuse for some of the things I have had to live down. My temper, as well as my tongue, still gets me in trouble from time to time. But, I praise the Lord for helping me keep them both in check most of the time! While I do fairly well at keeping the outward man in submission, the inward man is too often a mess.

Paul the apostle wrote these words, "For the good that I would I do not: but the evil which I would not, that I do (Romans 7:19)." I know we can all relate to Paul's dilemma. The only way we can be delivered from this body of death is through the Lord Jesus.

John, the disciple whom Jesus loved, knew we would need help from the Lord to walk the right way. So did the apostle Paul. Furthermore, so do we all. It is not always easy to walk in the Spirit, but it is always expedient.

Let's start today. Let's walk in the Spirit so we do not fulfill the lust of the flesh. Let us not be found guilty of living it up. That way, we will not have to worry about living anything down.

Jesus, help me walk as You walked. Help me live for You alone. Amen

OCTOBER 2nd *ANNIVERSARY CELEBRATION*

◆━━◆

"For this cause shall a man leave his father and mother, and cleave to his wife." Mark 10:7

In 2007, I began a prayer journal. I only write in the prayer journal whenever the Spirit moves me to do so. I did not want this journal to become one more thing I would need to check off my "to do" list each day. Even though I pray multiple times each day, I do not write down my prayers very frequently.

In January of 2008, I wrote down a prayer for some friends who were going through divorces. I also wrote down a prayer for a friend whose husband had recently passed away.

I wrote these words about my own situation: "Lord, I know how my divorce not only rocked my world, but shattered it. Lord, You know I did not want to face life without my mate. But,You kept me in the palm of Your hand. You brought me through it. You gave me friends to talk to and to pray with. Most importantly, you brought love back into my life when you sent George my way. Lord, I am so thankful to have a loving, caring husband who has stuck by me through thick and thin. No matter how mean, ugly, sickly, spiteful, etc. I am, he has always been right there beside me. Thank You that he tries his best to take care of me. I believe, Lord, he would give me his last dollar and he would go hungry before he'd let me be in want. I thank You for the example he is of Your unconditional love."

I also wrote, "I just pray for (my two friends) to find someone of their own who will be a godly husband to them. I certainly don't want to leave (another friend) out. I pray that the day will come when she will praise your name that (her husband) wanted out of their marriage. I pray that you'd just work all this together for her good. I love You, Lord. Amen"

Forty-one years ago today, I married my soul mate and the love of my life. I thank God every day for a good husband like George. He is truly a man who left his mother (his father was deceased) to cleave to his wife. We have had a wonderful marriage.

If you are hoping and praying for a spouse, I hope you find one like mine. If you are going through a divorce, I understand the stress that brings. But I am also living proof that God works everything together for good. It just takes a little time. When you feel hopeless, look to the Blessed Hope. He loves and cares for you like no other can.

Jesus, I am so thankful, especially today, for the man You sent my way. Thank You for our marriage. Help those who are struggling with relationship issues. Amen

OCTOBER 3rd   *THY WILL BE DONE*

"Saying, Father, if thou be willing, remove this cup from me: nevertheless, not my will but thine, be done." Luke 22:42

Hillary Scott of Lady Antebellum fame released her first solo single in 2016. The title of the song is "Thy Will Be Done." Scott says the song stems from a letter she wrote to God after a very traumatic life experience.

In the song, she says she knows God sees and hears her, she knows He is good, but "this" don't feel good right now. Have you been in a situation like this before? I know I have, and I believe all of us could say the same thing. It is hard to be joyful when the noise distracts us and we are trying to make sense of His promises. Like Scott's song says, "Sometimes I gotta stop, Remember You're God and I'm not."

Even when we hear God loud and clear, sometimes we may follow through and end up in a hurtful situation. We don't want to think our broken hearts are part of His plan! We want to know why, don't we?

Jesus heard God loud and clear and followed through all the way to the cross of Calvary. On the eve of that event, Jesus prayed the cup of suffering might pass from Him. Yet, He said, "Not my will, but thine be done." Not a single one of us will ever go through the agony that our Savior endured, but when we face devastating trials, we feel we are being crucified.

We beg for answers. We don't understand how God could possibly allow some things to happen to us. We can't see how He could work those things together to bring good out of them. That is when we must stop and remember He is God and we are not. The blessing comes when we submit to His will in spite of not having the answer.

Yes, some things are very painful, but God will see us through them. We can exercise our faith, knowing God will never fail us. When we can't understand, we can trust.

Father, Thy will be done. Amen

OCTOBER 4th *LEAF-LOOKING*
◆━━◆

"And by the river upon the bank thereof, on this side and on that side, shall grow all trees for meat, whose leaf shall not fade, neither shall the fruit thereof be consumed: it shall bring forth new fruit according to his months, because their waters they issued out of the sanctuary: and the fruit thereof shall be for meat, and the leaf thereof for medicine." Ezekiel 47:12

I love fall! It is my favorite season. My grandmother did not care for fall because she said everything was dying during this part of the year. While that may be true, I love the beautiful colors of fall and I love the cool, crisp air.

Every year, we join the throngs of people who head to the higher elevations to look at the leaves. One September, we went to Vermont to experience a New England autumn.

When he was driving, George did not appreciate my enthusiasm for the beautiful foliage. Every time I would gasp, he would automatically put on the brakes! Then he would tell me to stop scaring him!

I often tell people the colorful leaves make my heart sing. I never tire of seeing the red, orange or gold hillsides. I have probably snapped hundreds of pictures of them and have yet to see one that does justice to God's paintbrush.

My grandmother probably knew the chlorophyll disappeared from the leaves during the fall and that is what made the oranges and yellows visible. She probably knew the trees stopped producing food for the winter. She probably didn't know the glucose stored in the leaves made the maple leaves red and wastes stored in the oak leaves made them turn brown. But she definitely knew all this was part of "dying."

Ezekiel tells of a time when God will bring restoration. The river he wrote about will issue from under the threshold of the house and flow eastward. The river will bring life to the land. Ezekiel says, on each side of the river, there will be trees whose leaves will never fade. Furthermore, the leaves will be for medicine.

My grandmother and I would agree that will be a wonderful "season."

Lord God, thank You for the promise of a better time to come. Amen

OCTOBER 5th *BETTER THAN A BIRD*

"Are not two sparrows sold for a farthing? And one of them shall not fall on the ground without your Father." Matthew 10:29

As young boys, my sons had, at one time or another, almost every pet imaginable. Dogs, cats, hamsters, gerbils, turtles, fish, and birds were all a part of our family. I did draw the line, though, when it came to having a snake or a tarantula! My grandchildren Logan, Liam and Lainey do have a ball python, but that doesn't bother me. I just won't spend the night with them!

We had a parakeet which one of the boys named Flying Cloud. With the white on his head and his pale blue body, whenever he took flight he did remind us of a cloud flying through the house.

Then came the day Flying Cloud was no more. I can't remember exactly what caused his demise. I was working when the end came. I just remember coming home from work and as I began to prepare our dinner, I opened the trash can and there lay his dead body! I was livid.

I began to ask questions. I wondered who would be so heartless as to toss this pet into the garbage can? How could anyone be so cruel? I never handled the bird, nor cared for its flying around, but I was shocked to see it discarded in this manner. I insisted on a proper burial in the backyard.

In the gospel of Matthew, Jesus is telling the disciples how important they are to God. He tells His followers not to be afraid of those who can kill the body but cannot kill the soul. He assures them with this verse about the sparrows. He says God knows and consents every time a sparrow falls, and they are of much more value than many sparrows.

The same is true for us today. God knows even the number of hairs on our head (verse 30). He knows our days from beginning to end. He filters through His fingers of love everything that comes our way. The enemy cannot do anything to us that God has not allowed him to do. So, we can endure testing, even persecution, knowing we are precious in His sight.

When those times come, we can, as Jonny Diaz sings, breathe, just breathe. We can take into our lungs the peace of God that overcomes and let our weary spirits rest. God has got this and He has got us, too.

Father God, thank You that I am better than a bird in Your sight. Amen

OCTOBER 6th *FREQUENT FLUBS*

"For the Lord taketh pleasure in his people: he will beautify the meek with salvation." Psalm 149:4

If anyone has been keeping a record of all my mistakes in this book, I am sure the list is quite long. No one is perfect, and sometimes it is the imperfections that make people the most charming.

While I say things that are not grammatically correct, I sometimes cringe when I hear those same things come from the lips of others. For instance, I hate hearing anyone use "I" when the correct word is "me."
I hear it all the time in church when people say, "Jesus died for you and I." I want to scream out, "No, He didn't. He died for you and ME!" When talking to family and close friends, though, I often say, "Me and George," instead of, "George and I."

People also say, for instance, "She gave George and I a gift." In this sentence, the preposition is understood, not stated, so maybe that causes the confusion? I don't know. What I do know is we all try too hard to be proper and perfect and that is when we mess up the worst. I am just as guilty as anyone. I use words incorrectly even though I know better.

Some of the malapropisms I hear endear the speaker to me. I had a friend who used the word *pacific* when she meant *specific*. I have a family member who says *forgotten* instead of *begotten*. Maybe you have heard of the *confession* stand at the ball park?

We hate to have egg on our faces when we say the wrong thing. We are "absolutely humiliated" when we mispronounce a word, or we just want to "die" if we give an incorrect statistic. But, being able to laugh at ourselves and our frequent flubs helps keep us meek. When we admit our vulnerability to mess up, we don't take ourselves so seriously.

The Bible says God takes pleasure in his people. He sees and hears every wrong thing we do, yet He loves us. He beautifies the meek with salvation. We don't have to be perfect for the Lord to take pleasure in us. I am not at all suggesting sin is charming. My intent is to focus on our frequent flubs that we take too seriously. Let us, then, admit our imperfection. Let's lighten up and enjoy the day.

God gave you and I (no, ME!) the gift of laughter. Let's use that gift and laugh at ourselves because we are all imperfect.

Lord, help me stop trying to be so prim and proper that I lose the charm of imperfection. Amen

OCTOBER 7th *STANDING IN THE GAP*

"And I sought for a man among them, that should make up the hedge, and stand in the gap before me for the land, that I should not destroy it: but I found none." Ezekiel 22:30

God said He had looked for one to stand in the gap for the land so that He wouldn't destroy it, but He found none. "Therefore," He said, "have I poured out mine indignation upon them; I have consumed them with the fire of my wrath: their own way have I recompensed upon their heads."

I think of Abraham standing in the gap for Sodom and Gomorrah. He pleaded for the inhabitants of the cities. He asked God to spare them if only ten righteous people could be found there. The Lord agreed, but, unfortunately, not even ten could be found. Fire and brimstone came down from heaven and destroyed all the inhabitants and all which grew upon the ground (Genesis 18 & 19).

Did you realize we are still called to stand in the gap? To intercede for others is not just a suggestion, it is our job! In I Timothy, Paul wrote, "I exhort therefore, that, first of all, supplications, prayers, intercessions, and giving of thanks, be made for all men (2:1)."

Even though I pray for others every day, there is one instance I recall fondly. Many years ago, I prayed fervently for a particular young man at my church. Our friend Louise informed me this young man told the church I had stood in the gap for him. It made me feel good, of course, to know he recognized my intercession. Better still, it made me feel good to know his life had been spared and he had turned back to the Lord.

Take a look around you today. There are so many needs we can lift up to the Lord. Be an intercessor. Pray fervently for others. I can promise you there will come a time when you will need intercession for yourself or someone you love.

Lord, I want to stand in the gap for others. Have mercy on us all. Amen

OCTOBER 8th *FUTURE PLANS*

"A wicked man hardeneth his face: but as for the upright, he directeth his way." Proverbs 21:29

When I was growing up in Cumming, there was nothing much to do around this town. We have the lake, and we lived within walking distance, but my family never went there. I did go occasionally with my Stanford cousins, but I did not enjoy it that much because I don't swim.

Outside of Sunday school, my church did not have any activities for young people. However, I did take piano lessons for awhile, and I was in a Girl Scout troop led by Mrs. Alice Mashburn. I also bowled in a league on Saturday mornings when I was in junior high school. Back then, most of the neighborhood children were relatives, and we played outside games or rode our bicycles.

But, I suppose that is why I spent so much time reading. I was just bored, otherwise. I always dreamed of moving so far away my family could not even afford to call me long distance!

Now, long distance is basically a thing of the past and I no longer have a desire to move. Our sons have moved away, but they are all within an hour's drive. They have said we should sell and relocate, but we are so close to the church, the hospital, our doctors, Wal-Mart and Home Depot, that moving seems like a ridiculous idea!

Now, I can close my eyes and see my cousins and myself making a playhouse. We used pine straw to mark off the rooms. We used sand, sticks, grass and leaves to make our pretend meals. Or, I can see us lying on our backs and attempting to identify objects in the sky made from the fluffy, white clouds. Later, we daydreamed about who our future husbands might be and what we would name our children. We wished time would float on by, like the clouds, and we were grown-up already, living in some big city far away.

Yet, here I am. Less than five miles from the home I grew up in. I think back to those simpler times when I spent too much time wishing my life away. The mystery of being an adult is now history! Decades later, I am still right here where I never longed to be. But, I am content and thankful for the memories.

The Lord saw fit to leave me here. My thoughts about my future were not the same as His, but now our thoughts are reconciled. He had a plan for my life that was hidden from my view. Even now, I do not know what tomorrow holds, but I know who holds tomorrow. I know I can trust the Lord to direct my way.

Jesus I pray I never harden my face against You. Thank You for directing my life, step by step. Amen

OCTOBER 9th *AS THE TWIG IS BENT*

◆————————————————————————————◆

"I am forgotten as a dead man out of mind: I am like a broken vessel." Psalm 31:12

Eighteenth century poet Alexander Pope wrote, "As the twig is bent so grows the tree." This means early influences have a permanent effect on a person's life. Parents and peers, as well as the environment, have a huge impact on a child. In other words, both nurture and nature help shape a child's early development and affect how he acts later in life. Most often, a grown person will act the way he or she was taught as a child.

In *Uninvited,* Lysa Terkeurst wrote about her desire to know her dad loved her. She still twirls about, hating the insecurities and desperate for reassurance. "Brokenness is universal. We all have things in life that trigger deep insecurities and our personal 'twirling about,' searching for reassurance," she said. She realizes now her reassurance can only come from God. Terkeurst wrote, "The blanket of His presence and His protection is the only perfect fit for the deep creases and crevices carved inside me."

She went on to list some truths from God's word and she prays the truths will flood our hearts with peace as they do hers. These truths give us the permission to stop twirling and start living like we are loved. Look these verses up for yourself today: Psalm 36:5, Psalm 48:9, Zephaniah 3:17, and Ephesians 3:17b & 18.

Maybe your dad loved you very much. Maybe your brokenness was caused by something, or someone, else. Whatever you personally struggle with, bring it to Jesus. Don't feel that you have been forgotten. There is no need to continue feeling like a broken vessel. Let the Lord restore your soul.

When you feel less than, left out and lonely, just remember "set apart" does not mean "set aside." The enemy wants us to feel rejected, but Jesus said He would not turn anyone aside (John 6:37).

Sure, some of our deep-seated issues spring from our childhoods, but we can have the victory over those things that keep us bent down.

Jesus, thank You for Your unfailing, unconditional love. Regardless of what has had me bent or broken, I can stand tall in You. Amen

OCTOBER 10th *AS DEATH FINDS YOU*

"If the clouds be full of rain, they empty themselves upon the earth: and if the tree fall toward the south, or toward the north, in the place where the tree falleth, there it shall be." Ecclesiastes 11:3

Somerset Maugham, British author and playwright, retold an ancient Mesopotamian tale and titled the story "Appointment in Samarra." Here is my condensed version.

A merchant in Bagdad sent his servant to the market. When the servant returned he was white and trembling. He said a woman in the crowd jostled him and, when he turned, he saw it was Death. The servant said Death made a threatening gesture to him. He asked to borrow the merchant's horse so he could ride away to Samarra and avoid Death. The merchant agreed and the servant rode away. The merchant then went to the market, found Death and questioned her about the meeting with his servant. Death said she was just surprised to see the servant in Bagdad, for she had an appointment with him that night in Samarra!

This tale lets us know we cannot avoid death. It will come for us all. We can run from death, but we can't hide. And when death does find us, we will then be unable to change our destiny. The Bible says as a tree falls, there it shall be. In other words, in whatever condition you are found at death, you will face judgment accordingly.

We never know when our appointment with death will take place. Therefore, we should make preparations now. The Bible says, "Now is the accepted time; behold, now is the day of salvation (II Corinthians 6:2)." If the Holy Spirit is bidding you, "Come," please don't delay. Death may be lurking just around the corner, and it is not God's will that any should perish but that all should come to repentance (II Peter 3:9).

Lord, I am so thankful I have made my calling and election sure. When death finds me, I am prepared to meet You. Amen

OCTOBER 11th *A SOUND MIND*

"For God hath not given us the spirit of fear; but of power, and of love, and of a sound mind." II Timothy 1:7

We all make jokes about losing our minds. I saw a T-shirt that had this on the front, "Of all the things I've lost, I miss my mind the most." As we age, we do miss being able to remember things like we did when we were younger. We miss being able to multi-task like we did when our children were underfoot. We go into a room and forget why we went there. We can recall every detail of something that happened when we were children, but can't remember to buy milk when we pass by it in the store!

Losing our short-term memory is just a natural part of the aging process. Or so I have read. However, dementia and Alzheimer's are no laughing matter. Both cause a decline in the ability to think, and they are both debilitating. Although Alzheimer's is a form of dementia, they are a bit different.

A couple of years ago, I saw on the internet that the mother of a friend of mine had passed away. I had not seen this man in years, maybe not even since we graduated, but I had written about him in my first devotional book and wanted to let him know. I went to the funeral home to pay my respects and I took along a photocopy of the page where I'd mentioned him.

First of all, I did not even recognize him. Someone had to point him out to me. Sadly, he did not even remember me, much less the days I had written about. One of his aunts told me he was suffering from dementia. Hearing the news broke my heart.

But, why was Paul writing to Timothy about a sound mind? Timothy was the young pastor of the church in Ephesus. Paul, his mentor, was in prison almost one thousand miles away. Knowing he needed encouragement, Paul wrote this letter exhorting Timothy to use the gifts God had given him.

The sound mind in verse seven refers to self-discipline. Despite discouraging or fearful circumstances, we must be on guard and continue to be bold. When we feel our beliefs, or our lives, are threatened, we must hold on to God's word and keep walking in faith.

The spirit of fear does not come from God but from our enemy the devil. When fear stalks us, we can resist it in the name of Jesus. Throughout the Bible, we are repeatedly told not to fear, but to be of good courage.

God has given us the spirit of power, love and self-discipline. While our minds are still "sound," let's exercise the gifts God so freely gave us.

Father God, help me walk in power, love and self-discipline every day. Amen

"Therefore we are buried with him by baptism into death: that like as Christ was raised up from the dead by the glory of the Father, even so we also should walk in newness of life." Romans 6:4

Everyone knows NFL stands for National Football League. It was formed from the American Professional Football Association in 1922. For three years, it sputtered along until Red Grange was signed on in 1925. Today, the NFL is listed as America's favorite in sporting contests.

Several years ago, I read about a pastor who found himself in very difficult circumstances. Many people were afraid to try ministering to him because the pastor is the one who normally gives the supportive and encouraging words. Most of his congregation was hesitant to say anything at all. Not one burly, gruff ex-Army sergeant, though. He walked right up to the pastor and said, "What you need is just being normal. Come to my house Monday night. We'll watch football."

I just happened to be watching the Falcons play against the Giants the very night I was reading that story! I don't know how things turned out for the pastor, but I know I love football on Mondays, Thursdays and Sundays. Saturdays, too, during the play-offs! And that is why I loved the Bible covers at Heavenly Dove that had NFL on them.

But, on those Bible covers, the NFL stands for New Found Life, not National Football League. New Found Life is even better! Once we have been saved, the next step is to be baptized. As we are raised up from the "liquid grave," we are to walk in newness of life.

The Roman believers were in a quandary. They wondered whether they should sin more and more so God could pour out more and more grace upon them. Paul the apostle said, "God forbid." He asked, "How shall we, that are dead to sin, live any longer therein (verse 2)?" He went on to say, "Likewise reckon ye also yourselves to be dead indeed unto sin but alive unto God through Jesus Christ our Lord (verse 11)."

No, believers are not to let sin reign in their mortal bodies. We are to walk in newness of life because we are now servants to God. Yes, we still have a sin nature, but we are not to obey it any longer. Once we have this New Found Life, sin is not to have dominion over us. The New Found Life gives us fruit unto holiness and everlasting life.

The wages of sin is death, but the gift of God is eternal life through Jesus Christ our Lord (verse 23). Have you found this new life? If not, ask Jesus to save you today.

Jesus, I am so thankful for my New Found Life. Help me yield myself unto God as an instrument of righteousness. Amen

OCTOBER 13th *FAVORITES*

"Beloved, if God so loved us, we ought also to love one another."
I John 4:11

Just a few days ago, I wrote about John referring to himself as the disciple whom Jesus loved. Surely, John did not think Jesus did not love the others. This reminds me of the plaque that says, "Jesus loves you, but I'm His favorite." Why do you suppose John thought he was the favorite?

My granddaughter Jada asks me from time to time which grandchild I love best. Thankfully, I can tell her, "Ryan is my favorite young man, Tyler is my favorite teen-ager, Jake is my favorite little boy, you are my favorite little girl and Josi is my favorite baby!" That usually pacifies her.

Thinking Jesus has a favorite is outrageous, maybe even a little sacrilegious, but very human. I believe we all have an innate desire to be loved the best. No one wants to be "second fiddle" when it comes to the affections department.

But, the love Jesus has for us is so much greater than we can imagine. In Ephesians 3:18 & 19, Paul says he wants us to comprehend the breadth, length, and depth, and height; and to know the love of Christ, which passeth knowledge. We can't really understand a love like Jesus has for us. It is limitless, it is ineffable, it is unfailing.

Edward Grinnan, editor-in-chief and vice-president of *Guideposts,* says, "He loves all of us equally and infinitely. We are each His favorite." Our former pastor Craig Richard modeled this kind of love to the members of Pine Crest. I always told people, "Craig treats each one of us as if we are his favorite."

I ask myself, how am I doing at treating others this way? I have to admit, I am not doing so well. There are people at my church I hardly ever speak to. It is not because I don't care for them, it is just because it is hard to get around to everyone. Especially when they sit across the aisle and get out and gone before I do. Just yesterday, I was thinking of a young mother I need to reach out to more often.

When this life is over, we will see Jesus as He is, we will know as we are known and we will be able to love as Jesus does. Until then, we need to "practice" loving everyone with a love like His. We need to make each person in our lives think we love him or her best!

Jesus, Your love is so much greater than ours, but I want to model Your love to everyone. I need Your help. Amen

OCTOBER 14th *STEPPING STONES*

"My brethren, count it all joy when ye fall into divers temptations."
James 1:2

I am guilty of not counting divers temptations as joy. I admit it. I don't like trials and tests, even though I know God has a purpose for them. I have been through enough of them to know God works all of them together for my good. I have experienced enough in my life to fully realize how much better I am, spiritually, when I come through a trial victoriously. So what is the problem?

When money worries, job issues, family matters, health concerns or any other troubles come, I don't immediately utter, "Oh, joy!" But I should, I think. God has proven Himself faithful time and time again. I should be able to thank Him and trust Him regardless of the external circumstances.

Our son Joel recently posted a picture of his son Jake on Facebook. Jake was in the water at Poole's Mill. He had slipped on the rocks and the caption was, "Banana Split." Thankfully, he was not hurt, but the picture reminds me of my own slipping on the stepping stones God puts in front of me.

God is not trying to make me slip, but rather He is providing a means of sure-footing. James continued his thought with these words, "Knowing this, that the trying of your faith worketh patience (verse 3). Patience is another word for perseverance.

Temptations, then, are just a given for any follower of Christ. They are opportunities for growth. Challenges are stepping stones that guide us and prepare us for life's journey. So, I need to step on each one, knowing the path will be clearer with each step.

Are you facing a trial today? Just remember, this stepping stone is instruction for your soul. Count it all joy!

Jesus, I want to persevere. Help me step *on* these stones of temptations rather than try to step *over* or *around* them. Amen

OCTOBER 15th *OUTNUMBERED*

"And five of you shall chase an hundred, and an hundred of you shall put ten thousand to flight: and your enemies shall fall before you by the sword." Leviticus 26:8

Tyler's five-year-old soccer team was having fun running, kicking and trying to score, but they were struggling to win. Once, though, Tyler scored four goals and his coach said he was their "ace in the hole."

We thought we had a sure-fire victory ahead when we were scheduled to play a team with only three players. We thought for certain those little guys would soon be tired out. Would you believe they ran circles around our team and wore us out instead?

That result was quite different from the one God promised the nation of Israel if they obeyed His commandments. God said they would be victorious, no matter how outnumbered they were, if they would worship Him only. But they did not obey. They bowed before their gods of wood and stone.

God would have rewarded their obedience with tangible blessings, but they stiffened their necks and turned their backs on Him. They saw His anger poured out on them in diseases, disasters and defeats.

God is still displeased with idolatry. We may not bow down to gods of wood or stone, but we often put power, prestige, prosperity and our physical appearance first in our lives. The Bible says God is a jealous God (e.g. Exodus 20:5). Since He never changes (James 1:17), we must be on guard against idolatry in our own lives.

There is no need for us to be routed by our enemy. With God, one is a majority. Let us, then, outnumber our foes by putting God first.

Dear God, I want no other gods before You. Amen

OCTOBER 16th *SOBBING FOR A STRANGER*

"I am weary of my crying: my throat is dried: mine eyes fail while I wait for my God." Psalm 69:3

In October of 1982, Jerry West was diagnosed with inoperable brain cancer. I did not know Jerry West and he did not know me. I did not know any member of his family on a personal basis. But I had seen his wife once!

Marion Bond West had been invited to speak to a group of ladies at the Western Steer Steak House one evening. I was privileged to be among those who attended. Marion spoke about her marriage, her family and her walk with God. She told hilarious tales of mothering two daughters and a set of twin boys. Mostly, though, she talked about how she depended on God to get her through each day.

As a subscriber to *Guideposts*, I was thrilled each time an article appeared that she had written. Did I mention she was from Georgia? As I read more and more of her stories, I felt as if Marion were my good friend. I felt I knew her family quite well. That is why I was so upset when Jerry died.

I will never forget the day I found out about his death. I was living on Antioch Road at the time. I opened my latest edition of *Guideposts*, only to discover she had written about Jerry's passing. I was absolutely devastated. I can distinctly remember "crying my eyes out." I knew from Marion's writings that Jerry was a Christian. I was not crying for him because I knew his hope was in the Lord. I was crying for my "friend" Marion and her little family.

I suffered with her as her children grew up without their father. I ached when her twin boys got into trouble with substance abuse. I was sad when her daughter Julie got married too young. Years later, I was able to rejoice with her as she fell in love with a minister from Oklahoma.

Marion says the one word that God planted in her pounding heart was *nevertheless*. It is used more than two hundred times in the Bible. She says God is not a God of *what if,* but of *nevertheless.* She says the power of "nevertheless living" is what got her through.

I almost never cry anymore. It makes my eyes hurt, my nose gets stuffy and my throat gets dry. It is an uncomfortable thing to do. I do cry from time to time, but it is a rare thing for me. Plus, crying does not change anything at all.

I sometimes wish I could still cry like I once did. Tears, they say, are therapeutic. Tears show your empathy. But it seems I have no tears left. I know I cried out a good portion of them when I learned of the death of this stranger. *Nevertheless,* God sees my tears, even when they don't run down my face.

Father God, So many times I have become weary of crying. Nevertheless, I wait on You. Amen

OCTOBER 17th *EARS THAT HEAR*

"He that hath ears to hear, let him hear." Matthew 11:15

In October of 1994, a baby boy was born into the Hitt family in Tampa, Florida. My brother Danny and his wife Casie were the parents. This baby was named Hunter. I did not get to see him for awhile since he was so far away. When I did see him, I thought he was so precious. He had eyes that just sparkled!

In June of 1997, we heard such depressing news about Hunter. He was not hard of hearing, he was totally deaf. I thought about all the sounds he would never hear. He could hear no music, no birds singing, no laughter, no crack of the bat, no thunder, no tree frogs, no revving engines, no barking dogs, no "I love you." Nothing. Totally deaf.

I talked with George about possibly helping them get cochlear implants for him. Danny said the doctor told them those would be of no use in Hunter's situation. Danny and Casie learned sign language and taught Hunter to sign. Although I knew the manual alphabet in high school (and got into trouble by "talking" with my friend Kim Rucker during class!), I no longer remembered it. Besides, at age three, Hunter could not yet spell words anyway.

He managed quite well in spite of this. He thrived and I was the one who felt handicapped. I needed Danny or Casie to convey to him what I was trying to say. We did a lot of high-fives and thumbs-up. When he learned to read, we could write notes to each other. Now he uses the computer all the time! Technology really is wonderful.

In John 11, Jesus was talking to the multitudes about John the Baptist. Jesus said those who stand strong in their faith, despite their suffering, are blessed. He says John is the messenger who went before Him to prepare the way and, among those born by natural means, there is no one greater than John. However, he that is least in the kingdom of heaven is greater than John. Jesus said if the people would receive it, John is Elias, which was to come. In other words, a new day was coming for God's people and John's ministry was the harbinger.

Then Jesus spoke the words in verse fifteen. He realizes the truths He has just shared with the people are difficult to grasp, but He calls everyone who hears the message about Him to believe it! He is the Only Begotten Son of God who gave His life for our salvation.

Have you heard it? Do you believe it?

Jesus, I am so thankful for my ears that heard the gospel. I do believe. Amen

OCTOBER 18th *MISTAKEN IDENTITY*

◆————————————————————————————————————◆

"For now we see through a glass, darkly; but then face to face: now I know in part; but then shall I know even as also I am known."
I Corinthians 13:12

A funny thing happened to our son Justin several years ago. He was in Home Depot in another r town when he heard an announcement over the intercom. He heard, "Justin Sams, call extension 123 (or whatever the number was)." He was quite surprised. He thought, "Who knows I am here?" The announcement came again.

He located a phone and called the extension. The lady on the other end told him there was a suspicious person on aisle ten and she needed him to go check it out! Justin told her, "Ma'am, I don't even work here." Just then another guy came up wearing a name tag on his Home Depot apron. His name? Justin Sams, of course!

We have laughed over this little episode time and again. Naturally, the lady on the phone could not see Justin and did not know she was talking to the wrong fellow. Had she seen him, she would most certainly have known because the two men were nothing alike.

On the other hand, I have often been mistaken for my cousin, Deenie, and she for me. I was ushering one night at the Cumming Playhouse when I saw a lady who looked exactly like Hillary Clinton. In fact, I am always guilty of thinking someone looks like another person.

In his letter to the Corinthian church, Paul wrote he would one day see Jesus face to face. He said he would then know as he was also known. In other words, he would no longer see Jesus as if looking through a dark glass. He would fully behold Him in all His glory. Paul would no longer have a limited understanding, but a perfect one.

When we see Jesus, there will be no mistaken identities. We will know Him as well as He knows us.

Lord, I look forward to the day when I will see You face to face. Amen

OCTOBER 19th *MY SPOT*

"That he might present it to himself a glorious church, not having spot, or wrinkle, or any such thing; but that it should be holy and without blemish." Ephesians 5:27

In October of 2008, I heard on the news there had been no sunspots for two hundred days. That was the longest period of time without the spots since 1954. A sunspot is a dark area appearing from time to time on the surface of the sun. It is an area of reduced temperature caused by some magnetic field issues. I do not pretend to understand all that entails.

All this talk about spots reminds me of what Reverend Danny Bennett says. From time to time he will talk about the spot where he was made spotless! What he means by this is he has a spot where the Lord saved his soul and made him presentable to God. Like Paul wrote in Ephesians, the church (all those who are believers) has been made without spot or wrinkle or blemish. We have been counted as holy because Jesus' death paid the penalty for our sins.

I have a spot like Danny's. It is located in Roanoke Baptist Church. As you walk in the door, it would be the front bench on the left hand side. I knelt down at that bench on the end nearest the wall and asked Jesus to save my soul! At the time, I did not pretend to know all that might entail. I simply knew I was in need of His saving grace and I asked for it. I knew I did not want to die and go to hell.

That took place in 1961, when I was just ten years old. Since then, I guess you could compare my life to a sunspot. I have had many days when I was not on fire for the Lord. I certainly had times when my temperature, or fervor, for Him was reduced. I guess you could say I had issues with my magnetic field, because I was not drawing close enough to the Lord. I am praying I can go for two hundred days at a time now with none of these spots.

The blemishes on my life, like the sunspots, are evident to others, but God sees me as Holy. When He looks at me, He still sees me as spotless because the blood of Jesus has washed away my sins' stains. Have you been made spotless? Do you have a spot like ours? If not, I urge you to ask Jesus into your heart today.

Spotless Lamb, help me live a life that is pleasing to You. Help me not to be like a sunspot, but like You. Amen

OCTOBER 20th *NO VACATION FROM GOD*

"Preach the word; be instant in season, out of season; reprove, rebuke, exhort with all longsuffering and doctrine." II Timothy 4:2

Last year, for our fortieth anniversary, George and I took an eleven day trip to Canada. We toured in three of the ten provinces: Nova Scotia, New Brunswick, and Prince Edward Island. We walked on the ocean floor at the Flowerpot Rocks, we toured the Green Gables house, we had our picture made by the lighthouse at Peggy's Cove, we toured the graveyard where more than two hundred victims of the *Titanic* were buried, we ate lunch at a five-star resort and did so many other things I can't mention them all.

But I want to write about what happened when we were inside the sanctuary of St. Pierre's Catholic Church in Cheticamp, Nova Scotia. I was wandering around, taking pictures of everything. George sat down on a bench to rest. One of our fellow travelers approached George and asked him, "Do you believes in God?"

George told me he looked around and silently said, "God, I am on vacation!" But he told the man, "I believe in Jesus Christ. Without His blood applied to your heart, you will die and go to hell." The man was confused and said he did not know what God he believed in. George talked to him at length about the One True God.

After hearing the truth from George, the man began to get tears in his eyes and walked away. I told George how proud I am of him for speaking the truth in love to this gentleman. I told him that he planted a seed. Someone else may have to water it before God gives the increase.

George did exactly what Paul encouraged Timothy to do. He may have been on vacation, as he said, but he was instant "out of season." He spoke the word and he exhorted this guy with longsuffering and doctrine. He rebuked belief in any other god.

The *Life Application Study Bible* says, "It may be inconvenient to take a stand for Christ or to tell others about his love, but preaching the Word of God is the most important responsibility the church and its members have been given. Be prepared for, courageous in, and sensitive to God-given opportunities to tell the Good News."

A vacation may be the perfect opportunity to witness for the Lord. Are you ready?

Lord, I ask You to help me be prepared for, courageous in and sensitive to the opportunities You give me to tell the Good News. Amen

OCTOBER 21ˢᵗ *HOW SHALL WE FALL?*

"And David said unto Gad, I am in a great strait: let us fall now into the hand of the Lord; for his mercies are great: and let me not fall into the hand of man." II Samuel 24:14

Marty Hoey was considered to be the world's best female high-altitude mountaineer. She had scaled Mount Rainier in Washington over one hundred times. She had also led expeditions to Mount McKinley in Alaska.

In 1982, she was among a group attempting to ascend Mount Everest, the highest peak in the world, from Tibet. Had she been successful, she would have been the first American woman to have accomplished this feat. A Japanese woman, Junko Tabei, had been to the top of Everest in 1975, from the Nepal side.

Unfortunately, Hoey did not make it. Perched on a 45-degree slope, she had leaned back to allow her climbing partner to take the lead when her harness came undone and she fell to her death. Her body was never recovered. She was one of ten fatalities during the 1982 climbing season and the only American to perish.

In II Samuel 24, we read of a mistake King David made. He tried to number the people of Israel; in effect, putting his confidence in his military power instead of God's power. David realized what he had done was not pleasing to the Lord. He confessed his sin and asked for God's forgiveness.

Gad, the seer, came to David and offered him three options from the Lord. The choices were seven years of famine, three months of being routed by his enemies or three days of pestilence. David said he would rather fall into the hand of the Lord and not man. He was surely hoping God would relent.

The Bible tells us God did repent of the evil and stayed the hand of the angel who had stretched out his hand to destroy Jerusalem. However, seventy thousand people died.

Hebrews 10:31, says, "It is a fearful thing to tall into the hands of the living God." That is because God is so holy and so sovereign. He will judge people for their sins. For those who have rejected Him, it will be too late when they face that judgment.

But, for those who accept Christ as Savior, our sins were judged at Calvary and we have no reason to fear. We can have confident trust in the Lord and patiently endure whatever comes from the hand of man.

The book of Jude ends with these words, "Now unto him that is able to keep you from falling, and to present you faultless before the presence of his glory with exceeding joy, To the only wise God our Saviour, be glory and majesty, dominion and power, both now and ever. Amen."

Jesus, I am thankful for Your power to keep me from falling. You alone are worthy of glory and majesty, dominion and power, now and forever. Amen

OCTOBER 22nd   *AWAKENED BY PRAYING*

"Night and day praying exceedingly that we might see your face, and might perfect that which is lacking in your faith?" I Thessalonians 3:10

George and I had been married for several years before I ever heard him pray aloud. Sad to say, but truthful. We had gone to visit a church pastored by one of his co-workers. The pastor called on George to pray the benediction. What a blessing it was for me! I was so proud the man I loved was calling upon the name of the God I loved. I knew George had been saved, but he was not vocal about his faith at that time.

After a couple of experiences with the Lord, when George felt he was surely near-death, that all changed. He began to pray with me every morning and night. We began to pray every time we sat down to a meal. He began to be a witness for the Lord everywhere he happened to be.

Some mornings I would be awakened by his praying. Before my alarm had even gone off, I would become conscious of George asking God to bless me and take care of me. He would be thanking God for giving him a wonderful wife that he could trust. What wife could be upset for being awakened like that?

In the first letter to the church at Thessalonica, Paul, Silvanus and Timotheus wrote to let the people know they were comforted in their affliction and distress by the faith of the Thessalonian believers. The writers wondered what thanks they could render to God for all the joy they had before Him because of the Thessalonians.

Don't you think it was encouraging for the believers to receive this letter? Just knowing Paul, Silvanus and Timotheus recognized and appreciated their strengths had to boost their confidence in their own faith. At the same time, the letter issued challenges and instructions for their continued growth. They prayed night and day that they might travel again to Thessalonica and strengthen these new believers.

All Christians understand our lives are journeys wherein we grow, mature and learn to walk as Jesus did. We have encounters with the Holy Spirit, we worship and pray more, we deepen our relationships with others in the family of God, we are more willing to do humble service for the Lord and we lead holier lives. Paul and his traveling companions wanted all this for the church in Macedonia.

Much like the Thessalonians, I am encouraged by George's prayers for me. He appreciates my faith, he recognizes my strengths and he thanks God for them. He also wants me to continue growing closer to the Lord in my walk. He asks God to shower me with His best.

I could appreciate being awakened every morning hearing a prayer like that!

Lord God, thank You for a praying husband. I ask You to shower him with Your best and draw him ever closer to You. Amen

OCTOBER 23rd *POSITIVE vs. NEGATIVE*

"And the peace of God, which passeth all understanding, shall keep your hearts and minds through Christ Jesus." Philippians 4:7

Post Traumatic Stress Disorder is a mental disorder one may develop after experiencing a traumatic event. It can occur whether a person was involved in the trauma or was a witness to it. PTSD is serious and is potentially debilitating. PTSD has formerly been known as shell shock or battle fatigue. No matter what it is called, the condition can change a person's life, usually for the worst.

I am so sympathetic for soldiers who have experienced the trauma of war. I would not ever pretend to know what that is like. I am in no way comparing the traumas of my life to what they have encountered. However, I have had some traumatic experiences that have affected me for the worst. These events have persisted in my psyche for decades.

It has been impossible to drive the memories away. George will often tell me to stop thinking about them. I just wish it were that easy. It is not that I *want* to torture myself with the reminders, but I often do.

I know the Bible says, "forgetting those things which are behind, and reaching forth unto those things which are before (Philippians 3:13)." That is my goal. I want to turn my traumas into triumph for the Lord. I earnestly desire my life be one of purpose and faith. Frank Freed, World War II hero, said, "We don't have to love our past or even like it, but it is good mental health to accept it. It is only at this moment of acceptance that we will be set free."

It is my choice to accept the traumatic events and know that God is using them for good in my life. He will give me the power to live out that choice and His peace will keep my heart and my mind. You might say He will help me think positive about the negative! He will help you as well.

Dear God, please take the negative aspects of my life and turn them into positive examples of Your peace. Amen

OCTOBER 24th *WEATHER THE WEATHER*

"Who giveth rain upon the earth…" Job 5:10

When asked how we are doing, we often say, "I am a little under the weather." It is funny how the weather affects our well-being. On a sunny day, I feel good and am energized. When dark clouds roll in, I just want to stay indoors and curl up with a good book. No doubt about it, my body is affected by the weather. When the barometric pressure rises, I often have headaches.

Scientists really have no explanation as to why this happens, but they theorize it is due to changes in the oxygen levels. They believe the blood vessels in our heads contract or expand to compensate. Thankfully, my headaches are not severe, just bothersome

The Bible tells us God gives us the rain and sends waters upon the fields. He made a way for the lightning of the thunder (Job 28:26). He made a wind to pass over the earth (Genesis 8:1), He gives snow like wool: He scatters the hoarfrost like ashes (Psalm 147:16), He casts forth His ice like morsels (Psalm 147:17).

We have no control over the weather. There is nothing we can do to change the weather, but we often complain about it, don't we? Here is a little song I once read in *Daily Guideposts:* "Whether the weather be cold, whether the weather be hot, I will weather the weather, whatever the weather, whether I like it or not!"

God is in control. He sends rain on the just and the unjust alike. He makes the sun to rise on the evil and on the good. We all receive blessings from His hand, although none of us deserve one good thing from Him.

Whatever the weather in your corner of the world today, you can be strengthened and energized by the Holy Spirit. You may be surprised how well you can cope when you give God the glory for any kind of weather He sends.

Father God, help me weather the weather, today and every day. Amen

OCTOBER 25th *DAY TO DAY TASKS*

"And let us not be weary in well doing: for in due season we shall reap, if we faint not." Galatians 6:9

Well, she is gone for the rest of the week. Joel has just picked up Josi, and when she left my house was a mess. There were blocks, pieces to a playhouse, books and various other toys scattered about.

After I picked those things up and put them away, there was still a multitude of chores to be done. There were clothes to wash, mail to read, checks to write, dinner to cook, dishes to wash, etc. Sometimes it seems I will never get caught up. But my mountain of tasks is nothing when compared to Orville Worman's.

He helped carve the presidents on Mount Rushmore. He thought the idea was a crazy one, but he had a family to support and the job paid fifty cents an hour. He said when the job was finished, he did not just see the presidents, but also the other men who worked with him. His job was drilling and others had more important ones, but he learned a valuable lesson. He said, "Sometimes those tedious day-to-day tasks that seem unimportant right then add up to something you can look back on and be proud of."

One day I will look back and be proud I was able to clean food off the floor that fell, or was thrown, from Josi's high chair. I will be thankful I could pick up a basketful of toys, clean fingerprints off my storm door, or rock a baby to sleep. I will miss all these simple day-to-day tasks, just as I did when my own sons grew up and no longer needed me so much.

When we think our tasks are unimportant or tedious, just remember Orville Worman. If we do not grow weary in well doing, we will be able to look back one day and see they were all worthwhile. This applies especially to our Christian walk. We must keep doing good and trust God to bring good results from our labor. We can't see the end result from our vantage point, but God can.

God, I do not know what my monument may look like when it is finished, but I want to keep doing my part, no matter how unimportant it may seem. Amen

OCTOBER 26th *RUNNING INTO A RUNNING BACK*

"And the Lord sent Nathan unto David. And he came unto him, and said unto him, There were two men in one city; the one rich, and the other poor." II Samuel 12:1

We were on our way to Alaska. The forty-ninth state to join the union, but our fiftieth to visit. I could not contain my excitement. In Atlanta we boarded a Delta 757, and flew to Salt Lake City where we were to change planes for the last leg of our journey. We had about an hour lay-over there.

When we boarded the plane in Atlanta, Kevin had seen a man whom he thought looked like Larry Csonka. On the ground in Salt Lake City, we saw the man sitting a few seats away from us. Kevin decided to approach him and have a talk. Sure enough, it was ole #39, himself.

Csonka was the number one pick of the Miami Dolphins in the 1968 draft. Despite suffering a couple of concussions, a broken nose and a ruptured eardrum, he went on to become the offensive leader of the team. For four seasons, he never missed a game and he led the Dolphins in rushing for five straight seasons.

During the 1972 season Miami became the only team since the AFL-NFL merger to go undefeated, and Csonka was instrumental in making that happen. After retiring from football, he hosted several hunting and fishing shows. That is actually what sparked Kevin's interest in speaking with the legendary player. (Kevin is a die-hard fan of the Pittsburgh Steelers!)

As it turned out, Csonka was returning to his home in Alaska after attending the funeral of his father. Even though it was a sad time for him, he took the time to talk to Kevin and I was able to get a photo of him as they talked.

In II Samuel, the meeting of the rich man and the poor man was quite different. In this story, the rich man took advantage of the poor man. He took the only little lamb the poor man had, he killed it and served it to a guest. This was only a parable the prophet used to make King David understand the wrong he had done by taking the wife of Uriah the Hittite. When he first heard the story, David's anger was greatly kindled. He declared the guilty man must die. But then Nathan said unto him, "Thou art the man." David admitted his wrong doing and repented.

Whether we are rich or poor, when we realize we have sinned, we must do as David did. We must admit our faults and repent. Even if we have to suffer dire consequences, we must fall on our faces before God and worship Him. He loves the rich man and poor man equally, but He also equally hates sin by either one.

Father, I may not have much in the way of worldly wealth, but I am rich in love and grace. When I must face my own sin, help me confess and repent immediately. Amen

"And Absalom met the servants of David. And Absalom rode upon a mule, and the mule went under the thick boughs of a great oak, and his head caught hold of the oak, and he was taken up between the heaven and the earth; and the mule that was under him went away."
II Samuel 18:9

King David of Israel had many sons. More than one of them caused trouble for their father. The third son was Absalom. He was handsome and the people liked him. Also, he had, as they say, a fine head of hair! Every year he would get a haircut and the weight of what was cut off was two hundred shekels (or, about five pounds).

But, Absalom did not possess sound judgment. He was a schemer, he was independent and, you might say, conceited. He attempted to usurp the throne from David. He sent messengers to all the tribes of the nation to incite a rebellion. His followers began to increase in number.

A messenger told David the entire nation had joined with Absalom in a conspiracy against his reign. David and his household began at once to leave the city of Jerusalem. David mustered the men to prepare for a battle. He told Joab, commander of his army, to deal gently with Absalom.

During the battle, Absalom met David's men and tried to make an escape. However, just as his mule went under the boughs of a big oak tree, Absalom's hair got caught in the branches and he was lifted up off the mule as it kept going. He was left dangling in mid-air. When Joab heard about this, he took three daggers and plunged them into the heart of Absalom. Then, they threw his body into a pit and covered him with stones. The battle was over and David remained king.

The moral of the story is this: the thing that we take the most pride in may turn out to be the cause of our un-doing. I personally know of a young man who took great pride in his souped-up car. He wrecked that car one night and died in the accident.

There are many things we could take pride in. However, the Bible tells us pride goes before destruction. We all need to guard ourselves so we do not become prideful over our looks, our possessions, our jobs or anything else in this world. The only thing we need to boast about is our Lord and Savior. Without Him, nothing we have is meaningful anyway.

Don't be like Absalom. Don't be caught up or brought down by some object of your pride.

Lord, help me not to be puffed up with pride over anything in this world. Amen

OCTOBER 28th *JESSICA'S JOB*

"And all things, whatsoever ye shall ask in prayer, believing, ye shall receive." Matthew 21:22

My daughter-in-law Jessica knows I pray for her, but I have never before shared with her what I wrote in my prayer journal in 2007. She was going to interview for a new job and had asked me to pray. Here is what I asked the Lord to do for her.

I pray for Jessica as she goes to interview for the job tomorrow. I believe she will be praying about this appointment. Father, You said in Matthew 18:19, if two agree on earth as touching anything they ask it will be done by You. Therefore, I am agreeing with her that you would give her the job, it it's right for her. You may have something better in mind. If so, help her to trust you. Either way, I pray that she will be relaxed, not nervous; that she will be confident of her ability and will have the demeanor and vocabulary to convey that to the principal. I know she has a good vocabulary, but I mean just give her exactly the right words to speak. Give the principal the unbiased judgment to make a hiring decision. I just hope he doesn't have pre-conceived ideas of what he wants and may not consider Jessica if she doesn't fit his profile.

If she gets this job, I pray that she will be able to get to work on time. I pray that Jake will be safe in my care. I pray that she will have friends and mentors at the school. I pray for the students she will teach. I pray that she will make a big difference in their lives. I pray that you will keep her safe as she travels to and from work on a busy set of roads. I also pray that Joel will help her with Jake at night. I pray they will develop a routine of going to bed at a set time and get enough rest. In Jesus' name, Amen.

She did get the job! She has changed to a different position now, but still works for the Forsyth County school system. God answered every part of my prayer. (I don't think they ever get enough rest, though.)

Jesus told the disciples to *believe* when they pray for things. Our friend Calvin Bailey shared what God showed him about praying. He said he *believed* God when he prayed to be saved. Now that he *is* saved, he has to believe God just as much as he did when he prayed the sinner's prayer. If he doesn't, there is really no need to pray at all.

James tells us to ask in faith without wavering. He wrote, "For let not that man think that he shall receive any thing of the Lord (1:7)." Jessica and I believed God when we prayed about her job and she received what we prayed for. God will do the same for you. Only believe!

Jesus, when I pray, please help me not to waver, but to ask in faith. Amen

OCTOBER 29th *HEART ATTACK!*

"But I have trusted in thy mercy; my heart shall rejoice in thy salvation." Psalm 13:5

This is the way the story was told to me. My brother-in-law Tommy was at work when it happened. The pain awakened my sister-in-law Ethel from a sound sleep. Although her mother had been dead for several years, Ethel said she could feel her mother's presence in the room comforting her.

She did not call 911 because she had already been to the doctor once and was diagnosed with acid reflux. She did call Tommy's aunt, Jean Kirby, who hurried over to take Ethel to the emergency room. After some quick testing, the doctor determined she was having a myocardial infarction, or a heart attack. He told Ethel had she gone back to sleep, she most likely would not have survived the night.

Dr. Hudson, a leading cardiologist, was called in. He had Ethel transferred to St. Joseph's in an ambulance. Ethel said she felt so cold on the ride down, but she felt her mama was hugging her closely to help keep her warm. At St. Joseph's, Ethel had three stents inserted to keep her clogged arteries open.

Although she has had numerous health issues since that time, she trusts in God's mercy and her heart rejoices in His salvation. Much like David when he wrote these words, "Consider and hear me, O Lord my God: lighten mine eyes, lest I sleep the sleep of death (Psalm 13:3)." Ethel came close to sleeping the sleep of death, but, thankfully, the Lord heard her and restored her.

The heart is a muscle that keeps the body going. It is great to exercise to keep our other muscles toned and strong, but the essential thing is to keep the heart strong. The same goes for our spiritual hearts. We can strengthen and tone the heart through reading God's word and putting its message into practice in our daily lives. Hebrews 13:9 says, "For it is a good thing that the heart be established with grace." We also learn in II Chronicles 16:9, the eyes of the Lord run to and fro to shew himself strong in behalf of them whose heart is perfect toward him. Let's make sure our hearts are established with grace and that they are perfect toward the Lord.

Finally, let Ethel's experience be a lesson to all of us. When suffering severe chest pains, call 911 immediately. It is better to be safe than sorry. Also, when our lives are in danger, we should call on the Lord to come to our aid. He will help us, and He may also send comfort by way of a vision from beyond!

Lord, I trust in Your mercy. I rejoice in Thy salvation. Consider and hear me, O Lord my God. Amen

OCTOBER 30th *THROW AWAY THE CALENDARS*

"And sware by him that liveth for ever and ever, who created heaven, and the things that therein are, and the earth, and the things that therein are, and the sea, and the things which are therein, that there should be time no longer:" Revelation 10:6

We plan our lives around our calendars and our watches. Lately, it seems my calendar is filled with notes about appointments, functions at church, bowling dates, babysitting days, the days the therapists or nurses are coming to check on George, etc. There is hardly a day that has nothing special going on.

Each day, I am constantly checking my watch. I have to see what time the baby is coming, when George needs his medicines, what time I have to leave to get to wherever it is I am going, how much time I have before starting to cook and so on. I often feel like the White

Rabbit in *Alice in Wonderland.* I go around saying, "Oh dear! Oh dear! I shall be too late."

But, when this life is over, we will never need to consult our daily planners, our watches nor our calendars again. There will be no more time! Can you imagine that? I have to admit, I really can't. Nevertheless, in the book of Revelation, chapter ten, an angel will come down from heaven and declare that time will be no more.

The Bible tells us there will be no night in the new city, because Jesus is the light. We sing in church about an endless day, but have you stopped to consider what an endless day will be like? I honestly can't fathom it.

Reverend Mercer Williams thought about it, though. I know he did because, when I was a young girl, he always had us alter a song he liked to lead. He would often lead "I'll Live On," but he always told us we would not live THRU eternity but IN it. So, he told us when we sang the chorus to make sure we sang *"In* eternity, I'll live on."

We are called the human race, possibly because we are always rushing around! But Jesus knew rest was important. Take time out of your busy schedule today to rest in the Lord, physically, spiritually and emotionally. And remember, in eternity there will be no calendars and no watches.

I don't know what that will be like, but I know I will like it. I know it will be perfect because I will be in eternity with Jesus. I know it will be pure bliss to have no calendar to consult about how my days are planned for me. And what a blessing to stop checking a watch to see how much time is left!

Jesus, forgive me if I get *too* busy. Help me slow down and rest in You. Amen

OCTOBER 31st *PROTESTANT REFORMATION*

"And he said, The Lord is my rock, and my fortress, and my deliverer;" II Samuel 22:2

When George and I were on our vacation to Canada last year, we visited the Fortress of Louisburg. It is located on the rocky shoreline of Cape Breton, east of Sydney, Nova Scotia. In the eighteenth century, it was one of the busiest seaports. Founded by the French in 1713, it fell twice to the British as they laid siege to the fortress. Our tour guide reminded us of the difference between a fort and a fortress. A fortress encloses a town within its fortifications, while those of a fort do not.

As I thought about the difference, I could not help but think of the song, "A Mighty Fortress." The words and music were written by an Augustine monk who was also a professor of theology. His name? Martin Luther. On October 31, 1517, Luther posted on the doors of the Cathedral of Wittenberg, Germany, his 95 theses (complaints) against the medieval Roman church's teachings. The Protestant Reformation was born!

It is not known exactly when the song was written, but it is generally believed to have been around 1529. The song tells us our God is a mighty fortress, a bulwark never failing. I like the third verse which says *And tho this world, with devils filled, should threaten to undo us, we will not fear, for God hath willed His truth to triumph thru us.*

I thought about Martin Luther's choice of words for his song. I love that he called God our mighty fortress. God is not a fort, where "soldiers" come temporarily, but a fortress where His people *live.* We will experience battles with the enemy, but we are secure in Him. As I walked around the Fortress of Louisburg, all I could think of was God as a dwelling place. He intends for us to go about our daily lives *in Him.*

In the Bible, the books of Samuel, Psalms and Jeremiah all refer to the Lord as our fortress. We learn from Acts 17:28, "For in him we live, and move, and have our being." On this Reformation Day, be thankful for people like Martin Luther who helped to re-establish the Scriptures, clarify the means of salvation and restore congregational singing. Also, praise the Lord God because He is our mighty fortress.

Oh, God, You are my rock and my fortress. In You, I dwell securely. Amen

NOVEMBER

NOVEMBER 1st *HIGH TEA AT HILARY'S*

"And did eat and drink before the Lord on that day with great gladness." I Chronicles 29:22a

Hilary came to work at Heavenly Dove when I decided to leave my part-time job. She is from the United Kingdom and has a wonderful British accent. She also has a strong relationship with the Lord. She is a fabulous hostess, too. I found this out when I was invited, along with all the ladies from the Dove, to High Tea.

In typical English fashion, it was raining that day as I headed to her home. High tea is normally late in the afternoon, as the British eat their dinner around seven o'clock in the evening. Hilary served us quiche, cucumber sandwiches, Caesar salad, fruit cake, trifle and a Victoria sandwich (a dessert). I am sure I have probably left out something!

Since I do not drink any caffeine whatsoever, I asked if the tea was decaf. She said that is not something one would ever be offered at a proper high tea, so I only took a few sips of mine. I ate enough of the savories and pastries to make up for it though!

Not only did we have a wonderful time feeling like aristocrats, the tea was also a time to honor Angie, owner of the Dove. Each of us wrote a letter of tribute thanking her for her dedication to the Lord, her boldness to witness for Him and her concern for all of us. So, we did eat and drink before the Lord on that day with great gladness.

But why wait for high tea? We can eat and drink before the Lord with great gladness any day of the week. And we should! Nehemiah tells us, "the joy of the Lord is your strength (8:10)." I Corinthians 10:31 says, "Whether therefore ye eat or drink, or whatsoever ye do, do all to the glory of God."

I realize I have taken those verses out of context and there are stories behind them, but I believe the thoughts expressed in those verses are true even when standing alone. We need to stop going around with long faces and burdened down with cares. We need to smile and let the world know where our joy comes from. We need to do everything to the glory of God.

What better way to be a witness, even in the midst of hard times and troubles?

Jesus, help me to wear a smile and glorify You in all I do. Amen

"Keep thy heart with all diligence; for out of it are the issues of life." Proverbs 4:23

I have watched some commercials on television that cause me to pause and consider my spiritual condition. One is of a person with a pet in the car. The commercial says you may have gone nose-blind to the odor, but to others it smells awful. Then there is the one about the family in the kitchen. When the lady puts some garbage in the trashcan, the commercial shows a dumpster in the kitchen where the island once was. It is overflowing, a cat is climbing all over it and you can hear the flies buzzing around. The family has gone nose-blind to the smell.

After taking allergy shots for six years, I can no longer smell every odor as I once did. In some ways that is a blessing. On the other hand, I may have gone nose-blind to what others smell as they get into my car or come into my home. While I do not have pets, I do have garbage.

I began to think about how easily Christians become nose-blind to sin in their lives. How easy it is to fall into the traps of pride, arrogance, lust, gluttony, prejudice, hatred, envy and so on. None of these seem too bad when they first rear their ugly heads in our lives. Little by little we accept their offerings and little by little we begin to feel they are acceptable and we are completely justified in embracing them as everyday behavior.

We may not see our faults, but others, like the people in the tv ads, see right through us and are repelled by what they see. We don't realize the stench these sins are in the nostrils of our God. I had much rather be a sweet aroma to Him than a foul stench.

In Jeremiah chapter five, God said, "Your sins have withholden good things from you(verse 25)." When we feel we are down-on-our-luck, the whole world is against us or nobody understands, maybe, just maybe, it is our sin that has caused good to be withheld from us. We may have just gone nose-blind to what we are harboring in our hearts.

Solomon exhorted us to keep our hearts with all diligence. Jim Rohn once said, "There are two types of pain in this world, the short term pain of discipline and the long term pain of regret. One weighs ounces, the other tons. Choose your pain." We can discipline ourselves to put away every weight and the sin which so easily besets us, or we can clutch those to us and live with the pain of regret.

Guard your heart so the enemy does not creep in and take up residence. Resist him with daily discipline. Rely on the Holy Spirit to help you. Don't be deceived by the "sweet" smell of sin or pretty soon, you will become nose-blind to its awful stench.

Lord Jesus, help me keep my heart with all diligence. Help me resist the enemy so that I am not nose-blind to sin in my life. Amen

NOVEMBER 3rd   *THREE DAYS IN A LIFE*

"And David said, Is there yet any that is left of the house of Saul, that I may shew him kindness for Jonathan's sake?" II Samuel 9:1

David asked that question when he was king over the nation of Israel. He had been the best friend of Jonathan who was the son of Saul, the former king. Ziba, formerly Saul's servant, told David about Mephibosheth, Jonathan's son. David sent for this young man to be brought to his palace. Once he arrived, Mephibosheth ate at David's table continually.

There are three very important days in the life of Mephibosheth. We will look at each one and compare our lives with what happened to the king's grandson.

The first day is the day Mephibosheth was dropped. He was five years old when his nurse took him up and tried to flee with him. In her haste, he fell from her arms and became lame. We can compare this to the day Adam and Eve ate of the forbidden fruit and we were "dropped" from our perfect relationship with God. The entire human race has since been crippled by sin.

The second day is the day Mephibosheth was picked up. David sent for him and had him brought to the palace. Mephibosheth was in Lo-debar, far away from the king, just as we are far away from King Jesus when we are sinners. Like David, the Holy Spirit comes searching for our lost souls to save us. When we are saved, we are picked up by God. We are brought back into a right relationship with him.

Last, but not least, is the day Mephibosheth was restored. He ate at the king's table continually because he accepted the invitation. When we accept the invitation from Jesus, we will eat at His table continually. When Mephibosheth sat at the king's table, no one could tell he was lame. His legs were under the table and were covered. When we eat at the King's table, our sins are covered and no one can see them either.

When Mephibosheth came into the presence of King David, he fell on his face and did reverence unto him. He could have been bitter. He could have railed on David that he should have been king. But, he did the opposite. He humbled himself just as we must do when we come into the presence of the Lord. Mephibosheth had a repentant heart and we must have one as well.

David promised to show kindness to Mephibosheth for his father's sake and promised to restore the property the man should have inherited. God will take care of us, too. We will share in all the riches Jesus has because we become joint-heirs with Him when we are saved.

If you are far away from the King today, please understand that He is looking for you. He wants to invite you into His palace, He wants to restore you and He wants to take care of you continually. I do hope you will accept the invitation and humble yourself before Him. I am so thankful I did.

Lord Jesus, I pray today for all those who are far away from You. I know Your invitation is going out for them to join You at Your table. I pray for them to humbly bow before You. Amen

(My apologies to whoever taught me this lesson. I don't remember and therefore can't give credit where it is due, but I am thankful for you.)

NOVEMBER 4th *TICKETS REPLACED*

"Ask, and it shall be given you; seek, and ye shall find; knock, and it shall be opened unto you:" Matthew 7:7

Our son Justin had temporarily moved to California, but he had told me he was getting us tickets to the Cirque du Soleil for Christmas. While he was away, I was putting all his mail in his dresser drawer. I had no idea the tickets had come and were safely stashed away in his room.

I had been seeing the commercials about the Cirque coming to Atlanta. I knew it would soon be time to go, but I did not know the exact date *we* were supposed to attend. I had been intending to ask Justin about it as soon as we talked again. He called me early in November and we discovered we had missed the show. He had spent almost four hundred dollars on tickets which were for three days prior!

I had thought he was going with us when he came home for Thanksgiving. I never dreamed we were supposed to go so soon. He was just sick about it and so was I. He told me the tickets were sold to him with the stipulation there would be no refunds. Almost four hundred dollars down the drain.

The next day, I felt I should just call and *ask.* What could they do but say there was nothing they could do? I was placed on hold for thirty-five minutes without speaking to a live person, so I got annoyed and hung up. But a still, small voice kept urging me to just *ASK!*

I called again the next day. This time I got a man named Felix on the line. I explained our predicament. Felix asked for our confirmation number, which I had retrieved from Justin's room. He said he could see that the tickets had not been used. He could not give me the same seats, but he said he could give me comparable seats for the next show. *Glory to God!* I was ecstatic. I called Justin and he was just as thrilled as I was. Probably more so, since it was his four hundred dollars!

All I had to do was ask. In Matthew, chapter 7, Jesus told us to ask, seek and knock. He said when we do, "it shall be opened unto you." So many times we fail to receive blessings from God simply because we fail to ask, seek and knock. Bible scholars say the tense of these verbs means the action continues into the future. In other words, we are to keep on asking, seeking and knocking. We are not to give up but rather be persistent.

Jesus Himself promises, "For every one that asketh receiveth; and he that seeketh findeth; and to him that knocketh it shall be opened (verse 8)." Remember this acrostic, A. S. K., ask, seek, knock.

Father God, Your word tells me I have not because I ask not. Help me remember, if I but ask I will receive. Amen

"Upon this I awaked, and beheld; and my sleep was sweet unto me."
Jeremiah 31:26

I have always been a night owl. I have never enjoyed getting up early in the mornings. I am the kind of person who likes to hit the snooze button two or three times and gradually awaken. George, on the other hand, wakes up even before the clock alarms and wants to start talking.

In the Bible there are so many references to people who rose up early in the morning. The first time the word *early* is used in the KJV is in Genesis, chapter 19, where Lot invited the two angels to tarry all night at his house and rise up early to go on their way. In the same chapter Abraham rose up early and stood before the Lord.

In Genesis we also read Abimeleck, king of Gerar, rose up early. And there are more references to Abraham's early rising, most notably the morning he went to sacrifice his son Isaac to the Lord. If there were ever a morning for hitting the snooze, I believe that would have been the morning I would have chosen to do so. Not Abraham.

Jacob, Laban, Moses, Joshua, Gideon, Samuel, David, Hezekiah, the women who went to the tomb of Jesus, and yes, even Jesus Himself are all recorded as rising early.

I am sure all of us have heard, "Early to bed and early to rise makes a man healthy, wealthy and wise." Or what about, "The early bird gets the worm"? I didn't care. Let the early birds have the worms!

Then I read a quote by Father Edwards Hays that made me think a little differently. He said, "May my rising be a rehearsal for my resurrection from the dead. With gratitude for the wonder of this day, I enter into silent prayer." Now, I usually set my clock for 6:30 A.M. I like to wake up with gratitude for all the blessings I have been given. I use the extra time to pray and read God's word. Getting up early also gives me more time to write!

So, whether we hoot with the owls at night, soar with the eagles in the morning or are somewhere in between, let us rise up each day giving glory to God for all His blessings and focusing our attention on Him.

Father God, You created both sunset and dawn. I am thankful for both. Help me rise each day with a resurrection attitude of awe. Amen

NOVEMBER 6th *CHURCH CENTENNIAL*

"Not forsaking the assembling of ourselves together..." Hebrews 10:25

On November 6, 2010, George and I attended the celebration of the centennial of Roanoke Baptist Church. That is quite a milestone. I know many churches in our county are much older, but Roanoke is a very special place to my family and me.

Not only was I brought up in that church, I was saved there as a ten year old girl. I married George, the love of my life, in that church. Two of my children were saved there. Many members of my family are buried in the cemetery there.

The night was kicked off with a barbecue dinner with all the trimmings. Then, there was a video about the history of the church with many pictures of both former and current members. There was a time capsule being put together and I chose to contribute a newspaper article about the church honoring certain mothers on Mothers' Day.

There was a table with index cards and pens. We were asked to write a favorite memory about the church. Of course, I wrote about when I got saved. As I went to put my card in the collection box, I noticed someone had written about the time Joel let my car roll down the hill and crash into a tree! It was not signed, so I do not know who wrote it, but I loved seeing it in there!

My cousin, Katie Nix, was in charge of putting the celebration together and I thought she did a tremendous job. It was wonderful to be at the church on that special night and be with my friends and relatives. The next morning, many of the former pastors were going to be sharing about their ministries at Roanoke.

No church would be able to celebrate a centennial if the members failed to assemble themselves together. Without a constant gathering of people who come to worship the Lord, learn of Him and share the gospel with the lost, the church would die. The writer of Hebrews tells us to gather together and exhort one another even more as the day of Christ's return approaches.

Yes, fellowship with other believers is both necessary and significant for growth in our Christian walk. We need help from each other to stand strong in times of trouble. We support and encourage one another as we serve together. Last, but not least, believers are to love one another. That is how a church will continue for a hundred years or more!

Lord, I am thankful for churches, young and old, where we can assemble to worship You. I am thankful for the entire body of Christ, regardless of where we worship. Amen

NOVEMBER 7th *INCHING ALONG*

"For even hereunto were ye called: because Christ also suffered for us, leaving us an example, that ye should follow his steps:" I Peter 2:21

After breakfast, I enjoy pushing my granddaughter Josi in her stroller. Since our house is on a steep hill, I get plenty of exercise going up and down the section that we travel. Occasionally, we will see squirrels, birds and chipmunks. Many times we see earthworms wriggling across my driveway.

I always stop the stroller and point out the worm to Josi. She is amazed by the creeping, crawling creature. So am I. Mr. Worm works so hard just to make a very little progress. Sometimes, I feel my walk with the Lord is like that of the worm's attempt to cross the pavement.

I can picture God, from high above the earth, looking down on me just as I do Mr. Worm. He sees me struggling and trying my hardest. He knows I am doing my best to continue on my journey. He sees where I am going and He knows my progress is made little by little.

Seeing Mr. Worm inch along reminds me of a Three Stooges skit. In this particular one, Curly talks first with Moe, then Larry, about what happened between those two at Niagara Falls. Both men say, "Slowly I turned, step by step, inch by inch," and then they each, in turn, proceed to beat up Curly. I sometimes feel beaten up, too, as I go step by step along.

Sometimes the road we travel will feel like a fiery furnace. I am sure Mr. Worm feels my driveway is like that on a hot, summer day! It takes the times of trial and testing to help make us strong in our faith.

I have read, "Life by the yard is hard, life by the inch is a cinch." I do know God does not intend for us to leap through this life with not a care in the world. We are exhorted to follow in Jesus' steps. One. Step. At. A. Time. It may appear that we are inching along, but as long as we are inching, we are going forward.

When you feel you are not going forward fast enough in your walk with Christ, just remember Mr. Worm. He keeps on keeping on, little by little, and, eventually, he makes it all the way across. So will I and so will you.

Jesus, help me follow in Your steps. Help me not to be discouraged when my progress is slower than I'd like. Amen

NOVEMBER 8th   *AUNT IRENE'S CAKE*

"To what purpose cometh there to me incense from Sheba, and the sweet cane from a far country? Your burnt offerings are not acceptable, nor your sacrifices sweet unto me." Jeremiah 6:20

My Aunt Irene (my grandmother's sister) made the best chocolate cakes I have ever tasted. She did not use a mix, she made her cake from scratch. And the icing was the kind that breaks apart when cooled. Those cakes were "to die for!" Every time we went to visit her, I hoped all the way there she had a cake made!

I am sure you have a favorite dessert made by a certain family member. It is likely your mouth is watering for that dessert even now. Did you ever stop to think about God wanting a sweet treat from His people? He is not interested in a piece of cake or pie, He is interested in the sweet treat of our obedience.

In Jeremiah, chapter six, the prophet is giving Jerusalem a final warning. He is telling the people an enemy is coming from the north to destroy them. God is allowing this because the people have turned from Him. They are worshipping idols and are in constant rebellion against God. They have said, "Peace, peace," when there is no peace.

God has had enough. The people were not even ashamed of their sinful ways. Yet, they were still going through the motions of worship. They were still bringing sacrifices and burning incense, but these were a stench in God's nostrils.

Do you remember what God said to Saul through the prophet Samuel? He said, "Behold, to obey is better than sacrifice, and to hearken than the fat of rams. For rebellion is as the sin of witchcraft, and stubbornness is as iniquity and idolatry." Oh, my.

We are all guilty at some point in our lives of rebelling against God's commands. We are all guilty of being stubborn at times, right? I know I am. God said those sins are as bad as practicing witchcraft or bowing down to an idol. That is not sweet to Him at all.

David wrote in the fifty-first Psalm, "The sacrifices of God are a broken spirit: a broken and contrite heart, O God, thou wilt not despise (Verse 17)." The writer of Hebrews said, "Let us offer the sacrifice of praise to God continually, that is, the fruit of our lips giving thanks to his name (13: 15)."

So then, the sweetest treats we can offer God are obedience, a broken heart when we sin and the praise of our lips continually. And you know what? Jesus thought these treats were enough to "die for." Offer Him your sweetest and best today.

Lord, forgive me and cleanse me from every sin. I want to offer you my very best. Amen

AUNT IRENE'S CAKE RECIPE:
2 cups margarine
1 cup sugar
1 and ½ cups self rising flour
2 eggs
½ cup sweet milk
1teaspoon vanilla flavoring
Mix together. Pour into greased and floured pan. Bake at 350 degrees until an inserted toothpick comes out clean. (About 30-35 minutes)

CHOCOLATE ICING
1 cup sugar
Dash of salt
1 tablespoon cocoa powder
1/3 cup sweet milk
1/3 cup cream (pet milk)
Mix together. Cook over medium high heat until it forms a soft ball when dropped in cold water. Then cut off heat. Add:
2 tablespoons butter
1 teaspoon vanilla flavoring

Cool slightly and spread. Enjoy!

IN LOVING MEMORY OF IRENE HANSARD GARNER
Born: January 17, 1909   Died: August 15, 1995

NOVEMBER 9th *POWER FAILURE*

"He ruleth by his power for ever;" Psalm 66:7

On this day in 1965, there was a massive power failure in the northeastern section of the United States. Over thirty million people in portions of Connecticut, Rhode Island, Massachusetts, Vermont, New Hampshire, New Jersey, New York and Ontario, Canada, were without power for up to thirteen hours.

The cause of the blackout was human error! A few days before this happened, maintenance personnel had incorrectly set a safety relay switch. When a small surge of power caused the relay to trip, it set off a chain reaction. Within five minutes the power distribution system was in complete chaos.

There was some consolation, however. There was a full moon shining brightly that night and only five reports of looting were made. The blackout was mentioned in subsequent films, books, television shows and songs!

My sister has asked us to put a flashlight in her coffin. She has stipulated she wants it turned on and filled with Duracell batteries so she will not have to worry about being in the dark! Duracells, as you know, are supposed to keep going and going and going.

One thing we will never have to worry about is the power of God failing. God is omnipotent and the Bible says He rules by His power forever. Isn't that a great comfort to you? It is to me. I can rest securely in the knowledge God is in control. Nothing is too hard for Him at all.

Job tells us God is excellent in power (37:23). Psalm 106:8 says, "Nevertheless he saved them for his name's sake, that he might make his mighty power to be known." In Luke 9:43, we read, "And they were all amazed at the mighty power of God." Also, Colossians 1:11 says we are "strengthened with all might according to his glorious power."

God's power will never go out. Human error can never cause His power to fail. The moon will eventually fail to give light and crime is ever-increasing, but God's power is not threatened in any way. It will last.

Father God, in this uncertain world, Your power remains constant. Amen

"The rod and reproof give wisdom: but a child left to himself bringeth his mother to shame." Proverbs 29:15

All children are born into the world with a sinful nature. No one has to teach us to lie, to be selfish or to hate. We come into the world bent and broken. Our lives are not a clean slate waiting to be written upon by others. It is the job of parents to train a child in the right way to live. This job is a hard one and takes at least eighteen years!

It is the parents' job to restrain their children as well as train them. Parents must give their children both counsel and correction. The children must learn the connection between disobedience and discomfort! The Bible tells us, "Foolishness is bound up in the heart of a child, but the rod of correction will drive it far from him (Proverbs 22:15)." And Proverbs 19:18, says, "Chasten thy son while there is hope, and let not thy soul spare for his crying." In Proverbs 13:24, we learn, "He that spareth his rod hateth his son: but he that loveth him chasteneth him betimes."

I must say I often put these verses into practice with my sons! All of us have an anti-authority mindset. We don't like people telling us what to do. That is why we need not passive, or absent, but active parents. Correction delivers children from a greater pain to come.

When we mix Satan's counsel with human logic, we get a disaster every time. These two are a deadly combination. Look what happened to Adam and Eve in the Garden of Eden. When they listened to Satan's counsel, they wanted what he offered. It seemed logical so they disobeyed God. Their punishment was death.

Disobedience is the outward working of something amiss in the heart. Jesus said it is not what goes into a man that defiles him, but what comes out (Matthew 15). He said evil thoughts, murders, thefts, false witness and so on proceed out of the heart. We need our hearts healed and the only solution is accepting Jesus as our Savior.

Parents need to be righteous, just and good in the discharge of their duties. I often failed in doing so. I was unfair, unkind and unreal with my sons too many times. I regret that more than I can say. God, however, is always just, good and righteous. He is currently restraining evil until the day comes when He will remove it.

Meanwhile, parents, counsel and correct your children. They won't like it, but later they will be grateful you took the time to bring them up in the way they should go.

Lord, help all parents as they counsel and correct their children. Amen

Aside from the personal references, this devotion is taken largely from a sermon by Pastor Allen Cantrell of Jackson, South Carolina. I am grateful for his wisdom and his humble spirit.

NOVEMBER 11th *SALUTE TO VETERANS*

"And thou shalt come from thy place out of the north parts, thou, and many people with thee, all of them riding upon horses, a great company, and a mighty army: " Ezekiel 38:15

We are all familiar with Teddy Roosevelt, the twenty-sixth president of the United States. But how many of us know about his son, Theodore Roosevel, Jr.?

He served valiantly in the Army during World War I. When the United States declared war on Germany, he volunteered to be one of the first to go to France. He braved hostile fire and gas as he led his battalion in combat. In 1918, he was gassed and wounded at Soissons. He was awarded the Distinguished Service Cross for his actions. .

In 1940, he returned to the Army and was later promoted to Brigadier General. He preferred to be with his men in the heat of battle and repeatedly asked General Eisenhower for combat command. In 1944, he was ordered to help with the invasion of Normandy.

On D-Day, he was the only general to land by sea with the first wave of troops. Although their craft had drifted a mile south of the intended landing site, Roosevelt said, "We'll start the war from right here!"

Slightly over a month later, Roosevelt died of a heart attack just before the orders were approved for his promotion to Major General. He was posthumously awarded the Medal of Honor. In 1962, Henry Fonda portrayed Roosevelt's D-Day actions in *The Longest Day.*

This day is set aside to honor all veterans. I, for one, appreciate the service of each of the brave men and women who have served our country in times of peace as well as times of war.

One day, Jesus will return with His army. Revelation, chapter 19, tells us Jesus will return on a white horse and heaven's armies will follow him. Jesus will have many crowns on His head and He will be clothed in a vesture dipped in blood. On His vesture and on His thigh will be written, King of King and Lord of Lords. All His enemies will one day be defeated and Jesus will usher in unending peace.

As we reflect on our veterans today, let us also reflect on doing *OUR* jobs in the Lord's army. Let's be like Roosevelt and go out into the world to serve in the heat of the battle. Let's not get comfortable in our church pews. Let's start the battle against our enemy right here in our neighborhoods, schools and workplaces.

No, the devil won't like it at all; but Jesus will. Let's be witnesses for Him today.

Jesus, I want to be a soldier in Your army. Too often I have remained in the safety of the post. Help me advance to the front lines as I battle Satan. Amen

NOVEMBER 12th *GETTING IT ALL ORGANIZED*

"I have seen an end of all perfection:" Psalm 119:96

I have always liked to get things organized I have organized everything from dinner parties to cross-country trips. However, too often I have wanted to do things *my* way! I figured that was the only way to do them right! But as you might imagine, no matter how hard I tried to make everything perfect, it never, ever turned out just the way I had planned!

I saw this on Facebook one day: Can yuo raed this? Sopspedluy msot plepoe can. Aoccdrnig to rscheearch at Cmabrigde Uinervtisy, it dsen't mtaetr in waht oerdr the ltteres in a wrod are, the olny iproamtnt tnihg is taht the frsit and lsat ltteer be in the rghit pclae. The rset can be a taotl mses and yuo can sitll raed it whotuit a pboerlm. Tihs is jsut bcuseae the hmuan mnid deos not raed ervey lteter by istlef, but the wrod as a wlohe.

When I realized I could zip right through that paragraph without a problem, I understood everything doesn't have to be perfect. I decided the next time I have an important event coming up, I will ask for help. I will delegate. I will share the workload.

We have all heard, "Too many cooks spoil the broth." And in some cases that is true. When there are too many involved in a simple task, all the differing opinions about how the task should be done could cause chaos. Nevertheless, all of us could use help from time to time.

Guess what? When *I* realize *my* way isn't always best, when I listen to the opinion of others, when I step back and allow others to help, things turn out much better! Proverbs 24:6, says, "In multitude of counselors there is safety."

My "perfection" ends the minute I wake up each morning. I have come to realize I need all the help I can get. And now I appreciate it more than ever.

Lord, thank You for all the help I get from You, from my family and from my friends. Amen

NOVEMBER 13th *DEVOTIONAL PROJECT*

"Faithful is he that calleth you, who also will do it." I Thessalonians 5:24

Four years ago, God gave me a vision about putting together an Advent devotional for our church. Not necessarily *about* Christmas, but rather short testimonials written by members of our congregation about God at work in their lives. It was meant to give us pause in our hectic holiday lives to focus on Him.

Like Moses, I argued with God. I said I did not know how to do it. I said I knew nothing about the computer. I put the project out of my mind as I got busy with my own holiday preparations. But God was not so easily side-tracked.

In yesterday's writing, I said I would ask for help with the next important event. I said I would delegate. I said I would share the work. And that is just what I did. When God began to deal with me again the next year about this project, I stood at church and presented God's plan to them. No one objected, my pastor was enthusiastic, and the folks I asked readily agreed to write an entry. I even had a volunteer!

I also told my church family I knew nothing about how to actually put it together as my computer knowledge was severely limited. Both Nathan Waters and Jonathan Kirby volunteered their time and assistance with that aspect. An anonymous donor also offered to pay for the printing! All systems were set to go.

When God reveals His plan to us, there is no need to procrastinate or argue about our inability. If He calls us to it, He will bring it to pass. Our job is to take the first step and God will work out all the details. He did not cause the waters to roll back for the children of Israel until the feet of the priests bearing the ark were resting in the Jordan River.

When told I would need a title before the printing order was submitted, I had nothing in mind. While standing at the kitchen sink, I felt God saying, "Looking Unto Jesus." Later, I realized how perfect that title would be because Advent is a time of waiting and preparing for the coming of Jesus. Of course, when God does anything it is always perfect!

At the time of this writing, our church is still doing an Advent devotional every year. I was simply called to spearhead the project. It is a church-wide endeavor that has been a blessing to everyone each time it is published. All I had to do was obey God and He took care of the rest. Just as He always does.

Lord, You are always faithful and will accomplish all You have called us to do. Help us stop arguing and procrastinating. Help us be instantly obedient. Amen

NOVEMBER 14th *THE STRAIT GATE*

"Enter ye in at the strait gate: for wide is the gate, and broad is the way, that leadeth to destruction, and many there be which go in thereat." Matthew 7:13

My mother and two of my brothers live off Pilgrim Mill Road. As I turn down Impala Drive, heading to their house, I pass by a vacant lot on the right side of the road. This lot was once used for parking large trucks or heavy equipment.

Now, that is no longer possible. The owner has put up a chain link fence with a narrow gate and there is not enough room for large vehicles to turn in to the lot.

When I first saw the fence, my thoughts went immediately to this verse from Matthew, chapter seven. When Jesus spoke these words, He was referring to His kingdom. The strait gate is the gate that leads to eternal life with God. Few go in because His way is not popular. It is a narrow road and often difficult. On the other hand, the broad way is travelled by many. It is not as confining. It gives plenty of room for a person to do his own thing, go at his own pace and pursue worldly pleasures as he travels. The broad way leads to destruction.

Yes, while traveling the narrow road one may often encounter hardship or persecution. However, this road leads to Heaven, but the broad road leads to Hell.

We can look in the first chapter of Psalms for another picture of these two ways. The man who does not walk in the counsel of the ungodly, nor stand in the way of sinners, nor sit in the seat of the scornful is a blessed man. But the ungodly man is like chaff that is blown away by the wind. The ungodly man will not stand in the congregation of the righteous.

Which gate have you chosen to enter?

Jesus, I know there is just one way to the pearly gates. I pray for all those entering the wide gate and traveling the broad way leading them to destruction. Amen

NOVEMBER 15th *THE SENSE OF TOUCH*

"And the whole multitude sought to touch him: for there went virtue out of him, and healed them all." Luke 6:19

When I was a child, there was not much touching in my family. My parents seldom expressed their affection openly to each other, much less to us children. Therefore, I was not very demonstrative myself for a long time. When George and I met, we did not even hold hands for weeks!

George's folks, however, were huggers. They were not afraid or ashamed to show how much they love someone. The more I was around them, the more I began to understand touching could be a good thing. Since our marriage, I have come to appreciate a gentle back rub, a caress, or even a reassuring hug from George. These days, we hold hands as we say grace before our meals. All are simple, everyday touches that have healing power for someone with deep-seated hurts.

Jesus knew about the power of a touch. He touched blinded eyes, He touched a leper, He touched the tongue of a man with a speech impediment, He touched the ear of the high priest's servant, He touched the hand of Peter's mother-in-law and He touched the bier of a widow's only son. He was not ashamed or afraid to touch the sick and the hurting. He loved them and had compassion on them.

Furthermore, the people wanted to touch Jesus. They wanted to experience His healing power. The woman with the issue of blood knew if she could just touch His garment, she would be made whole. In Mark 3:10, we read many with plagues pressed upon Him to touch Him. In Mark 10:13, we find young children were brought to Jesus so He could touch them. Luke 6:19 tells us the whole multitude sought to touch Jesus and be healed.

On April 2, 1979, the Bell System released a new commercial with the invitation to "Reach out and touch someone." The ad implied it was a good way to keep the lines of communication open. Jesus' touch communicates God's love to us. Have you felt His healing touch? If not, reach out to Him today.

Jesus, help me never to be afraid or ashamed to show my affection to those I love. Help me to reach out and touch them often. Help me to always be "in touch" with You. Amen

NOVEMBER 16th *BABYSITTING FOR BETTY*

"Then saith he to the disciple, Behold thy mother! And from that hour that disciple took her unto his own home." John 19:27

The first "job" I ever recall having was babysitting for my cousin Betty. She had two children. Joey was a few years younger than I, but twice as strong. I had to constantly be on guard lest he grab me by my arm and twist it or hold it behind my back! He was just being playful, but he could hurt!

There was also her daughter, Betsy, who was just a toddler at the time. Betsy was a beautiful baby with dark hair and those big, blue eyes. I was instructed to put her to bed at a certain time and warned she might cry for a bit, but she would go to sleep. It broke my heart to close the door on her. Sure enough, she went to sleep fairly quickly.

There were two reasons I loved getting to babysit for Betty and her husband. First of all, they paid me well. For a young teenager, there were not many opportunities to make extra money back then. I did not get an allowance either. Sure, sometimes I would be given a quarter or maybe fifty cents for washing the dishes or doing some other chore, but, mostly, helping was *expected* of kids back then. I would go home clutching my money and wondering what I should buy first!

The second reason I enjoyed babysitting in their home was that it was *my* home first! My family had "traded houses" with them. When I lived in the house, it was old and run-down. There was no indoor plumbing, either. But they had remodeled the old homeplace and I loved it! What had been a spooky old attic to a young girl was now an additional bathroom, bedrooms and a long hallway. With paneling and bright lights, it was not spooky at all!

I never thought about it then, but I wonder now why Mary, mother of Jesus, did not go back to her own home after His crucifixion? She had other sons and daughters. I wonder why Jesus wanted John to care for her instead? The Bible is not clear on this, so I suppose I will never know for sure.

It is sufficient for us to know Jesus, even in His pain, saw Mary's hurt and helplessness. He made certain she was to be cared for when He was gone. Jesus entrusted her to John, and John fulfilled the request by taking Mary into his own home.

John, like the younger me, was taking care of someone's kin. He was also happy to do it. Mary, like Betty, was not living in her first home, but she made John's home her own. I find this account very moving and very merciful. Jesus takes care of His own, even in His hour of death.

Lord Jesus, thank You for providing an eternal home for me. Amen

NOVEMBER 17ᵗʰ   *TREASURES IN THE WORD*

"For where your treasure is, there will your heart be also." Luke 12:34

Have you ever hidden money somewhere for your children and hoped they would soon find it? Were you excited to see their reaction when they discovered the dough? Have you wondered who was more excited on the discovery, you or the children?

For several years, I played a treasure hunt game with my grandson Ryan at Christmas. I would hide his presents. Then I would seal up the first clue in an envelope. When he opened the envelope, he would have a hint as to where to look next. He would have to hunt for each successive clue until he was led to the presents themselves. It was a world of fun for all of us as we watched him search for the treasure.

Each year, I read the Christmas story to my family out of Luke, chapter two. One Christmas, I kept telling Ryan over and over, the Bible is my favorite book. I had made up a song and sang it to him saying he would find his first clue in my favorite book. He had listened to me talk about my favorite book and headed straight for my Bible to find the envelope!

Those were great times that I will always cherish. Now, I hide some treasure for someone every time we go on an overnight trip. I can't remember just how this came to be a tradition, but each time we check into a motel with a Gideon Bible in the nightstand, I place some money inside it. Usually, I will put the money in the pages of John, chapter three.

Since verse sixteen is the one that is most well-known around the world, I believe a lot of people would turn there if seeking the Lord. Sometimes, I may put a couple of dollars, sometimes a five or more. But every time I leave the room, there is treasure buried in God's Word.

When Jesus spoke the words in today's verse, He was talking to the people about coveting, worrying about basic needs, being fearful of not having enough and setting their affections on things of this earth. He was telling them to seek first the kingdom of God. For, He said, where your treasure is, there's where your heart is.

I hate to admit it, but I was already a young mother before I began to discover the real treasures of the Bible. After attending my first Bible study, I felt like the richest woman in the world! Even now, decades later, I find new treasures in the pages of God's Word every time I study it. I ask the Lord to open my eyes that I may behold wondrous things out of His book.

My treasure can be found in the pages of the Bible. My prayer is that someone may pick up a Bible in a motel room and find, not only a little earthly treasure, but a spiritual treasure that is priceless.

Jesus, I am so thankful for the treasures in Your Word. I am also thankful for the Gideon Bibles in motel rooms. I pray those Bibles will be opened this very day and someone will come to know You as You speak to their hearts. Amen

NOVEMBER 18th *CHOICES AND REGRETS*

"Remembering mine affliction and my misery, the wormwood and the gall, My soul hath them still in remembrance, and is humbled in me." Lamentations 3: 19, 20

Tonight, no doubt, there is a lottery drawing for some big jackpot. No doubt, people are waiting intently hoping their numbers will be drawn and their lives will be changed instantly. I have better news for ticket holders. Your life can be changed instantly. Not by any random numbers, but by the grace of God. With Him, nothing happens by chance, either. Everything is filtered through His fingers of love.

No matter where we have been, no matter what we have done, no matter how many times we tried to change and failed, God was gently calling us to turn to Him and receive forgiveness.

That is just what God was doing with the children of Israel. He was calling them to turn back to Him, but they refused. In Lamentations, the prophet Jeremiah was mourning the destruction of Jerusalem. God had chosen a people for Himself and this was their capital city. But, they insisted on bowing down to false gods. Just as we often do today.

Like Jeremiah, we remember our afflictions and our misery. The bitterness causes our souls to be downcast. But, we have hope because of verses twenty-two and twenty-three. God's mercies are new every morning. He offers us a brand new day and a brand new start for our lives. Why? Because of His great love for us.

We matter to God. Every choice, mistake and regret we have in our lives matters to Him. He can fix us! He can cleanse us and make us whole. Because of His mercy we are not consumed. His compassions never fail, they are new every morning. His faithfulness is great. Don't bet on random numbers to be your ticket to change. Bank on God's love and mercy.

God, let every bad choice and every regret point us to You. Forgive us and cleanse us I pray. Amen

NOVEMBER 19th *JUNK FOOD JUNKIE*

"There hath no temptation taken you but such as is common to man." I Corinthians 10:13

I love sweets! I am not sure just how I got hooked on them, but I have been crazy about candy since I was a small child. My grandmother worked in Atlanta and every payday she would bring me home a bag of malted milk balls from the dime store, or a candy bar. I could not wait until Friday!

Of course my affinity was not limited to candy. I also loved cakes, pies, brownies, cookies, puddings and ice cream. How could I leave out my addiction for Coca-Cola in the small, green bottles? At one time I was drinking six every day!

Then I was diagnosed with acid reflux. The doctor said I needed to cut out chocolate and caffeine! He did not know what he was asking of me. But, with God's help, I did it. Now, I only drink one caffeine-free coke per day and I limit myself to one dessert per day (usually). I try to eat healthier than ever. Chocolate still calls my name, but the acid reflux says, "No, no, no!"

No matter what temptation calls our name, the Holy Spirit is inside us saying, "No, no, no!" We cannot participate in any sin without experiencing the consequences. We may think we can handle it, but verse twelve says, "Wherefore let him that thinketh he standeth take heed lest he fall."

It is tough trying to stay healthy. It is tough to resist any temptation without the help of the Holy Spirit. The rest of our verse for today says, "but God is faithful, who will not suffer you to be tempted above that ye are able; but will with the temptation also make a way to escape, that ye may be able to bear it."

Sometimes we may think the temptation is too great and there is no way we can resist. That is the time we must remember: God promised to make a way to escape it. When we request His help, we can recognize the sin that so easily besets us, we can run away from all situations which we know are not pleasing to Him, we can rightly make the choice to obey and we can realize we need support and counsel from our family or friends.

It may help us to remember, being tempted is not sin. Even Jesus was tempted. Remember how the devil tempted Him in the wilderness in Matthew, chapter four? I understand two different Greek words were used for temptation in Matthew and Corinthians, but both mean to test thoroughly or put to proof. No, it is the yielding to temptation that is sinful.

Paul wrote to Timothy, "Flee also youthful lusts: but follow righteousness, faith, charity, peace, with them that call on the Lord out of a pure heart (II Timothy 2:22)." When sin calls your name, say, "No! No! No!" and flee from it.

Lord, help us all say no to temptations by fleeing from them and calling on Your name. Amen

NOVEMBER 20th   *OUR EBENEZER MOMENT*

"Then Samuel took a stone, and set it between Mizpeh and Shen, and called the name of it Ebenezer, saying Hitherto hath the Lord helped us." I Samuel 7:12

I had a goal to see all fifty states. That goal was accomplished in 1999 when we toured Alaska. One of my heart's desires was to see Mt. McKinley, or Denali, as it was officially named in 2015. Denali is the highest mountain in North America. It stands over twenty thousand feet high and is the third most isolated peak after Mt. Everest and Aconcagua.

There was only one problem. Denali is usually shrouded in clouds. Try as we might, we were unable to take the tiniest peek at the peak. I was extremely disappointed, so we did the next best thing. We watched the movie, *Song of the Land*, which was a photo-symphony; in other words a collection of photos of Denali and surrounding countryside set to classical music. Beautiful, naturally, but just not the thrill I was looking for.

Finally, on our last day in the state, the sun was shining brightly and our bus driver told us she had spotted Denali as we drove back to Anchorage. She said we should be able to see it very clearly once we arrived in town. And we could! I walked around snapping pictures left and right. The mountain was a magnificent sight to behold!

It towered above the city, its snow-capped peaks dazzling the bluest of skies. It was such an awesome presence and had been there all through our trip, but hidden from our sight. Just like God's powerful, protecting presence. He is always there, but clouds of doubt and despair often keep us from seeing Him.

I called this our Ebenezer moment. In Hebrew, Ebenezer means "stone of help." I knew God had helped us travel safely to all our states and He had granted my request to see Denali. In I Samuel, however, the prophet called the stone by that name because Israel had won the battles with the Philistines. Samuel realized God Himself had granted the victory. He was their Help.

The *Life Application Study Bible* says, "During tough times, we may need to remember the crucial turning points in our past to help us through the present. Memorials can help us remember God's past victories and gain confidence and strength for the present." I have many such memorials. Every time a new crisis arises, I can say, like Samuel, thus far the Lord has helped us. He will continue to help us when we call on His name. It doesn't take a mountain to remind me of God's help, it only takes a memory.

If you are experiencing any kind of hardship today, think back to the Ebenezer moments of your life. Think about the times God has helped you through, and remember He is ALWAYS faithful.

Lord God, You are my Ebenezer, my Helper. I look to You for confidence and strength. Amen

NOVEMBER 21st *MY TRIBUTE*

"I thank my God upon every remembrance of you." Philippians 1:3

Several years ago, my cousin Denise was putting together a newsletter for Roanoke Baptist Church in which people could publish a tribute to those church members who had impacted their lives in special ways. I wanted to have my own list included since I had spent so much of my life in that place.

My list included my grandmother, my aunts and uncles (especially my Aunt Grace), the piano players (my cousins JoAnn and Denise), the lady who encouraged me to sing (Sylvia) and my friends and supporters through thick and thin (Betty Tate, Betty Sexton, Linda Stowers and Louise Nix).

It also included my assistants in my Sunday school class (Margie and Deenie), the man who was preaching the night I was saved (Bobby Samples), my pastor and Bible teacher for years (Joe Hulsey), two ladies who were great prayer warriors (Annie Beth Samples and Louise Langley), our youth choir (the Roanoke Revivers) and one of our youth ministers (Lamar Day).

I do thank God upon every remembrance of these men and women who meant so much to me as I grew in grace and in the knowledge of the Lord. They were such an inspiration to me.

Paul wrote to the church at Philippi and said he thanked God upon every remembrance of the saints, the bishops and the deacons there. He went on to say he had all these folks in his heart and he longed for them. He told them whether he came to see them or whether he was absent, he wanted to hear of their affairs. He wanted to hear that they were standing fast in one spirit, with one mind striving together for the faith of the gospel.

I fondly recall those men and women who strove together for the faith of the gospel at Roanoke. I am sure you have those from your church to whom you could pay tribute. Why not let them know today, if possible, how much they mean to you and tell them you thank God every time you remember them.

Lord, I am thankful for the saints who have worked so tirelessly for You. Amen

NOVEMBER 22nd *SURFER DUDE*

"And I have put my words in thy mouth," Isaiah 51:16

A couple of years ago, a young minister from my church shared a story with me. I can't recall all the details exactly, but I will retell it to the best of my ability.

He was in another state, California I believe, for work. He went out to the beach one morning, feeling somewhat alone. The beach was almost deserted, but there was this older guy who looked like he might have been a surfer dude. With this setting being California, my friend did not know what type of conversation he might get involved in with this guy, but they started to talk. The surfer guy asked my friend if he knew the Lord! He was thrilled to answer yes! They had a wonderful conversation before parting company. This made my friend's day.

We never know when or where we may get the opportunity to talk about the Lord. It may be two thousand miles away or by our mailbox. We may talk with the cashier at the store, the garbage collector, or a complete stranger who looks like he would not even want to hear about Jesus!

It is our job to be ready to give an answer about the hope that is within us. It is our duty to be a witness for Him wherever we may go. The Lord God told Isaiah, "I have put my words in thy mouth." When we feel that gentle nudging from the Holy Spirit to speak to someone, we must obey.

Not only will it make our day a little brighter, our soul a little lighter, it may help the other someone want to live a little "righter!" Go and be a witness for Jesus this day.

Lord, put the words in my mouth that I may proclaim Your goodness and grace everywhere I go. Amen

NOVEMBER 23rd *COUNTING CORRECTLY*

"Enter into his gates with thanksgiving, and into his courts with praise: be thankful unto him, and bless his name." Psalm 100:4

The first thanksgiving was decreed in 1621, by Governor Bradford, to celebrate the Pilgrims' harvest in their new land. Later, George Washington proclaimed a national day of thanksgiving in 1789. After the presidency of Abraham Lincoln, the day was proclaimed annually by the president and governors of each state. Finally, in 1941, Congress passed into law a bill for the fourth Thursday of November each year to be Thanksgiving Day.

Today, as we celebrate the holiday with our family and friends, let us be mindful of counting our blessings. Here is a list of ways to correctly count:

> *Count your blessings instead of your crosses*
> *Count your gains instead of your losses*
> *Count your joys instead of your woes*
> *Count your friends instead of your foes*
> *Count your smiles instead of your tears*
> *Count your courage instead of your fears*
> *Count your full years instead of your lean*
> *Count your kind deeds instead of your mean*
> *Count your health instead of your wealth*
> *Count on God instead of yourself!*

Today would also be a good day to sing the song, "Count Your Blessings." Johnson Oatman, Jr., wrote the words. He was a Methodist lay preacher who wrote over five thousand hymns. He tells us counting our blessings is the antidote for all the cares and discouragements of this world. The last verse of the song tells us God will provide help and comfort until our journey here is ended.

If you don't know the song, you could do what my family does each year. We make a list of what each person around the table is most thankful for. However you decide to do it, make sure today is about giving thanks to God and blessing His name.

Father, I praise You and bless Your name. I am so thankful for all the many blessing You have bestowed upon my family and me. Amen

NOVEMBER 24th *HUMBLE WORK*

"But thus do unto them, that they may live, and not die, when they approach unto the most holy things: Aaron and his sons shall go in, and appoint them every one to his service and to his burden."
Numbers 4:19

Have you ever wished you had the job held by someone else instead of the one you have? I have been guilty of this. Especially when I carried mail on Route 13. I delivered to several mobile home parks, to South Forsyth High School and to multiple businesses. It was the pits. I longed for one of the easier routes and, finally, the day came when I was able to bid for one of them.

I wonder if the men assigned to carry all the materials and furnishings for the tabernacle felt as I did. During the forty years the children of Israel wandered in the wilderness, three clans from the tribe of Levi were assigned to do the transporting.

They were the "roadies," so to speak. When I read in the Bible about their work assignments, I think of "The Load Out," by Jackson Browne. The clans of Kohath, Gershon and Merari were to "pack it up, tear it down, set it up in another "town." They were the champs when it came to moving God's sanctuary. They repeated the process countless times.

Do you think they ever envied the priests who got to do the sacrificing and the offering? I am sure they felt the priests' jobs were easier and more thankworthy. But, both assignments were from the Lord and both were very important in the worship of God.

A lot of times, we do not get to choose the job we must do. If we are stuck in a lowly position we can at least choose to have a good attitude about it. The Bible tells us to do everything as unto the Lord (Colossians 3:23). I once read in *Our Daily Bread,* "How we do the job God gives us is the measure of our service to Him."

When God assigns us a task, it is important in His eyes. We can honor Him by doing the job well, regardless of how humble it may seem.

Lord, I want to honor You with all I do. Amen

NOVEMBER 25th *WHY WAIT TO GO TO CHURCH?*

"But when they departed from Perga, they came to Antioch in Pisidia, and went into the synagogue on the Sabbath day, and sat down." Acts 13:14

My first conversation with George about going to church took place in the Fox Theatre on our first outing together. George said he did not go because of all the hypocrites there. He is not the only one I have heard complain about hypocrites keeping them away from God's house.

Even if folks don't complain about them, they have a host of other reasons for staying away. Reasons like the weather, lack of appropriate clothing, the boring preacher, the uninspiring singing, etc. If people do not want to go worship God, they will justify their actions someway.

But, Pastor Walter Nuessle, of Port Orchard, Washington, urged people not to wait until the hearse hauls them to church. He wrote this list of results for those who do:

1. *You will go, regardless of the weather.*
2. *You will go, regardless of the condition of your body.*
3. *There will be beautiful flowers there, but you won't enjoy them.*
4. *You will go, regardless of how your family feels.*
5. *The minister may say many good things, but they will do you no good.*
6. *There will be beautiful music, but you won't hear it.*
7. *There will be heartfelt prayers, but they will not touch your heart.*

8. *There will be friends and relatives there, but you won't worship with them.*
9. *You will go, no matter how many hypocrites are there.*
10. *You will go, no matter how much you are needed at home or at work.*
11. *You will receive no blessing from the service.*
12. *You won't feel concerned about your clothes.*
13. *You will never have to decide about attending church again.*

He asked, "Aren't you glad to be alive and well and full of zest and able to choose to go to church?"

Did you know Jesus Himself was in the habit of going to the synagogue? Luke 4:16, tells us, "And he came to Nazareth, where he had been brought up: and, as his custom was, he went into the synagogue on the Sabbath day, and stood up for to read." In the book of Acts, we find the apostle Paul was also in the habit of going to the synagogue to reason with the Jews about Jesus Christ.

People say they can worship just as well at home as at church. If you are at home, whom are you asking to pray for you? With whom are you having fellowship? With whom are you praising Jesus or studying His word?

I realize many people are shut-in and can't attend church. The rest of us really have no excuse. The most important thing, though, is to know Jesus as Savior and Lord. With Him, you are safe for eternity but without Him, you are doomed for eternity.

At Roanoke Baptist Church, James Earl Hubbard once said, "For the saved, earth is the only hell they will go through. For the lost, earth is the only heaven they will ever know." A serious question to be considered by everyone is this: Is your heart right with God?

Jesus, I am thankful for the privilege of going to church. I pray for those who have no desire to go. I am thankful my heart is right with You and I pray for those whose hearts are not. Amen

NOVEMBER 26th *PRAYING AT BELK*

"I exhort therefore, that, first of all, supplications, prayers, intercessions, and giving of thanks be made for all men:"
I Timothy 2:1

It was Thanksgiving Day, 2015. George and I, having already celebrated with the family, decided to go shopping. We are not really keen on "Black Friday" shopping, even when it starts on Thursday evening! Nevertheless, there were deals at Belk we could not pass up.

The doors were to open at six, and we arrived at four forty-five. We were numbers eighty-nine and ninety when we got in line. As we are wont to do, we started talking with some people in line around us. One lady, Lisa, and her daughter were particularly friendly. We began to talk about the Lord.

Soon, Lisa was asking us to pray for her. Rather than make a promise to do so later, I told her we would pray right then and there. We all joined hands and I prayed aloud for her and for the issues she was having with her parents. Afterwards, she hugged and thanked us.

Paul, in his first letter to Timothy, wrote that Timothy should make all sorts of prayers for all amen. He also wrote that men should pray everywhere, lifting up holy hands, without wrath and doubting (verse 8). When a person asks us to pray, why hesitate? Why say you will and not go ahead and pray right away? If someone needs prayer, it will do both parties a world of good to share a prayer right then and there!

What a blessing it was to pray together on the sidewalk outside Belk. What a blessing, too, to get the bargains when we got inside the store. Maybe we should try Thanksgiving shopping more often. There is no telling what needs we may be called upon to pray about the next time!

Lord, thank You for the opportunity to pray for the needs of others. Amen

NOVEMBER 27th *THE SPOKEN WORD*
◆————————————————————————————◆

"In the beginning was the Word, and Word was with God, and the Word was God." John 1:1

There are several Greek words that are translated "word" in the New Testament. A few of them are used only once or twice. The two Greek words used most extensively are *logos* and *rhema.* Logos means principle of divine reason and creative order. Some scholars interpret *logos* as the total inspired word of God, or Jesus Himself. Most say it is the written word, whereas *rhema* is the spoken word, or an utterance.

John's gospel uses *Logos* exclusively when referring to Jesus. In chapter one, John says Jesus is eternal, He was with God and He is God (verse 1). He tells us Jesus is the Creator (verse 3) and He is the Giver of life (verse 4). We also learn Jesus became a human and dwelt among us (verse 14). In verse 31, John tells us Jesus is the Lamb of God which takes away the sin of the world.

Jefferson Bethke has a "spoken word" video that you should see and hear. It is entitled "Why I Hate Religion but Love Jesus." Look it up on YouTube. Bethke says, in part, "Religion says do, Jesus says done, Religion says slave, Jesus says son." He goes on to say our logic is unworthy, it is like saying you play for the Lakers just because you bought the jersey. He tells us Religion is like spraying perfume on a casket.

Jesus also hated religion. His desire was that men quit following all their rituals and follow Him instead. He told the Pharisees they were like whited sepulchres. Jesus knew they appeared righteous outwardly, but inside they were full of hypocrisy and iniquity. In other "words," He did not want to hear them *say* they were righteous, He wanted to see it in their lives.

I hope my life *speaks* for my relationship with Jesus.

Jesus, Logos, I do not want to be like the Pharisees, claiming I am righteous when my heart is far from You. I pray every rhema of mine will show my relationship with You. Amen

NOVEMBER 28th *THE END OF THE ESCORT*

"Nevertheless we made our prayer unto our God." Nehemiah 4:9

We bought the car without my having driven it. George and I went to Neal Pope Ford in the pouring rain to find a new car I could use on the mail route. George did the test drive, but I did not even sit in the front seat. Nevertheless, it worked out well for me

The 1985 Escort wagon was small enough that I could sit on the console and reach out the passenger window with my right hand to deliver the mail while driving with my left hand and my left foot. It also had power steering and brakes, making my job much easier. It had air conditioning which cooled me off after a hot day on the route. Best of all, it had a cassette player so I could jam out while delivering to about six hundred boxes each day.

It was fairly roomy, too, for a compact car. Some days, however, I had it so loaded down, the front tires almost came off the ground! Not good for a front-wheel drive! I have no idea how many miles my Escort and I traveled together, I wish I knew. I just know it was very dependable for transporting the mail and me.

In 1989, as you've already learned, that Escort accidently met up with a large pine tree! Nevertheless, my mechanically-minded mate fixed it, and my little red wagon and I were back on the road. Nevertheless, the end came.

A little later on, the fan quit working properly but George showed me how to jiggle the wire on the relay switch so it would start back. I also carried along some water to fill the radiator if the car started running hot. I almost made it back to the post office that day, but my poor little car had had enough. It died at the intersection of Kelly Mill Road and Highway 20. I had blown the head gasket.

At least it was close enough that I could turn on the flashers, lock it up and walk over to the post office to call for help. Nevertheless, George had a cousin on the police force who came and threatened to haul it away if not moved in just a few minutes! Thankfully, we lived close enough that George did come to the rescue immediately.

Nevertheless, I needed a car to deliver the mail the next day. My brother Johnny sold me a Reliant K for four hundred dollars and we were back on the route early the next morning. After driving that car for a time, I bought a mail jeep from a fellow carrier, Brian Wimpey. Once again, God had provided for me.

Whenever life seems to "crash" around me or when things "blow up" in my face, I make my prayer to God. He always provides all my needs. He constantly amazes me with answers to my prayers. He does not always answer the way I had hoped or expected; He comes through with something even better.

When surrounded by those who oppose us, when all hope seems lost, we must, nevertheless, make our prayer to God. We must trust in Him and ask Him what action we need to take. Read about Nehemiah and his people building the wall around Jerusalem while under much opposition. You will see the first line of defense is always to call upon God.

Father, no matter what happens, I will, nevertheless, make my prayer to You. Amen

NOVEMBER 29th *SHOEBOXES*

"Every good gift and every perfect gift is from above, and cometh down from the Father of lights, with whom is no variableness, neither shadow of turning." James 1:17

Each fall, our church participates in Operation Christmas Child. This is an outreach program of Samaritan's Purse, a Christian humanitarian organization which supplies help to people in physical need as a key part of their missionary work.

If you are not familiar with this program, it is for needy children to have gifts at Christmas. The idea is for donors to pack a shoebox with gifts, candies, toiletries and school supplies. Samaritan's Purse then delivers the boxes to children in countries around the world.

Included in each box is literature in the child's own language about Jesus. If the child so desires, he or she can enroll in a twelve lesson Bible study which will guide them in learning to faithfully follow Jesus. Samaritan's Purse asks each person who packs a box to pray for the child who will receive that box.

As a result, lives are being changed and new churches are springing up around the globe. Our WMU at Pine Crest takes care of distributing the empty boxes, collecting the filled boxes and we make sure the boxes are prayed over before they are sent to the collection site.

George and I look forward each year to filling some boxes. He buys for boys and I buy for the girls. It is amazing how many neat things you can actually fit inside a simple shoe box.

I love giving gifts every chance I get. Regardless of the occasion or the amount of money I have available, I enjoy giving. One of my favorite verses in the Bible is James 1:17. Every good and perfect gift comes down from the Father of lights.

Sometimes the gifts I give are not appreciated because they may be the wrong size, the wrong color or something the receiver is just not interested in. But God knows just what will be best for each and every one of us. He never changes and there are no shadows with Him, only light. He chose us to be born again, through the Word of Truth, so that we are the firstfruits of what He created.

Yes, the best gift ever given came from God. He gave us eternal life through Jesus Christ, His only begotten Son. I did not need a shoebox to learn this gospel message, but some children do. The boxes can be sent to Samaritan Purse year-round, too, not just in November. If you have never participated, why not pack a shoebox today? It might change a child's life for eternity.

Lord Jesus, I thank You for the gospel message going out into many countries by way of Operation Christmas Child shoeboxes. Bless all the efforts of Samaritan's Purse and others who participate in this endeavor. I am so thankful I heard the message when I was a child. Amen

NOVEMBER 30th *NOT BEST, BUT VALUABLE*

"They looked unto him, and were lightened; and their faces were not ashamed." Psalm 34:5

My husband George tells me multiple times every day he thinks I am the greatest. He constantly brags on me and builds me up. He says I am good at everything I do. Yeah, right.

I have never felt I am *good enough* at anything I do, much less the *best* at anything! I have always felt insignificant and worthless. At least that is how I felt until I took the Bible study, *Search for Significance.* Then I learned I do not have to be the *best* in order to be valuable to God or to anyone else.

I do not have to perform perfectly to be accepted in His sight. I do not have to be a high achiever in order to gain worth, security or confidence. I do not have to earn God's favor.

God loves me and He created me to be *me!* He rejoices over me with singing. Jesus loves me so much, He died on the cross for my sins. Furthermore, He has gone to prepare a place for me so that I can join Him when this life is over. God's love for me is unfailing.

My confidence is to be in the Lord, not myself. I am not to be wise in my own eyes. Also, God works everything together for good in my life. My cousin Heidi has said, "Even the dark threads are part of the pattern." I can't see the finished design right now, but I can rest in Him, knowing He continues to work in my life.

Don't fall into the same trap I once did. Do not feel you are unlovable or insignificant to God. You are valuable and so am I. I like to think about a little sentence I often hear: "God don't make no junk!" Let's all try to keep that thought in our minds.

Father God, I know I am loved by and I am valuable to You. Thank You for accepting me as I am, yet always working to make me more like You. Amen

DECEMBER

"For when we were in the flesh, the motions of sins, which were by the law, did work in our members to bring forth fruit unto death."
Romans 7:5

I wonder if any of you readers are feeling sorry for my husband George? As you have read, I am constantly signing us up for anything I think might help him with his health issues. I suppose you may wonder what I will have him doing next? Well, in 2014, it was Tai Chi.

Tai Chi is an ancient Chinese tradition that is now practiced as a form of exercise. People have taken up Tai Chi to fight stress and reduce anxiety. It is often described as meditation in motion. As it consists of flowing motions, it is easy on a person's joints and promotes serenity as well. When I heard it was recommended for folks with Parkinson's to help with their balance, I did not hesitate to sign us up.

We began our classes the first week of December at Central Park. It was an hour of exercise each week. The instructor was a male and there was another guy in the class, so George did not feel self-conscious. The instructor also told the class how important it is to get a good night's sleep and that we should try to sleep the same hours every night. We were already attempting to do that.

Neither of us really enjoyed the class that much and when our lessons were over, we were not interested in going for another session. I must confess, to me the exercises seemed pointless. For all of you tai chi lovers, I wish you well. Those motions were just not meant for George and me.

In Romans 7, Paul wrote about the motions of sin which were by the law. He said they worked in our members to bring forth fruit unto death. We know that no law has any hold over a dead person and since we have died to sin through our belief in Christ, the law can no longer condemn us. We are new creatures! Our service to God now is not through obeying a set of rules, but by having a changed heart. If we walk in the Spirit, we will not be guilty of the motions of sin.

The law showed us our sin, but it could not make us righteous. We were doomed until Jesus died on the cross for our sin and then rose from the tomb. Once we accept His forgiveness, we have the power of the Holy Spirit to help us resist temptation.

Tai Chi was like the law. It could not cure George of his disease. It often showed him his limitations, but was powerless to provide a lasting cure. Once we were "delivered" from the class, we had no desire to go back again, just as we have no desire to go back to trying to live by the law!

Like the law, Tai Chi seemed fine at first, but soon it became a burden. Like an albatross around our necks. We were thankful to be freed from the classes and we are thankful to be freed from the law!

Lord Jesus, Thank You that we are no longer "going through the motions." Thank You for setting us free to walk in newness of life. Amen

DECEMBER 2nd *THE TALENT SHOW*

"Yea doubtless, and I count all things but loss for the excellency of the knowledge of Christ Jesus my Lord: for whom I have suffered the loss of all things, and do count them but dung that I may win Christ," Philippians 3:8

Our son Joel and some of his friends put together an act for the talent show at Mashburn Elementary. They were a rock band and really dressed the part. Also, in the middle of their song, Joel and Chris Cook tossed their guitars across the stage to each other. It was, in my eyes, a fabulous performance.

The M. C. started by reading the third-place winner. *Great, it was not them.* I thought *surely they have second place in the bag.* Second place also went to someone else. *First place? Can it really be?* But no, the first place winner was Star Blanchard.

And it should have been Star. However, she sang last and I did not even realize she was a *contestant* in the talent show! She had been singing on stages for a long time and I thought she was our entertainment while the judges decided.

It was a disappointing ride home. Joel, Chris and the rest of their group had practiced and practiced as they learned their number. They took the stage full of confidence and never "missed a lick." But the prize went to someone else. In fact, *ALL* the prizes went to someone else. The loss weighed as heavily on me as it did on Joel.

But, he did his best. He tried his hardest. And, letting an elementary school contest ruin our night seemed silly. They had entertained the packed lunchroom and everyone had loved their performance. It was a great experience for the boys.

It was also a great lesson for Joel's mom. We may do our best and still not come out on top. But we are to count all things as loss for the excellency of the knowledge of Christ. Even if we suffer the loss of all things, we are to count them as nothing that we may win Christ.

Just as the apostle Paul did. He wrote to the church at Philippi about his change of attitude. He said he was circumcised the eighth day, he was of the stock of Israel and from the tribe of Benjamin, he was a Hebrew of the Hebrews and a Pharisee with a zeal for the law. Yet, he counted all those things as garbage. The most important thing to him was winning Jesus.

It is the most important thing to me as well. No prize this world could offer would ever be more meaningful. And certainly the prizes the world gives are not eternal either.

Jesus, We may not come in first place or win earthly trophies, but knowing You as Savior is the best "prize." Amen

DECEMBER 3rd   *JEZEBEL vs. ELIJAH*

"And it was so, when Elijah heard it, that he wrapped his face in his mantle, and went out, and stood in the entering in of the cave. And, behold, there came a voice unto him, and said, What doest thou here, Elijah?" I Kings 19:13

Elijah had defeated the prophets of Baal on Mt. Carmel. But Jezebel, wife of King Ahab of Israel, had threatened to kill Elijah. He quickly fled for his life. Along the way, he became depressed and he asked the Lord to take his life rather than save it.

As Elijah was sleeping, an angel came to him with food and water. Twice he was given nourishment for the journey ahead of him. Forty days later, he came to Mt. Horeb, where he lodged in a cave.

God told him to go out and stand on the mountain. Elijah experienced a great and strong wind, an earthquake and a fire. But the Lord was not in either of those things. Then Elijah heard a still small voice. It was the Lord speaking to him.

God let Elijah know he was not alone, and there were seven thousand who had not bowed down to Baal or kissed his image. When the time came, a chariot of fire and horses of fire appeared and Elijah went up by a whirlwind into Heaven.

Awhile later, Jezebel was thrown down from a window and killed. Only the palms of her hands, her feet and her skull were found. Just as God had said, "In the portion of Jezreel shall dogs eat the flesh of Jezebel (II Kings 9:36)." Jezebel reaped the evil she had sown.

Elijah, however, was rewarded for his faithfulness. He received a **treat** from the hand of an angel to sustain him (I Kings 19: 6 & 7). He received **treatment** for his depression when he heard the voice of God (12-18) and in spite of the **threat** against his life (verse 2), God granted him safe **travels** for about eighty miles until he was out of Jezebel's kingdom (verse 8).

God also presented Elijah with a **trainee** to take his place (verse 19). Later on, God carried Elijah to Heaven in a **tornado** (ok, a whirlwind! II Kings 2:11).

God asked Elijah **twice,** "What doest thou here, Elijah?" But God knows. He sees everything we do, He knows every thought we think. He understands our depression, even though it is certainly not His will for us to be depressed. He knows the enemy attacks us immediately after any kind of spiritual victory and tries to bring us down. That is when He whispers peace and encouragement in His still small voice.

Jezebel is the epitome of wickedness and Elijah of faithfulness. God rewarded both according to the life they had chosen. Have you chosen to follow after wickedness or faithfulness to God?

Lord, I choose You because You first chose me. Amen

DECEMBER 4th *BEYOND THE SUNSET*

"The sun also ariseth, and the sun goeth down, and hasteth to his place where he arose." Ecclesiastes 1:5

Christmas had always been her favorite time of the year. Her house was overflowing with presents, each one wrapped differently from the rest. She made all her bows herself. None of those stick-on kind was found on her gifts. She made certain no one in the family was short-changed. She spent equally on us all.

In 1982, Christmas day was three weeks away and Bodie lay in West Paces Ferry Hospital, dying from lung cancer. The call came early on that Saturday morning. The end was imminent. We rushed to be by her side.

I stood by her bedside, a helpless thirty-one-year-old, and watched her life ebb away. The white bed sheets seemed to swallow her up as the bleeps on the monitor became slower and slower. Suddenly, she was gone.

In the blink of an eye, her final breath left the pained and diseased body in which she had been trapped for several months. She had crossed over into the lovingkindness of God; into the land beyond us where she would never hurt again. She was, at last, safe in God's hands.

I thought about the song, "Beyond the Sunset." Virgil Brock, who co-wrote the song with his wife, Blanche, had this to say about its origin: "There we stood entranced, enjoying the hospitality of the householder at Rainbow Point, and watched the Householder of heaven draw down the multi-colored curtains over His latticed windows. Our rapture moved to the inescapable question. 'What lies beyond the wondrous sunset? What will it be like when our work is done and the experience of heaven begun?' So amid the afterglow of the sunset, and still in the wonderland of its beauty, the poem took form and was set to music." These words were quoted in *Forty Gospel Hymn Stories* by George W. Sanville.

We asked the Sawnee Mountain Trio to sing this song at her funeral. The first verse of the song says, "Beyond the sunset, O blissful morning, When with our Savior, Heav'n is begun, Earth's toiling ended, O glorious dawning, Beyond the sunset, when day is done." She had gone into that fair homeland where there is no parting. Bodie was at last in the glorious presence of God. His words of welcome were her portion on that fair shore and she was beyond the sunset forever more!

When our time comes to leave this world of pain and suffering, our Lord will take our hand and lead us beyond the sunset to our eternal home. We can comfort one another with these words.

Father God, thank You for the life beyond the sunset that You have planned and prepared for us. Thank You for carrying us through that doorway between here and there. Amen

DECEMBER 5th *THE SHADOW*

"And Hezekiah answered, It is a light thing for the shadow to go down ten degrees: nay, but let the shadow return backward ten degrees."
II Kings 20:10

As I write these words, my granddaughter Josi is thirteen months old. She loves to walk up and down my driveway. It is a long driveway for her little legs, but she thinks she is so big, strutting back and forth.

Just in the past few days, she has discovered her shadow. She doesn't quite know what to make of it, though. She has no idea why that black image goes everywhere she does! It stops when she stops and goes when she goes. She is amazed by it.

I am also amazed by a shadow. Not my own, but the one I read about in II Kings. Let me give you the background. Hezekiah was at the point of death and Isaiah the prophet had advised him to get his house in order for he would not live. Hezekiah prayed and the Lord promised to add fifteen more years to his life.

But Hezekiah wanted a sign. Isaiah asked which he would prefer: the shadow to go forward ten degrees or back ten degrees? Hezekiah knew it was normal for the shadow to go forward, so he asked for the thing only God could do. He asked that the shadow go backwards ten degrees and it was done.

I have read various speculations as to how this was accomplished. Some say God may have used atmospheric conditions, clouds that refracted light or the reversal of the earth's rotation. All I need to know is that God spoke the reversal into being just as surely as He spoke the sun into existence on the fourth day of creation.

I tend to be a bit like Billy Graham. When asked if he believed a whale could really swallow Jonah as the Bible says, Reverend Graham replied, "I believe Jonah could swallow a whale if the Bible says so." Sure, it is hard for our finite minds to grasp the miraculous workings of God. That is why we must live by faith. Regardless of which direction the shadows may fall.

Lord Jesus, You said an evil and adulterous generation seeks after a sign. Help me take You at Your word, never doubting but trusting. Amen

DECEMBER 6th   *ARE YOU WEARY?*

"But they that wait upon the Lord shall renew their strength; they shall mount up with wings as eagles; they shall run, and not be weary; and they shall walk, and not faint." Isaiah 40:31

The Christmas season is a busy, stressful time for people in the retail business or the postal service. The year our grandson Jackson entered the world was no exception.

When he was eight days old, I had some help in the office from a new substitute on my route, but my time on the road was still difficult. And it was bitterly cold that day. The wind cut like a knife.

After work, a co-worker and I met at the home of Lamar Nuckolls to wrap Christmas gifts for the needy. It was after seven o'clock when I got home. I then discovered I had a message from our son Joel. He was wondering if we were coming over.

I dragged my weary body back out into the cold and away we went. Joel and Jessica had just purchased a new car and they wanted us to sit with the baby while they went out for a ride. Jackson slept the entire time we were there, so he was no trouble at all. Plus, we got to eat some chocolate pie from the fridge. Rest and refreshment!

Our daughter-in-law is an avid photographer, so she wanted to snap some pictures of us before we left that night. When I saw myself in those pictures, weariness was showing all over my face. I looked as bone-tired as I felt.

The Bible tells us what to do to renew our strength. We must wait upon the Lord. We will be like an eagle if we do. An eagle can average up to thirty miles per hour in flight and its wing feathers are made to reduce turbulence. Also, eagles can soar for long distances on thermal winds without flapping their wings. This helps them conserve energy.

When we wait on the Lord, we can also rise above difficulties and reduce the stress, or turbulence, of everyday living. We can conserve our energy by trusting in Him to act, in His own good time, on our behalf.. Whenever we feel we cannot go on, that is when we must wait on Him. The Lord faints not and is never weary. He gives power to the faint and increases strength to those with no might (verses 28 & 29).

Although our bodies get tired and need rest, waiting on the Lord keeps us from becoming weary in our Spirit.

Lord, help me to wait upon You. Amen

DECEMBER 7th *BELIEVE AND RECEIVE*

◆————————————————————————◆

"But these are written, that ye might believe that Jesus is the Christ, the Son of God; and that believing ye might have life through his name." John 20:31

When I worked at Heavenly Dove, I became acquainted with a young man named Derrick. He would come in fairly regularly. He was always interested in our music selections.

Derrick and his wife adopted a baby boy. Timothy was born with a very rare disease and his prognosis was uncertain at best. I was told when Derrick heard the report, he went to the bank and opened a savings account for Timothy's college fund. Now that is faith! I am not sure how old Timothy is today, but I am guessing he is around seven years old.

There are statistics and diagnoses and then there is God. Although the gospel of John does not focus on the miracles Jesus performed, we find the words we need to believe Jesus is God's Son and that He is the only way to receive eternal life. The last verse in the book of John says, "And there are also many other things which Jesus did, the which, if they should be written every one, I suppose that even the world itself could not contain the books that should be written. Amen."

Jesus is the same yesterday, today and forever. He performed miracles while He was here on earth and He is still performing them today. According to Bill Gaither, to expect a miracle is to "anticipate the inevitable supernatural intervention of God." We must anticipate, or believe, to receive.

I saw one of those Mahalo Moments signs that read, "Our weakness is a chance for God to show up and show out. When we are down to nothing, He is up to something." His strength is made perfect in our weakness and all things are possible to him who believes.

If you need a miracle, remember you must believe to receive.

Jesus, I do believe. Amen

DECEMBER 8th *A LOVING NEIGHBOR*

"And he answering said, Thou shalt love the Lord thy God with all thy heart, and with all thy soul, and with all thy strength and with all thy mind; and thy neighbor as thyself." Luke 10:27

When George was a young boy, his family lived across the road from Catherine Samples, her family and her mother, Mrs. Martin. George fondly remembers Catherine's love and concern for the Sams family. She was always giving them fresh milk from her cows or giving them produce from the garden.

He also remembers, not quite so fondly, how one of Catherine's cows chased Mrs. Sams and Ethel. It ran them around a tree until Mrs. Martin and Catherine came to their rescue!

Little did George know he would be going to church later in life with Catherine and her husband, Billy Cowart. When we began attending Pine Crest, they were there. "Cat" never failed to tell us how much she loved us both.

She remembered me from Roanoke, but I had no recollection of her being there. That did not matter, though. Because it was so easy to love her, I felt I had known her all my life. Cat and I became very close friends.

She had been progressively suffering from the symptoms, but was not actually diagnosed with ALS until much later. She passed into the arms of Jesus on this day three years ago. George had talked with Cat and told her not to be afraid of dying. He shared his vision with her about going through the tunnel toward the light. He told her it was easy, and it did seem to be easy for her.

Her funeral was so spiritual, I just knew Catherine would have been shouting if she could have been there! All the words spoken over her perfectly described her. She loved God with all her heart and her neighbors as herself. She was a worshipper like Mary as well as a worker like Martha. She put her love for God into action by loving others.

In Luke, chapter ten, Jesus was talking with a young lawyer about how to inherit eternal life. He asked the young man what was written in the law. The man answered with the words in today's verse. Jesus said to him, "this do, and thou shalt live." But the lawyer wanted to know just who his neighbor was, so Jesus told him the story of the Good Samaritan.

Cat was like that Good Samaritan. She loved everybody and everybody loved her in return. I thank God for the privilege of knowing Cat. It is my desire to be more loving like she was; God first and my neighbor as myself.

Lord, help me share Your love with all my neighbors. Amen

DECEMBER 9th *MIRACLE MONEY*

"...thou shalt find a piece of money:" Matthew 17:27

When George had to stop working due to his disability, the Lord said to him, "Don't worry. I will take care of you." We had no idea at the time just how miraculously some of the funds we needed would be provided.

We were working on our budget that fall and trying to figure out how much money we could comfortably spend on Christmas gifts. One Friday, we received a letter in the mailbox about George's stock options with his employer. The letter said we needed to make a selection by a certain date or we would incur loss. When we called about this, we found out we would get a check for several thousand dollars!

This money was totally unexpected. We had no idea he even had stock of this kind anymore. What a total blessing from God. It was much more than we needed for Christmas money. After tithing, we also had enough to help a needy family have a merrier Christmas.

In Matthew, chapter seventeen, Jesus provided miracle money so Peter could pay tribute for Jesus and himself. Jesus told Peter to go to the sea, cast a hook, and take up the first fish he caught. When Peter opened the mouth of the fish, Jesus said a piece of money would be found inside! Peter was able to take that money and pay the taxes.

Our concern was not whether we could afford to buy gifts, but rather how much money we *could* spend on the gifts we wanted to buy. The money we got, while not totally necessary, was, nevertheless, a windfall. Although Jesus said paying the tribute money was not essential for them, He wanted Peter to pay the tax so as not to offend the ones who received the money.

Neither of these situations was a vital one, but the money came and things worked out well for everyone involved. Both times, the money came by miraculous means. I am thankful ours came by way of a letter in the mailbox and a telephone call and not by way of a fish with a coin in its mouth! Although had it done so, I know you would have been much more delighted to have read about it.

Lord, no matter what method You use, we are so thankful for the miracles You send our way. Amen

DECEMBER 10th *DRIVER'S LICENSE RENEWAL*

"For which cause we faint not; but though our outward man perish, yet the inward man is renewed day by day." II Corinthians 4:16

I can remember going several times to the State Patrol office in Lawrenceville to renew my driver's license. They were closed on Mondays, though. Since that was my day off for many years, going there was rather inconvenient. I would have to wait for a day when I finished my mail route early enough to make the drive over and arrive there in time to get it done.

That all changed when we got a State Patrol post off Georgia 400. I no longer had to make a drive outside the county, but you talk about inconvenient! There was almost always a room packed with people wanting a license and the wait times were horrendous.

Recently, the rules for renewal have changed. In addition to a birth certificate, you need a social security card, a bank statement, and a utility bill. A married woman also needs her marriage certificate. What an ordeal! But, George and I went to the Driver Services building off Pilgrim Mill Road, armed with all our documentation. As our birthdays are less than a month apart, we usually get our licenses at the same time.

This year there was a very short wait, we had no issues with our paperwork and the fee was just twenty dollars each! I guess there is some advantage to getting older; the new regulations only allow us to get a five year license! That sure makes a person think. We realize we have more years behind us than ahead of us.

There has not been any improvement with the pictures, however. The not-so-bad picture I had on the last license has given way to a photo of some old woman who was not even allowed to keep her glasses on!

Yet when I look at my life today, can I help but say it is *not-so-bad?* A lot has taken place since the last license renewal and more changes will come before the next one. But, God has been there with me through it all just as He will continue to be. Looking at the dates on the license makes me realize I am just that much closer to God than ever before. That is enough to put a big smile on my face.

In II Corinthians, Paul said, "our light affliction, which is but for a moment, worketh for us a far more exceeding and eternal weight of glory (4:17)." He also said the things that are seen are temporary, but the things which are not seen are eternal. One day, the earthly house of this tabernacle will be destroyed, but I have a building of God not made with hands, eternal in the heavens. Like Paul, "we groan, earnestly desiring to be clothed upon with our house which is in heaven (5:2)."

That renewal will not cost me one thin dime. Jesus paid for it with the blood He shed on the cross. Furthermore, that renewal is eternal.

Jesus, thank You for paying the fee for my ultimate renewal. Amen

DECEMBER 11th *WATERGATE SALAD*

◆————————————————————————————————◆

"And have tasted the good word of God, and the powers of the world to come," Hebrews 6:5

In 1980, the members of Juno Baptist Church published a cookbook that contains what is now one of my favorite recipes. The recipe was submitted by Annie Sue Chester and Judy Gee Sheffield. The dish is called Watergate Salad.

It is a great dish to take to a church social or a family dinner. I like to make it every year at Christmas because the pistachio instant pudding mix gives it a pretty green color which looks good on the table.

Almost everyone in the family loves the salad, although they consider it a dessert. My sister, however, refused to touch the stuff. She would turn up her nose at it and make fun of it year after year. She would always tell me, "I hope you are not making that green stuff again this year."

Then one year she decided to try it. It was love at first bite! She is actually puzzled as to why she refused to try it for so long. I really do understand, though. I can remember when I refused to try certain dishes but later came to crave the very ones I had previously "hated."

This made me think about those who spend the majority of their lives refusing God. They say He is not for them. They say they do not need Him. They want no part of Him and won't even consider trying Him. Yet once they have been enlightened and tasted of that heavenly gift, they never want to go back. They wonder how in the world they could have refused God for so long!

I have a brother-in-law who was not saved until he was sixty-seven years old. I saw a man in his nineties accept Jesus during a church service in the nursing home. God keeps trying and trying to woo lost souls with His Holy Spirit. It is not His will that any person die and go to hell.

He is asking you today to try His way. There is no promise any of us will live another minute, much less another year or decade. So, don't wait too long. Try God. I am sure You will love Him more than you ever thought possible.

Jesus, I have tasted the heavenly gift and the good word of God. I have been made a partaker of the Holy Ghost and I love it! Thank You for preparing these special treats for me. Amen

DECEMBER 12th *CHRISTMAS COOKIES*

◆————————————————————————————————◆

"And he shall take your daughters to be confectionaries, and to be cooks, and to be bakers." I Samuel 8:13

My mother was five years old when her mother passed away. My mother, along with her younger siblings, went from pillar to post after that, staying with first one relative and then another. I suppose that is one reason she never learned to bake. She had no one to teach her.

We never made cookies when I was growing up. Other girls would bring to school cookies they had made with their moms and I was so jealous! Although I did not make cookies with my sons, I vowed to change that when my grandchildren came along.

I would stare at the magazine covers while in the grocery-store checkout lines. I knew I could never make those picture perfect cookies shaped like snowmen, angels or candy canes. Slice and bake would be more my style!

Ryan, Tyler and I would bake the sugar cookies and then the fun began. We had frosting and sugar sprinkles in several different colors. I let the boys decide how they wanted to decorate each one. Sure, the kitchen table was a total mess when we were finished. Sure, the cookies bore no resemblance whatsoever to those on the magazine covers, but they tasted just fine and we had fun.

I have continued the tradition with Jake and Jada, and maybe soon I will be able to include Josi. I have found, though, Jake and Jada like to eat the raw cookie dough in spite of the warning on the package against it! One year, Tyler and I attempted to make gingerbread houses. I will confess, they fell down almost as soon as we were finished with them. Did we care? Not at all.

I have never learned the art of baking. However, just because I am not good at it does not stop me from trying. That is how we should be when it comes to serving Jesus. Just because we aren't accomplished singers, we should not be discouraged from making a joyful noise. Just because we do not pray eloquent prayers as some others do, that should not prevent us from simply talking to the Lord.

So what if we cannot play an instrument? We can use our hands to do other tasks that help our brothers and sisters in Christ. We can always witness for Him. We can volunteer at the food bank. That requires no talent at all! There are many ways to be of service to our King.

Our efforts may not look the best. We may make a mess of things from time to time, but the most important thing is to be found doing whatever we can to glorify Jesus and spread His love to those around us.

Jesus, I know I often make a mess of things, but my heart's desire is to serve You. I am far from perfect in anything, but thank You for blessing my humble attempts. Amen

DECEMBER 13th *OPENING THE DOOR*

"And Samuel lay until the morning, and opened the doors of the house of the Lord." I Samuel 3:15

Christmas is fast approaching. For some, the holiday is a lonely time. The loss of a loved one and the stress we put upon ourselves this

373

season contribute to making our world gray. Even though we are bombarded by bright and shiny decorations, even though we receive mounds of cards and even though we hear Christmas music played on every station and in every store, we may feel like a damp, dreary fog covers us.

But, if we wil look with our hearts and not just our eyes, we will see people earnestly spreading the love of Christ. If we will slow down enough to notice, small kindnesses abound around us. We see friends in the store and they give us a hug. Even though forbidden by their employers to say "Merry Christmas," harried clerks take the time to wish us a happy holiday and give us a smile. A person allows us to go ahead in the checkout line.

The tiniest kindness really does matter. I received a tiny, yet greatly appreciated, bit of kindness from an elderly gentlemen at the Dairy Queen. He looked to be well over eighty years old. He looked frail. Yet as we approached the door, he grabbed the handle, pulled the door open for me and stepped aside for me to enter ahead of him. Simple courtesy, you say? No, love in action if you ask me.

My grandsons have been trained to be gentlemen and I hope they never fail to be courteous to ladies. Yet, in this time of women's lib, when a lot of women resent a man opening a door for her, this aged soul did not hesitate to perform this task for me. I thanked him very much, and truly meant it. He made my day.

Even though Samuel had heard the very voice of God, he rose early and opened the doors of the house of the Lord. He was not puffed up with pride because the Lord had spoken to him, he went about performing a routine task he had been trained to do. He showed great humility. Opening the door and allowing another person to go ahead of you is still an instance of great humility, and an instance of kindness as well.

As you go about your tasks this holiday season, look for opportunities to perform even the tiniest of kindnesses. You never know how much it may mean to the other person. It may be just the act needed to lift a weary or downcast soul. It may be just what is needed to offer Christmas hope to someone.

Lord Jesus, help me perform random acts of kindness this holiday season and lift someone's spirit. Amen

"For consider him that endured such contradiction of sinners against himself, lest ye be wearied and faint in your minds." Hebrews 12:3

The new bowling season was not going well. My scores had taken a nose dive. I had tried everything I knew to correct that trend, but I was in a deep slump and could not seem to climb out of it. Nothing helped. Not standing in a different spot, not throwing a straight ball rather than a hook, not looking at the pins rather than the arrows. Nothing.

Finally, everything began to click. I don't even know what I did to correct my delivery, but the pins started to fall a little better in my favor. I was only hovering around the one fifty mark, but that was an improvement. Then my big day came.

The first game I had two open frames and scored 161; the second game I had two open frames and scored 168; the third game I started out with a four bagger, only had one open frame and rolled a 215. That is a five-forty-four series. At league's end, I had captured the first place award with that score.

I know. That is not so impressive. It is a long way from the six hundred series I could, at one time, bowl frequently. But it was such an improvement from my latest efforts and I was thrilled. I had become wearied and dreaded even going to the bowling center. I was about ready to give up and quit altogether. I am so glad I didn't.

The writer of Hebrews knew Christians would be tempted to give up and quit when times were hard. The writer knew suffering through persecution would be very difficult. That is why he encouraged the readers to consider Jesus and His example. Jesus, for the joy that was set before Him, endured the cross, despising the shame. He endured the opposition of sinners and is now seated at the right hand of God the Father.

The *Life Application Study Bible* tells us, "Suffering is the training ground for Christian maturity. It develops our patience and makes our final victory sweet." While my bowling in no way is comparable to the struggles of a Christian suffering persecution, I do know my suffering made my final victory (winning the high series scratch award) very sweet indeed!

Jesus, help us to fix our eyes on You and not our circumstances. Amen

"My mouth shall speak of wisdom; and the meditation of my heart shall be of understanding." Psalm 49:3

Every so often I begin to listen to the enemy. I begin to be like Eve in the garden. I question whether God's words really apply to me. I get down and out when I think of certain things and I dwell on them instead of what the Bible tells me about God and about myself. Every so often I need someone to speak wise words to me in love.

Can any one of my readers relate? Can *every* one of my readers relate? When I need a good counselor, I can always count on my friend Angie. As she has formerly practiced law, she is a no nonsense, get straight to the point kind of a friend. Just exactly what I need in those times.

She objects when I speak negative words about myself. She defends my position in Christ with the evidence of the Word. Her opening statements and closing arguments are always based on the facts. She will not listen to any hearsay.

A couple of years ago, I needed to hear wise words from her. She said no matter what had been spoken over me in the past, Jesus had *redeemed* me. He is working immeasurably more for me than I could ever ask or think. There were several other verses she quoted to me and I really needed to be reminded of each one at that time.

Why is that? After so long in the Way, why do I still have moments of weakness where I do not resist the devil as I should? I suppose we will always struggle as long as we are in this human body. In Romans, chapter seven, Paul said he struggled. But he went on to say Jesus is the One Who will deliver him from this body of death.

The jury is **not** still out. The verdict has come in and we are declared *Not Guilty* because Jesus took our place on the cross. I have spoken these words of wisdom time and again to others. My heart's meditation has been one of understanding. Yet, when I need to more fully heed those words, I know I can go to Angie and I will come away with an acquittal. Not just because of her words, but because of God's.

Lord Jesus, thank You for taking my place, for mercy and grace. Thank You for friends who will speak wise words when I need them most. Amen

DECEMBER 16th *REASONABLE SERVICE*

"I beseech you therefore, brethren, by the mercies of God, that ye present your bodies a living sacrifice, holy, acceptable unto God, which is your reasonable service." Romans 12:1

My son Justin designs the covers for my books. He doesn't charge me anything, of course, but I donate some books that he can give to his friends and colleagues. Last year, I shipped a box of books to him early in December. With insurance, tracking, priority mail fee, etc., it cost me $58.00, to mail them to California.

Eleven days later, Justin called to tell me his books had not yet arrived. I gave him all the information from my receipt so he could try and track the package. He found out the box sat in the Venice office for a solid week and had just arrived in Gardena that morning. No one could explain to him why the box sat there for an entire week. I certainly would not call that "reasonable service." Would you?

Paul besought us in today's verse to present our bodies a living sacrifice unto God. What does that mean exactly? It means living for God daily. It means putting our own wants, our own comforts and our own wills to death in order to serve God according to His plan for us.

Unlike the sacrifices under the old covenant where animals were slaughtered and the blood covered the sins of the people, a *living* sacrifice means no blood is shed. That is because Jesus shed His own blood for us on the cross of Calvary. His blood covered our sins once and for all time.

Paul said it is our reasonable service to be a living sacrifice. Reasonable means sensible, fair, not asking too much or not high in price. Reasonable is logical. It is rational. In other words, it is the least we can do. I beseech all of us to present our bodies a living sacrifice to the Lord. What a great Christmas present that would be for Him.

Lord, if You could die for me, then I can live for You. Teach me how, I pray. Amen

DECEMBER 17th *MY HIDING PLACE*

"Thou art my hiding place; thou shalt preserve me from trouble; thou shalt compass me about with songs of deliverance. Selah." Psalm 32:7

In Vancouver, British Columbia, the homeless have recently found some new sleeping arrangements. RainCity Housing, one of the local charities, created benches which convert to temporary shelters. The back of the bench can be pulled up to create a "roof" that will keep the wind and rain off the person sleeping there.The benches are easily spotted because of the message painted in glow-in-the-dark colors. The message says, THIS IS A BEDROOM. Or, others might say, FIND SHELTER HERE.

Whenever I read in the Bible about God's being our hiding place, I think of the book written by Corrie Ten Boom. She was Dutch, and the Nazi persecution of Jews had begun in her country. Corrie's family constructed a secret room in their home to shelter some of their Jewish neighbors. Their involvement was discovered. The terrified Jews managed to escape but the Ten Booms were arrested and sent to concentration camps. They were starved and they were beaten. All but Corrie died there, if I remember correctly.

While some people need physical protection from the elements or their enemies, David wrote about the spiritual protection he needed from his guilt. After his great sin concerning Bathsheba and her husband Uriah, David confessed and repented. Yet he said his sin was ever before him. In Psalm 32:1, David wrote, "Blessed is he whose sin is covered."

God is our hiding place. He is the One we can run to when the enemy bombards us with guilt, fear, condemnation, etc. We are hidden under the shadow of His wings (Psalm 17:8). In Psalm 27:5, David wrote, "He shall hide me in his pavilion: in the secret of his tabernacle shall he hide me; he shall set me up upon a rock."

In another place, the Bible tells us God is our strong tower. We can run to Him and be safe (Proverbs 18:10). If you are being threatened by the enemy today, run to the Lord. He will protect you, He will cover you, He will hide you.

Lord God, You are my hiding place. I know I am safe in You. Amen

DECEMBER 18TH *THE FAMILY CIRCLE*

"How often would I have gathered thy children together, even as a hen gathereth her chickens under her wings, and ye would not!"
Matthew 23:37

My paternal grandmother was a Hansard. In September every year there is a Hansard reunion held at Roanoke Baptist Church. Since my grandmother passed away, I don't think I have been one time. She would be very disappointed in me if she knew I am not holding fast to the tradition of attending.

She would be disappointed, too, if she knew our own little family is not getting together the way we once did. When her daughter, Eleanor (or "Bodie"), was living, her home was the gathering place. Bodie had the biggest living room and the biggest dining room, so we held all our family functions there.

Later, I hosted the entire family at my house for years. Until all the children grew up and had families of their own! Now my house is no longer able to hold everyone. It is sad that we have drifted away from each other. The love is still there, but no longer evidenced by the coming together like we did when these two ladies were here.

I began to think about the song, "Family Circle." The lyrics tell us the family circle has been broken and it is not the same anymore. But we will meet again on Heaven's shore. There we will never separate again and we will sing together around the throne. Once again the family circle will be together in a land where the soul shall never die.

Jesus knew the frustration of not being able to gather everyone as He would have liked to do. His own nation refused Him. Jerusalem was the center of worship for all the Jews, but they rejected God's Son. Jesus grieved over the coming destruction of the city and the people He loved so much.

I would encourage everyone to accept Jesus as your Lord and Savior. Please do not reject His love for you. I would also encourage you to celebrate and reaffirm the special bonds with your family this Christmas season. Even if you are separated by great distances and can't literally be gathered together, make a phone call or at least send a card. Let your family members know you love and support them. Stay in touch the best way you can. Keep the family circle together as much as possible. Don't wait until you all reach Heaven!

Lord, I grieve over the separations from family members whom I love. I do want my entire family circle to gather around Your throne one day. I pray for those who have not yet accepted Your love and forgiveness. Amen

DECEMBER 19th   *A HIPPO AND MY HEART*

"What shall I render unto the Lord for all his benefits toward me?"
Psalm 116:12

My favorite silly Christmas song is "I Want a Hippopotamus for Christmas." I enjoy not only singing the song, but acting it out as well. I have performed this number for my church's Secret Sister party, for my Aunt Grace and Uncle Herbert and for my own family's Christmas gathering. I have, in fact, received a few ceramic hippos for Christmas due to my affinity for singing this zany tune.

Quite a few years ago, James Taylor released, for a certain store, a CD of Christmas carols. I had not been familiar with one number prior to hearing Taylor's version. Although it was written a few generations before I was born, I fell in love with his rendition of "In the Bleak Midwinter."

This song was based on a poem written by Christina Rossetti, but was only published posthumously in 1904, when it was included in her *Poetic Works.* The first verse describes the supposed weather conditions when Jesus was born. Verse two contrasts the first and second coming of Jesus, while the third verse describes the humble surroundings of Jesus' birthplace. The fourth verse tells about the angels who appeared in the sky that night but says Mary was able to give the Baby her tender affection. The last verse is the narrator asking what can be given to this Child.

All verses of the poem are not included in the song I heard. But the last verse is the one that resonates most with me anyway. I had actually recited this part of the poem in a Christmas program when I was a child, but never knew its history. It asks, "What can I give Him, poor as I am? If I were a shepherd, I would bring a lamb; If I were a wise man, I would do my part; Yet what I can I give Him: give my heart."

That is what Jesus wants most from us. A heart fully surrendered to Him. It would be impossible to render enough to the Lord for all His benefits toward us, so the only thing we are able to do is give Him our heart. This simple act should result in our living for Him and praising His name. Have you given your heart to Christ? If not, now would be a great time.

Jesus, I am thankful I gave You my heart many years ago. Amen

"Then we which are alive and remain shall be caught up together with them in the clouds, to meet the Lord in the air: and so shall we ever be with the Lord." I Thessalonians 4:17

You probably haven't noticed, but on the twentieth day of each month I have written about some memory from one of our many trips. Today, however, I want to write about a trip I have yet to take.

My Aunt Birlyne was the next-to-youngest sister of my dad's mother. During her later years she lived just out the road from us. She and I became the best of friends. We loved to shop together, whether or not we had money to spend. We enjoyed the time we had to talk and to look around.

Aunt Birlyne also loved the mountains. In the summer of 1975, she was planning to take a short trip there with my mother and my siblings. However, God had other plans. He called her home that June.

My mother wrote and sang a song about her home-going. The title of the song was "You're Taking Your Vacation in Heaven." While I can no longer remember all the words to the song, I know it was about Aunt Birlyne enjoying the scenery of Heaven with the Lord. It was about her walking on the street of gold and seeing the pearly gates.

I have not seen that place yet, but one day I will. When Christ comes back for us, we who are alive will rise to meet Him in the air and will be with Him for eternity. If I should join the saints there prior to the resurrection, that is all the better.

I realize a vacation is usually a short break from our normal schedules. It is a temporary time of rest and freedom from work. But, the heavenly trip will be an endless vacation. As time doesn't exist in that place, our heavenly vacation will be eternal, yet will not seem to drag on. Sometimes George has been so tired from our trips, he would say he needed to go back to work to get some rest! The trip to Heaven will, I am certain, not be anything like that at all.

While I can't know exactly what the future holds, what we will be actually doing in eternity and so on, I do know we will be forever praising the One who died for us. He made the trip possible when He shed His blood on the cross for our sins. He made the itinerary for each and every one of us. He has every little detail planned to the jot and the tittle.

I am excited about taking the vacation with my Lord. How about you?

Jesus, You are the best Travel Agent. I trust You with all my "vacation" plans. Amen

DECEMBER 21st *JESUS ORNAMENTS*

"Neither is there salvation in any other; for there is none other name under heaven given among men, whereby we must be saved."
Acts 4:12

Lake Junaluska Conference and Retreat Center is located in Haywood County, North Carolina. The place is so named in honor of Mount Junaluska which is named after the famous Cherokee Indian leader, Chief Junaluska. The center is the headquarters of the World Methodist Council. But don't think that kept this Baptist girl from going there!

When I attended First Baptist Church, I sang in the choir with Jeanne Page. She was employed by the Methodists. Each December, Mrs. Page and a group of ladies went to Lake Junaluska for the annual Christmas concert. I was able to go with them several times.

We stayed in the Lambuth Inn. It was an absolutely beautiful hotel and the decorations were elaborate. I was particularly enthused over one Christmas tree. It was decorated with white ornaments. Each one had an outline of an open Bible. Written in gold letters were titles for Jesus. For example, Bread of Life, Son of God, King of Kings. I asked an employee if she knew where I might get some of those, but she did not know where they had been purchased.

Several years ago, I was finally able to buy some of those special ornaments for my own tree. They are the ones I most enjoy hanging on the branches. While we have many titles for Jesus, the Bible tells us there is no other name under heaven given among men whereby we must be saved. There is salvation in no other name. John recorded Jesus' own words, "no man cometh unto the Father, but by me (14:6)."

Craig Richard, our former pastor, once gave us a listing of titles for Jesus for every letter of the alphabet. I'd like to share those with you: Alpha and Omega, Bread, Chief Cornerstone, Door, Everlasting, Food for Our Souls, Good Shepherd, Head of the Church, I Am, Jesus, King of Kings, Lamb of God, Messiah, Nazarene, Only Begotten Son, Prince of Peace, Quiver, Resurrection, Savior, Truth, Unity, Vision, Word, Xperience, Yokefellow and Zion. I am sure there are many other examples as well.

Regardless of any other title for Him or any other description of Him, His name is Jesus. Do you know Him? If you have never listened to the sermon, "That's My King," by Dr. S. M. Lockridge, I encourage you to pull him up on YouTube and check it out. No matter how long you may have been a Christian, you will definitely feel you know Jesus better after having heard this sermon. And, if you don't already have them, you will probably want to hang Jesus ornaments on your tree this year!

Jesus, You are my King. Amen

DECEMBER 22nd *OTHER DECORATIONS*

"Saying, Where is he that is born King of the Jews? for we have seen his star in the east, and are come to worship him." Matthew 2:2

My daughter-in-law Jessica always has the most beautiful Christmas tree around. It always looks as if it should be gracing the window of the largest department store in some big city. Except for my Jesus ornaments you have just read about, the other decorations on my tree, for the most part, might be labeled "Tacky."

Nevertheless, they are my treasures. I have paper ornaments made by my sons when they were in kindergarten or first grade. I have some with their pictures on them. Then there are the wreaths made by wrapping red ribbon around a pipe cleaner.

I have many ornaments which always get placed on the front of the tree. They were given to me by my grandchildren. I also have the ones with different historic scenes of Forsyth County on them. Of course there are the angels, the stars and the miniature Nativities. I am sure you are picturing a conglomeration of odds and ends. You would be right.

My grandson Jake told me one year, "Grandmom, you have ugly ornaments." They may be ugly to him, but to me they are priceless because they were made and given to me with love. Furthermore, they all remind me of The Reason for The Season. There's the humble stable, the star of Bethlehem, the angels who announced His birth, the shepherds and the wise men with their rich gifts. Even the tree itself reminds me of the love Jesus showed when he died on the cross for our sins.

I may not celebrate in style, but I am celebrating my Savior's birth!

Jesus, I worship You. Thank You for loving us so much You became the propitiation for our sins. Amen

DECEMBER 23rd *LONGFELLOW'S POEM*

"Glory to God in the highest, and on earth peace, good will toward men." Luke 2:14

Henry Wadsworth Longfellow was born in Maine, lived in Europe for a time and later became a professor at Harvard. Before he was fifty, he retired from teaching to focus on his writing. Longfellow had some sorrowful circumstances with both his wives. His first wife, Mary, died after suffering a miscarriage. His second wife, Frances, died after her dress caught fire and she sustained serious burns.

The first Christmas after Frances' death, Longfellow wrote in his diary, "How inexpressibly sad are the holidays." The next year he wrote, "A merry Christmas say the children, but that is no more for me." Also, in 1863, his son joined the army and was injured during the Civil War. It would be another painful Christmas for him. However, as the church bells tolled that day, Longfellow began to write the poem *Christmas Bells.*

The first three stanzas are pleasant enough, but the next three turn a bit dark. He wrote about cannons thundering and drowning out the carols. He wrote about an earthquake renting the continent and making households forlorn. He also wrote about despair because hate is strong and no peace is found on earth.

But, there is a seventh stanza. Longfellow wrote: Then pealed the bells more loud and deep: "God is not dead nor doth He sleep; The Wrong shall fail, the Right prevail, With peace on earth, good-will to men."

Longfellow had found hope. He still had his memories of pain and loss, yet he finally realized and understood Christ had come to make all things new. This is the promise of Christmas. You might say it is the antidote for fear or turmoil in our lives.

Later, the poem gave birth to the carol, "I Heard the Bells on Christmas Day." A final stanza says, "Then ringing, singing on its way, the world revolved from night to day---a voice, a chime, a chant sublime of peace on earth, good will to men!"

Let's go forth with "Peace on earth, good will to men," on our lips and in our hearts. Not just at Christmas, but every day.

Lord Jesus, You are our Prince of Peace. You are the source of good will toward men. Amen

DECEMBER 24ᵗʰ *CHRISTMAS IN WORDS*

"And the Word was made flesh, and dwelt among us, (and we beheld his glory, the glory as of the only begotten of the Father,) full of grace and truth." John 1:14

My family celebrates Christmas on this night. The tradition began when I was a child. We gathered to open the gifts from each other, and on Christmas morning I was free to relish the gifts under the tree.

We did not often hug each other or say "I love you," yet the fun and the excitement gave us a special bond. We all sat in joy around the mound of presents and saw love expressed by the giving. My mother once said, "The love of Christmas should last all year!" And it should.

I have no knowledge of where the following originated, but I saw it in a church bulletin over thirty years ago. It is still pertinent for today. Joy, Grace, Hope-Love, Faith-Peace, Honor-Purity, Justice-Charity, Courage-Loyalty, Goodness-Prudence, Sympathy-Humility, Fortitude-Temperance, Brotherhood-Cooperation and God is Love. When you arrange these words just so, they make the shape of a Christmas tree. You start out with Joy at the top, add Grace underneath, then the next two words and then the next two and so on. The words have to be staggered so that Joy is centered at the top. You make the bottom of the tree by putting the last four words underneath each other. Try it. Not only do these words make a cute tree, but they are appropriate for any season of a Christian's life.

And, I saw this on a church sign in Cumming one year: "Life with Christ is an endless hope. Life without Christ is a hopeless end." Jesus is the Word who became flesh and lived among us to show us God's great love for us. God wants to give us an endless hope. He doesn't want anyone to face a hopeless end.

Christ is what this holiday is all about. His very name is spelled out in the first six letters of Christmas, which actually means Christ's mass. Take the Word at His word today, before it is too late. If you haven't already done so, accept Jesus as your Lord and Savior. Then, you will not have the Word dwelling among you, but *in* you!

Christ Jesus, everything good and holy about Christmas is truly summed up, not in words, but in the Word. You are the Word. Amen

DECEMBER 25th *THE PERFECT GIFT*

"For the wages of sin is death; but the gift of God is eternal life through Jesus Christ our Lord." Romans 6:23

At our house, Christmas celebrations are never perfect, no matter how much I plan for them to be so. Children argue over who gets to open a gift first. The gifts I have shopped for so diligently only receive half-hearted thanks. Part of the meal doesn't turn out exactly the way I had hoped. Sometimes, old arguments are rehashed.

However, we have not stopped celebrating together! None of us now are perfect, nor will we ever be. But our Christmas get-together is focused on the Only Perfect One who ever lived. We depend on Him because we are unable to live up to our own ideals, much less God's.

Before the world was spoken into existence, God, in His wisdom and foreknowledge, knew mankind would become sinful. He knew we would need someone to redeem us. He knew we could never satisfy our sin-debt. Again, in His omniscience, He knew exactly what was needed to reconcile sinful men and women with His demands of pure righteousness.

Jesus knew He would come to earth, live as one of us and die on the cross for our sins. He was conceived by the Holy Spirit, born of a virgin and never committed any sin. Therefore, His blood was the only blood suitable to satisfy God's requirements. And God made it so easy for us. All we have to do is believe on Jesus and His righteousness is credited to our account.

After we accept Jesus, God does not look upon our sins, but rather He sees the blood of Jesus covering those sins. He sees us as being washed white in the blood of the Lamb. He no longer holds us accountable for the wrongs we have done.

I personally cannot think of any gift more perfect. It is just right for any one of us. Regardless of our size or our situation, regardless of our gender or our generation, regardless of our looks or our likes, God's gift is just what we need. Eternal life through Jesus Christ is the best gift I have ever received. I hope you have received the same one. If not, just ask God. He will gladly give you the gift, too!

Jesus, thank You for being our Perfect Gift from God the Father. Amen

DECEMBER 26th *UNFAMILIAR SITUATIONS*

"And they were all amazed, and they glorified God, and were filled with fear, saying, We have seen strange things to day." Luke 5:26

I admit it. I am uncomfortable in unfamiliar situations. What if I use the wrong fork? What if I can't find someone to talk to? What if I don't understand the rules and make a fool of myself? Etc.

The night before George and I married, our friend Rick Lummus and his date carried us to the Midnight Sun Dinner Theatre in Atlanta. Neither one of us had ever been to a venue like that and we were out of our comfort zones. Completely. We were not exactly sure what we were expected to do. I quietly asked our waiter to give us the information we needed. Of course, he was happy to oblige and a good, no, make that *great,* time was had by all.

In Luke, chapter five, we learn of a man with palsy who is about to come face-to-face with an unfamiliar situation. This man was from the city of Capernaum. He was confined to his bed but he had some friends. These friends carried him, bed and all, to a house where Jesus was known to be healing the sick. The crowd was so large, the four men decided to take the tiles off the roof of the house in order to let the man down, bed and all, and place him at the feet of Jesus.

I have no idea how they carried the man and his bed up to the roof, but they did. The Bible doesn't tell us if they needed special tools to take off the tiles. Did they bring ropes with them to facilitate letting the bed down? Did they cause dust and debris to fall on the heads of those inside? The Bible doesn't say.

This was an unfamiliar situation for everyone involved. Yet, these friends were determined to get the sick man to Jesus. They knew He could help. Jesus, seeing their faith, said, "Man, thy sins are forgiven thee (verse 20)."

What? That was certainly unfamiliar. The friends expected Him to say, "Rise up and walk." Or something similar. But Jesus addressed the sick man's spiritual condition. Jesus said his sins were forgiven! It was also unfamiliar to the scribes. So much so, they accused Jesus of the sin of blasphemy. To prove He had the power to forgive sins, Jesus said to the palsied man, "Arise, and walk."

Walking was certainly unfamiliar to this man. At least it had been for quite some time. But he instantly obeyed, took up his bed and went back home. The situation was unfamiliar to the multitudes, but when they saw it, they glorified God for giving such power unto men.

I like my comfortable rut. So did the scribes in Capernaum. But, whenever we face an unfamiliar situation, we can rest assured Jesus is at work to bring us new experiences, new friends and new opportunities. Best of all, He just may be preparing us for a change in our lifestyle. Do you need to get off your bed of do-nothing and get busy? Rise up and walk!

Jesus, You are my familiar friend. Thank You for taking the unfamiliar situations and working them for good in my life. Amen

DECEMBER 27th *AFRAID OR DISMAYED?*

"And he said, Hearken ye, all Judah, and ye inhabitants of Jerusalem, and thou king Jehoshaphat, Thus saith the Lord unto you, Be not afraid nor dismayed by reason of this great multitude; for the battle is not yours, but God's." II Chronicles 20:15

The only football team to ever go undefeated all the way through the season, including winning the Super Bowl, was the 1972 Miami Dolphins. Others have come close. The 2007 Patriots won eighteen games in a row before losing to the Giants. In 2015, the Panthers had won every game until they played the Falcons in week sixteen.

Two weeks earlier, the Panthers crushed the Falcons 38-0. It was the first shut-out since 2004 for the Atlanta team. No one expected them to have a prayer for winning against Carolina when they came to the Georgia Dome.

Thanks to some nice catches by Roddy White, some tough runs by Devonta Freeman, the truly remarkable performance of Julio Jones and a Vic Beasley sack of Carolina quarterback Cam Newton which resulted in a fumble, the Falcons won 20-13. This loss was actually the first for the Panthers since November of 2014.

I contrasted this game to the invasion of Judah by the children of Moab and Ammon. When King Jehoshaphat heard of the multitudes coming against him, he was afraid. He proclaimed a fast and sought the Lord. All Judah joined him.

The king confessed to God, "We have no might against this great company that cometh against us; neither know we what to do: but our eyes are upon thee (verse 12)." The Lord sent encouraging words back to Jehoshaphat through Jahaziel. Those words are recorded in verses fifteen through seventeen. The Lord said Judah would only need to stand still and see the salvation of the Lord. There would be no need to fight. Neither were they to be afraid nor dismayed because the Lord would be with them.

Everything came to pass exactly as the Lord promised. There was so much spoil the people of Judah couldn't carry it away. It took them three days to gather it all. They returned to Jerusalem with joy because the Lord had caused them to rejoice over their enemies.

No one may have expected Judah to have a prayer for winning against this great multitude. They were afraid, they were dismayed; but the Lord caused them to triumph.

Back to the football game. I am not saying the Falcons were *afraid* of the Panthers, but surely they were a bit dismayed. I have no proof that any player fasted before this game. I am convinced, however, at least *some* of the players sought help from the Lord. There *was* a need for the Falcons to "come out fighting." Had they stood still, they would have been embarrassed, to say the least. The result was similar to Judah's though. The Falcons came away from that game full of joy because they had triumphed over their "enemies."

The king of Judah said he and his people did not know what to do, but their eyes were upon the Lord. That is exactly where our eyes should be. Whether facing an army or playing football, we need to look to the Lord. He is the source of our strength. He is our Defender and our Protector. He is in control.

Helen Lemmel wrote the words and the music to the song, "Turn Your Eyes Upon Jesus." In the chorus, Mrs. Lemmel urges us to "Look full in His wonderful face, and the things of earth will grow strangely dim in the light of His glory and grace." These words should remind us to face every situation with confidence in Him.

Lord, There is no reason for me to ever be afraid or dismayed. When the odds seem insurmountable and I do not know what to do, remind me to fix my eyes on You. Amen

DECEMBER 28th *WHAT'S MY TYPE?*

"For as the body is one, and hath many members, and all the members of that one body, being many, are one body: so also is Christ."
I Corinthians 12:12

Paul wrote to the church in Corinth about *the church.* He explained to them that each member, although different, is essential to the whole. Verse fourteen says, "For the body is not one member, but many." Some may be the foot, some the hand, some the ear or the eye, yet all are important.

Paul goes on to say, "But now hath God set the members every one of them in the body, as it hath pleased him (verse 18)." And also, "That there should be no schism in the body, but that the members should have the same care for one another (verse 25)." He tells the saints in Corinth if one member suffers, all suffer. Or, if one member is honored, all rejoice. We all make up the body of Christ, but we are members in particular.

However, too often we find some members have particular tendencies! Including me! For instance, some members are like wheelbarrows, they are no good unless pushed. Some are like canoes, they need to be paddled. Some are like kites, if you don't keep them on a string, they fly away. Some are like kittens, they are more contented when petted. Some are like footballs, you can't tell which way they are going to bounce next. Some are like balloons, full of wind and likely to blow up unless handled carefully. Some are like trailers, no good unless pulled. And then there are those who are like watches, having open faces, pure gold, quietly busy and full of good works.

Which type are you? I have probably been each type at some point in my journey, but my goal is to be the watch. Paul said we all have different gifts, and we are to covet earnestly the best gifts. However, the more excellent way to exercise any spiritual gift is by loving one another. Let's all serve one another in love.

Jesus, help me be quietly busy and full of good works. Help me serve others in love. Amen

DECEMBER 29th *PENCILS*

"Notwithstanding in this rejoice not, that the spirits are subject unto you; but rather rejoice, because your names are written in heaven."
Luke 10:20

I have always liked to write. I enjoyed seeing a pencil move across the lines of my paper capturing words and figures. Mrs. Coots, my high school French teacher, taught us that writing things down is the best way to remember them. I was already firm in that belief. I had been writing things down since I first learned to hold a pencil.

The Ticonderoga pencils were the pencils of choice. They were a distinctive yellow, with green lettering. They had #2 imprinted on the side, meaning the pencil was a soft grade. The pencils had a graphite core, were made of reforested cedar wood, had a satin smooth finish and were topped with a latex-free eraser.

Like so many other products, the Ticonderoga pencils are no longer produced in the United States. But, for at least two centuries, they were the most well-known and widely used pencils on the market.

Someone once used a simple pencil to teach an object lesson about the grace of God. Here are the main points.

1. The purpose of a pencil is to write a story. Our purpose is to live a godly life.
2. The lines on the paper represent God's laws. They are there to make your writing task easier. They are not meant to make you discouraged or to torment you.
3. The eraser is for mistakes. You can use it as often as you need it. With practice, you may need it less, but you will always need it. God's grace is your eraser. Since you will always make mistakes, you will always need His grace.

4. The important thing is to write a story. Don't get too hung up about the lines or about trying to see how little you can use the eraser.

Whenever I find I am being too intense about rule-keeping or when I am too worried about wearing out my eraser, I can remember this pencil lesson. I can tell myself to get on with the main task of writing the story. When I get out of the lines, I tell myself, "It happens." When I use my eraser, I am thankful to have it. The main thing I must remember is to do something pleasing for "God's eternal journal."

Father God, help me live a godly life so that my story pleases You. When I make mistakes, remind me Your grace is there to erase them. Amen

DECEMBER 30th *COMPLETED MISSION*

"I have fought a good fight, I have finished my course, I have kept the faith:" I Timothy 4:7

From 1966 through 1973, *Mission Impossible* was a popular television series. The show was about a team of secret government agents called the Impossible Missions Force, or IMF. Their covert mission was to fight dictators, evil organizations and crime lords. The leader would receive instructions on a recording.

The voice on the recording could be heard saying "This is your mission should you choose to accept it." It would always end with these words, "As usual, should any members of your Impossible Missions Force be caught or killed, the Secretary will disavow any knowledge of your actions. This tape will self-destruct in five seconds."

I thought about our missions for our Lord. He has a purpose for our lives. Sometimes we do not choose to accept it. We run from His call on our lives or deny Him altogether. Or, we take on the mission and won't let go of it, even when God's work for us is over in that particular ministry. We begin to feel it is *our* work, when in fact it is His.

It can be very difficult to say good-bye. However, we must trust God to keep things going without us. His purpose will prevail with us, or without us. We must be ready to move on when God says it is time.

During his final imprisonment in Rome, Paul wrote the second letter to Timothy, his son in the faith. Paul was preparing Timothy to keep the ministry going after he was gone. Paul knew his death would soon come, but he was resigned to that.

Paul had rejected the Lord at first, but after the encounter on the road to Damascus, he was gung-ho for the gospel. He fought a good fight against the crime lord, Satan, and his evil organization. He made certain God's instructions for his life were well known. He wrote about them to many churches and to many individuals. Paul did not secretly carry out his mission, but rather preached the gospel everywhere he went. Often, causing himself great peril.

Also, God's instructions never self-destruct. Since creation, He has been calling on men and women to follow and serve Him. His instructions are clearly spelled out for us in his Word. Furthermore, God will never disavow knowledge of us. In fact, He has laid up a crown of righteousness which He will give to all who love His appearing.

When our mission on this earth is completed, I pray we can all be like Paul and say, "I have fought a good fight, I have finished my course, I have kept the faith."

Jesus, help me to fight and finish with faith. Amen

DECEMBER 31st *YEAR'S END*

"And in the end of years they shall join themselves together;"
Daniel 11:6

New Year's Eve is the night the peach drops in Atlanta. It is the night the ball drops in New York City. Many people join themselves together to bring in the New Year while watching one of these events on the television. In 1997, George and I were invited to the home of Eddie and Connie Hitt for the occasion. But, we did not watch the tube.

There were people from Eddie's Sunday school class at Pine Crest gathered in their home. Everyone brought finger foods and we snacked almost all night. We talked, we played Name That Tune and we watched videos of church programs. My favorite part of the evening was playing Biblequest. I love that game!

393

When it was nearing twelve, I made certain I was near George so we could share a kiss at the stroke of midnight. But I don't believe we sang "Auld Lang Syne." We might have done "Amazing Grace," but I am not certain about that.

Auld Lang Syne is actually a poem, written by Robert Burns, and set to the tune of a traditional folk song. The title actually means "old long since" or, you might say, "days gone by." The song asks, "Should old acquaintance be forgot and never brought to mind?" I suppose the New Year *is* a good time to reflect on old friends and days gone by. We certainly enjoyed reflecting with our old friends.

But rather than looking back with fondness, I think it is better to look ahead to the wonders God has in store for us. Let us focus on the goodness and the mercy of God. Endings lead to new beginnings. God has been our Help in ages past and He will be our Hope in the years to come.

Let's not focus on the past. It is much more important, I think, to begin seeking a closer walk with Him in the year ahead. Let's accept His forgiveness for sins and shortcomings of the past year. Let's ask Him to guide our steps and use our lives to inspire others. That is the best way to ring out the old and ring in the new!

Lord God, thank You for all Your blessings this year. Help me to walk closer to You, to love my fellow man and to pray without ceasing. Amen

AUTHOR'S NOTE

This book was written for the sole purpose of giving God the glory for my life. He is my constant companion, my dearest friend, my Savior and my Lord.

Special thanks go to my husband George. He is my soul mate and the love of my life. George has endured many lonely days and nights while I sat at the computer composing these devotions. He has been such an encourager. He has never failed to say he is proud of me. When things were not going well, he would lift my spirits and remind me to trust God to work everything out. He is my hero in every sense of the word.

Since I began to write, a new daughter-in-law has come into our family. Kevin married DeAnn and three more grandchildren, Logan, Liam and Lainey, have been added as well. We welcomed them with open arms.

I would also like to thank every person mentioned or alluded to in this book. Thanks for giving me stories to write! Thanks for impacting my life in such profound ways.

Once again, I would like to thank our son Justin for designing the beautiful cover. Doesn't he do an amazing job?

Thank you to everyone who purchased this book. Every penny of my profits from its sale will be donated to the Lottie Moon Christmas offering for foreign missionaries.

My prayer is for God to bless you through the reading of these pages. He is constantly working, in everyday situations, to train us in the way we should go. Listen to the gentle nudges of the Holy Spirit. Look for God in every trial. Search for Him with your whole heart and you will certainly find Him (Jeremiah 29:13). Finally, always make certain you are *Giving God the Glory!*

Made in the USA
Charleston, SC
15 October 2016